TARGETING PEACE

To Klara Smedberg

Targeting Peace
Understanding UN and EU Targeted Sanctions

MIKAEL ERIKSSON

Routledge
Taylor & Francis Group
LONDON AND NEW YORK

First published 2011 by Ashgate Publishing

2 Park Square, Milton Park, Abingdon, Oxon OX14 4RN
711 Third Avenue, New York, NY 10017, USA

Routledge is an imprint of the Taylor & Francis Group, an informa business

First issued in paperback 2016

British Library Cataloguing in Publication Data
Eriksson, Mikael.
Targeting peace : understanding UN and EU targeted sanctions.
1. United Nations--Sanctions. 2. European Union countries--Foreign relations. 3. Sanctions (International law)
I. Title
327.1'17-dc22

Library of Congress Cataloging-in-Publication Data
Eriksson, Mikael.
Targeting peace : understanding UN and EU targeted sanctions / by Mikael Eriksson.
p. cm.
Includes index.
ISBN 978-1-4094-1932-7 (hardback)
1. Sanctions (International law) 2. Economic sanctions--European Union countries. I. Title.
KZ6373.E75 2010
341.5'82--dc22

2010028223

ISBN 978-1-4094-1932-7 (hbk)
ISBN 978-1-138-27378-8 (pbk)

Contents

List of Tables

Appendix 2

Acknowledgements

The Swedish Research Council (Vetenskapsrådet) and the European University Institute, Italy, have provided generous support to make this book possible. Without their financial and logistical support, this book would not have been written. Financial support has also been made available from the Swedish Institute and the Nordic Africa Institute (both in Sweden). Special gratitude is owed to Professor Pascal Vennesson. Without his comments, my study would be clouded in ambiguities. In addition, I would like to express my appreciation to Professor Friedrich Kratochwil for widening my scientific horizons.

Over the years, a numbers of scholars and experts have also commented or exchanged ideas on various drafts and conference papers throughout the writing process. A special thanks to Professor Peter Wallensteen for his support throughout my academic career. Not only is he an excellent global research entrepreneur and a norm diffuser, but also a close colleague and friend. Thanks also to Professor Thomas Biersteker, Professor David Cortright, the Honourable Sue Eckert, Professor George Lopez, Professor Iain Cameron and Associate Professor Peter Viggo Jakobsen. Along the way, several researchers at the European University Institute have provided me with excellent comments.

My research also included a number of field trips to study sanctions more closely (for example, to Angola, Zimbabwe, Moldova/Transdniestria, Malaysia, Thailand, Ivory Coast, Liberia and Sierra Leone). These missions were enabled by a combination of support from the Swedish Foreign Ministry, staff of the United Nations, and local NGOs (such as the Human Rights Trust of Southern Africa, SAHRIT). During the writing process I also had the chance to spend six months at the EU Commission/DG RELEX (Spring 2007). Not only did it bring new friendships, but also profound insights into the process of EU sanctions policies. In particular, I would like to thank Albertus Straver and Alyson King for taking the time to explain the logic of the EU's restrictive measures. In 2008, I was fortunate to spend time at New York University's Center on International Cooperation. My stay there was very enriching.

Many thanks, too, to the most helpful editorial staff at Ashgate publishing. Especially Elaine Couper, and to Huw Jones for his copy-editing

Last but not least, friendship is important when seas become stormy. Here I would like to mention Dr Niklas Rossbach, Stefan Borg, Dr Evelyn Huebscher, Dr Fredrik Thomasson, Dr Roland Kostić and Jesper Sundien, for their support.

Chapter 1
Targeting Peace

Following the end of the Cold War, the United Nations (UN) and the European Union (EU), as well as their respective member states in their own capacities, each shifted from comprehensive to targeted sanctions. This policy shift opened up a new area of sanctions research and invited new approaches to the analysis of this tool.[1] While multilateral sanctions practice during the Cold War was limited in scope, with only two sanctions regimes in place in the period 1945–90 (the economic sanctions on Southern Rhodesia 1965–79 and an mandatory arms embargo on South Africa 1977–94), there are currently nearly 30 EU and UN targeted sanctions regimes ongoing around the world.[2] Scholars have labelled the proliferation of UN sanctions regimes during the 1990s as the 'Sanctions Decade'.[3] The trend towards this new practice is also well summarised in the academic literature.[4]

Targeted sanctions involve measures such as financial sanctions, travel bans, arms embargoes, trade sanctions, flight bans, admissions restrictions, diplomatic sanctions, boycotts, as well as a number of specific measures applied on rough diamonds and timber, and so on. These measures are adopted and implemented in order to deal with domestic and international crises, as well as armed conflicts.[5] From traditionally having been state- and society-oriented (that is, 'conventional' or 'comprehensive'), the use of sanctions now entails targeting, by political and economic means, those individuals (entities) and groups involved in armed conflict,[6] terrorism,[7] threats to

---

1 Elliott and Hufbauer (1999): 405.

2 In addition, there have been many bilateral sanctions regimes as well as a number of non-mandatory economic embargoes in place. Charron notes, in a recent dataset, that an estimated 39 voluntary UN sanctions regimes in the period 1945–2007; see Charron (2009): 3.

3 Cortright and Lopez (2000).

4 *Ibid.*, Cortright and Lopez (2002a, 2002b), Doxey (1996, 1999), Tostensen and Bull (2002), Hufbauer et al. (2007), Portela (2008), Giumelli (2009) and Charron (2010).

5 Cortright and Lopez (2002b): 1–22.

6 According to the Uppsala Conflict Data Programme (UCDP), there were an estimated 30 ongoing armed conflicts around the world in 2008 (for the latest update, see Harbom and Wallensteen, 2010). Several armed conflicts have been profoundly shaped by decisions taken by charismatic leaders. Examples here include Jonas Samvimbi (Angola), John Garang (Sudan), Joseph Koney (Uganda), Yassir Arafat (Palestine) and Charles Taylor (Liberia).

7 Since 11 September 2001, a large number of terrorist entities have been placed on UN and EU sanctions lists. The relevance of imposing targeted sanctions follows the number of independent terrorist organisations and individuals posing a threat to international peace

peace and security,[8] and international crimes, political violence and human rights abuses.[9] Cameron (2008), who has written an important legal analysis of the use of this policy, suggests that targeted sanctions nowadays can achieve a number of different goals. The primary goals of targeted sanctions are to encourage democracy, stop human rights violations and suppression of internal opposition, enforce peace agreements, assist in the pursuit of individuals for prosecution before international courts, and ensure compliance with treaty obligations; the secondary goals concern the promotion of the sender's reputation domestically and internationally, and ultimately, to maintain international norms and structures.[10] To these observations, one could also add other sanctions objectives such as preventing and containing armed conflict, achieving compliance with international law, countering conflicting parties' military aggression, expressing outrage, building support for military action as a tool in negotiations, preventing the export of sensitive technologies, embarrassing the targets, restoring democratically elected governments, settling civil wars, containing conflict, compelling compliance, limiting the spread of weapons, constraining international rogue actors, and bringing suspected terrorists to justice.[11]

With all of the above in mind, what underpins the current use of targeted sanctions is the rationale of avoiding harm to those actors that are not responsible

---

and security. For an overview of the features and numbers of such groups, see Kreuger and Laitin (2004); Mack (2005); UCDP, <www.pcr.uu.se>; US Department of State (2008).

8 Over the last two decades, targeted sanctions have been imposed and concerted to bring perpetrators and former war criminals to international justice. Examples include the International Criminal Tribunal for former Yugoslavia, Liberia and Sierra Leone (all of which are currently subject to sanctions regimes). High-profile targets which have been previous or currently listed include: Slobodan Milošević (former Yugoslavia), Saddam Hussein (Iraq), Charles Taylor (Liberia) and the more recent establishment of the hybrid UN Special Tribunal for Lebanon (1 March 2009) following the killing of former Prime Minister Rafiq Hariri and 22 others. In addition, targeted sanctions have also been imposed to deal with more long-standing threats (for example, in the Democratic People's Republic of Korea, and in Iran when targeting the elite for its nuclear ambitions), as well as more short-term ones, for example to bring warring parties to peace negotiations (in Sudan/Darfur, for instance).

9 Targeted sanctions have also been implemented against those engaged in organised crime and political violence. A well-known entity here is Viktor Bout, or 'the merchant of death', an arms dealer and alleged holder of five passports active in conflicts such Iraq, Afghanistan, Liberia and Somalia. While many countries do not experience armed conflicts and terrorism per se, most countries do, however, experience organised crime and political violence; see Mack (2005): 50, and Andreas and Nadelmann (2006). Moreover, officials and government leaders inciting political violence have also been targeted with sanctions, usually for their failure to adhere to democratic and human rights practice (for example, President Robert Mugabe of Zimbabwe).

10 See Cameron (2008).

11 As noted by Gottemoeller: 'Nevertheless, "sanctions" may feel better than nothing: they are less feeble than scolding an ambassador and less bloody than sending in the marines. They provide a frisson of moral satisfaction"'; Gottemoeller (2008): 100.

for the policies which the sender intends to change.[12] By introducing targeted sanctions on carefully selected individuals and commodities, instead of entire countries and societies, the sender hopes to change, steer or control the political behaviour of the target. The way this is done is by hitting the political heart of decision-making power, thereby reducing the political and economic capabilities of those targeted.[13] Rather than inflicting collective punishment and suffering, which was embedded in the rationale of comprehensive sanctions, targeted entities – both so-called 'natural' entities (individuals) and legal entities (organisations and private operators) – are held accountable.[14] Based on this rationale, the shift in sanctions practice reflects the determination of the sender to make the sanctions policy more ethical, legally secure and justifiable than previous comprehensive sanctions.[15]

The shift in sanctions practice also makes it possible to differentiate between three different application areas. A distinction can be made between: (1) sanctions targeted against individuals, groups or corporate entities (such as against senior military officials in Burma/Myanmar, weapons traders such as Victor Bout, organisations like Hamas, or private companies like Iranian banks); (2) sanctions targeted against particular commodities or sectors of an economy (such as timber sanctions in Liberia, arms embargoes on former Yugoslavia, bans on rough diamonds under the Kimberly scheme, or the luxury goods ban in North Korea), and (3) sanctions targeted against certain regions of a country (such as the arms embargo against groups active in the Eastern Democratic Republic of Congo).[16]

In this study, I will limit the focus to sanctions adopted against individuals. Compared to conventional sanctions that are mostly applied to entire states, individually applied sanctions present a specific research puzzle compared to comprehensive sanctions, as they are able to 'think', 'act' and 'respond' to the polices adopted by the sender. This brings in a number of new factors in assessing the effectiveness of sanctions which have traditionally been left out of the literature. As noted by Chesterman and Pouligny: 'A micro sociology of local actors, of their interests and strategies, is necessary to understand their different reactions when sanctions are imposed.'[17] Not only do we need to account for personal perception and political behaviour, but also how the sender and the target interact with each

12 Biersteker and Eckert (2006).

13 Cortright et al. (2000a): 4.

14 One problem here is whether targets are listed as free agents under state protection or in their public capacity. Such separation is not entirely clear in international law.

15 Over the years, a number of governments have turned to targeted assassinations, the killing of political leaders for preventive purposes. For a legal discussion, see Lotrionte (2003) and Kretzmer (2005).

16 Biersteker (2004): 2.

17 Chesterman and Pouligny (2003): 511.

other. Most importantly, the focus on individuals is likely to affect the way scholars and practitioners assess the policy outcome of a sanctions regime.[18]

This shift in focus also jibes well with a 'humanisation' trend in international politics and contemporary international law, where there is a clear increase in the pursuit of personal responsibility and judicial accountability of natural entities and official decision-makers. Professor Sikkink, who refers to an ongoing international 'justice cascade' where attention is put on individual decision-makers, has also made a similar observation.[19] Interestingly, the imposition of targeted sanctions against individuals and groups also seems to form part of a longer and more established practice of holding government officials and individuals accountable for practices that are contrary to the will of the international community. In fact, the trend of individualising responsibility seems to go back at least as far as the First World War.[20] Since then, a number of regional and international institutions have been established to promote personal responsibility among decision-makers. Foremost, there has been the establishment of local, regional and international courts seeking to extradite, put on trial and convict individuals, both in their private and official capacities, involved in activities undermining human rights, democratic principles and/or posing a threat to peace and security.[21]

Returning to the shift in practice of targeted sanctions, as noted at the outset, there is still a fundamental puzzle that remains unsolved for sanctions scholars in understanding the utility of targeted sanctions. How should sanctions scholars go about evaluating this new form of sanctions practice? This and related questions make up the focus of this study, which will focus on the UN and the EU. This choice was made because they are the most significant multi-party actors in the sanctions field today.

A New Sanctions Practice

This book begins with the assumption that the shift in practice from comprehensive to targeted sanctions has invited a new way of understanding the role of this

18 Such interactions can be noted in mediation efforts, public diplomacy, political dialogues, and so on. See Conciliation Resources (2008).

19 Sikkink (2008).

20 See also Meron (2006).

21 Examples include the establishment of the Nuremberg trials (1945), the International Military Tribunal of the Far East/the Tokyo trials (1946), the establishment of the International Criminal Tribunal for Former Yugoslavia (1991), the Arusha Tribunal, (1994) and the Special Court for Sierra Leone (2002), the national process against former Chilean president Pinochet (1998–2006), the establishment of the International Criminal Tribunal (2002) and the Iraqi Interim Government's trial of Saddam Hussein (2003).

policy. As will be illustrated below, there are good reasons to argue that there is a need to re-think sanctions as a whole: the measures, the actors, as well as their relationships and goals. While comprehensive sanctions have traditionally been broad-based and state- and society-oriented; targeted sanctions are actor- and issue-oriented. Moreover, while comprehensive sanctions were enacted in a climate of superpower rivalry, targeted sanctions now exist in the era of globalisation. Not only do such differences in contexts create a new dynamic, they also introduce new kinds of relationships among the constitutive elements of a targeted sanctions regime. Consequently, sanctions call for a redefinition of the elements and how they fit into scholars' analysis of sanctions, not least when the goal is to evaluate their effectiveness. This also requires a new way of thinking and a new theoretical approach. More specifically, one could think of five reasons why such a re-thinking is needed.

First, the engagement between senders and listed entities has increased dramatically over the last decade. This follows a shift in the level of analysis. While previously the sender in its adoption of a sanctions policy was mostly dealing with the behaviour of a government, one can now notice the sender is far more engaged in a sanctions practice that concerns the political behaviour of a specific decision-making actor. There are currently several individuals and groups 'interacting' with the sender, both in its official and private capacity. Thus, as will be argued here, one cannot investigate impact in terms of unitary state behaviour alone, but the behaviour of each listed target.

Second, the increasing management by senders of so-called 'sanctions lists' is likely to change the practice and process of sanctions compared to past practice. The sender needs to engage in a more refined administrative policy approach, as it will increasingly come to focus on individual members. In this context, the sender need to ensure that its policies have personal impact on the listed entity to persuade it to change its behaviour. As sanctions' impact can both be direct and symbolic, the sender needs a strategy to tackle this.

Third, targeted sanctions open up new ways of thinking about the 'strategic' rationale of imposing sanctions. While comprehensive sanctions traditionally meant an indiscriminate security governance approach – making no distinction between those clearly responsible and those that had nothing to do with the unwanted political behaviour – the impact of targeted sanctions is more easily understood if we take into consideration their function in a broader strategic setting, where the merit of this policy can be seen in light of the many other policy measures. Consequently, if examining targeted sanctions, without including the broader strategic scope in which sanctions are embedded, one is not likely to explain the logic of sanctions' impact or their effectiveness. Strategies that go hand in hand with sanctions seem increasingly important. For example, to evaluate the effectiveness and impact of sanctions, one needs also to take into account how they play an integral part in the sender's overall policy (accounting for other policies such as the role of peacekeeping missions, aid programmes, security sector reforms, demobilisation and reintegration measures, and so on).

Fourth, to arrive at a better sense of how targeted sanctions result in a particular impact (as opposed to comprehensive sanctions), there is also a need to take a 'multivariate' approach that accounts for the micro-dynamic and complex processes that go on throughout a sanctions regime. In contrast to comprehensive sanctions, which mainly focused on the official reaction by the state following sanctions, factors such as human behaviour, emotional reactions, perceptions, decision-making patterns etc., will have to be accounted for in a sanctions assessment.

Finally – and perhaps the most important contrast which has followed the shift in practice and philosophy of sanctions – there is the question of how one addresses sanctions' 'effectiveness'. While conventional studies have approached the evaluation of sanctions regimes by comparing official goals and policy outcomes – and conventionally assigning successes and failures – an alternative proposal will be advanced in this study. This stems from a conviction that conventional assessment approaches have often taken too narrow a methodological approach when engaging in assessment, in which the factors considered are simply too few, too connected to the outcome of the sanctions case (for example, often only comparing the goals and observable outcomes of the established sanctions regime) or ignore temporal and contextual changes. Rather than judging the effectiveness of sanctions policy at the end of a sanctions regime, which has been a common traditional approach, each sanctions regime should be divided into a number of temporal episodes, which may then much better explain the impact of sanctions. Above all, such episodic evaluations will contribute towards an understanding of the effectiveness of targeted sanctions. This will be discussed further in later chapters.

Contribution and Relevance

The objective here is to make a theoretical and methodological contribution to the existing sanctions literature, especially in the area of sanctions assessment. This will be done by constructing a theoretical bridge between parts of the comprehensive and targeted sanctions literature that deal with the question of sanctions' effectiveness. While the general theory of sanctions has mostly been concerned with state-based sanctions, the shifting practice towards individually applied sanctions has been investigated to a lesser degree. Consequently, the theory of sanctions needs to be amended.

In summary, sanctions are likely to be determined and shaped by a number of factors from the time of adoption to the time of their daily management and implementation. Such factors include the role of the sender and target in shaping the sanctions outcome (formal and informal decision-making rules, perception and understandings of the tool); the role of sender–target interaction; the importance of accounting for the overall strategy within which sanctions are embedded, and the importance of seeing sanctions regimes as a combination of a number of specific episodes. While I have restricted myself to these crucial factors – often overlooked, or at least not combined in the same analysis – there may be many more factors shaping sanctions outcomes.

Organisation of the Book

Having outlined in this chapter the need to reconsider the way in which sanctions are currently examined, Chapter 2 introduces the theoretical framework and the context of the trend towards targeted sanctions.

Chapter 3 makes a case for reconsidering sanctions assessment by shifting attention to 'sanctions episodes'. Unlike previous sanctions studies, such as the classical sanctions assessment study *Economic Sanctions Reconsidered*, the chapter seeks to demonstrate how to analyse a sanctions case by taking into account the political dynamics at crucial points in time (here called episodes).[22] The second part of the chapter proposes an argument for bringing into the analysis the enabling strategic logics that accompany targeted sanctions and that are likely to feed into the explanation of sanctions' impact. Underlying this claim is the notion that a targeted sanctions regime cannot be understood as a stand-alone policy in itself.

Chapter 4 turns to contemporary trends in targeted sanctions practice by presenting new data on the number of entities targeted with sanctions by the UN and the EU. The pool of cases examined consists of the sanctions regimes active in 2009 involving lists of individuals to be targeted with asset freezes and/or travel bans. The purpose of presenting these data is to illustrate present-day examples of trends in targeting and to show how significant targeting has become as a policy tool in international politics today. The chapter also examines the broader strategic framework in which targeted sanctions are embedded. As it demonstrates, targeted sanctions are usually accompanied by a number of other policy measures that are likely to effect sanctions' impact. The aim is to identify the main factors and political 'interventions' which the sender (in this case, the UN and the EU) relies on in order to achieve behavioural change in the target.

Chapter 5 offers an analytical perspective that brings the sender's formal and informal decision-making into the sanctions assessment methodology. It discusses the complexity of decision-making in sanctions processes, and how the structure and agency of a sanctions sender is, at an early stage, likely to determine the outcome of sanctions.

Subsequently, Chapter 6 investigates formal and informal UN decision-making, drawing on a number of interviews with desk officers working on targeted sanctions on a daily basis. By focusing upon formal/informal sanctions procedures,

22 Three editions of *Economic Sanctions Reconsidered* are available, published in 1985, 1990 and 2007.

I will try to demonstrate that sanctions enforcement is not such a straightforward enterprise as several efficacy studies that ignore these factors seem to imply.

Chapter 7 presents an in-depth investigation into the UN's targeted sanctions regime against UNITA (Angola). The examination of this case is structured by disaggregating the sanctions regime into a specific number of episodes where key developments are examined in conjunction with the sender's policy engagements made prior to and immediately after the introduction of sanctions. This allows us not only to better analyse the bargaining situation between the sender and the target (and its specific listed entities), but also provides for a more systematic overview of sender–target interaction in these cases. Another element included is an examination of the listed targets' perception and behavioural attitude towards the senders. This element is based on analysis of interviews conducted with some formed listed entities.

Chapter 8 consists of an investigation into the formal and informal decision-making concerning EU targeted sanctions. As in Chapter 7 on the UN, the aim here is to illustrate how sanctions' impact is likely to shaped as early as the design and management stage.

Chapter 9 turns to the EU's targeted sanctions (restrictive measures) against Zimbabwe, paying attention both to sender and target perspectives, and analysing a number of target interviews.

Finally, Chapter 10 summarises the insights from each previous chapter, along with some closing remarks. Given the complexity of implementing targeted sanctions, it will outline what more can be done in order to strengthen this policy, both from a theoretical and policy perspective.

Chapter 2
Rethinking Targeted Sanctions

Over the course of history, sanctions in general have frequently been resorted to in order to deal with complex political, economic and military challenges. Consequently, the policy has attracted much academic attention.[1] A review of the conventional sanctions literature since the First World War reveals that studies and academic debates over various aspects of sanctions are often triggered by the efficacy of newly established sanctions regimes. In particular, sanctions scholars have shown interest in evaluating success and failure. These and related themes will be examined first in this chapter, followed by an examination of how the literature on conventional sanctions has tackled the issue of sanctions' effectiveness. I will then move on to discuss the principal factors which have motivated and enabled the shift from conventional sanctions towards targeted sanctions, before exploring some of the new challenges in understanding sanctions' impact.

Conventional Sanctions Theory

An overview of the sanctions literature suggests that six types of sanctions debates have so far ensued during the twentieth century. The first wave of sanctions literature began in the 1930s, when scholars debated means to contain aggression in the context of international politics prior to the Second World War. This naturally included the use of sanctions. The second wave in the 1960s and early 1970s mostly studied sanctions as a means to speed up decolonisation. In the debate, it was often claimed that sanctions, while being less effective than military violence, was always a more attractive option than military force to deal with international crises because of the policy's non-violent character.[2] A number of scholars have provided empirical evidence as to why conventional economic sanctions did not achieve their goals.[3] In the 1980s, a third sanctions debate was initiated. Analysts now generally began to reconsider sanctions in a more positive light, arguing more favourably for the use of sanctions to put pressure on states that did not live up

1 For bibliographies and a literature overview, see <www.smartsanctions.se>, Van Brabant (1999a), Wallensteen (2000), Rudolf (2007) and Watson Institute (2007).

2 Pape (1997): 91. Note that other scholars taking such a position include Galtung (1967); Doxey (1968, 1971a, 1971b, 1972, 1976) and Knorr (1975).

3 Hoffman (1967); Wallensteen (1968); Nincic and Wallensteen (1983).

to international obligations.[4] Following this, in the 1990s, a fourth debate wave could be distinguished. This debate was primarily triggered by the UN sanctions imposed upon Iraq.[5] It was marked by the many critical findings regarding the side-effects and unintended consequences of UN sanctions, in particular the blunt implementation applications and the negative humanitarian consequences.[6] The literature also sparked a reconsideration of the conventional forms of sanctions, arguing for more 'intelligent', later 'smart', and nowadays 'targeted' forms of sanctions. This period can also be characterised as optimistic about the possibilities of this new tool.[7] Today, a fifth debate has begun. This is marked by a more detailed examination of targeted sanctions, how the various restrictive measures are implemented, and how they can be refined and complemented by other strategic approaches and studies investigating the unintended consequences of targeted sanctions.[8] This latest interest takes a more critical approach to the use of sanctions. In fact, some scholars have even suggested that sanctions are today one of the most contentious issues in international relations literature.[9]

Concisely, the sanctions literature can be categorised into those scholars who find conventional sanctions to be an ineffective tool (the negative perspective), and those who consider sanctions to be rather effective in dealing with unwanted political behaviour (also commonly referred to as the revisionist or positive perspective). Among the positions critical of the effectiveness of sanctions, one encounters in particular the work of Professor Pape.[10] His view is well articulated in his article 'Why Economic Sanctions Do Not Work' (Pape, 1997). This view has also come to be synonymous with a more sceptical view of sanctions. He is not alone, however, as some scholars go so far as to call conventional forms of economic sanctions 'sanctions of mass-destruction', primarily pointing to the policy's inability to coerce those responsible.[11] On the other side of the argument, there is the position of Professor Baldwin, who articulates a more positive view of the effects of conventional sanctions. In his influential book *Economic Statecraft* (1985), Baldwin criticised the negative analysis of sanctions that had prevailed in the literature to date, arguing that they were more effective than was often

4 Pape (1997): 91. Note also that those scholars taking such 'optimistic' position include: Daoudi and Danjai (1983), Baldwin (1985), Kaempfer and Lowenberg (1988) and Martin (1992).

5 Wallensteen (2000).

6 See references in Weiss et al. (1997) and Van Genugten and De Groot (1999).

7 See Cortright and Lopez (1995).

8 In a unique scholarly collaboration, sanctions analysts have formed an international consortium with the aim of evaluating targeted sanctions. Results from this research are expected to be seen in 2011–12.

9 Jentleson (2000): 123.

10 Baldwin cites a number of 'sanctions-sceptic' scholars; Baldwin (1985): 57. A list of statements on sanctions sceptics is also given in Drezner (1999): 10–11, and Jentleson (2000): 123. See also Hovi et al. (2005): 480.

11 Mueller and Mueller (1999).

considered: 'The two most salient characteristics of the literature on economic statecraft are scarcity and the nearly universal tendency to denigrate the utility of such tools of foreign policy.'[12] Moreover, he stated that it was 'difficult to find any proposition in the international relations literature more widely accepted than those belittling the utility of economic techniques of statecraft'.[13]

Following these debates and categorical positions, how then do conventional sanctions work, and what spurred the change to targeted sanctions?

Common Understanding of Sanctions

The 'general theory of sanctions' as we know it today was introduced by Galtung in 1967.[14] In his article published in Journal of *World Politics*, based on a case study on the situation in Rhodesia (now Zimbabwe) following the UN-imposed sanctions in 1965–79, Galtung defined sanctions as actions initiated by one or more international actors (the senders) against one or more others (the receivers) with either or both of two purposes: to punish the receivers by depriving them of some value, and to make receivers comply with certain norms the senders deem important.[15] In this definition, sanctions are understood to be comprehensive and state-oriented, as opposed to individually oriented, like the contemporary form of targeted sanctions.[16] Galtung systematically criticised existing assumptions of sanctions at the time, which foresaw that an outside economic interruption would transform into political pressure, which then would induce the current regime of the target country to alter or modify its policies (or at best, lead to its complete removal from power). To Galtung, however, the idea that greater economic and social hardship would cause compliance by the regime (that economic pain would lead to political gain) was 'naïve' (hence the expression 'the naïve theory of sanctions').[17] Rather than redirecting the pain onto the regime, he found instead that the regime was more likely to generate support, since it would be in a position to use domestic propaganda against the sender. This would also cause a 'rally around the flag' effect. In addition to enabling the use of counter-propaganda, the regime would also likely be in a position endure the hardship imposed by the sender, unlike the civilians of the target country (the problem of adaptability).[18]

---

12 Baldwin (1985): 51.

13 *Ibid.*: 57.

14 Galtung (1967): 379.

15 *Ibid.*

16 Galtung makes an interesting reference to targeted individual sanctions: 'For simplicity we may disregard … sanctions directed at individuals: with the present structure of the international system, territorial integrity makes such actions – unilateral, multilateral or universal – impossible unless they are combined with a military presence. In a future world, the supranational structure may include permanent enforcement machinery, stationed in all nations like police stations in the nations today – but this is for the future; ibid.: 383.

17 *Ibid.*: 388.

18 *Ibid.*

In recent years, though, this way of understanding sanctions has been modified. Tostensen and Bull (2002), for example, have argued that the pain-gain principle – generally including elements such as 'financial cost-benefit' calculations, the 'costs of casualties', 'political gains and losses' and 'trade-offs between future human rights gains and immediate violations' – does not hold true because the sanctions target may treat costs and weights differently in different situations.[19] Such refinement of Galtung's theory makes a welcome contribution to the field. However, as will be argued in this study, the conceptualisation of conventional sanctions differs quite substantially from targeted sanctions, as it deals with a different unit of analysis as well as with different instrumental tools.

Another characteristic of the debate over sanctions is that today there is no real agreement among scholars on how to define them.[20] This is not to say that there have not been some good and solid attempts by scholars to do so. While Galtung outlined the general theory of sanctions, Baldwin (1985) defined the contours of sanctions in general in greater depth by referring to the use of economic statecraft.[21] For Baldwin, there were at least three common understandings of the term 'economic sanctions': (1) a more narrow view of state-based economic measures to enforce international law; (2) one referring to the types of values that are intended to be reduced or augmented in the target state, and (3) an understanding corresponding to the concept of economic techniques of statecraft. While the two first understandings refer to the goals of the policy, the third seems to relate more specifically to the strategic means to pursue certain interests.[22] Regrettably, Baldwin never explicitly defines sanctions per se. Instead, he notes that 'The term "economic sanctions" is used in so many different ways that there is much to

19 Tostensen and Bull (2002): 375.

20 The UN refers to sanctions as a political action that can be taken in cases of threat to international peace and security: 'Should the Security Council consider that measures provided for in Article 41 would be inadequate or have proved to be inadequate, it may take such action by air, sea, or land forces as may be necessary to maintain or restore international peace and security. Such action may include demonstrations, blockade, and other operations by air, sea, or land forces of Members of the United Nations'; UN Charter, art. 42. The EU defines sanctions in terms of restrictive measures: 'Sanctions are an instrument of a diplomatic or economic nature which seeks to bring about a change in activities or policies such as violations of international law or human rights, or policies that do not respect the rule of law or democratic principles'; definition from EU Commission Website, 'Sanctions or restrictive measures', <http://ec.europa.eu/external_relations/cfsp/sanctions/index_en.htm>. While legal scholars have provided different definitions, there is no commonly accepted or legal agreement regarding the definition of sanctions; Abi-Saab (2001).

21 There have been other attempts to define sanctions: see, for instance, Wallensteen (1968, 1969).

22 Baldwin (1985): 35–6.

be said for avoiding it altogether.'[23] Thus, he never specifically defines sanctions except as an inclusive form of economic statecraft.

Besides Galtung and Baldwin's understanding of sanctions, the literature has been greatly shaped by Hufbauer et al.'s (1985) accounts of how to define economic sanctions. In their view, sanctions 'mean the deliberate government-inspired withdrawal or threat of withdrawal, or "customary' trade or financial relations"'.[24] The authors also provide us with a solid account of various independent variables operating under such a policy.[25] Yet these efforts leave us with little understanding of how to conceptualise the more recent form of targeted sanctions. In fact, conventional understandings of sanctions need to be rethought. Rather than being considered a general and broader policy of coercion, as the general theory of sanctions suggests, targeted sanctions need to be redefined. Not only does this entail redefining restrictive measures (financial sanctions, travel bans and so on), but also how they are applied within a broader policy strategy. Another problem with the conventional understanding of sanctions is that it is too state-centric, leaving little room for its disaggregation into individuals, groups or other non-state actors. Recognising the limits of conventional sanctions, Crawford and Klotz (1999) note that 'much of the literature focuses on *economic* sanctions imposed by states against states. This conceptualization is simply too narrow. Sanctions may be undertaken by international organizations, alliances, single countries, corporations, universities, municipalities, or individuals.'[26]

In sum, the conventional approach to state-oriented sanctions does not really fit the multi-level approach that targeted sanctions currently call for. However, the legacy of such a conventional approach still seems to dominate the current

23 *Ibid.*

24 Hufbauer et al. (1985): 2.

25 The definition provided by Hufbauer et al. (1990) is often used as the main reference point for sanctions scholars. Later scholars (such as Drezner 1999) have also used their definition as well as methodology. A common distinction is made between political and economic types of measures. For instance, Blanchard et al. (2000) define economic sanctions as 'actions taken by one state – the sender – to interfere with the economy of another state – the target – for the purpose of coercing its compliance with the sender's wishes. Economic inducements, or incentives, are rewards that a sender extends to a target to secure the target's compliance or alter its interests'; Blanchard et al. (2000): 3. Definitions can also be more or less open-ended, leaving room for both political and economic measures. For example, Tostensen and Bull define international sanctions as 'the temporary abrogation of normal state-to-state relations to pressure target states into changing specified policies or modifying behaviour in suggested directions'; Tostensen and Bull (2002): 374. Similarly, Chan and Drury understand sanctions as 'attempts at exercising international influence whose goal is to seek a specific change in a target country's policy'; Chan and Drury (2000): 8. Most definitions of sanctions, however, remains largely state-centric. This is also likely to determine the measures of success or failure which one can attribute to sanctions regimes. This has also been the main theme of recent sanctions debates; see Daoudi and Danjani (1983); Baldwin (1985), Doxey (1996): 8; Askari et al. (2003): 76–85.

26 Crawford and Klotz (1999): 5.

research on targeted sanctions. This may also cause confusion in terms of how to go about investigating sanctions' effectiveness. Besides definitional aspects of sanctions, there is also the question of the *intent* of sanctions. A distinction can here be made between goals of the sender (the behavioural change) and the realisation of such goals.

With regard to the goals and purposes of sanctions, the field has seen innovative proposals and observations. For instance, a common view of sanctions is that they can be designed to alter the target's behaviour and bring about a complete change of policy, compliance, modification or a reversal of policy.[27] Barber (1979) suggested that the use of sanctions can be categorised into three types of principal goals of the sender *vis-à-vis* the target.[28] The primary objectives concern the actions and behaviour of the target state; the secondary objectives relate to the status, behaviour and expectations of the sender, and the tertiary objectives focus on broader international considerations, such as the structure of the international system. Clearly, these categories help us frame the policy significance of sanctions. Yet they could be criticised for being too analytically broad, and therefore of little value. Yet, to realise the plethora of goals mentioned with regard to conventional sanctions, actions by the sender to achieve these may need to be applied along with different, broader classical strategies, such as deterrence, compulsion, retribution, disapproval, punishment, stigmatisation, symbolic actions, threats, destabilisation, signalling, containment and general deterrence.[29] Regrettably, though, the sanctions literature rarely investigates how sanctions fit into such broader strategic paradigms.

Beyond shifting understandings of sanctions, there are also a whole host of problems with the conventional approach to understand comprehensive sanctions. These differences need to be highlighted when trying to understand targeted sanctions more profoundly.

Epistemological Problems

Much of the contemporary sanctions literature has been greatly influenced by the work of Hufbauer et al. (1990). Their methodology and approach (and those of other scholars working in this tradition) pose a number of problems and challenges with regard to how to understand sanctions, in particular when it comes to 'measurement' of efficiency. Three theoretical problems will be addressed in the following section: the close and vulnerable dependency between the definition of sanctions and their outcomes; the problem of what factors to include in a sanctions evaluation that attempts to demonstrate 'success' and 'failure', and the role strategic contextual factors play in shaping sanctions outcomes. These three

27 See Lindsay (1986).
28 Barber (1979): 370.
29 See Mack and Khan (2000): 285–6; Nossal (1989): 313.

aspects have been chosen because they bring to the forefront the main challenges that sanctions assessment studies needs to overcome or 'solve'.

The dependency between the definition of sanctions and sanctions outcome Symptomatic of some of the conventional research approaches to sanctions is that the sanctions outcome is highly dependent both on the definition of sanctions and the methodology chosen to demonstrate success and failure. This approach is very problematic. Definitions that are very narrow ('exclusive') tend to miss out on a number of factors that can explain outcomes. This makes such studies less relevant for policy makers, as they are likely to be seen as too one-dimensional. Yet even with more open and inclusive definitions of sanctions, the usefulness of arriving at such a policy 'verdict' is problematic, as including additional variables will not reflect the actuality of sanctions performance (for example, they may still not make the case for a casual relationship between input and output). A slight definitional change of sanctions can dramatically change the assessment of sanctions effectiveness. The sanctions debate between Pape and Elliott during 1997–98 over Hufbauer et al.'s rather 'optimistic' findings of success and failure of sanctions makes this first problem clear. This debate will be briefly revisited below.

Hufbauer et al.'s large-*n* database presented an optimistic conclusion regarding sanctions' effectiveness, claiming a success rate of 34 per cent for all sanctions cases coded for the period 1914–90. However, rather than the alleged success rate, Pape could only find five sanctions cases that could be considered successful, given that military force directly or indirectly contributed to achieving the sender's goal (which Hufbauer et al., according to Pape, excluded from their definition). The problem was, according to Pape, that Hufbauer et al. conceived of sanctions as a substitute for other instruments of statecraft – something separate from other stand-alone measures (that is, not in combination with other policy instruments).[30] However, Elliott, in response, meant that Pape treated economic sanctions as an effective *alternative* to military force, not taking into account the role that sanctions could play in *combination* with military force. According to Elliott, this view was simply too narrow.[31] Therefore, Elliott argued that Pape's more pessimistic findings on the data, at the heart of his argument, were the result of him placing the bar of success too high following stricter definition.[32] This exchange is symptomatic of the limitations of adopting a too narrow and inflexible definition of sanctions.[33]

The definitional understandings of sanctions have also been at core of another well-cited debate on the subject: Pape's critique of Baldwin's work on economic statecraft. Here, Pape criticised Baldwin's definition of economic statecraft for being far too conceptually wide. This, to his mind, invited several conceptual and methodological problems (for example, a mix of economic sanctions, trade wars

30 Pape (1998): 69.
31 *Ibid.*: 68.
32 Elliott (1998): 51.
33 A similar debate is discussed in Jentleson and Whytock (2006).

and economic warfare creates confusion).[34] To Pape, political goals need to be kept clear from economic goals:[35] 'What is at stake here is whether we should distinguish among different uses of international economic pressure, or whether we should blur them all together.'[36] Baldwin argued that economic statecraft is preferable to notions such as economic coercion and economic warfare, 'on the grounds that such concepts usually fail to maintain a clear distinction between ends and means'.[37]

In sum, the problem of adopting too narrow a definition and a static (as opposed to flexible) understanding of sanctions is that assessment of the tool becomes vulnerable to exogenous factors which could easily give rise to alternative explanations of outcomes. It also underlines the more fundamental problem of trying to measure 'success' and 'failure' in the first place, because each definition and interpretation of sanctions will affect the number of such observations one can make.[38] In fact, the limitation of such an approach – assigning a sanctions outcome on basis of success or failure – begs the question of the utility of taking such a research method in the first place. One way to avoid this predicament is to abandon the approach of trying to single out or 'rank' better or worse sanctions policies, or simply to abandon such research programmes altogether. Another alternative is to re-think the question of sanctions effectiveness by operationalising sanctions more specifically, disaggregating them into more refined sub-goals and considering degrees of sanction *impact* instead of effectiveness. The use of impact leaves more room for flexible interpretation and allows for different conclusions about sanctions outcomes.

Methodological challenges in the measure of success and failure Closely tied into the first problem of a too static and narrow definition of sanctions are the conventional sanctions assessment approaches that explicitly seek to evaluate the policy in terms of success and failure. Evaluating sanctions along these lines have received criticism for a variety of reasons. Jentleson (2000) summarises these main arguments by referring to the problem of defining what economic sanctions encompass, the different roles sanctions and sanctions objectives can play, the common problem of selection bias, the reliability and validity problems that a policy outcome is confronted with, the problems of attributing causality, the standard for success rates, and so on.[39]

Another problem with arriving at patterns of success and failure, in the tradition of Hufbauer et al. (1990), is the use of so-called scoring systems that grades sanctions' efficacy. The main methodological problems here include the

34 Pape (1997): 95.
35 Baldwin and Pape (1998): 191.
36 *Ibid.*: 196.
37 *Ibid.*: 190.
38 This is a long-standing debate: see, for instance, Mastanduno (1999).
39 Jentleson (2000): 126.

subjectivity of the individual coder when evaluating the policy, selection bias, relational problems (what one measures effectiveness in relation to) and the lack of consideration of alternative goals than those officially stated.[40]

On numerical scoring methods, success and failure depends upon the subjectivity of the individual coder and imposes both weakness and a challenge to the merits of assigning success and failure to sanctions regimes. Obviously, these considerations are not news in any sense for the social sciences, but they are worth keeping in mind when drawing policy conclusions.[41] The point of the dangers of subjectivity is also made by Pape in his response to Elliott's defence of the Hufbauer et al. study: 'Optimism and pessimism are relative concepts; whether one should be considered optimistic about a certain policy instrument depends in part on how one's views compare with the judgments of others.'[42] However, this is not unique to sanctions scoring, but applies to most quantitative approaches in which political behaviour must be categorised and defined rigidly. Yet it is worth remembering that it adds to the weakness of the conclusions.

There is also a problem of selection bias.[43] The problem is that the data being analysed – for example, by Hufbauer et al. – cannot account for all those situations where sanctions have been used as a threat, but never imposed, because of their successes. This leads to an underestimation of the data collected.[44] For example, by using a game theory approach, Blake and Klemm (2006) have found that sanctions may rarely be applied in those cases where they are most likely to be effective because the mere *threat* of sanctions generates the desired policy outcome.[45] Thus, sanctions are least likely to be implemented precisely when they are most likely to succeed (and conversely, if the sender is likely to gain through easy compliance by the target, the sender is likely to impose and keep sanctions in place for a long time).[46] An example like this contributes to the weakness of the scoring argument, as it is always likely to underestimate certain factors. This fact leads to a severe problem for accuracy in attempts to provide accurate scientific 'evidence'. Moreover, the goals of a sanctions policy may be manifold. This suggests that there are evident risks with scoring a policy as failure when, in the end, it could be a success.[47] But even more problematic than this, it is also likely that the measurement will not capture all factors that constrain and enable a sanctions policy in the first place.

---

40 In this context, Crawford and Klotz introduce five potential variables that affect the likelihood of successful sanctions: (1) government as a collection of decision making elites; (2) the target state as a collection of institutions that require material resources; (3) the target state as vulnerable as a result of its economy; (4) civil society and non-state groups and individuals, and (5) regional and global contexts; Crawford and Klotz (1999): 29.

41 Hufbauer et al. (1990): 41.

42 Pape (1998): 67.

43 See Blake and Klemm (2006); see also Drury (1998).

44 Drezner (2003): 644.

45 Blake and Klemm (2006): 134.

46 *Ibid.*: 136

47 Also noted by Van Bergeijk (1999): 103.

Finally, the problem with measuring success and failure is that success is *relative* to other policy goals that are often unstated. Thus, specifying the conditions for success and failure is very important – success and failure in relation to what?[48] For instance, what does a workable sanction mean?[49] It is problematic to say, as Hufbauer et al. do, that economic sanctions have a success rate of 35 per cent. This begs a follow-up question: 35 per cent in regard to what? The success of diplomacy? The success of the use of military force? The success of negotiations?[50] The need for specification derives from the fact that senders often consider a number of goals and actors. Goals may change over time for different actors and for different policy interests (for example, regime-specific, country-specific, regional considerations or the domestic reasons of the sender). Effectiveness in this context is also conditional upon the basis of the 'costs' of sanctions for the target, which was emphasised by Baldwin.[51]

While some of these factors are more important than others, the outcome matters in the end. Baldwin provides a good analogy of a company. The success of a company is measured in terms of profit. Some departments in the company may lose money while others make it. At the end of the day, it is the work of the entire company that matters when counting costs and gains.[52]

The role of contextual factors Finally, there is a problem with conventional sanctions studies, which pay too little systematic attention to other contextual factors when scoring the policy by a 'success or failure' approach. While Pape attributed the success of economic sanctions in the absence of other policies such as military threat or covert action, Hufbauer et al. argued that it did not confine them to consideration of whether sanctions is an effective alternative to military force (instead, they included aspects of 'economic warfare' in their definition of economic sanctions: 'economic and military pressure can act together synergistically').[53] In asserting that their methodology for understanding success and failure did take into account "companion policies', Elliott noted: 'We explicitly take into account the presence of these other policies and call an episode a sanctions success only if sanctions – relative to these other tools – contributed at

48 Baldwin (2000): 167.

49 *Ibid.*: 169.

50 *Ibid.*: 171.

51 Baldwin stresses the importance of the fact that if effectiveness of sanctions is to be understood one needs to account for the many different goals and actors that a sanctions policy aims at, not only one factor per se. Also in this context it is worth noting the findings made by Eaton and Engers: 'We find success more likely when the threatened measure costs the sender little relative to the gain from modifying the target's behaviour, while the damage to the target is large relative to his cost of complying with the sender's will – results consistent with both in tuition and empirical evidence'; Eaton and Engers (1999): 409.

52 Baldwin (2000): 172.

53 Elliott (1998): 54.

least modestly to the outcome.'[54] Accordingly, sanctions in this sense are seldom expected to achieve ambitious foreign policy goals in the absence of other policy tools.[55] Yet while the contextual aspect of any sanctions evaluation is relevant and necessary, such variables seem not to be accounted for systematically in the conventional sanctions assessments actually being made. One explanation may simply be that it is epistemologically difficult to account for contextual factors in any database, because actors and context change constantly, and the amount of data that would be needed to develop a realistic picture of reality in different periods of the sanctions regime would be overwhelming.

In summary, the conventional approach to evaluating sanctions is clearly problematic, for several reasons. In particular, there are a number of problems relating to data, methodology and the overall sanctions research agenda when seeking to demonstrate sanctions' effectiveness. However, one way to avoid many of the problems of evaluating sanctions cases is to reconsider using a 'success or failure' approach in the first place, and to consider instead the role of sanctions' *impact*. Here one could think of targeted sanctions' impact in separate ways: target impact (the actual effect), the target's behavioural impact (for example, behavioural change) and overall conflict impact (for example, whether the conflict was resolved). Such distinctions are not usually drawn.[56]

Having outlined the theoretical problem underlying the classical notion of sanctions, I will now illustrate how and why actors such as the UN and the EU have turned to targeted sanctions. We will also seek to answer what this trend has entailed for theory and practice and for the ontology of the subject.

Emergence of a New Policy Norm

In the mid-1990s, a growing sentiment against comprehensive sanctions began to root itself in public debate. The debate, which came to focus on the role and the effects of comprehensive UN sanctions, was commonly referred to as the 'humanitarianism' debate. It originated partly in the criticism voiced by organisations like the Catholic Church and the United Nations Children's Fund (UNICEF) against the negative effects of comprehensive sanctions.[57] This criticism was based on a number of negative and unintended side-effects of sanctions, which had increasingly become socially visible in countries such as Iraq, Haiti and Cuba. In the latter half of the 1990s, the critics included many NGOs, businesses and experts typically having humanitarian aid and human rights interests.[58] The UN sanctions imposed on Iraq (August 1990–May 2003) perhaps contributed most to

---

54 *Ibid.*: 52.

55 *Ibid.*: 58.

56 One could also argue that that the application of targeted sanctions is always a 'success' if one can avoid the use of military force (violence).

57 Hawkins and Lloyd (2003): 443.

58 *Ibid.*: 445.

this criticism.[59] An explanation for this increased criticism should probably include a number of early studies by the World Health Organisation (WHO) and UNICEF investigating the negative impact of comprehensive sanctions on Iraq.[60]

More specifically, following the first Gulf War in Iraq and the subsequent imposition of comprehensive sanctions, a number of humanitarian assessments of the impact of the Iraq sanctions were made, including studies conducted by the UN Food and Agriculture Organisation (FAO), Martti Ahtisaari's *Report to the Secretary-General* (1991), the Harvard Study Team, the Center for Economic and Social Rights (1996), and a number of articles in *The Lancet*. For instance, the findings by the FAO were published in the *Lancet* and received much attention. The FAO study, which compared pre-sanctions periods with social situations under ongoing sanctions regimes, estimated that by December 1995 about 500,000 Iraqi children had died following malnutrition and disease resulting from the sanctions (in total 1 million persons).[61] Two years later, the figure was said to have doubled.[62] Other research findings that were well cited was the data from Garfield, who reassessed many of the studies conducted during the 1990s. One of his aims was to establish minimum estimates for the magnitude of mortality changes among under-five-year-olds. He found that there was a clear link between child mortality and sanctions, although data supporting such claim are fraught with problems (mainly access to reliable Iraqi health data).[63] Several of these reports also attracted considerable political attention. For instance, they led Madeleine Albright to publish in *Annals of Internal Medicine* a view from the State Department on the effect of sanctions and the findings on child mortality.[64] Essentially, the article sought to highlight that in the regions of Iraq where the UN was in control, the children were better off than those living in areas under direct control of the Iraqi president, Saddam Hussein.[65]

Despite being well received overall, a scholarly debate ensued concerning the accuracy of the sanctions assessments. Several articles were published which questioned the results of some of these studies, pinpointing potential

59 A collection of 'critical' voices is presented in Arnove (2003).

60 Hawkins and Lloyd (2003): 443.

61 See Food and Agriculture Organization (FAO) (1995, 1996), and Zaidi and Smith-Faz (1995).

62 FAO (1998).

63 The debate on the impact of the comprehensive sanctions on Iraq is now largely over. No systematic reassessment of these data has since been carried out. Meanwhile, the previous Iraq sanctions regime continues to be an important reference point for the kind of unintended consequences that may follow when no differentiation is made between the decision-making elite and the people.

64 Albright (2000): 155–7. Yet her view may be contrasted with a TV comment in 1996 where she was prepared to assert that the killing of 500,000 children was justified to protect US interests; Simons (1999): 179.

65 Ali and Shah (2000): 1,851.

exaggerations in the findings.[66] In particular, the number of mortalities following the comprehensive sanctions became the subject a lively scholarly debate, focusing on the use of questionable official population figures, as well as some methodological concerns.[67]

Besides research findings on negative population impacts, the UN sanctions on Iraq also gave new insights into the problems of enforcing sanctions not least with regard to evasion and implementation. For instance, during the Iraq sanctions regime there was an illicit smuggling trade via Turkey and Iran (with earnings of more than $800 million).[68] Although the import/export restriction regime on Iraq was strong, countries in the region saw Iraq as too important an oil trading partner for a full cessation of trade to be put in place. Especially following the establishment of the Oil-for Food Programme (1995–2003), the illegal trade in oil encouraged much corruption. To clear it from these and other accusations, the independent Volcker Commission was established to bring to light the severity and problems of the Iraq sanctions.[69] The commission presented its findings, which included lists of several sanctions violators (naming and shaming both companies and individuals), and even connected the corruption to the UN Secretary-General's office.[70]

Following the many objections, both to the impact and to implementation problems, in 1998 the UN Secretary-General took increasing note of the objections concerning comprehensive sanctions, stating, inter alia,[71] that:

> I have in the past underlined the need for a mechanism that renders sanctions a less blunt and more effective instrument. Therefore, I welcome the fact that the concept of 'smart sanctions', which seeks to pressure regimes rather than peoples and thus reduce humanitarian costs, has been gaining support among Member States.

---

66 See, for instance, London School of Hygiene and Tropical Medicine (1996) and Baram (2000).

67 The legacy of the comprehensive sanctions debate on Iraq seems today be that the sanctions regime relentlessly eroded both the physical and psychological well-being of an entire generation of Iraqis following the sanctions; Alsnasrawi (2001). On the other hand, there is also a sense among sanctions scholars that measures imposed on Iraq were successful in effectively disarming and preventing the Iraq regime from developing and using WMD; Lopez and Cortright (2004): 94.

68 Cortright and Lopez (1999): 743–4; Lopez and Cortright (2004): 97–8.

69 A number of reports have focused on the Oil-for-Food Programme, including *Report on the Manipulation of the Oil-for-Food Programme*, referring to former UN Secretary-General Boutros Boutros-Ghali; Oil-for-Food Programme (2005): 519.

70 See also the Second Interim Report issued by the *Independent Inquiry Committee into the United Nations Oil-for-Food Programme*, referring to former UN Secretary-General Kofi Annan's son, Kojo Annan: <www.iic-offp.org/documents.htm>: 4.

71 Annan (1998).

Yet it would take until early 2000 before the UN Security Council (UNSC) began to respond more forcefully to international campaigns against comprehensive sanctions.[72] One such move was the establishment at the UNSC of a standing working group on sanctions with the aim of looking into ways to improve sanctions. This standing group was initially led by the Canadian government under Lloyd Axworthy, later followed by the UN Permanent Representative for Bangladesh, Anwarul Chowdhury.[73] The group finalised its work in 2008. However, while initially promising, the work of the standing group hit an impasse: it was simply easier to oppose comprehensive sanctions than devise a politically tolerable option. However, the humanitarian situation in Iraq – created, at least in part, as a result of the sanctions in place against it – would speed the transition away from comprehensive sanctions. Another more explicit factor that also promoted the shift to targeted sanctions in this context was the resignation of two senior UN officials, Denis Halliday and Hans von Sponeck in frustration at the negative impact of sanctions on the Iraqi population.[74] They would later also become involved in awareness campaigns against the Iraq sanctions.[75]

Following the widespread criticism of Iraqi sanctions by various actors both inside and outside the UN, member states began to look more seriously into ways to improve the sanctions tool. For instance, in response to the humanitarian impact of the comprehensive Iraq sanctions, the ambassadors of China, France, the Russian Federation, the UK and the US wrote to the UNSC that sanctions 'should be directed to minimize unintended adverse side effects of sanctions on the most vulnerable segments of targeted countries'.[76] While initially having been quite stubborn proponents of keeping maximum pressure on Iraq, even the US began to change tack. In November 2001, both the US and UK begun to lift certain export prohibitions in order to ease the sanctions. France, for its part, wanted a complete end to sanctions. The failure of the Iraq sanctions in the end provided for such a shift in the norm that the UN has not implemented comprehensive sanctions on such a scale ever since.[77]

The turn to more intelligent and 'smart sanctions' reflected a changing attitude in the UNSC.[78] The shift in this regard was also as much an ethical one. However, this had less to do with the value per se of the sanctions instrument than the actual political consensus at this time.[79]

---

72 Hawkins and Lloyd (2003): 446.

73 Cortright and Lopez (2002a): 7–11.

74 Hawkins and Lloyd (2003): 447.

75 See, for instance, Halliday (1999) and von Sponeck (2000, 2006).

76 UN Report S/1995/300.

77 Gottemoeller (2008): 101.

78 Craven (2002): 44.

79 Chesterman and Pouligny (2003): 504. Another explanation as to why sanctions have become an accepted and well-used practice may be the shift in attitude towards state sovereignty. Moreover, sanctions have often been a good option to a military risky (militarily, economically and politically) intervention; Weiss (1999): 500.

In conclusion, conventional sanctions have involved a number of theoretical problems over the years. As discussed, these have to do with some methodological issues as well as epistemological problems regarding how to define and measure the impact of sanctions. One common problem involves the efficacy of sanctions in terms of success and failure, and how to measure these. More importantly nowadays seem to be under what conditions they do so, and the implications of asking such kinds questions in the first place.[80]

Moreover, conventional forms of sanctions encounter a number of practical challenges. Some of these have been corrected over time, while some may endure. While conventional sanctions have been used by states in a number of complex emergencies throughout history, the negative side-effects now seem to outweigh the positive outcomes. This does not only imply that comprehensive sanctions will never be applied again, but that the argument for imposing targeted sanctions in most cases is always likely to prevail from an ethical point of view, thus making this approach more acceptable to policy makers. Yet, with the introduction of targeted sanctions, several issues relating to practice as well as theory need to be reconsidered, as they are far from being the panacea they seek to be. While the first optimistic wave of targeted sanctions literature has now firmly established itself in the sanctions debate, there are, regrettably, a number of problems that are increasingly becoming known. Before elaborating on these issues, we will embark on a review of more recent thinking and policy practice regarding targeted sanctions.

The Turn to Targeted Sanctions

In view of the practical as well as ethical problems of imposing comprehensive sanctions – with the UN sanctions on Iraq being the tipping point – the shift to targeted sanctions was a logical development. However, despite the ending of the Iraq sanctions regime and the move among leading powers, particularly at the UN level, towards targeted sanctions, by the mid-1990s this process was far from complete. Even today, scholars and practitioners consider how targeted sanctions should be designed and to what extent they should be applied to force targets to change their behaviour if it comes at the expense of general suffering among the population. As observed by Weiss et al.: 'Civilian pain is justified by the imposition of sanctions on the grounds that it makes an indispensable contribution toward agreed changes in policy by a targeted government. Suffering associated with a failed political strategy is more difficult to justify …'.[81] Yet a real push for targeted sanctions at the UN and the EU level followed a number of international processes

80 Such questions have been addressed by Haass (1998) and Blanchard and Ripsman (1999).

81 Weiss et al. (1997): 218.

related to the implementation of targeted sanctions (2000–2006).[82] More precisely, a number of government-sponsored processes considered ways to improve the tool: the Interlaken Process, the Bonn-Berlin Process and the Stockholm Process.[83] While both the Interlaken and Bonn-Berlin Processes considered various ways to design targeted sanctions, the Stockholm Process looked into implementation difficulties. Not only did these processes push for increasing practical measures, they also prompted a number of academic studies on the subject.

Recent Studies of Targeted Sanctions

Over the last decade, an increasing body of literature dealing exclusively with targeted sanctions has been published.[84] The lion's share of this literature has been policy-oriented and empirically rich, while less focused upon theory per se. In all, much of the debate on targeted sanctions since the turn from conventional sanctions, has been rather technical, in the sense that primary attention has been paid to the actual management of targeted sanctions policies. Another such interest has also been the implementation aspect. It is also worth noting that most studies have been sender-oriented.

Today, the literature on targeted sanctions mostly meets at the crossroads of political science and law. One can also note an increasing number of case-specific studies looking at targeted sanctions by explicit actors (such as the European Union or the African Union),[85] or studies reviewing particular sanctions regimes.[86] Over the last few years, a number of evaluations of particular sanctions measures (such as arms embargoes)[87] and particular features of sanctions have been made (such as the impact of targeted sanctions on civil war).[88]

The difficulties of ensuring a correct sanctions policy performance have also recently been the main theme in the field of targeted sanctions and counter-terrorism. Notably, a number of legal challenges by listed entities against a number of EU and UN governments have led to academic attention. For instance, following vague sanctions procedures, listed individuals, groups and companies have expressed numerous complaints about unclear listing and de-listing

82 Tostensen and Bull (2002); Brzoska (2001, 2003); Biersteker (2005).

83 For a summary of these processes, see Brzoska (2001, 2003) and Wallensteen et al. (2003).

84 Cortright and Lopez (2000, 2002a, 2002b); Mack and Khan (2000); Wallensteen and Staibano (2005).

85 Hazelzet (2001); Anthony (2002); Kreutz (2005); Rackow and Stegmiller (2007); Portela (2006, 2008).

86 De Vries (2002); Wallensteen et al. (2004); Wallensteen et al. (2006); Eriksson (2007b).

87 Luck (1999); Rydell (1999); Brzoska (2002); Knight (2004); Tierney (2005); Vines (2007); Fruchart et al. (2007).

88 Strandow (2006).

procedures.[89] In this sense, one could perhaps conclude that the very politics of targeting has somewhat collided with legal realities. In particular, one could distinguish a rather expansive research domain dealing with: legal, institutional and human rights practices of targeted sanctions;[90] studies evaluating the aspects of the UNSC's efforts to counter terrorism practices (institutional procedures of sanctions committees) and the general applicability of international law to these circumstances;[91] the implementation of counter-terrorism measures,[92] and institutional responses to dealing with problems of implementation.[93] One of the main observations stemming from these studies is that the codification of sanctions measures into institutional and legal practices has only very recently reached a satisfactory level of legal safeguards in terms of protecting the human rights of those on the lists on the one hand, while on the other safeguarding political goals. Another observation is that while targeted sanctions have been considered almost immune to the scourges that afflict comprehensive sanctions regimes, scholars and practitioners have begun to conceive of targeted sanctions as being in a state of crisis or entering a period of lost momentum.

What, then, is at core of the targeted sanctions rationale? Cortright and Lopez, who have worked extensively in the field, offer perhaps the best account of what targeted sanctions are:

> In our definition, a smart sanctions policy is one that imposes coercive pressures on specific individuals and entities and that restricts selective products or activities, while minimizing unintended economic and social consequences for vulnerable populations and innocent bystanders.[94]

This definition suggests both an instrumental as well as an actor-specific approach with ethical undertones. It also implies an efficiency argument, in that targeted sanctions can achieve better results more rapidly since they are more effective

89 See, for instance, the *Kadi* case and the judgment of the EU Court on 3 September 2008.

90 Gowlland-Debbas (2001); Cameron (2003a, 2003b, 2006, 2008); Andersson and Cameron (2003); Ward (2005); Geiss (2005); Biersteker and Eckert (2006); Dewulf and Pacuée (2006); Lavranos (2006, 2007); Fassbender (2006); Fitzgerald (2007); Foot (2007); Conte (2008); Almqvist (2008); Shagabutdinova and Berejikian (2007); Marty (2007); Porretto (2008); Rosand et al. (2008).

91 Rosand (2004); Bianchi (2007); Eeckhout (2007); Farrall (2007); Flynn (2007); Franck et al. (2007), ch. 7; Rosand et al. (2007); Chesterman (2008); Stenhammar (2008).

92 Jimeno-Bulnes (2004); Gregory (2005); Lopez et al. (2006); Millar and Rosand (2006); Bures (2006); Stiles and Thayne (2006); Biersteker and Eckert (2007); Cortright and Lopez (2007); Rackow and Stegmiller (2007).

93 Sutterlin (2003); Hurd (2007); Allen (2008).

94 Cortright and Lopez (2002b): 2.

in achieving goals and undercutting specific group support for the target government.[95]

Unlike comprehensive sanctions, targeted sanctions are more refined, both in terms of relating to specific actors and specific goals. The policy also opens up a different strategic instrumentality, enabling them to be used in specific contextual settings rather than for broader goals. This goes in line with what, for example, the former UN special envoy to Sudan, Jan Eliasson, recalled as using targeted sanctions as 'drums beating in the background' when mediating in the Sudan/Darfur peace process.[96] Similarly, the former Special Representative of the UN Secretary-General in Côte d'Ivoire, Pierre Schori, used targeted sanctions as part of a conscious strategy of coercion against the individuals placed on the UN's list.[97]

In sum, the literature on targeted sanctions has proliferated in recent years. This increase is notable in many different disciplines. Before discussing more precisely the challenges that lie ahead in assessing targeted sanctions as opposed to conventional sanctions, we will review a variety of dimensions of what targeted sanctions entail.

New Targets

Much of the literature on conventional sanctions takes a state-based approach.[98] As a result, this earlier approach took the state as the primary analytical unit. In sanctions theory, then, impact was calculated on the basis of the net effect sanctions were likely to have on the society – the extent to which the political behaviour of the citizenry resulting from the pressure of sanctions was likely to change the attitude of the state. While the question of civilian pain and political gain has received much attention in the literature, less political distinction has been made between the effects on the government and society in general.

Targeted sanctions encompass many different categories of targets. For example, listed individuals can be those entities associated with terrorism, or individual members of a ruling regime (in those situations where ministers are included on sanctions lists, this is done both in terms of being government officials and in their private capacities). Measures are also applied against different groups and companies (for example, companies and organisations may serve to legitimise other subversive activities, for instance cultural organisations or local

---

95 See, for instance, Cosgrove (2005); Kaempfer and Lowenberg (2003).

96 Interview with Ambassador Jan Eliasson, former Special Envoy of the UN Secretary-General for Darfur, in Eriksson (2008).

97 'Interview with Pierre Schori, UN Special Representative to the Côte D'Ivoire'; Eriksson (2007a).

98 See, for example, Van Bergeijk (1999); Blanchard and Ripsman (1999); Cortright and Lopez (2002); Crawford and Klotz (1999); Drezner (2003); Hovi et al. (2005); Lektzian (2003); Mack and Khan (2000); Niblock (2001); Tostensen and Bull (2002); O'Sullivan (2003).

bank associations involved in money laundering or collecting money intended for rebel groups or terrorist organisations). Thus, in a number of situations, states and collective security bodies impose lists of specially designated individuals and non-state-actors to be targeted with sanctions.[99] Closely linked, targeted sanctions can also be imposed on private operators. These private operators may be linked to states, or they may operate independently.

New Measures and Application Areas

Besides new targets, the strategic rationale for using sanctions has also changed dramatically. Targeting now involves a variety of strategic devices, usually put into effect through a combination of corrective measures such as travel bans and financial sanctions, incentives and conditionality. More specifically, targeted sanctions involve different types of restrictive measures: financial sanctions, assets freezes, travel bans, rough diamond bans, timber sanctions, arms embargoes and luxury goods bans. More so, the rationale of targeted sanctions against individuals is to put pressure on, and hold politically and legally accountable, those individual decision-makers of the ruling elite who are formally or informally responsible for the unwanted behaviour (for example, the president, the spouse of the president, the party secretary), and/or groups involved in local armed conflicts, terrorism and political violence. Such measures involve, for example, the deterrence and prevention of specific local actors from engaging in unwanted behaviour by placing them on a sanctions list, imposing a travel ban and targeting their assets. Personal accountability by listing can also be applied during ongoing armed conflicts in order to promote conflict resolution, or in post-conflict situations to contain and deter active or potential spoilers.

Furthermore, targeted sanctions always involve embedding them within larger strategic contexts, where other political tools are used in combination with strategic measures such as the deployment of peacekeeping troops, mediation, humanitarian assistance and the dispatch of special representatives.

Financial sanctions and targeted assets freezes One of the most common forms of targeted sanctions by the UN and the EU is the application of financial sanctions and the freezing of assets. The benefit of using financial sanctions as opposed to a conventional economic boycott to coerce targeted entities is that they have less unintended consequences and are to some extent less costly to impose.[100] While financial sanctions in general have been applied throughout history, the UN introduced targeted financial sanctions on individuals (as opposed to more broad

99 Such lists often serve as general 'wanted lists' for a variety of purposes (such as combating terrorism, the drug trade, smuggling or money laundering).

100 Cortright and Lopez (2002): 93.

financial sanctions against a regime) for the first time with the establishment of the Haiti sanctions adopted in June 1993 (UNSCR 841).[101] However, this sanctions regime was not binding as is often the case, and did not include a sanctions list.[102] On the other hand, it singled out sanctions on the regime, as opposed to Haiti as a whole. While increasingly adopted in a number of sanctions regimes during the 1990s, the events of 11 September 2001 gave this instrument an imperative role in the US-led so-called 'global war on terror'.[103] Imposing financial sanctions has been an important tool for policy makers because it can perform preventive, deterrent, investigative and analytical functions.[104]

Financial sanctions commonly refer to three types of measures: suspension of loans or aid withdrawal by the sender; denial of access to international financial markets, and bans on capital investment into the targeted state.[105] In addition, financial sanctions often involve sector-specific bans, such as an oil ban, textile ban or a ban on using a particular currency or engaging with particular financial operators such as banks.

During the Interlaken Process, much attention was dedicated to enhancing the efficacy of the financial sanctions tool.[106] Contributors to the process treated considered financial sanctions as 'financial' in that they involve the freezing or blocking of funds and other financial resources, and as 'sanctions' in that they are coercive measures applied to effect change. In this sense, targeted financial sanctions represent an impending alternative to general trade sanctions. They are generally used in conjunction with other coercive measures (such as diplomatic initiatives, travel bans or the threat or use of military force) as part of a multilateral strategy towards a target country.[107]

Targeted assets freezes are applied in order to deny or deprive particular entities, whether an individual, group, company or institution, of their assets or property (as opposed a group punishment).[108] Further to this, these types of sanctions are enacted either to undermine the activities of the target or to irritate the target by 'naming and shaming' it in a more symbolic way. A policy problem in this context is whether one is targeting the person in his or her private/personal capacity or

101 Note that governments on a bilateral scale have used targeted financial sanctions.

102 See discussion in Cortright et al. (2002): 26.

103 For a good introduction to the literature of targeted financial sanctions as well as an overview of sanctions regimes applying such measures, see Biersteker et al. (2000): 2–12.

104 Biersteker and Eckert (2008): 2.

105 Tostensen and Bull (2002).

106 See Interlaken Process (1998b).

107 Definition used by the sanctions project at Watson, Brown University: <http://www.watsoninstitute.org>.

108 Using a military analogy, Newcomb notes: 'the target must be defined with enough specificity so that those who are sent to attack it will know both what they need to attack and whether they have hit it'; Newcomb (2002): 47.

in his or her official capacity. Similar to the problem of adopting travel ban lists, policy makers today do not seem particular clear on this, and nor does international law provide a clear answer. This poses a severe challenge to the entire policy. However, it is not wrong, given the rationale of the shift to targeted sanctions, to consider it as a tool to deal with the person in his or her private capacity if he or she has misused an official position.

Moreover, a targeted assets freeze is often meant to be temporary in nature and to have a surprise effect (at least this often seems to be the aspiration).[109] Usually, though, an assets freeze is put in force until it has been deemed by the sender that the targeted actor has changed its political behaviour or been proven innocent, or that the political reason for which sanctions have been imposed is resolved. An important aspect in achieving maximum impact, though – which is also relevant for other restrictive measures – is rapid implementation combined with decisiveness, as listed entities can quickly their move assets and thereby evade the policy measure.[110] It has also been suggested that that financial sanctions should give targets an opportunity to comply (an incitement policy), and if they fail to do so, fine them heavily, which would have a deterrent effect.[111] This would be a gradual approach as opposed to a surprise one.

While many recommendations in the Interlaken Process focused mainly on the sender, a call was also made to conduct further research on targeted actors, for instance through a personal 'cost' analysis.[112] In the end, a target has the choice to respond to the policy adopted by the sender. Yet while the number of individuals subject to financial sanctions has increased dramatically in recent years, research has been modest. Thus, an important research lacuna remains in the literature with regard to the kind of impact this has on those entities listed.[113] The only detailed study on the role financial sanctions and assets freeze measures in this area has been made by Biersteker and Eckert (2008), and to some extent Elliott and Hufbauer (1999).[114] Most studies have focused on implementation aspects rather than on efficiency. Elliott and Hufbauer, for example, examined the many problems which targeted financial sanctions and assets freezes have encountered when being implemented, stating, inter alia:[115]

> The question, of course, is whether assets freezes can inflict sufficient pain to cause regime leaders to comply with the demands of the sender or even to send

---

109 The surprise effect has also been pointed at in some legal judgments on the imposition of EU sanctions: see 'Judgment of the European Court of Justice in Joined Cases C-402/05 P and C-415/05 P, September 3' (2008).

110 Cortright and Lopez (2002a): 103.

111 See Interlaken Process (1998a): 127.

112 As suggested by Doxey in *ibid.*: 129.

113 As also raised by Brooks (2002).

114 Elliott and Hufbauer (1999); Biersteker and Eckert (2008).

115 Interlaken Process (1998b): 194.

> a strong signal of disapproval. To have any success: regime leaders must hold assets abroad; the assets must be identifiable; and, in cases where compliance is the goal, the assets must be a large enough proportion of the targeted individuals' total assets that the costs of defiance – the value of the blocked assets – must be perceived as being larger than the political, economic, or other costs of complying with the sender's demands.

In noting these problems, Elliott and Hufbauer came up with a number of conditions that need to be accounted for in any sanctions analysis: the targets' access to new incomes and financial flows; whether the targeted individuals are more interested in wealth than power, and whether the targeted elites value wealth over the direct exercise of power.[116] An important question that remains on top of this is whether the target is vulnerable to targeted sanctions in the first place. For instance, is it justifiable to list specific individuals with targeted financial sanctions despite the fact that they are not part of the global commercial network?

In summary, while increasing attention has been paid to the problem of implementation, there is still little theory building on the role of target impact when it comes to targeted financial sanctions and targeted assets freezes. Few efforts has been made to aggregate the number of assets that have actually been frozen by various sanctions regimes (although some efforts have been made in the anti-terrorism and money laundering areas). Such data collection and accompanying analysis could give a sense of direction regarding degrees of impact.[117] It is worth noting, however, that such investigation only constitutes one aspect of impact, since imposing financial sanctions may also have additional types of impact (such as psychological ones). To date, there have been few systematic studies investigating the effect of targeted financial sanctions on those being targeted – that is, how they work and what kind of impact they have on the target and the management of the overall conflict.

Travel bans Alongside targeted financial sanctions, a travel ban measure is also one of the most popular tools of political statecraft to deal with individuals and groups posing a threat to or a problem for the sender. Over the years, travel bans have been applied with multiple goals, such as halting support to terrorism, extraditing criminals, having actors comply with peace agreements, preventing access to weapons of mass destruction (WMD) knowledge and technology, and restoring governments.[118] Travel bans have been imposed in several contexts, beginning with the UN sanctions regime on the military junta in Haiti in May 1994

116 See also Newcomb (2002): 48–50.

117 In testimony to the House of Lords (2007), EU Commission officials said that such figures were provided by the private sector and that these reports were 'being compiled'. No official figure has been given.

118 Conroy (2002): 162.

(UNSCR 914, 1994), and most recently applied to Iranian government members and official associates (UNSCR 1737, 2006).

Travel bans commonly refer to two types of measures. A travel ban can be applied to individuals who are either part of a regime or acting totally independently.[119] A travel ban measure may prevent an individual from getting a visa (also referred to as a visa ban) or from entering the country of the sender. Such measures do not cause striking negative economic damage to the target, but are mainly an irritant and of symbolic effect.[120] Secondly, a travel restriction, which is somewhat distinct, can also include aviation sanctions. Such measures restrict or ban international flights in and out of a designated target country, and may include all flights or specific airlines, covering both passenger traffic and/or cargo.[121] It has also been proposed that travel bans can be imposed gradually – that is, the sender takes incremental steps against the target, such as restricting travel, denying travel completely, or the withdrawal of passports.[122]

According to Conroy, travel sanctions have two main operational effects: (1) to cause a symbolic sense of isolation and/or signal a policy of disapproval, isolating the target from international processes in order to de-legitimise the target's behaviour and/or claims to authority, and (2) to make the target's policy of a non-compliance more costly and difficult to sustain, in the hope that these costs may reduce the benefits of non-compliance.[123] However, Conroy's view is not ideal, as each target is likely to calculate differently the value of complying or not complying with such measures.

A travel ban is difficult to implement and enforce, as targets can evade measures intentionally or contravene them inadvertently.[124] It is therefore up to each member state of the sending body to ensure the effectiveness of the measure, for instance by deploying international observers at airfields, ports and crossing points.[125] As noted by several sanctions experts, a travel ban seems to be most effective when applied in combination with other measures or as part of an overall sound strategy.[126]

One problem with imposing a travel ban or an assets freeze measure is determining whether they are imposed on an official agent of a state or in the target's private capacity. It is likely that most listed entities travel in the interests of their state, for instance to attend conferences that will be of benefit to the public. On the other hand (or at the same time), targets may travel to advance their private interests, for example to attend their child's graduation at a foreign university (which would require travel arrangements) or to visit luxurious shops.

---

119 Brzoska (2001): 52.
120 Tostensen and Bull (2002).
121 *Ibid.*
122 Van Brabant (1999b): 3.
123 Conroy (1999): 1.
124 Brzoska (2001): 94.
125 UN Department of Political Affairs, DPA (2000): 27.
126 Cortright et al. (2000a): 27, Kulessa (2000): 6; DPA (2000): 28.

To date, little investigation has carried out into travel bans and their effects. While during the Bonn-Berlin Process a number of cases were reviewed, little attention has yet been given to the actual impact that the target may experience when subjected to this measure. However, a few observations have been noted. Targeted travel-related sanctions, like assets freeze measures, can have both a direct and a psychological impact on the target (acting as an irritant for those targeted). In this way, they may also reduce targets' ability to conduct business as usual.[127] It has also been noted that targeted travel-related sanctions are only meaningful when applied to individuals or categories of people who wish to travel internationally and openly, and/or who benefit from the operations of international commercial flights.[128] However, these conclusions need to be further based on in-depth empirical investigations.

Other targeted sanctions measures Besides targeted sanctions imposed on individuals, groups and companies, actors such as the UN and the EU have also imposed sanctions on particular commodities which sustain political activities of listed actors. For example, in order to break the link between armed conflict and the trade in illicit high-value resources, the UNSC has on a number of occasions introduced targeted sanctions on 'unpolished' diamonds (as in the case of Angola, Sierra Leone, Liberia and the Ivory Coast). The aim with such a policy has mainly been to block sources of finance for insurgents, criminal networks and other warring parties. For example, experience from a number of civil wars in Africa during the 1990s shows that in many cases, local warlords have been dependent on securing natural resources in order to sustain their military machinery (paying for arms, soldiers/militia salaries, and so on).[129] Dealing with money is often a vulnerable and difficult logistical matter. Minerals such as diamonds, on the other hand, are easier to carry around, to smuggle and to hide from the regular financial system. Thus, in cases where valuable natural resources exist, actors tend to deal in high-value minerals such as diamonds instead. The many complications involved in preventing this kind of rough diamond trade have led collective security actors such as the UNSC to actively support the development of a strong monitoring mechanism in order to ensure that conflict diamonds are being correctly certified through the Kimberley Process.[130]

127 Brzoska (2001): 48.

128 *Ibid.*

129 For a good introduction to the illicit trade in rough diamonds, see Farah (2008), who looks specifically at the activities of al-Qaeda.

130 For the EU, the work with the Kimberley Process started with the Council Regulation established in December 2002: Council Regulation (EC) No. 2002/2368, of 20 December 2002. The Regulation specifies how community members should work together to establish effective control of the international trade in rough diamonds – that is, how to 'prevent the trade in conflict diamonds from financing the efforts of rebel movements and their allies to undermine legitimate governments'.

Besides using targeted sanctions on rough diamonds, the UN and the EU have also increased their methods to target trade in high-value timber.[131] Like rough diamonds, timber is also considered to be a source for funding local armed conflicts, and has therefore been considered worthy of control. As in the case of the civil war in Liberia, timber became a substitute source of income when trading in conflict diamonds became more difficult following the travel ban.[132] Here, the export of timber provided the financial means to prolong the war. Consequently, the UN and EU imposed sanctions on the timber trade.

In most sanctions regimes, the UN and the EU have adopted arms embargoes. According to the report *United Nations Arms Embargoes: Their Impact on Arms Flows and Target Behaviour* (Fruchart et al., 2007), arms embargoes are one of the more frequently used sanctions measures.[133] In the period 1990–2005, 74 arms embargoes were introduced, and they continue to proliferate as an important policy to deal with conflicts.[134] The main purpose of an arms embargo is to deny or reduce access to weapons for parties to the conflict. Usually both parties are targeted, sometimes only one. Like other targeted measures, the implementation of arms embargoes is very difficult as it entails a complex process. Not only is the arms trade a lucrative market generating much money, and thereby attracting many actors (legitimate as well as illegitimate), but monitoring and implementation requires extensive resources and political will to be fully effective. At the UN, sanctions can be mandatory, or voluntary pending the stipulations of the UNSC Resolution establishing such a regime. In the EU context, arms embargoes are typically provided for in a Common Position, since they are not covered by the common market principles (community regulations). Thus, the imposition of EU arms embargoes is carried out at the member state level.[135]

Finally, the UNSC, and later the EU, also adopted a luxury goods ban as part of the targeted sanctions rationale. The imposition of trade in luxurious commodities, however, is a unique action rather than a common practice. Recently, the UN and

131 For instance, the EU has introduced an action plan, called the EU Action Plan for Forest Law Enforcement, Governance and Trade (FLEGT), specified in Council Regulation (EC) No. 2173/2005 of 20 December 2005.

132 This spurred, inter alia, the UN Security Council to include on the sanctions list the arms and timber trader Guus Kouwenhoven (an associate of the warlord Charles Taylor). He was brought to the District Court of The Hague on 24 April 2006. In March 2008 he was acquitted, but his case is under appeal.

133 Fruchart et al. (2007).

134 Brzoska (2008).

135 Most of the time, its operative provision refers to the EU Code of Conduct, which sets the common standards for arms transfers by an EU member state; *European Union Code of Conduct on Arms Exports* (1998). Whenever an arms embargo is implemented, the *Common Military List of the European Union* is likely to be consulted. For more on this, consult the *Official Journal* of the European Union 2006/17/3, 2006/C66: 01. Another reference point is the *Council Common Position on the Control of Arms Brokering and the List of Dual-use Items and Technology*.

the EU imposed such a policy measure against the Democratic People's Republic of Korea (North Korea). Sanctions targeting particular luxury commodities are mostly intended to cause annoyance and irritation, and therefore mostly of symbolic value. This does not mean that they do not effect the target, as they may have a strong psychological impact. Luxury goods sanctions, however, generally tend to have several implementation problems in terms of what commodities to include in such a regime, and because such bans may easily harm the sender's own export interests.

Unintended Consequences

While targeted sanctions have increasingly come to replace conventional sanctions, at least in the application of UN and EU sanctions, this shift has not come about with ease.[136] While the theoretical rationale for targeted sanctions seems fairly logical and straightforward, the practicalities of targeted sanctions are complex and problematic.[137] Some scholars even argue that targeted sanctions are more complex than comprehensive ones.[138]

One of the main problems with listing individuals is, as Haass has pointed out, that the opportunities to employ effective sanctions are rare, since one is dealing with individual targets that can easily isolate themselves from the sanctions measures.[139] Another closely related problem is that targeted sanctions do not always achieve their planned objectives, thereby producing a number of unintended consequences. This could lead to what Jentleson has described as 'backfiring' (strengthening the will of the target), 'misfiring' (humanitarian pain), 'cross-firing' (straining relations with allies) and 'shooting in the foot' (self-inflicted costs).[140] While several side-effects occurring during the early 1990s were discounted as early implementation problems, recent experiences of side-effects seem to display a structural problem.[141] Craven even criticises the kind of attention that problems of targeted sanctions have received in this regard:[142]

> In the absence of any such admission, however, it might be reasonably argued that the new initiatives seems to be more concerned with an intent to disguise persistent anxieties as to effectiveness of sanctions or the legitimacy of Security

---

136 The manuals provided by the Interlaken, Bonn-Berlin and Stockholm Processes best summarise the many complex aspects of sanctions implementation and management.

137 Several sanctions studies have portrayed sanctions as inefficient; Doxey (2000): 210.

138 Chesterman and Pouligny (2003): 507.

139 Haass (1997): 79.

140 Jentleson (2000).

141 Mack and Khan (2000): 288–90.

142 Craven (2002): 60.

> Council actions, by shifting its focus of attention towards the managerial questions of design and implementation under the banner of 'humanitarianism'.

A number of studies are currently under way that look at this aspect in more detail. Regrettably, targeted sanctions are never likely to get rid of the problems altogether.

Problems and Under-studied Areas

While there are an increasingly large number of studies on targeted sanctions, there are also a number of problem areas that remain unresolved or under-studied. As alluded to earlier, one such area has to do with the *impact* of targeted sanctions. More specifically, there seems to be a tendency in the literature to generalise too broadly based on too few single factors, rather than recognising the complexity of targeted sanctions in terms of achieving a desired outcome. Often sanctions are treated as a stand-alone measure where direct causal links between input and output are operating. However, experience shows that not only is there a need to integrate several strategic and contextual factors in any sanctions assessment, but it also needs to take into account resources, institutional capacities, technical knowledge, administrative capabilities, and executive and monitoring assessments.[143] One could talk about the need to include formal and institutional competencies and informal factors such as the knowledge and skills of personnel working with sanctions in any targeted sanctions analysis. This is important both for the theory of targeted sanctions as well as for an understanding of their role in practice.

This leads us to the conclusion that there is a need, in any serious sanctions assessment, to take a 'multi-factor' approach when seeking to understand the utility of sanctions. If we only examine the institutional capacities of the sender (for example, the UNSC, the Sanctions Committee and the Secretariat) or implementation practices alone, we are not likely to be able to explain sanctions' efficacy. In fact, there are even good reasons to question whether targeted sanctions can be evaluated at all, given that there are a multitude of intervening or background variables that can effect sanctions' outcome, and that all these may not be entirely encapsulated in any analysis. To conclude, it would be more prudent to illustrate the complexity of targeted sanctions rather than make absolute assertions.

Following the shift from comprehensive to targeted sanctions, I will turn to examining the role of formal and informal decision-making processes: sanctions episodes, the role of strategic contexts, target behaviour, sender–target interaction and the impact of sanctions. These particular aspects are examined as they seem to contribute, in a profound way, to the shape of a sanctions policy outcomes.

---

143 Haass's *Economic Sanctions and American Diplomacy* (1998) also seems to lean towards this when arguing that the complexity of sanctions often leads to unpredictable types of impact; see esp. Haass's concluding chapter.

The role of formal and informal decision-making One important area often left out of conventional sanctions studies seeking to assess sanctions regimes is the role that the decision-making structures of the sanctions imposing body play in shaping the sanctions regime. This is a problem given that one could assume that sanctions' impact is very much likely to be enabled and constrained by formal as well as informal decision-making procedures of the sending bodies. Any study involved in evaluating the impact of sanctions needs to take a closer look at the dynamics thereof. What is of particular relevance is the individual desk officer's perception of the targeted sanctions, and how this perception is translated into policy implementation. Experience suggests that there are officials working with daily sanctions management in sending bodies that seem to treat sanctions more as a symbolic measure, as opposed to leading to a direct effect – that the imposed restrictive measures do not lead the target to actually change its behaviour. To understand this process in more detail, one also needs to analyse the perceptions of the practitioners of sanctions. By doing so, one can better identify the particular narratives (the constructed understandings of how targeted sanctions are expected to work) that exist throughout the sanctions decision and implementation chain. In fact, it is likely that many different types of norms and institutional cultures of understanding sanctions are likely to exist along the sanctions implementation chain. For example, diplomats (permanent staff) are likely to have certain perceptions and expectations regarding what targeting is and what to expect from it – views that are likely to differ from other decision-makers and implementers – and thereby shape the policy effectively (for example, banking regulations or customs officials). In all, it would be strange if these did not affect the implementation of targeted sanctions.

Sanctions episodes A common problem in many current sanctions studies is the tendency to analyse each sanctions regime too broadly. For example, in the influential study by Hufbauer et al. (2007), a sanctions regime is understood as a case or an episode. Each case is thereafter evaluated according to its key events, goals, responses, economic costs, and a general assessment.[144] As described by Hufbauer et al.:[145]

> Our approach in dating episodes is to start the episode with the first recorded sanctions threat from official sources or the first recorded sanctions event, whether or not the threat or sanctions was made public at the time. We treat the episode as ended when the sender or the target country changes its policies in a significant way or when the campaign simply withers away.

This approach is clearly problematic. A sanctions case in this traditional approach seems to ignore the ongoing policy interventions undertaken by different actors

144 Hufbauer et al. (2007).

145 *Ibid.*

during the course of a sanctions practice. Such interventions in the end contribute to sanctions impact and sanctions outcome (the number and the degree of successes and failures). While the Hufbauer et al. database looks at different policy interventions, these seem to be collected randomly, as opposed to systematically. The problem with taking too broad an approach when assessing the effect of sanctions by looking at individual sanctions cases is not unique to Hufbauer et al., but also present in many other studies.[146] For instance, Cortright and Lopez (2000) also use sanctions regimes and cases as their analytical objects: 'The twelve cases of sanctions analyzed in this book did not develop in a vacuum. The assessment and derivation of "lessons" from each sanctions episode was an ongoing enterprise that shaped how subsequent cases unfolded,'[147] and 'Our small data set includes fourteen cases of UN sanctions imposed since 1990, including two different Yugoslavia episodes (Bosnia, 1992–1995, and Kosovo, 1998–2000).'[148] In order to address this problem, an alternative approach to understanding the impact of sanctions is discussed. This approach will better account for the ongoing interactions between target and sender. Moreover, in this new approach the perception of targets will also ultimately contribute to the resolution of the crisis or conflict for which it was originally implemented.

Strategic context The impact of targeted sanctions cannot be addressed analytically unless the broader strategic context in which targeted sanctions are embedded is also taken into account. Similar to the finding that many different variables can affect the sender's policy making, context is also likely to affect target behaviour. First, the success or failure of a sanctions regime does not automatically follow the imposition of restrictive measures alone, but can follow other political actions taken by the UN or the EU, such as military interventions and peacekeeping missions. Usually, these measures are only understood by taking into account for the broader strategic context within which targeted sanctions are embedded. Thus, in order to understand how a sanctions sending body operates and what constitutes

146 Despite the fact they are often referred to, definitions of the sanctions cases themselves are seldom used in sanctions studies other than in more descriptive and general terms. For example, while O'Sullivan (2003) uses the case as a unit of analysis, she does not provide a specific definition of what such a case means. The treatment of what a case is could be distilled from the multi-part analysis put forward which is designed to examine impact, effectiveness utility and comparative utility of sanctions; O'Sullivan (2003): 30. This analysis includes: the historical context, the effectiveness and utility of sanctions (addressing economic and political impact of sanctions on the target), the analysis of sanctions utility in a broader sense, and the future of the case; *ibid.*: 30–32. Doxey's understanding of the case is most clearly set out by the following comments: 'Details are given of the sponsoring power(s) or organization, the conduct which provoked an international response, the measures selected and their duration, followed in each case by a very brief summary on the main economic and political effect insofar as the are ascertainable'; Doxey (1996): 12.

147 Cortright and Lopez (2000): 3.

148 Cortright and Lopez (2002b): 3.

impact, one needs to implement a broader and more integrated sanctions strategy. For instance, as alluded to by de Chazournes (2007), there is an increasing need to take a more holistic approach when analysing political, legal and economic intervention (such as sanctions) in target states by the UNSC, as these operate in conjunction with one another.[149] Moreover, the impact of targeted sanctions alone cannot be explained unless we also take into account the political and economic actions taken by other actors in the international system. The type and number of international and regional actors may play a decisive role in the behaviour of the target, such as the involvement of actors like the US, Russia, China, the Commonwealth and the African Union. Particularly important in this regard is the role of neighbouring countries, since they may be decisive in determining whether sanctions are implemented or not, which in the end will affect the ability of targets to travel and access their personal finances.[150]

Finally, the location of the targeted actor at the time of the sanctions is likely to shape the impact of sanctions. Here one may consider targets' cognitive location and physical location at the time of targeting. The target's cognitive location refers to the perception of the target at the time of the imposition of the targeted sanctions; for example, the kind of information that is available to the target, the perception of risk associated with evading sanctions, or prior experience with the sender. The target's physical location refers to his or her actual geographical location, the proximity of regional actors or support from neighbouring states, the political stability of the country of location, and the integration of the target in the financial infrastructure.[151]

Target behaviour The conventional literature has so far had a tendency to be heavily state-centred. More attention is therefore needed to understand the reaction of the listed individual. Until now, sanctions studies interested in target behaviour have mostly examined regime or group behaviour, rather than individual behaviour.[152] This is somewhat misleading. Political behaviour refers to the reaction that the individual or the group displays when the travel or frozen

---

149 De Chazournes (2007): 25–6.

150 This was a noted feature in a sanctions study conducted on Burma/Myanmar; see Wallensteen et al. (2004).

151 As the geographical context of each sanctions regime is completely different, one could assume that each sanctions regime has its specific dynamics and therefore cannot be generalised beyond the specific context. For instance, if we are to explain the behaviour of a targeted actor in Myanmar (EU sanctions), we need to consider that there is a geographical and mental proximity between Myanmar's leadership and the leadership in China (the regional superpower which is currently supportive of Myanmar's political decisions). Were we, for instance, to consider targeted sanctions on the former Yugoslavia, then the proximity of the EU and Russia would be relevant. In particular, the EU's engagement would enable a stronger sanctions implementation, and therefore also the impact on the target. This also provides an explanation for sanctions outcomes.

152 Allen (2008).

assets measure are imposed – the response *vis-à-vis* the sanctions sending body. What is important to take into account when trying to understand why particular target behaviour is displayed and how it comes about?[153] A behavioural change can be achieved by sender actions such as threats, punishment and positive incentives. This can be done by using methods that alter the target's activities, whether they impede or stop them completely.[154] Thus, the sender needs to select the most appropriate instrument to change the calculus of the target. While the sender may expect to achieve a behavioural change, it cannot expect to realise its overarching goal with such a measure unless it also takes into account the broader strategic context within which the target operates.[155] Thus, practitioners also need to account for the underlying conditions promoting the need for a behavioural change, such as conflict resolution, regional stability, democratisation and state building. In addition, the sender needs to make sure that the specific sanctions tool and the strategic context operate in tandem. However, the political behaviour of a listed entity can be observed. What, then, are the likely impacts on political behaviour?

Following conventional sanctions and state reactions to sanctions, Doxey has identified a number of common political reactions that can either be short-term or long-term: anticipatory action, defence of economy, reliance on non-participants, sanctions evasions, counter-measures, political and psychological effects, and mitigation of hardships.[156] Most of these forms of reactions also seem plausible to translate to the individual level. In a more refined way, one could observe effects such as sobering, restraint, repentance, victimisation or repellence.[157] Such reactions have not been investigated systematically.

Sender–target interaction The political behaviour of a target *vis-à-vis* the sender may also be observed as a factor of sender–target interaction. This interaction is also likely to influence the success or failure of any sanctions regime. Yet this kind of dynamic is usually left out of many studies evaluating the success or failure of sanctions. Interaction typically takes place in the form of both target and sender's

153 Kelley makes a distinction between the methods for achieving such change, and the actual behaviour to be changed; Kelley (2004): 29).

154 Freedman (1998): 44. In this context, one could also think of aspects relevant to the target, such as status, resources, authority, values (social and financial), interests, ideology, principles, and so on.

155 George has found eight contextual factors affecting a policy maker's coercive diplomacy; George (1991): 70. In a similar way, this book argues that the political behaviour of the target – the sender is similarly to be effected (by variables such as types of provocation, magnitude of conflict interest, image of war, time pressure, type of coercive diplomacy, strong leadership, isolation of adversary and preferred post-crisis relationship with adversary).

156 Doxey (1996): 97–110.

157 Some of these effects have also been noted in some UN targeted sanctions regimes; see Wallensteen et al. (2006).

policy reactions, modifications and updates regarding each other. Such interaction can be observed by looking at speeches and policy documents issued by the sender and the target (for example, in the media). When it comes to sender–target interaction, such a factor may follow because of a historical tie, such as a particular conflict, or based on an expected future relationship. For instance, in the case of the EU's sanctions on Zimbabwe, mostly driven by the UK, there are colonial ties, a strong sanction pre-history, and a need for future normalisation between the two.

To bring this aspect into the sanctions analysis, two cases studies illustrate how this can be accounted for. The two cases are the EU's targeted sanctions on the government of Zimbabwe, and the UN's imposition of sanctions upon UNITA. By including these cases, the aim is to illustrate how such an interaction can unfold, and why it matters for any analysis of sanctions' impact.

Impact An important aspect of sanctions evaluation is the kind of political result a sanctions policy can lead to. As noted above, this has led scholars in the field to demonstrate degrees of efficacy, and develop scores of success and failure. However, as also noted, such verdicts are problematic. Hence, the term 'impact', as opposed to 'effectiveness', will be applied. As outlined above, conventional sanctions studies have typically referred to economic pain and an increase in the proportion of the population who oppose their leaders in the target country.[158] Most studies of this kind have looked at state-based sanctions, conceptualising targets as unitary actors. This also reflects a general assumption in the literature on international politics as consisting of purposive acts of unified governments.[159] However, with the shift to targeted sanctions there is a need for another focus that includes listed individuals and their behaviour as part of the policy outcome.[160] One of the more interesting exceptions in this regard is Cosgrove's interviews with actors targeted by UN sanctions (listed by the Sanctions Committees in Liberia and Sierra Leone).[161] Based on interviews with entities targeted with sanctions, and a broader review of 10 cases of travel bans, some of Cosgrove's more notable conclusions are that: (1) travel bans are more likely to have an impact upon individuals who need to carry out their work; (2) the psychological impact of travel bans varies widely, and may in part depend upon whether individuals feel singled out for inclusion in the ban or whether they see themselves as natural targets based on their official positions or group affiliations; (3) individuals on travel ban lists may feel political pressure to limit or end their support for the target governments or entities, not only because of the travel ban, but also because of additional pressures or suspicions about them on the part of their superiors in target regimes, and (4) travel bans have the potential to inflict severe economic harm upon individuals included on the lists, since their professional reputation

158 Hufbauer et al. (1990); Dashti-Gibson et al. (1997).

159 Allison and Halperin (1972): 41.

160 Kirshner (1997).

161 Cosgrove (2005).

suffers from the stigma of being listed, even if lax enforcement or exemptions permit them to continue to travel (this is more likely if the target is in the private sector, where he or she will be affected by a bad reputation).[162] While seeking to determine how the target felt about being listed and whether it changed his or her behaviour, with reference to the expectations and demands of the sender, Cosgrove also found that this was 'an extremely difficult area about which to draw firm conclusions'.[163] However, the target's perception is essential in determining whether EU and UN sanctions are a success or failure, not least because this can be used to identify different categories of political behaviour.

In this study, impact is understood in three ways: the impact on the target (physical or psychological impact), such as blocking an account or preventing a target from entering a country; the impact on the sender (for example, side-effects and unintended consequences), and the impact on the overall conflict/crisis (for example, resolution). In the first two cases, impact can be observed on the basis of behaviour (such as change in political behaviour through actions, verbal or written comments by the sender/target), while the third type can be observed through, for example, a change in policy, a change of government, or the signing a peace agreement. Of particular interest here is the role of target impact, which seems to shape sanctions' outcome.

Thus, for further research on targeted sanctions, psychological impact and target perception will continue to be of interest in explaining impact. This will also feature as an important aspect in the rest of this book.

Operationalisation of the Targeted Sanctions Process

In order to better delineate sanctions in a more conceptual way and to emphasis the shift from conventional sanctions, some of the main elements discuss so far has been put together into a working definition of targeted sanctions:

> The implementation of targeted sanctions is a flexible and multivariate process embedded in a larger strategic context involving a sender and a target, where the decision-making, perception and interactions between these actors, during well-defined episodes in a sanctions regime, shape political outcome.

This characterisation is deliberately flexible in order to be applicable to a large number of cases. One operationalisation is offered in Appendix 1. The definition and its operationalisation may also serve as a reference tool for factors to take into account when imposing targeted sanctions.

---

162 *Ibid.*: 226.
163 *Ibid.*: 217.

Conclusion

Given that targeted sanctions have only been imposed for about two decades, this relatively short period has not yet allowed for much systematic investigation. However, a number of scholarly attempts have begun to observe the efficacy of targeted sanctions more systematically. For instance, as concluded by Hufbauer et al. (2007): 'the evidence seems to suggest that sanctions targeted very narrowly against rough regimes and their leaders can serve useful symbolic purposes but may not be adequate to achieve coercive goals, such as regime change'.[164] Yet a judgement like this needs to be treated with caution, because it is likely to have been reached using a methodology described earlier that does not do justice to the material investigated. What is more important than seeking definite conclusions or explanations of sanctions' efficacy is to demonstrate how and why sanctions have worked as they have. This point of departure follows the suggestion of Kratochwil (2007): 'The issue is not a test versus non-test but what "can count" as a test or provide sufficient evidence to establish a proposition (or to justify a particular judgment) at least presumptively.'[165] Instead, a middle path is taken here by offering illustrations of the complexity of sanctions implementation, and the implications of this complexity for the general approach to achieving target impact (that is, addressing shortcomings). These illustrations are also intended to make informed empirical comments on a broader theoretical argument that emphasises the intricacy of using targeted sanctions. The aim is to contribute to theory building. Given that the social world does not offer any ostensible basis for generalisation, the methodology will also partly involve offering some case studies to illustrate and 'trace constitutive and regulative rules' that help to explain practices.[166]

Having outlined the broader problem of sanctions, the next chapter will commence an examination of what a new sanctions assessment programme might look like and what aspects to consider in any serious sanctions assessment.

164 Hufbauer et al. (2007): 133.
165 Kratochwil (2007): 30.
166 *Ibid.*: 33.

Chapter 3
Refining Sanctions Assessment

Targeted sanctions can achieve a wide range of strategic objectives for governments and collective security bodies.[1] This has been noted in different contexts. For example, a study by the US Defence Research and Development Corporation (RAND) states: 'When it comes to pursuing some international issues, diplomacy is too little and war is too much. Sanctions help fill the gap.'[2] While often considered as a stand-alone strategy, targeted sanctions are seldom imposed in isolation. On the contrary, hosts of other strategies as well as a number of goals always accompany restrictive measures. As observed by Doxey (2007), the sender is most likely to have multiple goals, and sanctions may form just one strategy to accomplish these goals.[3] The role of targeted sanctions, and their embedding in a larger strategic framework, have also been noted by the United Nations Secretary-General Ban Ki-moon: 'sanctions [have] enormous potential to contribute to the maintenance of international peace and security when not used as an end in themselves, but in support of a holistic conflict resolution approach'.[4]

Moreover, applying targeted sanctions is seldom a straightforward process. As noted in the theoretical framework outlined in Chapter 2, there are good reasons to question the logic that suggests that the imposition of targeted sanctions will automatically cause a direct impact on a regime member. On the contrary, several constraining and enabling factors are likely to shape the policy outcome. Hence, treating targeted sanctions as a stand-alone measure is problematic for several reasons. Not only are sanctions regimes complex, context-specific, random and for the most part incomparable, but the methodological approach to evaluate sanctions in a stand-alone capacity is usually also problematic in itself.

Therefore, this chapter will make a case for the need to examine targeted sanctions as part of a larger strategic logic. The rationale is that this will better explain those factors contributing to shaping this policy's strengths and weaknesses.[5]

---

1 In this context, Barber (1979) proposed three types of objectives: primary goals dealing with the particular crisis or conflict, secondary goals promoting own interest and reputation, and tertiary goals using sanctions to uphold a particular structure or system of norms.

2 Speier et al. (2001): 1.

3 Doxey (2000): 213.

4 Statement by UN Secretary-General Ban Ki-moon, UN News Center, 30 April 2007.

5 Rules of the game enabling targeted sanctions might include components such as intent, resolve, goals, investments, signalling, willingness, preparedness, rationale, effusiveness, support, sophistication, follow-up, capabilities, commitment and sacrifice.

As touched upon earlier, there is a need today to rethink the very contemporary conceptualisation in the literature of the sanctions 'case'. More specifically, the issue is how to define and methodologically assess sanctions within such an analytical construct. As such, I will present an alternative approach to how to conceptualise a sanctions case. This new approach will allow for comparisons that are more systematic across such cases, as well as within these sanctions regimes. We will introduce the idea of 'sanctions episodes' and explore how such episodes play into our understanding of targeted sanctions.

A New Approach in the Study of Sanctions Regimes

This section will propose a different way of evaluating targeted sanctions than has traditionally been the case, by addressing two types of problems that are typically embedded in studies that seek to evaluate sanctions' effectiveness by using scoring criteria for success or failure.

First, some of the current theoretical literature on economic and political sanctions suffers from a level-of-analysis problem. As noted, the targeted sanctions literature has yet to shift its full attention to the role of personal targeting within a state, and refrain from taking a unitary group approach when seeking to determine sanctions' effectiveness.[6] Given the new context of targeted sanctions, the existing crude approach is likely to skew our knowledge about the functions of sanctions, as it does not reflect the attitudes, perceptions and behaviours of those individuals being pressured by measures like a targeted assets freezes or travel bans. Shifting the level of analysis to account for sender–target interaction will better explain the usefulness as well as the applicability of targeted sanctions than studies to date.

Second, a more refined methodological approach to address the sanctions case will be made. This alternative approach accounts for the ongoing interactions that take place between the sending bodies and the targeted actors. As will be explained, senders make constant evaluations of the listed entities' behaviour, as well as the situation on the ground, and extend or de-list actors accordingly. Thus, in practice, the sender is 'evaluating' the performance of the policy imposed. As such, each interaction with the target may be characterised as a policy intervention, and marks the start or end of a new episode. Each of these episodes can then be seen as an instance of 'success' or 'failure' rather than the entire case per se. This sharply contrasts with methodological approaches such as the one used by Hufbauer et al. (1990). They rely on a broad account of the interaction between sender and target by looking at the case as equal to a sanctions regime. To begin with, however, I will discuss the level-of-analysis problem closely aligned with this approach.

6 Examples of scholars primarily looking at states, groups and cases include Hufbauer et al. (1990), Cortright and Lopez (2000) and Portela (2008).

The Conventional Sanctions Case

Besides rethinking the ontology of targeted sanctions by acknowledging new actors, new strategic logics, new relationships between these, and shifts in level of analysis (especially in the assessment of targeted sanctions), there is also a need to take a more refined approach in assessing the effectiveness of sanctions. To date, there have been many attempts to classify moments of sanctions policies into particular periods, events and occurrences. In most contemporary sanctions studies, though, the unit of focus has been the sanctions case or the sanctions regime. While some studies do include a number of observations of what takes place, most often it is the sanctions regime that serves as the point of reference when determining the success or failure of the policy.[7] While several scholars look at the dynamics of sanctions regimes, efforts to define or even establish comparative turning points within sanctions cases are seldom given any specific weight, and are therefore either obsolete, absent or at best carried out in an unsystematic and random manner.[8]

A review of the literature suggests that the main studies engaged in assessing the utility of sanctions since the late 1980s have used a similar definition of the case to that given in the classic study by Hufbauer et al. (1985). The praxis is that scholars refer to the sanctions case as a natural given unit of analysis. Cortright and Lopez (1995), despite having carried out the most extensive research on targeted sanctions, leave us without a proper definition of a sanctions case.[9] For instance: 'The twelve cases of sanctions analyzed in this book did not develop in a vacuum. The assessment and derivation of "lessons" from each sanctions episode was an ongoing enterprise that shaped how subsequent cases unfolded,'[10] and 'Our small data set includes fourteen cases of UN sanctions imposed since 1990, including two different Yugoslavia episodes (Bosnia, 1992–1995, and Kosovo, 1998–2000).'[11] Similarly, in her rigid analytical study of sanctions, Doxey (1996) uses the notion of sanctions cases when describing her method, albeit not explicitly defining it:

> Details are given of the sponsoring power(s) or organization, the conduct which provoked an international response, the measures selected and their duration, followed in each case by a very brief summary of the main economic and political effects insofar as they are ascertainable.[12]

---

7 See the introduction to Hufbauer et al. (2007). Here a case is constituted and based on such factors as key events, goals, responses, economic costs and a general assessment.

8 Zucconi (2001).

9 Cortright and Lopez (1995).

10 Cortright and Lopez (2000): 3.

11 Cortright and Lopez (2002b): 3.

12 Doxey (1996): 12.

These operationalisations are inadequate.

Yet there are some studies which elaborate more specifically how to go about the process of targeting within a case.[13] Crawford and Klotz (1999) have offered the closest explanation to such a refined understanding of sanctions episodes accounting for sender–target interaction. Having conducted a literature review on theories of sanctions, they conclude, inter alia: 'much of the literature focuses on *economic* sanctions imposed by states against states. This conceptualization is too narrow.'[14] Instead, they suggest: 'The target of sanctions may be simply the state, but sanctions are better understood if targets are disaggregated.'[15] While acknowledging the importance of further disaggregation as well as taking into account the impact of individual decision-makers' reactions to the sender's sanctions policy, their advice is not really operationalised, which makes their treatment of South Africa (which is the focus of their study) difficult to compare with other cases. However, this case is treated within the conventional debate on sanctions, and is unable to account for the shift to targeted sanctions where other mechanisms are at play.

Commonly, sanctions regimes are defined and studied the on basis of the duration between the decision being taken to enforce sanctions and the point in time at which the sender decides to remove particular sanctions measures. For example, the UN sanctions on Iraq (1990s) represent such a sanctions period, lasting from August 1990 until May 2003.[16] The reason for demarcating a sanctions case in such a way is based on the epistemological advantages. It is fruitful to use sanctions episodes when analysing, demarcating and comparing instances of sanctions. The approach has also proven useful for quantitative purposes, where it provides a clear-cut way of delineating the frequency of sanctions events in the international system. For instance, the categorisation of sanctions episodes, similar to that of sanction regimes, has led to finding patterns of occurrences as well as designating their success and failure. Through such conventional clarification of the constitution of a 'case', one can make the observation that the UN has been involved in two sanctions episodes in the period 1945–90 (Rhodesia and South

13 One example is Chan and Drury (2000). These authors note that there are generally three clusters of policy processes to consider from the point of view of a case when studying sanctions: those pertaining to the sender and targets respectively, those pertaining to the interaction between the two actors, and those pertaining to their respective coalition politics. Similarly, O'Sullivan (2003) offers ways of operationalising cases. In her view, a methodology of analysing cases should incorporate an examination of impact, effectiveness and the comparative utility of sanctions. These should be based on the historical context, the economic and political impact of sanctions on the target, an analysis of sanctions' utility in a broader sense, and the future of the case. Despite the relevance and clarification, these informed comments are introduced in the context of a conventional state-based sanctions approach, where the unit of analysis is the case, and thus by definition does not contribute specifically to knowing how to deal with individuals subjected to targeted sanctions.

14 Crawford and Klotz (1999): 5.

15 *Ibid.*

16 For details of the Iraq sanctions, see von Sponeck (2006).

Africa), and as many as 16 sanctions episodes during the 1990s.[17] Similarly, one can observe that 116 sanctions episodes occurred during the years 1914–90.[18]

While this practice is generally a cogent one in terms of demarcating and separating specific sanctions events, the case approach is problematic if one wants to account for targeted sanctions, and especially what actually takes place during such episodes. By analysing and focusing on the dynamic within a regime, one can easily depict decisive moments that could be considered as episodes in themselves. For example, all instances of the issuing of sanctions lists constitute sanctions episodes, or more specifically, the turning point from one episode to another. It follows that in all such instances, the sender is likely to review and examine whether their policy is effective in achieving a behavioural change and likely to succeed overall. While the traditional broad-based view of what constitutes a review of an episode does not account for the frequent interactions taking place between a sender and a target, the more refined approach to sanctions episodes offered here does.

The Constitution of a Sanctions Episode

Unlike previous sanctions studies, an episode is defined here as one out of many interventions made by members of the international community in interacting with specific targets.[19] More precisely a sanctions episode is seen here as a specific period within a sanctions case, which is defined as the basis of a sender's decision to change, extend or update a policy position based on a judgement of the impact and the efficiency of its policy in achieving a behavioural change. A number of sanctions episodes form part of a sanctions regime (or a sanctions case). In this definition, an episode starts with the first point of entry into the sanctions regime, in which an actor such as the UN or the EU enters or initiates its policy against a particular entity. As noted, this could be marked by a decision by the sender to initiate, extend or review a sanctions list. The episode then terminates or re-starts sanctions with every decision to implement, broaden or suspend its restrictive measure against a listed entity.

As can be found in examinations of approaches to targeting, it seems that the sender is continuously engaged in an evaluation of the behaviour of the target. In some sanctions regimes this evaluation is based on a more general approach, while in others it is based on the behaviour of each specific target. An evaluation is based on how successful or unsuccessful a policy is, according to the sender. The assessment is dependent upon different factors associated with the sender's original goal in imposing sanctions (for example, the evaluation may be based on

17 Tostensen and Bull (2002): 373.

18 Hufbauer et al. (1990): 93. However, in their 2007 edition they have added nearly 170 sanctions cases. Most of these involve a mix of unilateral and multilateral sanctions.

19 Note that my definition of an episode not only concerns targeted personal sanctions, it can also be defined to account for interactions over commodity sanctions.

the sender's examination of the target's behaviour; the positive or negative effect that this behaviour has on the conflict; the ability to get the target and target groups to the negotiating table, and so on). Thus, each decision that the sender makes to review the list (for example, by listing or de-listing particular entities) is based on such an assessment.

The outcome of this assessment is often noted in UNSC Resolutions or, for example, in reports by UN panels of experts, or in EU Common Positions or EC Regulations. These assessments then make it possible to identify natural 'start' and 'end' dates of the episodes. While this alternative approach stems in part from a critique of the quantification of sanctions research, the benefit of a further refinement of the concept is that it will be more exact and detailed with regard to the effectiveness of the policy. The reason is that each episode can help to reveal the type of implementation that takes place; the type of situation that exists at a given point in the time of the sanctions regime; the type of change, if any, that occurs during the sanctions regime; the type and gradual change of the mandate that is taking place, and the type of exit strategy that both the sender and the target are likely to choose. This should be contrasted with the more general references and scopes of conventional approaches and conceptualisations of the case.

More specifically, the re-classification of sanctions regimes into particular episodes provides identifiable and structurally definable events of sender–target interaction. So far, this seems only to have occurred in ways that are more random. Each such event is given a start and end date. While Hufbauer et al. identified 116 sanctions cases in the post-1945 Cold War era, the episode approach offered here would instead have generated thousands episodes. These episodes could then be scored, if that was desired. Although there is no intention here to do so, criteria for sanctions episode evaluation could be based on the elements forming the definition of targeted sanctions.[20] Clearly, such a refinement would change the established results of the number of successes and failures of targeted sanctions. It would similarly be more accurate and precise, casting the utility of sanctions in a new light. For instance, a case that traditionally would have been considered a failure could now be considered a success through this deconstruction and reinterpretation. The main point is that the reinterpretation of the sanctions case through the lens of more refined episodes will show that there are many kinds of successes and failures taking place over time, and not only one, as the conventional literature

20 Criteria and questions that could be used for each sanctions episode include: new types of measures; implementation difficulties/challenges; types and numbers of main senders; other senders (actions, types of measures, co-operation, roles, and so on); decision-making and implementation capacities; types of bodies active in administrating sanctions; types and numbers of targeted entities; perceptions of sanctions (by senders and targets); political behaviour by targets; the 'quality' of sender–target interactions (with regard to sanctions and other forms of co-operation); the existing strategic contexts and rationales; types and degrees of impact (senders and targets); types and degrees of impact on conflicts, and other multivariate processes (changes in nature of the international system, location of the targeted actor in the international system).

would argue. In all, however, the re-codification should be dealt with cautiously, as it is very dependent upon a precise definition that does not really have to reflect reality in a precise sense.

Second, dividing sanctions regimes into more clearly demarcated episodes has the advantage of identifying patterns of interaction between the sender and the target. The events observed can then be examined and brought into a more informed analysis of the impact and efficacy of sanctions. While this has been done before, it has not been carried out very systematically for ongoing targeted sanctions regimes. Similarly, the interaction pattern will also help in understanding how the structure agent or the sender target is mutually constituted and self-referential in circumstances of targeting (that is, how they affect and shape each other's policies).[21] In fact, the imposition of targeted sanctions on a specific entity is likely to affect the behaviour and activities of the sender.

Third, disaggregating the sanctions regimes into a number of episodes will also contribute to demarcating situations of target impact. Not only can the sender examine through the assessment *whether* the specific target has modified its behaviour towards the other participants in the conflict (or towards the sender), but also determine *how* the target has modified its behaviour in response to the sanctions policy of the sender. In all, disaggregation of this kind also becomes very context-sensitive, as it makes it easier to demonstrate what affects, if any, targeted sanctions have during these episodes, and how they fit into the broader conflict process. By refining the approach to assessing a sanctions regime, the account of the target's reaction towards the sender will become easier to demarcate and analyse following revisions of the sanctions lists (that is, the policy decision), which will give the outside observer a specific reference point in time to compare how the sender has judged a target's behavioural change from one period to another. The reaction of the target can also be scrutinised by observing the target's statements and behaviour towards the sender's action of listing or de-listing the target (for example, by observing whether the target is travelling, making speeches/propaganda, or engaged in battles or unwarranted financial actions).[22]

The ability to influence a particular entity is also dependent upon multiple restraints and enablers shaping the kind of impact that will take place once a targeted sanction is adopted and imposed. Yet the kind of analysis that is being pursued is very much dependent on the kind of analytical paradigm one adopts. For example, while classical notions of coercion often take rationalist-consequentialist approaches, paying specific attention to cost-benefit calculations, there are also more recent analytical social-constructivist approaches suggesting that coercion needs to be further advanced by looking at the role of norms, rules, cultures, attitudes and perceptions in order to better understand the role sanctions can play. This needs to be kept in mind when analysing the larger strategic frameworks that usually embed

21 For more on the structure agent, see Wendt (1987).

22 This can be done by observing the behaviour of the target one month prior and one month after the sender renews, limits or extends the sanctions list.

sanctions. In particular, there seem to be three central factors that cut across all cases and contribute to determining the type and degree of sanctions impact.

First, the sender's strategic goal changes over time. Rather than being fixed, the sender is likely to shift its preferences over the course of a sanctions regime and thus enact new mechanisms and policy measures to meet these. Often such changes follow changing attitudes and behaviours of targets. For example, the North Korean regime has changed its positions concerning its nuclear enrichment ambitions over the years. While sometimes co-operative and accommodating, decision-makers in the government have at other times been more hostile. Thus, depending on the target government's policy of the day, the sender may strategically downgrade or upgrade its goals *vis-à-vis* the target. While the strategic concern originally may have been to impose pressure on targets, it can later shift to other threats and challenges that may be more demanding. For instance, new actors may invite or force the sender to adjust its policies so that it can face new dynamics on the ground. Another factor is that the conflict dynamic may have changed.

Second, and closely connected to time, the sender is also likely to have multiple goals. The level of threat, the number of actors, the level of complexity – in connection to political will and interest – may rank the targeted sanctions policy differently. For instance, while targets engaged in military hostilities have been listed, the main concern of the sender, besides seeking to achieve a behavioural change, may first and foremost be to achieve regional stability, or even to deter other targets (in the same or other contexts) from pursuing the same path. The sender may also have to change its allies, or confront new groups threatening its interests. Moreover, a sender may not only account for challenges to its strategic interest in the specific country, but also in the region. Goals and preferences can also be negotiated for to address threats and concerns in other contexts. Sometimes goals can even be contradictory or declared with other intentions in mind. For instance, while sanctions can be imposed to promote a human rights cause, the same actor could also be prepared to ignore instances of human rights abuses if, say, their military interest in the target country is more important (for example, the EU's sanctions against Uzbekistan). This makes sanctions assessment difficult. One case that illustrates this is the recent UN targeted sanctions resolution imposed upon the Democratic People's Republic of Korea (DPRK). While imposing targeted sanctions on the DPRK may be important from a negotiation standpoint, the tough UN sanctions resolution against the DPRK was partly designed with a forthcoming UN sanctions resolution on Iran in mind.[23] This example implies that targeting cannot be evaluated exclusively in terms of a single goal, but must be interpreted within changing and overlapping strategic goals. In all, it suggests that sanctions assessment studies which consider targeted sanctions as a stand-alone policy are very problematic.

---

23 Beehner (2006).

Finally, strategic efforts are, as noted above, usually implemented at different intervals (phases) of a crisis or an armed conflict. Thus, depending on the stage of the conflict (that is, what the conflict history looks like), the target may be more or less receptive to a particular measure. For example, in a sanctions regime in which measures are repeatedly extended, like the EU sanctions on the Zimbabwe elite, the sender may not be able to achieve the goal that was originally set, since the circumstances may have radically changed beyond what was achieved the first time sanctions were threatened or imposed. The sender therefore needs to be aware not only of how targeted sanctions are likely to work in a particular phase of a conflict (whether the right measure is being put in place), but also how sanctions will work as the conflict enters subsequent conflict stages. Sanctions measures are likely to have a variable impact during the conflict process, as the situation is likely to exhibit different kinds of responses depending on when measures are introduced. For instance, a 'surprise' effect is not likely to occur, as commonly assumed, if targeting has been implemented over a number of years pursuant to slow conflict resolution processes.[24]

In sum, these three notions suggest, contrary to traditional sanctions assessment approaches, that both the policy of targeted sanctions and the overall strategy in which targeted sanctions are embedded change over time and in context, and that it is difficult to categorise a specific sanctions measure in a fixed sense. Thus, having now identified and unravelled an alternative understanding of the sanctions case, we will offer a brief treatment of the problem of treating targeted sanctions as a stand-alone policy when assessing them. As will be argued, targeted sanctions are often embedded in a larger strategic policy logic that both promotes and constrains sanctions' efficiency.

Embedding Targeted Sanctions in a Broader Policy Framework

The use of targeted sanctions as an embedded form of strategic coercion is not new. Although the shift from comprehensive to targeted sanctions dates back to the 1990s, the strategic philosophy of targeted sanctions dates from far earlier. In fact, the practice of blacklisting enemies as a form of economic statecraft can be traced to the economic warfare of the First and Second World Wars. During this era, the Allies used selective sanctions as an integral part of their campaigns. For example, the British government used the first form of official blacklists against entities trading with its enemies. As noted by Stenhammar (2008), the British Trading with the Enemy Act arrogated for itself considerable power: under subsection 2 of the Trading with the Enemy Act 1939, the British Board of Trade

24 In one of its decisions on the *Organisation des Modjahedines du Peuple d'Iran* (OMPI), the EU Court decided that the sender may 'benefit from a surprise effect' by not informing the listed entity (in this case OMPI was listed by the EU as a terrorist organisation, but was removed from the EU Council's list of terrorist organisations in January 2009).

issued so-called 'Black Lists' containing names of persons and firms carrying on business in neutral countries deemed to be enemies.[25] Britain was not alone. Later, during the Second World War, the use of sanctions lists by the US government became an established part of its strategic warfare.[26] In this regard, it is worth noting how targeting has played a role as part of a broader strategic campaign of US administrations in order to counter threats to its interests. As noted by the current US Office of Foreign Assets Control (OFAC):[27]

> Dating back prior to the War of 1812, Secretary of the Treasury Gallatin administered sanctions imposed against Great Britain for the harassment of American sailors. During the Civil War, Congress approved a law which prohibited transactions with the Confederacy, called for the forfeiture of goods involved in such transactions, and provided a licensing regime under rules and regulations administered by Treasury. OFAC is the successor to the Office of Foreign Funds Control (the 'FFC'), which was established at the advent of World War II following the German invasion of Norway in 1940. The Secretary of the Treasury throughout the war administered the FFC program. The FFC's initial purpose was to prevent Nazi use of the occupied countries' holdings of foreign exchange and securities and to prevent forced repatriation of funds belonging to nationals of those countries. These controls were later extended to protect assets of other invaded countries. After the United States formally entered World War II, the FFC played a leading role in economic warfare against the Axis powers by blocking enemy assets and prohibiting foreign trade and financial transactions. OFAC itself was formally created in December 1950, following the entry of China into the Korean War, when President Truman declared a national emergency and blocked all Chinese and North Korean assets subject to US jurisdiction.

What is remarkable is that the sanctions literature seldom makes an explicit connection between targeted sanctions and these other strategic measures.[28] On the

25 See Stenhammar (2008): 295.

26 Both the US and the UK are heavily engaged in pursuing this policy, both unilaterally and multilaterally. The US government, for instance, continues to use the Office of Foreign Assets Control (OFAC) as part of its tactic to designate entities on sanctions lists, which it sometimes also introduces at the UNSC. Most notably, the US government has been active in applying global counter-terrorism measures against members of al-Qaeda, the Taliban and their associates following the 11 September 2001 attack.

27 Citation from the OFAC website, <www.ustreas.gov/offices/enforcement/ofac> (accessed 7 April 2009).

28 Most discussion on the strategic aspects of influence is found in studies on aspects of political and economic statecraft. See, for instance, Baldwin (1971), Schelling (1976), Craig and George (1990), George et al. (1994) and Jakobsen (1998a, 1998b). However, few if any studies look at targeted sanctions under such strategic umbrellas. Some studies, such as Speier et al. (2001), only touch upon the issue when discussing non-proliferation

contrary, targeted sanctions are often assessed in isolation, or if in connection with other strategies, only on an ad hoc basis. However, by assessing targeted sanctions in isolation, one will not be in a position to explain the inherent ability to pursue statecraft, nor to explain a particular policy outcome.

Recent practices in international politics show that targeted sanctions can be a valuable tool in contributing to objectives such as preventing armed conflict, stopping military aggression, restoring democratically elected governments, protecting human rights, settling civil wars, limiting the spread of weapons, constraining international spoilers, bringing suspected terrorists to justice and countering the threat of terrorism.[29] Despite the capacity to accomplish such goals, the strategic stand-alone impact of targeted sanctions is difficult to verify scientifically. One reason for this is that classical sanctions assessment approaches tend to ignore the strategic logic in which sanctions are embedded, focusing mainly on the instrument in isolation.[30]

The embedding of targeted sanctions in a larger strategic framework is not only a theoretical and methodological problem of more recent sanctions literature. However, in fact, the practice of the policy is seldom made explicit by policy makers themselves regarding how they see targeted sanctions fitting into a broader strategic logic. In fact, sanctions practitioners rarely seem to have the capacity to streamline such policies with other broader strategies (lacking time, information, capacity, and so on). As observed by Doxey: 'Well-chosen measures effectively applied can often play a useful role in encouraging policy change, but in most cases they need to be part of a broader strategy which includes sustained and skilful diplomatic initiatives …'.[31] This suggests that other features beyond strict sanctions factors also need to be taken into account when assessing a sanctions regime.

Given the various ongoing UN and EU sanctions regimes currently targeting specific individuals involved in politically complex environments, how are these to be understood in the wider strategic context?

Targeted Sanctions as a Context-specific Strategy

In addition, there are also a number of more specific strategic paradigms that also enable control over the degree of target impact. These include strategies typically described under paradigms such as deterrence, containment, compellence, coercive

sanctions, or in particular case studies, such as De Vries (2002), Cortright et al. (2002b), Rodman (2001) and Wallensteen (2005). This is simply because targeted sanctions is still a rather young research field.

29 For a good overview of related strategies, see *Accord* no. 19 (2008).

30 A good exception in this regard is Haass and O'Sullivan (2000), who argue for a more strategic approach to the use of sanctions. Another exception is Baldwin (1971), given the fact that he devotes his study to sanctions in a strategic context, yet he does not claim to evaluate sanctions. See also Portela (2006), who examined all autonomous EU sanctions cases during 1987–2003.

31 Doxey (2007): 59.

diplomacy, pre-emption and prevention, and the strategic role that targeted sanctions can play on their own merits. These paradigms also need to be borne in mind when evaluating sanctions. Unless this is done, one will not be in position to fully understand the underlying logic on which targeting is built. Regrettably, sanctions assessment studies tend to ignore such strategic perspectives, while over-emphasising the role of targeted sanctions as a stand-alone measure.

Beyond these more specific and conventional strategic paradigms, policies for achieving behavioural change and maintaining pressure, there are a number of closely related strategies that could embrace targeted sanctions. Here one could think of softer although equally effective strategies like conditionality, norms, naming-and-shaming and socialisation.[32] For instance, Kelley has highlighted the role of norms and incentives in the context of EU conditionality.[33] Of the different processes discussed here, conditionality, at least in the context of EU enlargement, is the main form of pressure. As will be shown, the EU has on a number of occasions used future membership of the union as a reward if actors in target countries or those with influence upon targets meet certain EU demands.

For Kelley, conditionality could be operationalised as an instance in which an institution links *admission* to the fulfilment of a recommendation.[34] However, these forms of pressure tend to be more general and imprecise than a declared strategic doctrine like deterrence. Moreover, they may not be as concrete as those strategic paradigms reviewed here; on the contrary, they could easily fit into other different strategic paradigms. With regard to conditionality more specifically, several cases above seem to fit such a strategy. For example, the sanctions regime which intends to bring indicted entities to the International Criminal Tribunal for the former Yugoslavia (ICTY) or impose targeted sanctions on those who engage in helping ICTY targets to evade decisions by the UN cannot be understood unless one takes into account the EU enlargement programmes towards the Balkans (such as the stabilisation and accession programmes).[35]

None the less, the strength of these normative strategies is that they may help to coerce actors to gradually conform to a common goal without the sender having to rely on or challenge the target by imposing specific goals, deadlines and threats. Instead of firm deadlines and detailed behavioural criteria in the context of sanctions (often perceived as confrontational and negative), the sender can operate in the background with general conditions for membership, aid, and political and economic backing if adjustment is made. Such conditional offers, as well as normative and cultural influences, may be linked to country programmes,

32 The EU's use of these softer forms of pressure with the goal of inducing change and achieving influence and compliance can be found in Finnemore and Sikkink (1998), Checkel (2001), Manners (2002), Schimmelfennig et al. (2006) and Schimmelfennig and Sedelmeier (2005).

33 Kelley (2004).

34 *Ibid.*: 55.

35 In particular through the EU's Neighbourhood Programme.

dialogues, exchanges, assistance, and so on. Thus, the goals of the sender can be accomplished by means other than the sanctions per se. The advantage is that the sender can operate at different levels by using such indirect and softer strategies. In doing so, the sender does not have to confront just the target (which targeted sanctions do), it is also possible for the sender to deal with different actors at different levels, and therefore harmonise an overall policy. The problem with not relying on targeted sanctions as a stand-alone measure is that conditionality and socialisation processes may look imprecise, contradictory and not as forceful in a context where such force may be needed.

While much has been written about broader sanctions strategies – carrots versus sticks, honey versus vinegar, engagement versus disengagement, positive and negative sanctions – little research has yet looked at the microcosm of targeted sanctions in more specific settings.[36] While it has been illustrated in this section how targeted sanctions are enabled by the larger strategic settings and the need for them to be assessed in those contexts, it is also possible to see targeted sanctions as an independent strategy on their own. Although they can seldom be analytically detached from a larger strategic paradigm, it is likely that the more local and the more context-specific the policy becomes, the more effective it can be on its own. That is to say, targeted sanctions can also be used independently as a strategy to address specific challenges, such as negotiating a peace agreement. For instance, mediators use the logic of personal accountability to engage specific individuals engulfed in warfare and commit them to peace agreements. In this context, much could be learnt from the literature on intra-state peace negotiations.[37]

As noted by Griffiths and Barnes in a study on incentives, sanctions and conditionality, measures such as targeted sanctions can be valuable during peacemaking to help shift the underlying dynamic of a conflict, and thereby assist with conflict resolution.[38] For example, targeted sanctions may play a useful role during different phases of peacemaking. In particular, these measures may be used to get parties to the pre-negotiation table, encourage parties to remain at the negotiation table, and to exert pressure on the parties to reach and implement peace agreements. Examples of such practices include Macedonia (FYROM), the Ivory Coast, the Federal Republic of Yugoslavia (Serbia and Montenegro) and Sudan.

In Macedonia, a peace agreement had already been signed when EU targeted sanctions were imposed, therefore the implementation of targeted sanctions was clearly intended to prevent potential spoilers from derailing the agreement. In the

36 For instance, a number of case studies have also looked at how the international community can interact with target governments and local communities during times of war, for instance in Iraq (Niblock, 2001) and Yugoslavia (De Vries, 2002). Advancing the theory in this direction has also been achieved by Crumm (1995), Kirshner (1997) and Abdelal and Kirshner (2000).

37 See Greenhill and Major (2007).

38 Griffiths and Barnes (2008).

Ivory Coast, UN targeted sanctions were put in place even after an agreement had been signed, because the agreement was implemented slowly. In the case of Yugoslavia, targeted sanctions were connected to the Rambouille Agreement, and implemented with the expectation that targeting would dissuade listed entities from persisting in violence. In Sudan (in the context of Darfur), the UN Special Representative, Jan Eliasson, used targeted sanctions as drumbeats in the background to pressurise groups still engaged in combat to commit themselves to a comprehensive peace agreement. Cases like these suggest that sanctions can be very useful in local and specific micro-level contexts, not least to hold individuals (such as rebels) accountable for their actions.

Moreover, as noted by Griffiths and Barnes (2008), there is a spectrum of measures along which incentives, sanctions and conditionality can be used in combination:[39]

> At one end of the spectrum are the most coercive measures, from outright force to various forms of restriction or punitive pressure. Lower down are measures that are less coercive but based on a similar logic of reward and punishment, aimed at encouraging changes in behaviour through offering positive incentives. Towards the bottom of the spectrum are non-coercive and non-conditional measures to facilitate changes in the parties' relationships and mindsets, such as the creation of forums, training or tools for negotiation for parties that are receptive to engaging in negotiations.

Similarly, one could argue that when dealing with individuals and when there is the possibility of using a number of strategies, as in state-to-state interaction, a number of personal pressure strategies during specific phases of peacemaking can be applied. For instance, the sender can reward the target if it decides to comply partially, by offering de-listing or invitations to conferences and dialogues. There are several possibilities for the gradual, partial and/or time-limited or contingent lifting of certain provisions of the imposed targeted sanctions.[40]

In sum, larger strategic frameworks play a role in determining sanctions outcomes. As argued here, larger strategic frameworks often enable targeted sanctions to function according to certain rationales. One could consider these kinds of strategies to be norms, enabling and predicting the impact of sanctions. While several scholarly attempts have been made to come up with methods of sanctions assessment, most studies often ignore or underestimate these broader strategic frameworks. Studies that seek to establish the 'success' and 'failure' of targeted sanctions in isolation, without taking into account the broader rules of the game, are fundamentally problematic.

Targeted sanctions play different roles in different contexts. While the same type of restrictive measure, whether a travel ban or an assets freeze, may be put

39 *Ibid.*: 9.

40 Cosgrove (2005).

in place across different sanctions regimes, the outcome will vary considerably. It follows that each measure is carried out within a broader strategic framework, and that there is a constant interplay between the sanctions instrument and this general strategic logic. These frameworks both directly and indirectly contribute to the credibility of the sanctions. Thus, following the strategic paradigm within which the policy of targeted sanctions is carried out, the impact will vary. More specifically, and seen through an illustrative empirical example, while targeted sanctions in the form of travel bans have been imposed in both the Iranian and Zimbabwean contexts, it is simply not possible to compare the success and failure of personal sanctions against the elite in Iran with the efficacy of personal sanctions against the elite in Zimbabwe alone, as the former case is based on the logic of deterrence, while the latter is being carried out as a preventive strategy. Accordingly, the larger strategic rationale of coercion matters, and as such needs to be accounted for.

Conclusion

This chapter has discussed new ways to assess the impact of sanctions. The aim has been to offer an alternative that can better account for sanctions' impact compared to those approaches currently on offer in the sanctions literature. In doing so, it argued for a need to rethink the way the literature on targeted sanctions conceptualises sanctions cases. The aim here was to show not only how existing findings on the utility of targeted sanctions policy can be completely rethought, but also the dangers of leaning too heavily on a larger conceptualisation of a sanctions regime. As opposed to large-*n* studies or particular case studies based on traditional sanctions approaches, each episode reflects the sender's viewpoint on the efficacy of sanctions. Thus, a sanctions regime will comprise a collection of such sender judgements. In doing so, the series of episodes will on their own better explain how targeted sanctions contribute to conflict resolution. This will give us a fairer sense of success and failure (if this is what we really want to do in the first place).

This chapter also sought to criticise the conventional approach that seeks to assess targeted sanctions as a stand-alone measure. Thus, an argument was also made for the need to account for the larger strategic framework that usually embeds targeted sanctions, given that this operating background process (rules and norms) both enable and constrain sanctions outcomes. As argued, assessing targeted sanctions in isolation is unlikely to explain their utility. Instead, one needs to account for the enabling process that contributes to setting the rules of the games for the policy. By doing so, we will be in better position to understand why the same types of measures (travel bans and targeted assets freezes) can have different outcomes.

Chapter 4
Trends in Targeted UN and EU Sanctions

This chapter will offer a sample overview of contemporary UN and EU sanctions practice. The aim is to demonstrate how sanctions regimes could be assessed using a new approach in which greater emphasis is put on distinct episodes of a case, rather than on a sanctions regimes as such. The analysis of a case into episodes will also illustrate the kind of interaction that goes on between sender and target during the course of a sanctions regime. The pool of cases typified here includes all those ongoing UN and EU sanctions regimes that have ever adopted sanctions against individuals and that were active in mid-2009. Data on episodes is included in Appendix 2.

The information presented here includes tables showing the number of entities being targeted with assets freezes and travel bans; the role of target engagements; the presence and dynamics of ongoing targeted sanctions regimes; the encapsulation of political strategies embedding targeted sanctions, as well as some targeted entities' perception of the sanctions.[1] In addition to illustrating trends in targeting, the data analysis also includes sender strategies. The purpose of including such data is to demonstrate how targeted sanctions are strategically embedded. It should be emphasised that no attempt will be made to assess the success or failure of the sanctions regimes covered here. Instead, the primary motive is to illustrate the complexity of each sanctions regime, and how this contributes to shaping the overall sanctions outcome.

The chapter is structured in the following way. First, it will give a general note on the number of actors listed. This will be followed by a case overview, structured by: (1) general background to the establishment of the sanctions regime; (2) how the sanctions interactions look, and (3) what other strategic tools senders use to put pressure on targets.

Sanctions Regimes and their Episodes: Contemporary Samples

In early April 2009, there were nearly 30 ongoing UN and EU sanctions regimes.[2] Of these, 18 sanctions regimes had at some point issued lists of individuals to be subjected

---

1 Note that the establishment of the sanctions episodes is based on the implementation of sanctions on *natural* targets (physical persons, as opposed to *judicial* entities, companies, groups or other agents).

2 Ongoing sanctions regimes active at this time include: the al-Qaeda and the Taliban sanctions, Belarus, Bosnia and Herzegovina, Burma, China, Democratic Republic of Congo,

to travel bans and/or financial sanctions.[3] Eight of these 18 sanctions regimes targeted individuals in Africa, 5 in Europe, 2 in Central Asia, 2 in the Middle East and 1 in South-East Asia.[4] This should be compared with the number of sanctions regimes adopted in the period 1945–2007, when there were a total of 39 different UNSC sanctions regimes (voluntary and mandatory).[5] Compared to previous decades in the post-Cold War era, the number of sanctions regimes has increased dramatically.[6]

A general overview of the number of UN and EU sanctions regimes suggests that Myanmar (Burma) in 2009 has the highest number of entities listed. This could be compared to the ICTY regimes, which over the last ten years have had the highest numbers of entities subject to travel bans and asset freezes (however, the ICTY

Ivory Coast, Croatia, Haiti, Iran, Iraq, Democratic People's Republic of Korea, Lebanon, Liberia, Libya, Former Yugoslav Republic of Macedonia, Moldova, Myanmar (Burma), North Korea, Serbia and Montenegro, Sierra Leone, Somalia, Sudan, Syria, Uzbekistan and Zimbabwe. Some of these did not include targeted sanctions against individuals. In the period 2009–10, an additional number of episodes of each case have developed (as most of them are still ongoing). Moreover, a number of sanctions regimes have been established by the UN and/or by the EU. For example, on 23 December 2009 UNSCR 1907 (2009) adopted sanctions on Eritrea (including targeted sanctions against individuals: violating the arms embargo against Eritrea; providing support from Eritrea to armed opposition groups; obstructing UNSCR 1862 (2009) on Djibouti; supporters of individuals or groups involved in violence or terrorist acts against other States or their citizens in the region, and against individuals obstructing the Monitoring Group established by UNSCR 1853 (2008); see Council Decision 2010/127/CFSP. In addition, on 27 October 2009 the EU established targeted sanctions against the Republic of Guinea; see Common Position 2009/788/CFSP. This followed, inter alia, severe human rights abuses and lack of constitutional rule of law.

3 Terrorist sanctions are not included, although they are comparable to 'political' sanctions and often presented by the sender in the same context (for example, both the EU and the UN include travel bans and targeted assets freezes as means to address terrorism). Terrorism sanctions are quite different from geographically based sanctions. Terrorism-based sanctions (notably the al-Qaeda and the Taliban sanctions regime UNSCR 1267 (1999), as well as UNSCR 1373 (2001) are closely related to the attacks of 11 September 2001. Following the so-called 'war on terror', the US government has lent the UN particular political support, notably through institutional support and political will. This has given 'terrorist sanctions' a particular institutional standing and role, both at the EU and the UN (and also to respective member states of these institutions). Also, in the period following the launch on the 'war on terror', 'terrorist sanctions' have become considerably more politicised then other sanctions regimes. A final reason for leaving terrorist sanctions out of this study is that the terrorism lists published by the UN and the EU are much more comprehensive and would require a separate analysis on their own. It should be repeated that much research, both in the legal but also the political science literature, has already been conducted on EU and UN institutional responses to terrorism.

4 Neither the Lebanon/Syria regime nor the DPRK (North Korea) sanctions regimes are included, as separate tables had not been drawn up in mid-2009.

5 Charron (2009): 3.

6 Various scholars, such as Hufbauer et al. (2007), and Cortright and Lopez (2000), have noted this.

regimes are currently being phased out). In contrast, the Ivory Coast, Macedonia, Sudan and Uzbekistan sanctions regimes only have a handful of entities listed. Finally, it is worth noting that both the Sierra Leone and the Iraq sanctions regimes remain dormant. There follows a closer analysis of these ongoing sanctions regimes. They have been grouped together both by issue and geographic context.

Belarus

In the period 2004–2009 (and prior than that as well), the diplomatic relationship between the EU and Belarus has been frosty because of the EU's decision to downsize its political relations with the regime. In fact, diplomatic contacts were reduced early on to being held solely 'through the Presidency, the SG/HR, the Commission and the Troika'.[7] The moderation followed the implementation of individual sanctions against the Belarus leadership in September 2004 (Episode 1). This was the second time in recent years that the EU targeted the elite. A previous set of targeted sanctions was introduced in November 2002 following the political crisis regarding the Belarusian government's attitude towards the Organization for Security and Co-operation in Europe (OSCE).[8] However, this sanctions regime was terminated when the government at the time conceded to the EU's demands for continued co-operation with the OSCE.[9]

Sanctions episodes The autonomous EU sanctions measures against some leading members of the Belarusian elite are illustrated in Table 1 (see Appendix 2). A travel ban was put in place because of the serious concerns the EU had about the deterioration of democracy, the rule of law and human rights in the country. One reason for this political action by the EU was the Belarusian authorities' lack of co-operation in investigations of the disappearances of four well-known opposition figures (a case examined by the Parliamentary Assembly of the Council of Europe and reported on 28 April 2004 in the Pourgourides Report).[10]

An examination of Table 1 reveals that the number of targets increased over time, having begun with few targets placed on the list. Interaction between the sender and the target regime took place a number of times throughout the year. Having targeted four individuals in 2004, more extensive targeting occurred in 2006. The second episode of targeting expanded the sanctions list by adding two more names (making a total of six). The list seems to have been modified to reflect two political viewpoints. First, the EU judged the Belarusian authorities as having been complicit in a number of disappearances of opposition members. Second, the EU judged the overall democratic situation to have deteriorated further. This

7 General Affairs and External Relations Council (GAERC) Conclusions, 7 November 2005.

8 The OSCE had criticised the government of Belarus for its democratic practices.

9 See Eriksson (2005).

10 Council Common Position 2004/661/CFSP.

political view, spurred by the conclusion of the International Election Observation Mission, held that the parliamentary elections and referendum held on 17 October 2004 had fallen short of Belarus's basic OSCE commitments, and that the authorities were directly responsible for these shortcomings. Two individuals were therefore added to the list.[11]

On 23 March 2006, the European Council condemned the Belarusian government for having, inter alia, arrested a number of opposition members who had led demonstrations against the regime.[12] Consequently, the EU decided to adopt restrictive measures against those individuals responsible for the violations of international electoral standards. Restrictive measures were adopted against the Belarusian leadership as well as against officials responsible for violations of international electoral standards and their crackdown on civil society and the democratic opposition, including President Lukashenko. Targeted sanctions in this episode applied to 31 persons, mostly government officials on a travel ban list. Those on this list included the president and several of his closest aids, ministers, judges, officers and election commissioners.[13]

In an effort to bring further pressure to bear on those the EU and the OSCE considered responsible for the violations of international electoral standards and the suppression of civil society and the democratic opposition, the sanctions instrument was expanded to cover a mandatory assets freeze on the leaders. Also included on this list were another five persons who had not been included on the first one (a decision taken on 18 May 2006).[14] As part of the dynamic regarding the sender–target interactions, and more specifically given the lack of progress with regard to the reasons for imposing the sanctions in the first place, the EU Council on 18 May 2006 again expanded the list of individuals responsible for the concentrated effort to repress members of civil society and the democratic opposition.[15]

Despite the imposition of targeted sanctions, the human rights situation continued to deteriorate during 2007. For example, this worsening situation led the UN Human Rights Council (UNHRC) to decide not to renew the mandate for its human rights rapporteur, on the grounds that the Belarusian government had disregarded the UNHRC's previous concerns. In April 2007, a decision was taken to extend the sanctions regime against certain Belarusian officials. The extension was put in place for a period of 12 months.[16] In November 2007, the UN General Assembly voted in favour of a resolution criticising the human rights violations.[17]

---

11 Council Common Position 2004/848/CFSP.

12 The demonstrators had protested against the conduct of the presidential elections held in Belarus on 19 March 2006.

13 Council Common Position 2006/276/CFSP.

14 Council Common Position 2006/362/CFSP.

15 Council Decision 2006/718/CFSP.

16 Council Common Position 2007/173/CFSP.

17 *Keesing's* (Belarus), vol. 53, November 2007: 48,262.

Interestingly, though, sanctions were extended by the EU again during 2008, though later suspended. The reason was a EU Council decision on 13 October 2008 to uphold the restrictive sanctions against Belarus for a period of six months following some progress made during the parliamentary elections held on 28 September. The EU Council also noted Belarus's co-operation with the OSCE (although the election did not meet democratic criteria).[18] Another reason may have been the decision by the Belarusian government to allow the establishment of an EU Commission Delegation in Minsk. In all, the EU signalled preparedness to improve its relations with Belarus and to open up further dialogue. This shifting attitude, although somewhat relaxed, was sharply criticised by the democratic opposition. In contrast, the US did at the same time expand its financial sanctions measures, partly to cover Belarus's largest petrochemical corporation.[19] This move by the US led to a situation where the US ambassador to Belarus was considered *persona non grata* for a few months.[20]

On 27 January 2009, a ministerial troika met with the Belarus regime (the troika included the EU Commissioner for External Relations). The issues discussed involved economic matters, energy, food, customs, environment, transport and regional matters. The discussions took place in the midst of the EU's review of the democratic progress of the Belarusian authorities.

Auxiliary strategic tools While targeted sanctions remained in place, the EU's policy mix included a number of other instruments to engage the authorities in Minsk. In principle, the EU took a two-track approach towards Belarus. On the one hand, targeted sanctions were put in place against individual members of the regime. However, this policy placed the EU in a dilemma, as there were a number of issues of strategic concern for the EU which required dialogue with the Belarusian regime, in particular in areas such as justice, freedom and security (JFS); migration; border management, and the fight against organised crime, including trafficking in human beings and drugs.[21] This strategy partly forced the Belarusian elite to keep the dialogue open and not to adopt an entirely isolationist approach. The second track pursued by the EU was to move the primary political engagement away from the Belarusian government to the people of Belarus. Halting direct assistance to the government, the EU opted to concentrate assistance on humanitarian or regional projects, or those which directly supported the democratisation process.[22]

---

18 Council of the European Union, Council Conclusions on Belarus, 2897th External Relations Council Meeting, Luxembourg, 13 October 2008.

19 *Ibid.*

20 *Keesing's* (Belarus), vol. 54, April 2008: 48,604.

21 European Commission, *European Neighbourhood and Partnership Instrument: Belarus Country Strategy Paper 2007–2013 and National Indicative Programme 2007–2010*: 15.

22 *Ibid.*

This strategy was pursued by supporting the needs of the population and by the effort to:

> promote shared democratic values between the people of the EU and Belarus by intensifying people-to-people contacts and by strengthening good neighbourly relations across borders (e.g. through student and scientific exchanges, scholarships, youth travel, contacts between small- and medium-sized enterprises, training local authority officials, etc.).[23]

This support takes effect under different instruments.

One of the more recent policy inventions of strategic concern for the EU has been the instrument regulating the EU's policy towards Belarus is the European Neighbourhood Policy (ENP). Another instrument is the completion of negotiations on a Partnership and Co-operation Agreement (PCA) that was put in place in 1995. However, the conclusion and ratification of this agreement have been frozen since 1997 because of the EU's dismay over the introduction of an 'authoritarian' system by President Lukashenka (1996–97). Moreover, other instruments include the European Neighbourhood and Partnership Instrument (ENPI) (2007) covering the period 2007–13, thematic components (essentially support for democracy and transnational projects) and the Stability Instrument. The Stability Instrument allows for the provision of EU technical and financial assistance to deal with situations in which political crises exist or in the event of disasters, whether man-made or natural; to support policies that prevent violent conflicts, and to finance EC measures accompanying initiatives taken by the European Security and Defence Policy (ESDP), including activities concerning non-proliferation issues.[24]

In late 2008, the EU offered a new form of partnership to its eastern neighbours, the New Partnership for the East. The aim of the policy was to invite a number of countries, including Belarus, to sign EU Association Agreements that would promote free trade and free movement of people, guarantee mutual energy security (or energy interdependence), promote sustainable development as well as a new multilateral framework for joint interest, and the signing of additional institution-building agreements. However, the New Partnership for the East is based on Belarus's own will to participate and adhere to the democratic principles, as well as deal with the issues of human rights raised by the EU. Thus, the proposed initiatives are clearly conditional.

While the EU used sticks against the regime, it seemingly also offered a number of carrots such as those put forward by former EU Commissioner Ferrero-Waldner in the non-paper *What the European Union could Bring to Belarus*.[25] This document

---

23 *GAERC Conclusions*, November 2005.

24 European Commission: *European Neighbourhood and Partnership Instrument: Belarus 2007–2013*,: 19–21.

25 See Ferrero-Waldner (2006). Note also the Stability Instrument in Regulation 1717/2006.

presents in bullet points what the EU can offer the people of Belarus, as well as what the government of Belarus has to do in order to gain the support of the EU.

Overall, as illustrated above, there are a number of policies which the EU has used in its relations with the Belarus regime. It is clear that targeted sanctions play a very crucial role in all of these strategies.

Former Yugoslav Republic of Macedonia (FYROM)

During the 1998–99 armed conflict in Kosovo, many (Macedonian) Albanians joined the Kosovo Liberation Army in its fight for independence from Yugoslavia.[26] This context also saw the formation of the Macedonian UCK (Ushtria Clirimtare ë Kombëtare/National Liberation Army). Part of the goal was to launch support for the Albanians in Kosovo. Segments of the UCK, however, also engaged in a campaign for secession from Macedonia and the formation of a Greater Albania. On 11 January 2001, fighting with the Macedonian government erupted. The violence, which led to more than 100 casualties, was later settled with the Ohrid Framework Agreement, signed on 28 July 2001. Yet it was not until 13 August in the same year that a more formal accord was signed. However, mediation attempts did not succeed fully, which led a number of parties to the conflict to opt out of the framework.

Sanctions episodes Disapproving of renegade spoilers of the agreement, the EU decided to impose an autonomous travel ban on those who actively sought to:[27]

> promote or take part in violent extremist activities and as such challenging the Ohrid Framework Agreement's basic principles of stability, territorial integrity and the unitary and multi-ethnic character of FYROM. Measures were also to be imposed on those who were deliberately, repeatedly and 'illegitimately' undermining and obstructing the concrete implementation of the Framework Agreement by actions outside the democratic process.

The number of entities identified as posing such a challenge is included in Table 2 (Appendix 2). Since the establishment of the agreement, the number of targets has remained limited. However, in 2004, as was determined by the EU Council, there were still a number of individuals considered a threat to the overall situation as well as the general Macedonian peace accord.[28] Consequently, the list of targets was expanded. Table 2 also illustrates a reduction in the number of persons targeted over time (Episodes 4–7). This reveals partial achievements in terms of overall conflict resolution.

---

26 Uppsala Conflict Database (UCDP) (accessed 23 February 2008).

27 Council Common Position 2004/133/CFSP.

28 *Ibid.*

Auxiliary strategic tools Besides imposing a travel ban, the EU also engaged Macedonia in a number of strategic ways. Some policies are likely to have had an important impact on the way monitoring and implementation of these sanctions has been shaped.

In 2001, a Stabilisation and Association Agreement (SAA) was signed, which entered into force in 2004.[29] The SAA is subject to annual review to evaluate political and economic progress. Since 2002, the European Agency for Reconstruction (EAR) has been assisting FYROM in a wide range of areas, including those of democracy and the rule of law, economic and social development, justice and home affairs, and the environment and natural resources. In the field of democracy and the rule of law, EAR has supported the implementation of the Ohrid Framework Agreement, and in particular the equitable representation of the country's ethnic communities. In the field of justice and home affairs, EAR has supported, inter alia, the police reform process, improving policing capacities as well as increasing border security. In 2008, the EU adopted another enlargement strategy and progress report for FYROM. In this, it was concluded that further steps had to be taken before it could meet the political criteria set out by the EU. The progress report also noted the implementation of the Ohrid Agreement and the continued fight against terrorism. Because of the political steps taken, FYROM was able to submit an application for EU membership in early 2004. After review by the EU Commission, the EU Council decided in late 2005 to grant FYROM the status of a candidate country.[30] Moreover, in early June 2008 Macedonia held elections. However, these were partly marred by violence; this was noted by the EU Commission, which officially deplored the incidents, also claiming that the elections did not meet international standards.

While a number of measures have been taken to put pressure on peace spoilers, a number of other strategic measures by the EU have, as noted, been implemented to force the government to settle the remaining difficulties with these spoilers (or at least encourage the government put further pressure on these entities). Thus, not only does the EU as a sender seek to interact directly with the targets, it also seeks to have the government interact with them. This provides for a very subtle political game.

The Former Yugoslavia, Serbia and the ICTY

The war in the former Yugoslavia has so far posed the single most direct strategic challenge to the stability of Europe. In fact, one could argue that the EU's strategic attention on the Balkans has been a high priority ever since the declaration of independence of Slovenia in June 1991 and the start of the Balkan War. While the EU has been active in imposing sanctions ever since, it has not been alone. The US government also embraced sanctions as part of its overall strategy. For instance, in

29 Council and Commission 2004/239/EC.

30 European Council, Presidency Conclusions, 15/16 December 2005.

the early 1990s it pushed the UNSC to impose a comprehensive sanctions regime on Serbia following the war in Bosnia.[31]

More precisely, it was during the war in Bosnia that the Milošević government experienced its first round of international sanctions. These early comprehensive sanctions measures have been considered by some studies as remarkably effective, and one of the reasons why Belgrade changed its political behaviour and joined the Dayton Peace Process.[32] Yet the targeted sanctions regime currently in place relates to Serbia's political behaviour towards Kosovo. In this context, sanctions measures were not imposed until the armed conflict between the Kosovo Liberation Army (KLA) and the Serb-dominated Yugoslav security forces began in early 1996.

Episodes The first sanctions measure to be put in place was an arms embargo.[33] However, it took nearly two years before the EU agreed on a first list of names to be targeted with an assets freeze and travel ban. Targeted sanctions were imposed on 19 April 1998, during what was known as the first Kosovo War.[34] The initial motivation for targeted sanctions was to oppose the use of force against the Kosovo Albanian community in Kosovo. The first Kosovo War ended in early 1999, leaving room for negotiations under the Rambouillet Agreement.[35] Kosovo declared independence on 17 February 2008.

In March 1999, the later conflict between Yugoslavia and NATO began. At this time, the EU also dramatically increased the number of targets subject to sanctions.[36] At the time, the EU deemed President Milošević, all ministers and senior officials of the FRY and Serbian governments, as well as persons close to the regime, responsible for the 'pursuance of extreme and criminally irresponsible policies'.[37] During this sanctions regime, there were a number of episodes that displayed how the EU and the UN regarded Serbian actions.

---

31 See Stedman (1997) for a more detailed review of US sanctions on Serbia during the 1990s.

32 Cortright (2001): 119; Weiss et al. (1997): 217.

33 For the earlier sanctions history, including other EU measures, see Woodward (1995), ch. 12. Note also that the arms embargo was introduced by 1996/134/CFSP.

34 Council Common Position 1998/240/CFSP.

35 This also related to the future status of Kosovo. Note also that the 1996 decision dealt with the first round of UN sanctions and maintained the arms embargo. In 1998, the second round of EU sanctions imposed some new sanctions. For instance, on 19 June 1999, the assets freeze also covered companies (Regulation 1999/1294) in order to deal with social ownership (state-owned and socially owned entities in Serbia). Lists were modified by means of regulation 2000/723 (the 'black list' regarding Kosovo and Montenegro and the 'white list' regarding Serbia). Most of the measures were repealed after the 24 September 2000 elections in which President Kostunica was brought to power (Regulation 2000/2488).

36 For a good analysis of the EU's sanctions against the former Yugoslavia in the period 1998–2000, see De Vries (2002): 87–108.

37 Council Common Position 1999/318/CFSP.

As shown in Tables 3, 4 and 5 (Appendix 2), the sanctions regime in place against the Serbian elite has gone through two distinct phases. On the one hand, a sanctions regime was put in place to target and arrest leaders of the federal Serbia and Montenegro government. On the other hand, measures were meant to put additional pressure on those individuals being indicted by the ICTY.[38] Table 4 (Appendix 2) illustrates the EU's policy of targeting those individuals involved in supporting and hiding those indicted. The targeting of the Serbian elite definitely represents the largest sanctions operation put in place by the EU. At times more than 800 individuals, were identified and placed on the EU's sanctions list.

Symptomatic of the categories of targets included on the list was the parallel with the strategic concerns on the ground. During the first Kosovo War, the sanctions episodes targeted those the EU held accountable for the Yugoslav decisions (early 1998); the second cluster of sanctions episodes (mid- to late 1999) targeted those decision-makers who objected to the conditions prescribed by the sender,[39] and the third cluster was part of the overall military campaign and its aftermath.

Another characteristic worth noting, given the large number of entities subjected to a travel bans and assets freezes, was the fact that the EU never really seemed to engage specific targets per se, but rather to treat most of them as a group.

Auxiliary strategic tools What is not illustrated here, though, is how the measures imposed actually fit into an overall strategy involving military pressure: the imminent threat of a NATO attack, UN force deployment, EU force deployment, the active involvement of EU High Representatives, UN mediation, EU mediation, OSCE involvement, a complete or partial oil embargo ('oil for democracy'), an arms embargo, comprehensive financial sanctions, an aviation ban, a sports ban, and so on. While specific targeting was based on autonomous EU decisions, all other types of mechanisms of coercion involved a mix of a variety of stakeholders in the Balkan conflict with the aim of putting pressure on Serbia and individual members of the elite. In this context, it is difficult to separate the strategy of the EU from that of NATO or the OSCE and other bodies. One reason is that several influential EU governments, such as those of the UK, France, Germany, Italy and Spain, also participated in these forums. Notably, then, evaluation of sanctions impact cannot be carried out without including these other strategies. The other two sanctions regimes included the same targeted measures, although the overall strategic rationale was different.

The ICTY was established in late May 1993,[40] with the first hearing taking place on 8 November 1994. Yet, despite of the indictment of nearly 160 persons,

38 Several names included in this list were identical to the names included in the first sanctions regime.

39 Council Common Position 1999/318/CFSP. Principles referred to are also located at UN S/1999/516.

40 UNSCR 827 (1993).

a number of these never even showed up in court. Adopting a policy of assistance to the ICTY, in mid-March 2003 the EU decided to implement a travel ban on a number of individuals it considered had helped the indictees evade court appearance, stating, inter alia, that:[41]

> Persons indicted by the ICTY are still at large, and there is evidence that they are being assisted in their efforts to continue to evade justice. Such assistance is unacceptable, is an affront to the international order and fundamental standards of justice, and undermines the work of the ICTY, the success of which is essential to a stable and prosperous future for the region of former Yugoslavia.

This decision is marks the first episode. The list continued to be expanded gradually over time. Moreover, in further support of the ICTY, the EU also imposed a sanctions regime against those indicted individuals who were still at large. This sanctions regime consisted of an assets freeze policy.

What is interesting about these sanctions lists is that they seem more target-oriented. Both the EU and the UN have kept a close eye on the political behaviour of the targets included. For each of the targets placed on the list, extensive information was collected (not least in collaboration with the ICTY Chief Prosecutor, Carla Del Ponte).

While sanctions against Serbia have been terminated, the EU's strategy of exercising pressure continued through the imposition of travel bans and assets freezes. In addition, the EU continued to keep the Serbian government engaged in order to persuade it to do everything it could to ensure that all ICTY indictees still at large were brought to the Hague. With this in mind, a pertinent question with regard to the implementation question may be posed. As explained in one of the EU's Serbia Progress Reports at the time, assets were frozen, 'but the procedures are highly complex and the current legal framework leaves potential loopholes and shortcomings in enforcement'.[42]

Yet there was also a broader strategic framework in place with regard to Serbia. Based on decisions taken at the Thessaloniki Summit in June 2003, Serbia was considered a potential candidate country for EU accession. This was later laid out in a communication from the European Commission on its policy on enlargement towards the Western Balkans.[43] The possibility of Serbian EU accession has been managed under the European Partnership Dialogue (EPD) (preceded by the EU-FRY Consultative Task Force and the Enhanced Permanent Dialogue) and the SAA negotiations with Serbia (and early on, with Montenegro). The EPD included some key conditions the Serbian government had to fulfil. These included full co-operation with the ICTY.[44] In addition, the SAA, starting on 10 October 2005,

41 Council Common Position 2003/280/CFSP.

42 Commission Staff Working Document, *Serbia 2008 Progress Report* (2008): 21.

43 European Commission Communication, Brussels, 9 November 2005.

44 Council Decision 2006/56/EC, 30 January 2006.

included a number of provisions which had to be met (the SAA is assessed on a yearly basis). In 2006, the assessment report indicated that only limited co-operation between the government of Serbia and the ICTY had taken place. This led the EU Commission at the time (May 2006) to call off the SAA negotiations.[45] Negotiations were later reopened on 7 November 2007, following the formation of a new government. According to the EU, the new Serbian government had taken concrete action to improve co-operation with the ICTY. While negotiations advanced rapidly, the EU continued to maintain the condition of full co-operation with the ICTY before a final SAA could be signed, stating:

> The Council recalled that the pace and conclusion of the negotiations would depend, in particular, on Serbia's progress in developing the necessary legislative framework and administrative capacity to implement its obligations under the Agreement, and on full cooperation with ICTY.[46]

Following the co-operation, the EU established a new partnership agreement with Serbia in mid-February 2008. Furthermore, on 28 April 2008, the EU signed an SAA with Serbia. The SAA includes a number of references to co-operation with the ICTY. The Serbian Parliament ratified the SAA on 9 September the same year.

Today, the ICTY sanctions regimes are being phased out. During Spring 2008, an election campaign was held in Serbia. This led to the formation of a new pro-EU government on 26 June 2008, under President Boris Tadić. One month later, on 21 July, the new government had captured the ICTY-wanted suspect Radovan Karadzic in Serbia (following the earlier arrest of another ICTY suspect, Stojan Zupljanin). This is also noted in Episodes 19–23. The move pushed Serbia and the EU to their closest point in decades, and fulfilled the requirements for speedy integration into the EU.

Moldova

Targeted EU sanctions were imposed on the Transdniestrian leadership due to a long-standing political crisis between Moldova proper and the renegade province of Transdniestria. The crisis erupted when the Moldovan authorities declared Moldova's independence during the break-up of the Soviet Union in August 1991, which triggered local decision-makers in the Transdniestrian province to declare their loyalty to Moscow.[47] At its peak, the political crisis led to a number of human causalities from the two territories. For most of the 1990s, the conflict remained

---

45 COM (2006) 649 final, SEC (2006) 1389 (11 August 2006): 5.

46 Commission Staff Working Document, *Serbia 2007 Progress Report* (2007): 5.

47 Following the rotation system of the Red Army during the Soviet Empire, a number of Moscow loyalist officers had been stationed in Transdniestria. During independence, their influence was still strong.

deadlocked, with actors like the EU and the US backing Moldova proper, and Russia backing Transdniestria.

Over the years, the EU, as well as other actors, has made efforts to get the two parties to commit to a long-term solution based on an agreed constitution recognising Moldova's sovereignty. Yet because of what the EU considered to be continued obstruction by the Transdniestrian leadership with regard to changing the status quo, a travel ban was imposed on a number of leading decision-makers in Transdniestria. Actors were identified based on obstruction of engagement in co-operative talks.[48]

Episodes Initially, 17 persons of the Transdniestrian leadership were identified and targeted with sanctions (see Episodes 1–2 in Table 6 in Appendix 2). In 2004, the EU's sanctions were expanded. This decision followed on observations made by the EU Council of those members of the Transdniestrian government who had been involved in an intimidation and closure campaign against Latin-script Moldovan schools.[49] Consequently, in late August another set of individual decision-makers were placed on the list (Episode 3).[50] Because of the political deadlock between Moldova proper and the self-declared regime in Transdniestria, and based on close monitoring of the situation, the EU thereafter repeatedly renewed its decisions at timely intervals. The number of targets during the episodes has remained constant over the years.

Auxiliary strategic tools The settlement of the conflict in Transdniestria remains one of the EU's top priorities.[51] To expand its efforts to solve the dispute, on 15 February 2007 the EU appointed a Special Envoy to Moldova. One year later, on 11 April 2008, a meeting was held between Moldova's President Voronin and Igor Smirnov, the Dniester leader. The meeting was mediated by Russia, the Ukraine and the OSCE, with the EU and the US as observers. The aim was to work on confidence-building measures. Reports suggest that Russia was prepared to support unification between Moldova and Transdniestria if Moldova gave up its ambitions to join NATO.[52]

The EU's strategy towards Transdniestria has been implemented on many different levels. Since the fighting in 1992, and the subsequent signing of a cease-fire agreement between Moscow and Chisinau in July of the same year, a joint peacekeeping force has been patrolling the Dniester River border zone.[53]

48 Council Common Position 2003/139/CFSP.

49 The self-declared government of Transdniestria has promoted the Cyrillic alphabet, while the Latin script is preferred by Moldova.

50 Council Common Position 2004/622/CFSP.

51 European Neighbourhood and Partnership Instrument, *Republic of Moldova Country Strategy Paper 2007–2013* (2007): 3.

52 *Keesing's* (Moldova), vol. 54, April 2008: 48,548; *ibid.*, May 2008: 48,593.

53 Originally including Russian, Transdniestrian and Moldovan Units.

Since 2005, this Joint Control Commission (JCC) peacekeeping force has included both EU and US troops. Also of significance, the EU has been part of the mediation talks led by the OSCE, Russia and the Ukraine (since October 2005, also including the EU and the US as observers).[54] In recent years, the border between Transdniestria and the Ukraine has been of increasing concern, as Moldova, the EU and the US have feared that much smuggling is going on there, sustaining the Transdniestrian economy.

While there were some attempts by Transdniestrian leaders to travel to European capitals, the strongest pressure on the regime is likely to have been caused these other strategic means. For instance, the strategy of the EU to mount pressure on the Transdniestrian side has involved making the social, political and economic conditions so favourable on the Moldovan side that joining Russia, from the Transdniestrian people's point of view, would never be an alternative. Hence, while keeping pressure on a number of influential leaders on the Transdniestrian side who proclaim the distinctiveness of Transdniestria, the EU has also supported the Moldovan government through political and financial engagement. The instruments through which the EU operates in this context include: the ENP and the new European Neighbourhood and Partnership Instrument (ENPI) (aimed at promoting prosperity and a good neighbourhood atmosphere); the *EU-Moldova Country Strategy Paper 2007–2013*; the PCA; the EU-Moldova ENP Action Plan, and support through the Stability Instrument (which includes promotion of democratic values and respect for human rights, and the elimination of the excessive accumulation of conventional weapons such as small arms, light weapons and explosive remnants of Soviet war materials), and the *Economic Growth and Poverty Reduction Strategy Paper*. In several of these, as well as additional official documents, the key strategic objectives have been helpful in resolving the Transdniestrian conflict by the inclusion of a number of specific actions and mechanisms at various political and economic levels. For instance, in December 2008 the EU Commission, at the request of the EU Council, launched a new initiative: the New Eastern Partnership. The aim was to bring Moldova and other countries in its region closer to the EU through measures such as working towards concluding new association agreements; establishing comprehensive programmes for building institutions; gradual integration into the EU's economy; agreeing mobility and security pacts; enhancing energy security co-operation, and creating multilateral platforms based on democracy, governance, stability, economic integration and convergence, energy security, and increased people-to-people contact.[55] Finally, it is worth noting that the EU has also provided more specific forms of support for the resolution of the conflict through the deployment of an EU

---

54 European Neighbourhood and Partnership Instrument, *Republic of Moldova Country Strategy Paper 2007–2013* (2007).

55 EU Commission, *The Eastern Partnership: An Ambitious New Chapter in the EU's Relations with its Eastern neighbours* (2008).

Border Assistance Mission on the Moldovan–Ukrainian border (EUBAM).[56] The mission was launched on 30 November 2005.

Measures like these clearly need to be built into any analysis seeking to demonstrate sanctions' effectiveness, as different policy pressures are likely to shape the political outcome. However, the intricacy of factors affecting the policy makers of Transdniestria (and Moscow) may never reveal which factors will yield the most effect in constraining or achieving a behavioural change among the listed entities.

Perceptions of targeted actors In an interview with one of the deputy ministers of the government of the Dniester Moldovan Republic (DMR), it became clear that the targeted sanctions were an essential component in the political dynamic on the ground.[57] According to the DMR representative the conflict was between Chisinau and Tiraspol, despite the involvement of the EU, the US and Russia. According to him, the sanctions imposed formed part of a more general blockade imposed by Moldova against Transdniestria. Moreover, the official held that the support Moldova received from the EU's sanctions policy had to be placed in a broader context. It formed part of Moldova's general 'information warfare' that was accompanied by 'widespread accusations'. In this propaganda machine, Transdniestria was according to him considered a 'black hole' in terms of lacking judicial enforcement, and that 'we are an anti-democratic government violating human rights'.[58]

With regard to the specific travel ban imposed by the EU, the DMR representative held that his government had responded to this policy by issuing several notes to the EU and the US. However, the deputy minister did not expect the EU to lift its sanctions. Moreover, according to the deputy minister, the Transdniestrian government had also at times reacted 'adequately' towards Chisinau. For instance, 'On 21 March [2003], the Transdniestrian government limited the access, and the entering or transition, through its territory a number of government representatives from Chisinau. These actions are also described on the Internet. It is a national ban.'[59]

When the official was asked whether the sanctions had affected their work, he gave an example of how some Transdniestrian officials had been asked to attend a workshop in Belgium in 2004. However, they had not been granted visas, 'because

56 The argument is that the porous border between the Ukraine and Moldova (on the Transdniestrian side) has helped organised crime to flourish. This in turn has helped the renegade government to sustain itself economically. One interpretation for why the EUBAM has been set in place is that tighter control of the border will deprive the Transdniestrian government of important routes for illicit smuggling, which in the end will undermine its capacity to serve as a viable alternative to the legitimate government in Moldova proper.

57 Interview conducted on 2 February 2006.

58 *Ibid.*

59 At the time of the interview, I observed a list with names and pictures at the Transdniestrian border passage of members of the Moldovan government who were not allowed to travel into Transdniestria.

of Germany [reasons unclear]. This we consider is against established principles. Why should a German embassy refuse granting a visa to Belgium?'[60]

The kind of impact that could be felt by listed entities was also exemplified when interviewing one person included on the EU sanctions list. Here it was observed that the EU's personal sanctions measure had not been communicated clearly to the target. On asking the official when he realised that he was on the sanctions list, he stated: 'This is the first time I've heard about the lists, at this particular moment.'[61] Clearly dishonoured by seeing this information, he went on to say: 'I thought the EU was a serious organisation. If they now have lists in place, I would at least expect them to be serious enough to contact me personally. The EU could place whomever they want on the lists. I have no idea why I am placed on the list. I can only guess.'[62]

It is difficult to tell whether this really was the first time he was made aware of the EU sanctions list. None the less, the interviewee was clearly upset, commenting on the list: 'Isn't it so that the EU is working hard with maintaining human rights across the world? But by being listed, I am prevented from travelling. It is an assault on my right to free movement,' and 'Being listed is like being convicted for a crime, it is like a punishment.'[63]

Whether comments like these explain impact and behavioural change requires further systematic investigation. It may not be representative of all targets. Yet it constitutes an example of how a listed actor could be unaware of his inclusion on the sanctions list (on the other hand, it is worth noting that this by no means rules out that he actually did know about the sanctions).

Iraq

While for most of the 1990s the UNSC had imposed comprehensive sanctions against Iraq, the Iraqi people would witness a new type of sanctions policy when an entirely different sanctions regime was set up in May 2003.[64] The shift to targeted sanctions came a few weeks after the beginning of the artillery bombardment of Baghdad (beginning on 19 March 2003), which later forced Saddam Hussein's government out of office (and provided for President Bush's famous 'Mission Accomplished' speech in early May 2003).[65] While a number of listed entities were killed, others were taken into custody or deliberately forced into exile.

---

60 Interview conducted on 2 February 2006.

61 *Ibid.*

62 *Ibid.*

63 *Ibid.*

64 For a pre-history of targeted sanctions on the Saddam Hussein government, see Cortright et al. (2002b): 210–12.

65 The speech on 1 May 2003 declared the Iraq battle had been won; see White House transcript, May 2003.

Episodes The first resolution to reflect the shift from comprehensive sanctions to targeted sanctions was UNSCR 1483 (2003), deciding, under Chapter 7, that an assets freeze on members of the former Iraqi government and their families should be enforced (see Table 7 in Appendix 2).[66]

At the time of writing, the UN Sanctions Committee on Iraq handles the designation and management of the sanctions list. Whereas the committee is meant to actively review and update the list of individuals targeted, the work seems beset by fatigue. Few targeted sanctions measures have been imposed since 2005. One example illustrating this is the fact that as late as February 2008, Saddam Hussein was still included on the list of targets whose assets should be frozen. Yet he had been hanged on 30 December 2006, and should therefore have been removed immediately if the list had been managed properly. If the UN Sanctions Committee was as proactive in pursuing its tasks properly, he would have been removed from the sanctions list.

Iran

By adopting UNSCR 1737 (2006), the UNSC decided to impose targeted sanctions on some members of the Iranian elite. As in the case of Iraq, the predominant sponsor of the resolution was the US government. The motivation was assumptions by both the US and EU that the Iranian government was actively seeking knowledge and components to acquire nuclear capacities and to create nuclear weapons for military purposes.[67] Such indications not only posed a threat to US interests (and to its allies such as Israel), but also to international peace and security. The timing of the resolution should also be read against the background of the talks being held meanwhile with the DPRK on issues relating to the Non-Proliferation Treaty (NPT).[68] In fact, at the time of the Iranian

66 Designated members were Saddam Hussein and other senior officials of the former Iraqi regime and their immediate family members, including entities owned or controlled directly or indirectly by actors acting on their behalf. See EU position: Council Common Position 2003/495/CFSP. Note also that part of the strategy of imposing an assets freeze was to help the new government to gain control over lost money.

67 In this context, it is worth noting that the US government has imposed various forms of bilateral sanctions on Iran (as a whole) following the seizure of the US embassy in Tehran in 1979; see Bahgat (2001).

68 The nuclear issue has been a long-standing one. Worried about the Pyongyang regime's ability to develop nuclear weapons, the US opened bilateral negotiations with the DPRK in June 1993. An agreement was reached in October 1994 with the Agreed Framework. In principle, the DPRK and the US agreed to a facility, financed by an international consortium (the Korean Peninsula Energy Development Organization, KEDO), that would help the DPRK government solve some of its long-standing energy issues. After a policy review, the Bush administration announcement on 6 June 2001 that it was prepared to pursue a dialogue with North Korea on a broader agenda, including North Korea's conventional force posture, missile development and export programmes, human rights practices and

resolution, a UNSCR against the DPRK had also been put up for support to the UNSC and been approved (UNSCR 1718).[69]

Episodes Targeted sanctions were at the initial stage primarily aimed at members of the elite who were involved in the nuclear programme. Targets included members of the military and the research intelligentsia dealing with nuclear physics.

However, the adoption by the EU of necessary legislation for community implementation of the UNSCR against Iran was delayed due to internal political differences between the UK and Spain regarding the status of Gibraltar as well as about the tabled proposal of a far-reaching EU sanctions package than had been adopted by the UNSC.[70] In terms of targeting particular persons, the EU Council decided to go further than the UNSCR had stipulated. While the UN Sanctions Committee on Iran, on the basis of UNSCR 1737, 1747 and 1803, provided for a specific number of decision-makers to be subjected to a travel ban and assets freeze, the EU included provisions for further targeting (making it possible to identify and target more individuals than the UN had done). This had not occurred before when implementing UN sanctions. The reason was primarily that at the time, the governments of France and the UK believed that the UNSC had not gone far enough in its resolution (as further measures would have been blocked by Russia and China). EU sanctions actions thus opened

---

humanitarian issues. However, as events progressed, in October 2002 the US delegation presented the Pyongyang regime with information that suggested the latter was pursuing a uranium enrichment programme. The DPRK claimed it had a legal right to pursue such a programme (indirectly acknowledging its existence). These conflicting views led to a political crisis that in late 2002 led the DPRK government to announce its withdrawal from the Non-Proliferation Treaty, arguing that it wanted to provide itself with a deterrent force in the face of a hostile US policy. In 2003, however, the US government proposed multilateral talks on the nuclear issue. The DPRK accepted the proposal, and in late 2003, six-party talks were held between the US, the DPRK, China, the Republic of Korea, Japan and Russia. The six nations met on several occasions. In November 2005, these talks ended inconclusively, as the Pyongyang regime began a boycott of the six-party talks, citing the 'US's hostile policy' and specifically the US's imposition of an assets freeze on DPRK bank accounts in Macau's Banco Delta Asia. In mid-July 2006, the UNSC imposed selective sanctions designed to address the DPRK's technical capacities to further develop its nuclear technology. A UNSC Resolution was triggered because of the DPRK's decision to test-launch seven ballistic missiles. On 9 October 2006, the DPRK further tested a nuclear explosive device, prompting the UNSC to adopt UNSCR 1718. This resolution imposed, inter alia, personal sanctions such as a luxury goods ban on the DPRK government, and further sanctions on trade in certain military materiel, WMD and missile-related parts, as well as technology transfers (note, however, that the export ban concerns the entire country, so one cannot talk about targeted sanctions in the very strict sense).

69 At time of writing, no sanctions list has been issued, therefore no separate table for the DPRK sanctions regime has been included.

70 An article in *The Financial Times* on 2 February 2007 features this story: 'N Korea leader raises a glass to Gibraltar'.

the possibility of targeting more natural entities than the original UNSCR stipulated.[71] As illustrated in Table 8 in Appendix 2, the Iranian sanctions are fairly new, although they received much attention over a fairly short period (the table accumulates the number of targets listed over time).

Auxiliary strategic tools Both the Iran sanctions regime and the sanctions regime on the DPRK followed developments at the International Atomic Energy Agency (IAEA). It was the reports and conclusions reached by this body that lay the ground for the UNSC actions. Thus, an assessment of the impact of sanctions cannot be carried out without taking into account the role of the IAEA and its assessments of Iran's nuclear research programme.

In terms of the EU's broader strategic relationship with Iran, a review suggests that engagement during the past decade has remained low. In general, the EU has engaged in soft carrot-and-stick diplomacy on the energy issue in its dealings with the regime. This has taken place primarily within the EU3 framework (France, Germany and the UK). In 2003, the EU3 group offered Iran economic incentives should it agree to suspend its uranium enrichment programme, allow inspections by the IAEA and sign the Additional Protocol to the NPT. Iran, having initially accepted the offer, later breached the agreement (at least according to the EU); then the EU presented to the Iranian authorities a new set of proposals from the UN for opening negotiations on Iran's nuclear programme. On 1 June 2006, China, France, Germany, the Russian Federation, the UK, the US and the EU adopted a number of proposals for continued talks. The proposal recognised Iran's development of nuclear energy for peaceful purposes as well as expectations that Iran would co-operate fully with the IAEA.[72] On 2 May 2008, these proposals were reviewed and subsequently updated. Elements of the new proposal were only made available to the Iranian government, not to the public. The Iranian response was that it wanted wider talks on security. On 8 August 2008, the EU imposed additional targeted sanctions on members of the Iranian regime. The US followed by expanding its financial sanctions against companies supporting Iran's nuclear programme. In early March 2009, the IAEA Board of Governors concluded that: 'Regrettably, as a result of the continued lack of cooperation by Iran in connection with the remaining issues which give rise to

71 A travel ban was imposed on those directly associated with or providing support for Iran's proliferation-sensitive nuclear activities, and for the development of nuclear weapon delivery systems, including through involvement in procurement of the prohibited items, goods, equipment, materials and technology. An assets freeze was also imposed on those additional persons or entities designated by the UNSC or by the UN Sanctions Committee as being 'engaged in, directly associated with or providing support for Iran's proliferation sensitive nuclear activities or the development of nuclear weapon delivery systems, or by persons or entities acting on their behalf or at their direction, or by entities owned or controlled by them, including through illicit means'; based on paras 10 and 12 of UNSCR 1737 (2006).

72 Spokesperson of the Secretary-General, High Representative for CFSP/S202/06.

concerns about possible military dimensions of Iran's nuclear programme, the agency has not made any substantive progress on these issues.'[73]

In the absence of any framework agreements between the EU and the Iranian government, there are various forms of side-dialogues. These include the Comprehensive Dialogue established in 1997 (through troika meetings), which covers issues such as regional affairs, the Middle East peace process, non-proliferation, human rights and the fight against terrorism; the High-level Working Group on Energy and Transport; the High-level Working Group on Trade and Investment, and the Political Dialogue Agreement (PDA) established in late 2002. The EU has also held troika meetings on the NGO roundtable in Tehran on human rights, as part of a newly instituted Human Rights Dialogue. However, in December 2003, the Comprehensive Dialogue between the EU and Iran was suspended since Iran was considered reluctant to compromise on the nuclear question. However, international engagement, especially through the UN, has been undertaken through talks between Iran and the IAEA over Iran's nuclear processing capabilities.

West Africa (Sierra Leone, Liberia and the Ivory Coast)

Targeted sanctions against certain individuals in Sierra Leone, Liberia and the Ivory Coast all rest on UNSCR Chapter 7 decisions. While having experienced their own distinct wars, they are deeply intertwined as a conflict complex.

The civil war in Sierra Leone started in mid-March 1991 following an invasion from Liberia by the Revolutionary United Front (RUF) led by rebel leader Foday Sankoh. Through much of the conflict, Sankoh was very dependent on Charles Taylor, the leader of the National Patriotic Front of Liberia (NPFL). Through political support and a strong financial backbone (especially through the gem trade), Taylor was able to lend territorial support to the RUF's incursion.[74] After several years of indiscriminate killing, the RUF succeeded in gaining power in Sierra Leone. This followed a *coup d'état* in May 1997. Ahmad Tejan Kabbah, the elected president of Sierra Leone at the time, fled to Guinea, while the leader of the Armed Forces Revolutionary Council (AFRC), Johnny Paul Koroma, and the RUF together formed a military junta.[75] Initially, the UNSC imposed targeted travel bans against the junta and its family members.[76] At the

---

73 IAEA Board of Governors, GOV/2009/8.

74 Taylor, a proclaimed warlord, had been active in the illegal sale and smuggling of arms and diamonds throughout western Africa during the 1990s. The Taylor factor, though, is important for understanding the political and civil war dynamic throughout the region. The Taylor regime would also come to receive much attention from a sanctions point of view.

75 The AFRC was an alliance between the RUF and former Sierra Leone army soldiers.

76 UNSCR 1132 (1997).

time, no sanctions list was issued, and enforcement was very weak. It would take until late January 1998 to come up with the first sanctions list, which included names and personal identifiers of those to be targeted.[77]

Meanwhile, in neighbouring Liberia, Charles Taylor was elected president. In this capacity, Taylor continued to support the war in Sierra Leone. However, his support for various ethnic groups and loyal tribes at the expense of others made him vulnerable to a series of attacks, not least from neighbouring Guinea. These attacks would also see Taylor engaged in warfare throughout his entire presidency in Liberia.

Episodes Reacting to Taylor's activities, the UNSC imposed a travel ban on members of his government on 7 May 2001 (see Table 10 in Appendix 2).[78] As a counter-move, Taylor placed a domestic travel ban on UN officials, forbidding them to travel more than 27 miles outside Monrovia.[79] In June, the UN Sanctions Committee on Liberia issued a list of 136 persons to be targeted with sanctions.

Fighting in Liberia lasted until late 2002, when Taylor left Liberia for exile in Nigeria. In August 2003, ECOMIL (Economic Community of West African States [ECOWAS] Mission in Liberia) was deployed, providing for the deployment of UNMIL (UN Mission in Liberia) two years later.[80] The mandate of UNMIL was set to end on 30 September 2009.[81]

Back in Sierra Lone, a counter-attack by the previously ousted leader Kabbah with support from Nigeria and the Kamajor tribe brought him back to power in March 1998. In the process, the RUF and the AFRC re-engaged in guerrilla warfare. A peace agreement was subsequently signed in Lomé, Togo in July 1999 without the AFRC. However, what was supposed to be a complete end to the civil war soon turned out to be only a temporary interruption.

As it turned out, the RUF was not genuine in its commitment to peace. In May 2001, the RUF re-engaged in fighting, exchanging fire both with UNMIL forces in Sierra Leone and later with deployed British forces. The fighting severely weakened the RUF. Later, the capture of Sankoh and installation of the new RUF leader, Issa Sesay, saw a re-commitment to the previously signed peace agreements. With President Kabbah reinstated as a democratically elected president, the sanctions list, as illustrated in Table 9 (Appendix 2), was put in place to deal with the remnants of the AFRC. Strangely, however, a large number of the persons included on the list at the time were currently outside Sierra Leone, dead, or imprisoned by the International Criminal Court of Sierra Leone (for instance,

77 SC/6472 (28 January 1998). Note that this sanctions regime was terminated, as the government was later toppled (and is therefore not included).

78 UNSCR 1343 (2001).

79 Cortright and Lopez (2002a): 146.

80 *Annual Review of Peace Operations* (2008): 58.

81 UNSCR 1836 (2008).

at least one target had even begun work for the UN). Thus, the public sanctions list at the time did not accurately reflect the political situation on the ground. On 1 October 2008, the UN Integrated Peace-building Office (UNIPSIL) began its work in Sierra Leone.[82] The aim was partly to identify and resolve potential conflicts before they turned out to be violent. UN targeted individual sanctions continued to remain in place, but in a dormant mode.

With the departure of Taylor from power and peace installed in both Sierra Leone and Liberia, the UNSC introduced a new sanctions regime in mid-February 2004 to reflect this new political situation. Targets included individuals who were still considered a threat to the stability of the region: senior members of former President Taylor's government and their spouses, former members of Liberia's armed forces, and any other individuals associated with the entities providing financial or military support to armed rebel groups in Liberia or other countries in the region.[83]

The first Liberia sanctions lists produced by the Sanctions Committee were presented in mid-March 2004 (see Tables 11 and 12 in Appendix 2). A number of listing and de-listing measures have since followed. Overall, the number of targets has remained constant following the episodes starting in 2004. The Liberia sanctions still remain in place, although an increasing number of targets have been de-listed. While targets may not pose a direct security threat today as they did before, their inclusion on the sanctions list may be useful as a deterrent.

Noteworthy with the introduction of the Liberia sanctions list was the fact that a number of associates of Taylor placed on this sanctions list joined the Liberian Parliament (Senate), probably to secure a political future (note that one listed actor even took office as the Speaker of Parliament, a position that he resigned from in mid-February 2007 following corruption charges).[84] Some even seemed to see their seats in the Senate as a way to become immune from targeted sanctions. Later, the UN Sanctions Committee strengthened its regime by establishing a parallel assets freeze measure on an additional number of targets.[85] However, this list included a more limited number of targets compared to the travel sanctions regime.

Before reviewing subsequent sanctions regimes, some further and more in-depth views from some of the entities included on the Liberia sanctions list will

82 UNSCR 1829 (2008)

83 See Council Common Position 2004/137/CFSP and UNSCR 1521 (2003).

84 Although the Comprehensive Peace Agreement was signed in August 2004, there were, as late as mid-July 2007, reports of plans to overthrow the new democratic government; *Annual Review of Peace Operations* (2008): 58.

85 At time of writing, a number of countries have frozen assets connected to entities placed on the Liberia sanctions list (for example, France, Germany, Ghana, Lebanon, Syria and the US), according to the UN Panel of Experts on Liberia. However, Liberia has not yet implemented the necessary laws to ensure that the UN assets freezes are also being implemented in Liberia; Boucher and Holt (2009): 93–4. One reason for this may be that some members of parliament are themselves on the sanctions list.

be examined.[86] Attention will be devoted to their perception of the UN's targeted sanctions. Their perception is relevant to a better understanding of how sanctions work, not least in connection to the many other kinds of strategic interventions that take place.

Listed Entities' Perception of being on the UN Liberia Sanctions List

According to the first interviewee, his inclusion on the first UN travel ban list had come as a complete surprise:[87]

> I was previously in Charles Taylor's Cabinet. During the heat of the war, I worked close with the UN. I thought the listing of me was wrong. However, I did not do anything to get off the list. I was placed on the list, and then I was suddenly taken off the .... I was very disillusioned and sad when I first heard about the list. Innocent people should not be targeted, one should target those that are criminals. I have no idea how I was placed on the list.

The interviewee also considered the sanctions imposed on him as unfair, arguing that: 'Why should the US government not bring their soldiers to The Hague, but we need to? If we protest, then we are placed on a travel ban ... it is not fair'.[88] The unfairness of the personal sanctions was also illustrated by an anecdote:[89]

> My father once told me a story. A family had a farm where they had recently been sowing grains. The farmer was irritated however, because some birds were picking them. One day, the farmer decided to put an end to this. To do so, he threw out a big net in which he managed to capture all the birds in one throw. One by one, the farmer picked out each bird and broke its neck. When he finally reached the last bird, the little fellow said 'Wait ... wait don't kill me! I was working very hard to keep the other birds from stealing the grains. I knew it would not be beneficial for us to do so, and besides, I have not been stealing a single grain myself.' The farmer responded: 'How am I supposed to know that you are telling the truth? Since I don't have any proof that you are innocent, and

86 In 2006, a number of interviews were conducted with members of the UN sanctions lists. The goal was to get in touch with as many members subjected to sanctions as possible. However, targets had to be located on an ad hoc basis since it was impossible to locate some targets on the official sanctions list(s). For instance, some had been jailed, some had been killed, and some were out of the country or had simply 'vanished'. Thereafter, a number of persons were simply unwilling to participate. The goal of these interviews was to explore an extra dimension, often overlooked in the literature, about the role and perception of targets *vis-à-vis* the senders and their policies.

87 Interview conducted on 7 June 2006.

88 *Ibid.*

89 *Ibid.*

> since I have broken the neck of all your other friends, I might as well break yours as well.' And so the farmer did.

While noting his general discomfort with the sanctions list, he was much more open to the other forms of sanctions imposed on Liberia. In particular, he was rather pleased with how the Governance and Economic Management Assistance Programme (GEMAP) and the other sanctions measures (arms embargo, timber ban, diamond ban, an so on.) were working. As he mentioned:[90]

> The international community has brought about two tools for pressure: sanctions and the GEMAP. Firstly, sanctions have worked and they have reached their aim. The sanctions have good intentions. Secondly, GEMAP provides a framework for providing help to a failed state. GEMAP will help Liberia to be accommodated in international society, to become a serious actor. As for now, Liberia will not accept a receivership or being occupied. One should see GEMAP as recognition of sovereignty and to what extent can we tolerate involvement of foreigners in our affairs? Nevertheless, GEMAP is led by a steering committee, a sharing of power between the international community and us. We need to manage the power formation, otherwise there is a big risk that the executive neglects the legislature of Liberia.

He further noted: 'I believe sanctions have worked well. It has made us behave. When GEMAP is fully working, the comprehensive sanctions could be lifted. I don't mind the linkage between sanctions and this GEMAP implementation. GEMAP is a good tool, but it needs to be guided.'[91]

In an interview with another listed entity, the scepticism was much more pronounced.[92] In his responses to my questions, he uttered strong criticism both of the UNMIL and the sanctions. With regard to the travel ban, he held that it was very strange that he had been put on the list: 'I was placed on the list [in] 2004. The listing of me is so strange. It says that I am a renegade supporter. This is very very strange … it is not justified. I don't know where to go.' The interviewee felt that even members of UNMIL and the Special Representative of the Secretary General (SRSG) had doubts about the UNSC's fairness in including him on the sanctions list (he also suggested that I speak to an UN Force Commander who, according to him, shared his view). The sense of unfairness was also expressed in the following way: 'I don't want to know who placed me on the list. The only thing I want to know is if it is justifiable to place me on the list.' Moreover, the interviewee also expressed a sense of abandonment: 'You cannot undo your deeds, can you? It is

90 *Ibid.*
91 *Ibid.*
92 *Ibid.*

pointless to make use of a lawyer. Where should this attorney go? I can't even afford having a lawyer.'

Asking the third interviewee how he got to know that he was on the list, he said: 'I woke up that morning and someone said they seen my name on a sanctions list. I went out on the Internet and I saw my name.'[93] Moreover, when asked about why he thought he was placed on the sanctions list, the interviewee said it must have been for political reasons: 'I think I am placed on the list for political reasons, because I am on the other political [side to] the ruling party. Being popular I pose a threat to the sitting government. Everyone knows that I and the president don't [get] along.' Later in the interview he also added: 'I was contacted by foreign embassies which advised me not to run in the election. [If] I did not participate, I would in return be taken off the list.' What became clear throughout the interview was that the listed entity felt the effects of sanctions on his life. Several comments illustrated this. First, he held that he had always been a public figure, and in that capacity he had been travelling a lot, but that the travel ban now prevented him and his family from doing so. This was not acceptable, according to him. Moreover:[94]

> The sanctions harm me in many ways. For instance, one of my children had an accident and hit his head. He needed to go to [country A] … for x-ray. My wife took him there. But afterwards the embassy of [country A] said that I sent my wife to connect with Mr Taylor. I was very sad and angry. As a response I showed them airplane tickets, the x-ray pictures and medical statements so that they would know that I was not lying.

With regard to sanctions having an impact on his family, he also stated:

> My family does not understand why I am placed on the list. I have no contact with Mr. Charles Taylor, whatsoever. My wife is an American. She has a green card. She can come and go as she wants. My children now live in the US, they can come here every now and then.[95]

In addition, he stated that he wanted to engage with those imposing sanctions on him:

> I would like to face my accusers. It feels now as if I am accused by the ghost. On the one hand perhaps the sanctions placed against me made me good, as it deterred me from being tempted to join Mr Taylor. But again, Taylor is not around any longer, and therefore the list should be reviewed.

93 Interview conducted on 8 June 2006.

94 *Ibid.*

95 *Ibid.*

In this context, he also noted that the Chairman of the Sanctions Committee had been in Monrovia to meet officials at the UN Headquarters and to speak about sanctions with members of the parliament, but that the chairman did not want to meet with him.

Finally, the presence of sanctions was also noted by his reference to reports on his financial activities (following targeted financial sanctions):

> There are reports that say I have US$10 million on my account! I had an account in ... with US$10,000, but this account I have no more. Since 1998, I have had an account in the [redacted] ... but this account has been left untouched. I can use this as I want, I can write a cheque with it.[96]

With a different interviewee, it was also clear that sanctions had a personal impact.[97] Asked how she had been informed, she stated:[98]

> I was shocked when I learned that we were placed on the travel ban list. Our names were out on the Internet. I was surprised that I was placed on the list since I had nothing to do with the war. I have never supported or taken part in the war. It is sad. I cannot travel to meet my daughters. A time ago, I sent US$1,600 to the US so that my daughter could attend a summer school, but the US took them. If I am sick, then I have to write to the [UNSC] committee to be exempted from the travel ban. But that does not happen. And *I am* sick. I have problems with my chest. I am guilty by association ....

Later, she also described her notification in the following way:

> The first list was the American travel ban list ... then came the UN lists. The UN list was both put on the Internet but also published in the newspaper. The first thing I did when I learned that I was placed on the list was to make an inquiry to understand what it meant to be placed on the list. What had I done to deserve to be placed on this list?

Finally, it is worth noting that, similar to other entities, she also felt that the listing of individuals for sanctions was unjust: 'The lists are very biased. Many people out there have been killing innocent children. Therefore I also support a war crimes tribunal, so that people could face charges.' In addition, she noted a number of errors of the UN list, such as information on birthdates. She also noted the fact that some persons on the sanctions lists were not in the country (at least one being in the US).

---

96 *Ibid.*
97 *Ibid.*
98 *Ibid.*

In the fifth interview, the listed individual made it clear that no form of sanctions was appreciated.[99] In fact, the interviewee was critical of most forms of targeted sanctions, not only individual ones. For instance, the timber and diamond bans had negative side-effects and did not accomplish their purpose: 'Timber and diamond mines are mostly owned by tribes, and sanctions effects the tribes and not the government.' Usually revenues were taken by international co-operation rather than handed back to the people of Liberia. In addition, it was her view that sanctions had no effect in stopping the war. Moreover, in terms of the existing arms embargo, in her mind, this should have been lifted, as the situation demanded it:[100]

> The arms embargo needs to be lifted so that the police force can be able to master street violence, robberies and murders. In general, it needs to be pointed out that weapons on the African continent come from abroad. We do not produce weapons ourselves. One should not only look at the end-result, one needs to look at the source, and importantly, also on weapons smuggling.

Above all, she felt that the UN sanctions had come about too late. In her understanding, it was not the former government of Charles Taylor that was the problem, but the rebel movement that had tried to overthrow them:[101]

> It was the rebels that brought about the war. LURD [Liberians United for Reconciliation and Democracy] and MODEL [Movement for Democracy in Liberia] killed people. For some reason everyone came to blame Taylor. It is all the time 'Taylor this' and 'Taylor that'. I thought the first round of war would lead to peace. But then suddenly sanctions were placed on us. He just wanted to help the population. Charles Taylor never got a chance to accomplish his mission, sanctions hit him. Don't forget that he was elected in free and fair elections, something that the international community even recognised.

When asked about the travel ban and the assets freeze, she said she had been informed by reading about them on the Internet, and that no one had told her in person. Like many other targets, she experienced the sanctions as unjust, referring to them as 'arbitrary sanctions'. She also said that some of the persons on the list did not belong there and had to be taken off. Similarly, there were individuals who clearly belonged on the list but were not on it.

What kind of impact did the sanctions have? There were a variety of examples of how they had affected her, both in her official and her private capacities. In terms of impact on her professional life, she offered the following remark: 'I am

99 *Ibid.*
100 *Ibid.*
101 *Ibid.*

a senator. How can I interact with other countries? How can people be invited to meet with me if I am on a sanctions list? It limits my work.' When referring to how sanctions had affected her in private, she stated:

> I am very sick. I have problems with my heart. I need a doctor, I have also been forced to make several operations. So, sanctions also had a humanitarian impact. For instance, I have also taken away several tumours in my chest. In 2003 I went to the US for a tumour check. I am a human being.

She also stated that she had written to the UNSC on repeated occasions to seek exemptions to travel to other countries for medical checkups. In addition to the travel ban, she also gave examples of how the assets freeze had affected her and her family. For instance, she noted that friends gave money to her children, who would otherwise 'starve'. Some of her children lived in London and some in Africa.

Asked about the measures she had taken to try to remove her name from the list, she claimed that she had written to the UNSC on a number of occasions stating that: 'I would like to be removed and to be exempted. But it feels as if I am talking to a computer. But they are humans.' She also came back to the fact there are no procedures to be removed from the list:

> The constitution says that you need to go to court to be charged. I have personally never been charged [for the reasons that have led to my being targeted]. The life we live today is not the Ice Age. You cannot judge someone just because of an affiliation. I am discriminated against. My chance of surviving was hampered. I was not given a job as I was placed on the sanctions list.

In another comment, she stated: 'If they want to freeze my assets then I have to go to court to be charged first. This is the arrangement of the law. One talks about peace, democracy, etc. But why do some of us get punished in this way? Why?' Besides personal action in an attempt to be removed from the sanctions list, the interviewee noted that consultations had also taken place with other listed individuals about what to do: 'Me and other listed individuals have spoken to each other on different occasions on how we should deal with these issues on a senate level.'

Turning now from the comments made by individuals placed on the Liberia sanctions list, I will briefly review the Ivory Coast sanctions case.

The Ivory Coast

While violence in the region was brought to an end under a cease-fire agreement as well as the signing of a comprehensive peace agreement in Liberia, signs of a deteriorating situation in the Ivory Coast had begun in 2000. Having enjoyed political stability for many decades, as well as being a model country for African development, the Ivory Coast's worsening conditions culminated in a *coup d'état* in 1999. The coup-maker, General Guei, promised to hold elections in late 2000, which he subsequently lost. Two years later, after some further political turmoil, in particular because of a widening north–south divide based on exacerbated ethnic differences, on 19 September 2002 mutinous northern soldiers launched a rebellion against acting President Laurent Gbagbo.[102] The conflict quickly spread to involve other groups.

After several broken cease-fires, such as the one brokered in the latter part of Autumn 2002, as well as half-hearted peace agreements, a larger peace accord, the Linas-Marcoussis Agreement, was signed in Paris in January 2003. The agreement stipulated the creation of a new government of national reconciliation (March 2003). As one of its main tasks, the government would set out to disarm the rebel groups and to restructure the national armed forces. Yet weak commitment from the parties to the agreed principles eventually led certain signatories to leave the government. Concern about the deteriorating situation led to another peace summit being arranged under the auspices of the UN, the African Union (AU) and the Economic Community of West African States (ECOWAS). The outcome of this summit, held in July 2004, led to the Accra III Agreement, in which the parties re-confirmed their commitment to the Linas-Marcoussis Agreement. In April 2004, a UN operation (United Nations Operation in Côte d'Ivoire, UNOCI) was mandated to oversee the accord (the peacekeeping mission mandate to remain in force until the end of July 2009).[103] The rebels and the opposition re-joined the government on 9 August 2004.

Episodes Slow political improvement and inflexibility by the concerned parties prompted the UNSC to impose targeted sanctions on individuals on both sides of the conflict (see Table 13 in Appendix 2). The goal of the sanctions was to target individuals who 'constitute a threat to the peace and national reconciliation process, in particular those who block the implementation of the Linas Marcoussis and Accra Agreements, and any other person determined as responsible for serious violations of human rights'.[104] However, it would take the UN, and then later the EU, almost two years to designate three individuals with a targeted assets freeze and travel ban. Problematically, however, the parties did not reconcile following the sanctions. In March 2007, the fourteenth partial peace agreement was signed between parties (the Ouagadougou Accord). Sanctions Episode 11 suggests that sanctions are still a necessary instrument in putting pressure on the actors involved.

Although the UN has been heavily involved on the ground, for example through the deployment of the UN peacekeeping force and through the appointment of a

102 Part of the root cause of the conflict had to do with regional economic and political imbalances (expressed in ethnic terms).

103 *Annual Review of Peace Operations* (2008): 105. See also UNSCR 1865 (2009).

104 See UNSCR 1572 (2004) and Council Common Position 2004/852/CFSP.

UN special representative, the number of UN targeted entities has remained fairly limited (only three individuals placed on the sanctions list). On the other hand, the targets have been carefully selected, choosing individuals from both sides. In order to better understand the impact of the sanctions, an account from one of the individuals on the UN's Ivory Coast sanctions list is given below.

Targeted sanctions from the perspective of a listed entity An interview was conducted with one subject of the UN Ivory Coast sanctions list.[105] The interview made it clear that sanctions had an impact on the target, both directly and indirectly (psychologically).[106] While the travel ban may have reduced his political room for manoeuvre, the interview did not make explicit to what extent it had contributed to a behavioural change with regard to the other parties to the conflict or to the UN. In this context, he stated: 'Sanctions were placed against me to make me change behaviour. But I won't change. I have my ideas and my principles. I keep cool now, but this is not because of the sanctions.' His actions and activities also seemed deeply related to his beliefs and convictions: 'In Abidjan I mobilised people in the street as one does in Europe, I worked hard with this. I also took part in a hunger strike.'

When asked how sanctions were affecting his life, the interviewee answered:

> I cannot travel. But my aim is not to travel. Earlier I travelled to Italy and Belgium. I was arrested in Brussels. The French have sent copies of my arrest to different embassies, before I was even placed on sanctions travel list.

At one point, he also stated that his family had some concerns about his being on the sanctions list, but that they were 'not annoyed' as they understood the underlying reason for his inclusion.

How, then, did he perceive the sanctions measures imposed by the UN? His perception was that it was mostly a 'game of personalities' and that the list would not endanger his future career: 'Politics is politics. Time will tell that they are wrong.' He also believed that they came about as a result of France's political will. France mattered: 'they have the real power'. In this context, he stated:

> France accuses me of wanting to kill their nationals. I want to have proof that I have been involved in the killings. I wrote them for an answer to the accusations. By they are cowards. They hide behind their bureaucracy. I have never been given the chance to tell explaining my case. I am a fighter. I fight for peace in my country.

During the interview, he said he would 'turn to France', as it was France that had the power. It was also France that would have the say about his removal from the

105 The Ivory Coast sanctions regime (under UNSCR 1572, 2004) targeted three persons included on its sanctions lists. Two of these were unreachable since they were in rebel-held territory at the time of the interviews.

106 Interview conducted in late May 2006.

list: 'I would not be able to turn to France in order to be relieved from the list. They are not neutral, and they don't see me as a human. And to have the Ivorian government to present my case will be difficult.'

Although the listed entity was in contact with officials of the UN mission, there were few signs of direct interaction with him and explanations of what he needed to do to be taken off the list. In fact, he had little information regarding what was expected of him:

> I have not personally been notified about the sanctions. I don't know about the criteria. I need to know what sanctions are about. I don't know why there are sanctions in place. I heard about the sanctions through the TV and the radio. I asked for lawyers as to know why.

While one goal with the sanctions would be to change his behaviour, for instance by forcing him to keep a low profile or to abandon the political course he had taken, there were also other factors in play at the same time. For instance, friends and equals expected him to continue to be a voice for their concerns: 'Many are tired of me just speaking. There are those that want me to take up arms.'

Clearly, sanctions mattered for the interviewee. It is difficult to say whether they contributed to changing his behaviour. Comments suggest that they may even have hardened his attitude, and that they may even have united his followers. However, the UN sanctions seem to have at least engaged the target, which in the end gives both sender and target a framework for interaction.

The perception noted above only reflects the attitude of one entity, speaking from one side of the conflict. There are two other entities on the list who may perceive sanctions quite differently (one being out in the field, while the other is publicly visible). Their presence and integration into public life differs. Yet the sanctions approach from the UN side does not differ much.

Auxiliary strategic tools It is worth noting that in all of the above cases, there have been a number of accompanying strategic measures to engage and also put pressure on listed actors. A number of peacekeeping missions have been deployed in the region: UNMIL, the UN Observer Mission in Sierra Leone (UNOMSIL), the UN Mission in Sierra Leone (UNAMSIL), the UN Mission in Côte d'Ivoire (MINUCI), and as noted, UNOCI.[107] While having the primary aim of ensuring peace in these countries, these missions have also been able to enforce aspects of sanctions. For instance, UNMIL has been able to monitor different areas of direct relevance to the sanctions, for example the status of the diamond trade, arms embargoes and political activities of targets. None of these were made public nor

107 A recent study noted that UNOCI has established a unique (in a positive sense) example of substantive co-operation with the UN Panel of Experts with regard to monitoring the implementation of targeted sanctions; Boucher and Holt (2009): 62.

on a systematic level. Besides various military and civilian missions, there have also been other instruments, such as the deployment of various good offices, EU and UN special representatives, and so on. For instance, in July 2006, the EU launched in Liberia an Interim Poverty Reduction Strategy Programme aiming, inter alia, to consolidate national peace (although it makes some reference to sanctions on natural resources, it makes no mention of the travel ban and the assets freeze on some leading politicians in the country).[108] Thus, targeted sanctions fit well under a broader strategy which, I argue, entails having other political measures in place, such as the International Criminal Court, and having UNMIL on the ground, as well as a constant monitoring of key stakeholders (for example, through the Peace Building Commission and Governance and Economic Management Assistance Programme GEMAP).[109] Although political connections have not been formally established between the various missions, they seem to have been complementary in the sense of keeping pressure on possibly violent political elites. Scholars have argued that various peace support missions should also have it in their mandate to formally oversee aspects of sanctions implementation.[110]

Democratic Republic of Congo (DRC)

Following an arms embargo imposed in late October 2002, a number of persons actively involved in the DRC conflict have been included on a sanctions list (especially with regard to the crisis in Kivu Province) (see Table 14 in Appendix 2). Despite various atrocities over the years – the conflict goes back to the 1960s – the targeting of specific individuals remains limited. Targeting has primarily been imposed on a number of key actors who have acted in violation of the arms embargo. Measures include both a travel ban as well as an assets freeze. While these measures were adopted by the UN in mid-2005, it took the UN almost five months to come up with the first set of targets, and the EU nine days more to incorporate this decision into EC law.[111] The updates of the sanctions list featured in Table 14 were made on the basis of decisions taken by the UN Sanctions Committee on the recommendations of the reports of the UN special representatives on the ground (and indirectly by some concerned UN member states).[112]

108 See, inter alia, *Republic of Liberia-European Community: Country Strategy Paper and Indicative Programme for the period 2008–2013*.

109 For more on the UN's involvement in Liberia from a sanctions point of view, see Wallensteen et al. (2006).

110 Wallensteen (2008).

111 The UNSC issues lists of individuals targeted by sanctions; see UN Press Release SC/8546.

112 One way to further account for the interaction taking place between the sender and the target is to include the number of reports sent by the UN Special Representative and the Sanctions Committee (including Panel of Expert reports).

Episodes The goal of implementing targeted sanctions in the first place (Episode 7) was to stop a certain number of targets violating the general UN arms embargo put in place in the DRC. Initially, the UN arms embargo was selective in character and implemented against all armed groups and militias operating in the territories of North and South Kivu and Ituri, as well as against groups not party to the global and All-inclusive Agreement. A UNSCR later expanded this scope to cover the whole territory of the DRC.[113] However, evasion and circumvention of the arms embargo forced the UN to single out particular persons as responsible for the breaches.[114] The main targets were leaders and former leaders of armed militias.[115] However, the frequencies of interaction between senders and targets have been low, judging from the tables. This implies that the Sanctions Committees as well as the Panel of Experts have not been active in monitoring the activities of some of the entities involved in arms trafficking. What is noteworthy, though, is that two years passed between the introduction of the first list and the second list (Episodes 7 and 12). The conflict in the DRC is continuing, as are the targeted sanctions measures. It is difficult to establish how personal measures affect the overall conflict and its resolution. Further systematic assessment is needed, but depends on data collected on the ground.

Auxiliary strategic tools Targeted sanctions have not been the only means to put pressure on the parties. According to Vaux et al. (2007), international security actors have also engaged the DRC through various forms of state-building support (involving institutions, staff capacities and legislation).[116] The number of security support programmes in the field of conflict prevention, management and resolution are too many to be covered here, but all fit into the broader picture of exercising pressure on key stakeholders to the conflict.[117] For instance, both the EU and the UN conducted several missions aimed at separating the parties and supporting conflict resolution. For instance, in June 2003, following UNSCR 1484, the EU agreed to launch Operation Artemis. This military mission was set up to support the UN Mission in the Democratic Republic of Congo (Mission des Nations Unies en République Démocratique du Congo, MONUC) and to

113 Measures are detailed in UNSCR 1493 (2003), UNSCR 1552 (2004) and UNSCR 1596 (2005). The EU establishes these measures in Council Regulation (EC) 2005/889.

114 These measures are put in place in paras 14 and 15 of UNSCR 1596 (2005).

115 Some of the targets belong to the main fighting groups. Several of these are already identified in UNSCR 1493 (2003). Some of the most noteworthy targets are: former RCD-ML leader, former President of UCD/FAPC, FRPI Chief, President of the UPC/L, ex-President of PUSIC, FDLR Commander, President of FDLR, former FARDC Deputy Military Regional Commander of 10th MR, FNI Chief of Staff and former Chief of Staff of the FRPI, President of FNI, former RCD-G General, President of FEC in Aru territory and UPC/L Military Commander.

116 See Vaux et al. (2007).

117 A good introduction to current peace-building programmes can be found in the *Annual Review of Global Peace Operations* (2008), ch. 3.2.

stabilise the security situation in the country, particularly with regard to Bunia, the capital of the province of Ituri.[118] From April 2005 to June 2007, the EU also deployed a police mission, the Integrated Police Unit (EUPOL KINSHASA). Part of its mandate was to ensure that a general election could be conducted without violence. Moreover, the EU also launched an advisory and assistance mission for DRC security reform (EUSEC RD Congo).[119] Perhaps even more significantly, though, on 25 April 2006 the EU launched a military operation in support of MONUC to support the election process (Operation EUFOR RD Congo).[120] The deployment of troops came after the UN asked for support under UNSCR 1671 (2006). The operation was concluded on 30 November 2006. Clearly, these other strategic tools have had an influence by putting pressure on actors who spoil peace and promote war. Regrettably, however, the UNSC has not provided the UN missions with the necessary mandate to ensure that sanctions are implemented properly. Had it done so, a number of synergies between the UN peacekeepers, the Panel of Experts and the Sanctions Committees could have been brought into play. What can thus be seen is a number of missed opportunities by the senders to act effectively and coherently.

Moreover, collective security actors have also been putting pressure on targeted entities through the International Criminal Court (ICC) and its warrants. In June 2004, the ICC opened its first war crimes investigation for the DRC. Since then, a number of warrants and arrests have been made, and trials conducted, against individuals involved in the conflict. For instance, on 28 April 2008, the ICC in The Hague issued an arrest warrant for Bosco Ntaganda, a militia leader, for his role in forcing children under the age of 15 into the Forces Patriotiques pour la Libération du Congo (FPLC). Ntaganda was also placed on the consolidated sanctions list. Three other Congolese rebels also included on the sanctions list are currently in custody: Thomas Lubanga and Germain Katanga, both transferred to The Hague in October 2006, and Mathieu Ngudjolo Chui, transferred to The Hague on 6 February 2008. Despite their arrest, they still remain on the sanctions list. However, the sanctions lists also look as though they have been put together arbitrarily compared to ICC warrants. For example, on 10 June 2008, the ICC issued a request to Belgium for the arrest and surrender of Jean-Pierre Bemba, leader of the Congolese Liberation Movement (MLC). Fleeing the DRC in April 2007, he was on the run until he was arrested on 24 May 2008.[121]

Sudan

Sudan has been the scene of violence for many decades, and as a result has been the focus of a number of UNSC resolutions. The specific sanctions regime is

118 Already established in 2000 through UNSCR 1291 (2000).

119 EU Council Secretariat, 28 April 2005.

120 See EU Council Joint Action 2006/319/CFSP, 27 April 2006.

121 *Keesing's* (DRC), vol. 54, April 2008: 48,505; *ibid.*, June 2008: 48,622.

illustrated in Table 15 (Appendix 2); however, its results are primarily from the decision and command by the UN to end the violence in the Sudanese province of Darfur.

Episodes Targeted sanctions, in the form of a general travel ban and assets freeze measure, were put in place in accordance with UNSCR 1591 (2005) (measures were imposed by the UN on 29 March 2005, and one month later, decided upon by the EU).[122]

In March 2005, the UNSC referred aspects of the Darfur conflict to the ICC (which would later issue an arrest warrant for two high-ranking officials in the Sudan). With regard to targeted sanctions, the UNSC agreed to target those who had: impeded the peace process; constituted a threat to stability in Darfur and the region; committed violations of international humanitarian or human rights law or other atrocities; violated the arms embargo, and/or were responsible for offensive military overflights in the Darfur region.[123] The terms that such violations would entail were first laid out in the UN Expert Panel Report on Darfur on 30 January 2006.[124] In the second report, dated 19 April 2006, the Panel of Experts concluded: 'The Security Council Committee should act swiftly to designate members of the senior leadership within Sudan Liberation Army (SLA) and the Government of the Sudan ....'[125] This action was also designed to 'provide additional momentum to the entire peace process in Darfur, particularly given the enhanced attention being given by all parties to the situation in Darfur ...'.[126]

---

122 Council Common Position 2005/411/CFSP and Council Regulation 2005/1184.

123 UNSCR 1591.

124 The Panel of Experts identified in their first report nine categories of actions which, in their view, would meet the criteria for being placed on the travel ban and assets freeze lists. Moreover, after having carried out investigations on the ground in Darfur and hearing a number of key participants to the conflict speak, the panel came up with recommendations on who to put on the list (which was attached in a confidential annex to the Sudan Sanctions Committee). The nine categories which, according to them, would constitute a violation of the peace process were: ongoing hostilities and violations of the N'Djamena Humanitarian Ceasefire Agreement; failure to comply with the provisions of the Protocol on the Enhancement of the Security Situation in Darfur signed at Abuja on 9 November 2004; failure of the government of the Sudan to identify, neutralise and disarm armed militia groups in Darfur; exacerbation of tribal/ethnic tensions; provision of support to parties that engage in ongoing hostilities; hostile acts against AMIS personnel; failure to enforce accountability for violations of international humanitarian law and international human rights law; failure to fully implement UNSC resolutions concerning Darfur, and acts that impede the actual process of negotiations. For more specific information, consult S/2006/65, *Final Report of the Panel of Experts: Report Submitted in Accordance with Resolution 1591 (2005)* (30 January 2006).

125 S/2006/250, 2006: 43.

126 *Ibid.*: 4.

On 18 May 2006, the European Commission established a list of four individuals to be targeted with sanctions, following the UN action on the matter (Episode 10). The number of listed targets has remained constant over time.

Auxiliary strategic tools The EU has tied its support for Sudan to the effective implementation of the Sudanese Comprehensive Peace Agreement signed on 9 January 2005. With this support, commonly referred to as 'Peace Dividends', the EU is pursuing a gradual resumption of talks. The strategy is to monitor closely the implementation of the peace agreement, while allowing for progressive disbursement of political and economic support upon its implementation. In addition, the EU is supporting common humanitarian interests.

As in the case of the DRC, the UN and EU also rely on a policy mix making use of the ICC. For example, on February 2007 the ICC accused a former Sudanese minister of war crimes in Sudan's Darfur region (also called for under UNSCR 1593 (2005). According to the ICC prosecutor, there was evidence that Ahmad Mohammed Harun, former Minister of State for the Interior, and Ali Muhammad Ali Abd-al-Rahman had committed crimes against the civilian population in Darfur.[127] On 14 October 2008, the Sudanese government announced it had arrested one of these accused, Ali Muhammad Ali Abd-al-Rahman.[128] However, the Sudanese government refused to hand him over to the ICC, insisting that it would handle potential criminals in its own national courts. In another related case, the Sudanese government announced in mid-January 2008 that Sheikh Musa Hilal, paramount of the Jalul tribe in north Darfur, had been named as his adviser. The appointment was made despite his facing UN sanctions under UNSCR 1672 (2006).[129] In addition to this, on 14 July 2008 evidence was presented that President Omar Hassan Ahmed al-Bashir had committed the crimes of genocide, crimes against humanity and war crimes in Sudan's Darfur region.[130] An arrest warrant for President Bashir was formally handed over to the Sudanese government on 4 March 2009.

Besides political and legal pressure, the use of targeted sanctions also needs also to be analysed further through a strategic context involving military pressure. Both the EU and the UN have been actively involved in resolving issues on the ground through the deployment of personnel. In 2004, the UNSC adopted UNSCR 1564 (2004), setting up the peacekeeping force the Africa Mission in Sudan (AMIS).[131] AMIS was expected to co-operate with the UN force already established in Sudan, UNMIS. AMIS was deployed in June 2004.[132] In 2005, at

---

127 *Keesing's* (Sudan), vol. 53, February 2007: 47,734.

128 *Ibid.*, vol. 54, October 2008: 48,814.

129 *Ibid.*, January 2008: 48,337.

130 *Ibid.*, July 2008: 48,676.

131 For a good overview of international initiatives, see *Annual Review of Global Peace Operations* (2008), ch. 3.6.

132 *Ibid.*: 73.

the request of the AU, the EU deployed military personnel (as well as financial assistance) to support the AMIS force (this support would last until 2007).[133] In late December 2007, AMIS was replaced by UNAMID (UN-AU Mission in Darfur), comprising 26,000 troops.[134] The mandate for UNAMID was set to expire on 31 July 2009, but it was expected to be extended. As for the DRC, the UN and the EU seem to miss important synergies to provide its forces with mandates to implement and enforce sanctions. Interestingly, though, targeted sanctions came to play a role in the mediation attempts.

With the ensuing fighting on the ground, and in the search for ways to solve the Darfur crisis, the AU and the UN undertook mediation efforts.[135] The Darfur Peace Agreement was signed in May 2008.[136] However, because of the failure to bring on board all fighting forces under the agreement, the UN and the AU decided to establish a Joint Mediation Support Team on 16 November 2006 (acting as a form of secretariat). The aim was to re-energise the Darfur peace process. The mediation team was composed of the AU Representative, Salim Salim, and the UN Representative, Jan Eliasson.

During the mediation talks, Ambassador Eliasson, also reporting to the UNSC, used targeted sanctions as a way of pressurising parties to sign a peace deal. Although sceptical of sanctions as a tool for punishment, Eliasson held that targeted sanctions had an impact during the negotiations:[137]

> The UN targeted sanctions on Darfur have, I must admit, been mostly symbolic. But what is important is that they seem to have had a stigmatising effect. Being sanctioned in person is not something that any political or military actor welcomes. Being placed on a sanctions list means that you become an international pariah. Moreover, when the International Criminal Court mentions names in public, it creates waves of concern among those engaged in obstructing the peace, which hopefully affects the behaviour of listed targets and presumed future targets. Even the most stubborn political actors are sensitive to being identified as possible war criminals.

---

133 Joint Action 2005/557/CFSP.

134 UNSCR 1769 (2007).

135 In late 2005, the seventh round of the Inter-Sudanese Peace Talks on the Conflict in Darfur was held in Abuja, Nigeria. A peace agreement was later signed on 5 May 2006 – the so-called Darfur Peace Agreement (DPA) – by the government and by Minni Minawi, the leader of one of the two SLM factions. However, the DPA was rejected by JEM and Abdel ahid al Nur, the leader of the other SLM faction. Later, the Darfur Peace Agreement Implementation Team supported the DPA. However, in an effort to deal with the issues which the DPA had not covered, the AU also launched the Darfur-Darfur Dialogue and Consultation (DDDC Forum).

136 It also established the DDDC.

137 Griffiths and Barnes (2008).

Eliasson went on to say that his preferred option during the negotiations was to have sanctions work as 'drumbeating in the background':[138]

> For instance, the Tripoli Declaration of July 2006 increased pressure on the parties, which was good from a negotiating point of view. But the drums should not make so much noise that they overwhelm my voice. Another strategy is that certain conditions or sanctions could be introduced during the process, but not implemented until one has evaluated if the concerned parties' behaviour has changed. At the moment though we do not want to impose more sanctions as it risks deadlocking the dialogue.

In the end, the mediation efforts did not succeed. In late June 2008, Eliasson from the UN and Ahmed Salim from the AU, both being special envoys, resigned following the collapse of the peace talks held in Libya in October 2007.

Finally, besides connecting sanctions with ICC threats, troop deployment and mediation, the UN has also been engaged in placing mounting pressure on specific decision-makers by focusing attention on the human rights situation in Darfur. Such actions have included setting up an investigatory team of special representatives to look into various aspects of the conflict in 2007.[139]

The Sudan example illustrates a good case where different strategies have been applied to put pressure on the regime. While there seem to be some linkages between sanctions and these other measures, no clear and defined co-ordination strategy seems to exist. Further co-ordination, both at UN Headquarters (New York) and at the EU Commission (Brussels), and also with ongoing efforts on the ground, could enhance the impact of sanctions.

Zimbabwe

The Zimbabwean sanctions regime was introduced by the EU to prevent the election in 2002 from failing to fulfil certain democratic standards. However, in the absence of evidence of the behavioural modifications of listed entities in the days following the election, the EU increased its pressure. The focus of EU sanctions, however, falls not only on a general criticism of presidential and parliamentary elections, but also on the regime's violent and repressive behaviour,

---

138 *Ibid.*

139 The investigatory team was constituted by the: Special Rapporteur on the situation of human rights in the Sudan; the Special Rapporteur on extrajudicial, summary or arbitrary executions; the Special Representative of the Secretary-General for children and armed conflict; the Special Rapporteur on violence against women, its causes and consequences; the Special Representative of the Secretary-General on the situation of human rights defenders; the Representative of the Secretary-General on the human rights of internally-displaced persons, and the Special Rapporteur on the question of torture and other cruel, inhuman or degrading treatment or punishment.

not least against the opposition, the Movement for Democratic Change (MDC). As illustrated in Table 16 (Appendix 2), the total number of targets for the Zimbabwean case has now reached more than 100, having originally only listed approximately 20 persons in the first episode (the impact will be further discussed in the case study on Zimbabwe).

While it is unclear whether the EU anticipated any immediate behavioural change through the establishment of the first round of sanctions, it seems that one purpose was to contain the Zimbabwean government and signal that the EU was monitoring the situation closely. A problem for the EU, given the trend depicted in Table 16, is that while there has been an increase in targeting over time, the situation on the ground has continuously deteriorated. When linking sanctions to political outcomes, the effectiveness seems rather poor. None the less, the main question is whether further targeting will yield more pressure, or whether the increase in targeting and routine updates will simply lead the sender to become further bogged down in a political entrenchment 'war' *vis-à-vis* the sender. One problem with the sanctions strategy for Zimbabwe is that it does not seem to be as context-sensitive as it should be. While some policy adjustments have taken place (such as new categories of targets), the travel ban and assets freeze measures remain the dominant means. However, given the political changes that have occurred over the years, the EU could have engaged in a more refined push and pull strategy: involving the elite in more bargaining, using enhanced tools to put pressure on the elite, co-ordinating actors in the region, and so on.

First of all, a number of elections have been held in Zimbabwe over the years. These elections, although always falling short of proper democratic standards, have changed the reference points for sanctions as well as providing for new goals to have sanctions lifted. Secondly, support for the Zimbabwean regime has changed since 2002. For instance, while having originally enjoyed support not only in the immediate neighbourhood but also throughout the African continent, support for Mugabe has weakened. Recently, the AU adopted resolutions stating that the Spring and Summer elections during 2008 did not meet its standards. Another difference, compared to the previous situation when sanctions were imposed in 2002, is that the MDC leader has been able to take office as Prime Minister following mediation by Mbeki under SADC sponsorship (11 February 2009). Factors like these have significantly changed the conditions both motivating sanctions, and underlying their implementation and management.[140]

Despite these changes in the political landscape, the imposed EU sanctions remain more or less in the same. This also highlights the problem of having an excessively static approach. Given that the political situation changes over the years, the sender needs to change its strategy as well. However, sanctions, as in this

140 Council of the European Union, 'Council Conclusions on Zimbabwe' (September 2008); Council of the European Union, 'Council Conclusions on Zimbabwe' (2008); Presidency of the European Union, 'Declaration by the Presidency on behalf of the European Union on Zimbabwe' (Brussels, 4 July 2008).

case, do remain constant, which affects the credibility of the sender. Moreover, an excessively static sanctions approach also makes it difficult for the sender to take a decision to lift the sanctions, since a strikingly early suspension of the sanctions could send the wrong signal should targets continue to defy the sender. Similarly, if the sender maintains sanctions despite reconciling the behavioural attitudes of the targets, its credibility is likely to be undermined.

Uzbekistan

Targeted sanctions against members of the Uzbek elite were imposed in mid-November 2005, and ended in October 2009.[141] The EU's sanctions policy was triggered by the government's involvement in the Andijan killings on 13 May 2005. Allegedly, the government had been involved in decisions that led the Uzbekistan Special Forces to fire into a crowd of demonstrating opposition members (civilians), which led to several protestors being killed or wounded. The killings, which some called a massacre, caused an international outcry, prompting the UN to call for an independent investigation into the events. Against this background, on 23 May 2005 the EU Council strongly condemned what it judged to be the excessive, disproportionate and indiscriminate use of force by the Uzbek security forces, supporting the UN's call for an independent inquiry into these incidents. A few months later, on 13 June 2005, the EU Council again reiterated its condemnation of the Uzbek authorities, noting that no independent investigation had been opened. A month later, the EU made a similar call, this time also including a threat of sanctions.

Episodes Targeted sanctions were put in place in November 2005 (see Episode 1 in Table 17 in Appendix 2). These were directed against members of the elite who 'were directly responsible for the indiscriminate and disproportionate use of force in Andijan and the obstruction of an independent inquiry'.[142]

The travel ban imposed by the EU on members of the Uzbekistan regime was guided by a variety of considerations: the conduct and outcome of trials of those accused of precipitating and participating in the disturbances in Andijan; the situation regarding the detention and harassment of those who questioned the Uzbek authorities' version of events in Andijan; Uzbek co-operation with an independent international rapporteur appointed to investigate the disturbances in Andijan; the outcome of an independent, international inquiry, and any action that demonstrated the willingness of the Uzbek authorities to adhere to the principles of respect for human rights, the rule of law and fundamental freedoms. Despite a number of clear-cut concerns of the EU, the responses to the sanctions were

141 For the motivation of the sanctions policy, see Council Common Position 2005/792/CFSP. The sanctions regime was completely suspended (lifted) in October 2009. The case is included as it was still active in mid-2009.

142 The EU also imposed an arms embargo.

not encouraging. Rather than seeking a more co-operative path, the imposition of sanctions led Uzbekistan to build up its alliance with Russia (for instance, a mutual defence agreement was signed). Given the war in Afghanistan and the need for allies, and the gas crisis between the EU and Russia, member states of the EU called for a more conciliatory approach towards the Uzbek authorities. Thus, ahead of a renewal of sanctions and an upcoming EU-Uzbekistan partnership co-operation meeting in November 2007, a number of official visits by EU Council presidencies were made, as well as the dispatch of an EU special representative. These meetings were initiated by Germany in August 2006, and were later continued by the Finnish government. In November 2006, however, the EU Council decided to extend the travel ban for six months, concluding that an independent inquiry had not been opened.[143] Yet during the Spring of 2007, under German chairmanship, the EU eased the tensions with the Uzbek regime.[144] For instance, the Council noted that the Uzbek authorities had taken positive steps.[145] One reason for the more relaxed approach from the EU side was that the EU agreed to reduce its demand for an international inquiry to the dispatch of a study group to look into the events.[146] Second, the EU would accept further de-escalation if Uzbekistan accepted the agreement to hold human rights dialogues. The formula sent to the Uzbek authorities was thus: 'we are watching and we want to move quickly: if things move in the right direction, that's the end of the sanctions'.[147] In late May 2007, the Council nevertheless decided for a second time to extend the sanctions. This time, the list was shortened from 12 to 8 persons.[148] The human rights and democratic situations remained as they were prior to the sanctions.[149] In March 2008, NATO officials stated that US troops had moved into the German NATO base of Termez in Uzbekistan (the US had previously had bases in Uzbekistan, but had been expelled following human rights complaints in 2005). The base was used to support NATO operations in Afghanistan.[150]

In late October 2008, the EU Council decided to suspend targeted sanctions for a period of six months, following a Council conclusion that progress had been

---

143 Council Common Position 2006/787/CFSP. The EU Council also decided to open low-level talks with the regime, as it saw some movement on the part of Uzbek authorities to address the Andijan incidents; BBC World News, 23 November 2006.

144 The EU had strategic reasons to be on a good footing with the regime, as it planned to support oil and gas pipelines in the country. Moreover, Germany had strategic concerns for its forces operating in Afghanistan.

145 *Turkish Weekly*, 9 April 2007.

146 Portela (2008): 143.

147 *Ibid.*

148 Council Common Position 2007/338/CFSP.

149 For more on the democratic standards during the years of sanctions implementation, see *Freedom House Score* at: <www.freedomhouse.org/uploads/fiw08launch/FIW08Tables.pdf>.

150 *Keesing's* (Uzbekistan), vol. 54, March 2008: 48,472.

achieved in Uzbekistan with regard to human rights (Episode 6).[151] At this time, the four-year arms embargo was also lifted.

The main voice inside the EU in favour of removing the sanctions was Germany, following its need to develop good relations with the Uzbek officials as it had a military base there from which it supported missions in Afghanistan. On 29 April 2008, the suspension of personal sanctions was extended for another six months.[152]

Auxiliary strategic tools In terms of the broader strategic context, the EU put in place a number of agreements. In 1999, the PCA between the EU and Uzbekistan entered into force. This agreement was based on three pillars: political dialogue, trade and economic relations, and co-operation in a variety of sectors.[153] However, the PCA was partially suspended when targeted sanctions were imposed in 2005. In 2007, full operation resumed. The EU also assisted Uzbekistan through the TACIS (Technical Aid to the Commonwealth of Independent States) Central Asia Action Programme.[154] On 27 April 2007, the EU concluded the *Strategy Paper for Assistance to Central Asia for 2007–2013*, which set out a number of regional and bilateral priorities including democracy, governance, security and human rights.[155] Later the same year, the EU launched a new strategy called *The European Union and Central Asia: Strategy for a New Partnership*.[156] This addressed human rights, good governance, democracy and social development.[157] A year into the partnership, the EU concluded that there had been moves towards progress, and encouraged further development. For instance, all countries agreed

151 Council of the European Union, 'Council Conclusions on Uzbekistan' (2008).

152 In October 2009, the sanctions was removed completely.

153 More specifically, the agreement was drawn up: to support the independence and sovereignty of Uzbekistan; to support Uzbekistan's efforts to consolidate its democracy, develop its economy and complete the transition to a market economy; to provide an appropriate framework for political dialogue between the parties allowing the development of political relations; to promote trade and investment and harmonious economic relations between the parties, and to foster their sustainable economic development; to provide a basis for legislative, economic, social, financial, civil, scientific, technological and cultural co-operation, and to assist in the construction of a civil society in Uzbekistan based upon the rule of law; see EU Commission, *EU-Uzbekistan: The Partnership and Cooperation Agreement*.

154 This included: support for institutional, legal and administrative reform; support to the private sector and assistance for economic development; support in addressing the social consequences of transition; development of infrastructure networks; promotion of environmental protection and management of natural resources; development of the rural economy, and support for nuclear safety, where applicable.

155 European Community, *Regional Strategy Paper for Assistance to Central Asia for the period 2007–2013*.

156 EU Council Secretariat (October 2007).

157 *Ibid.*: 6.

to hold talks on the issue of human rights.[158] Besides regional and bilateral co-operation between the EU and Uzbekistan, there were a number of other co-operation forums, such as the Baku Initiative. Co-operation also took place with the UN, the OSCE, the Venice Commission of the Council of Europe, NATO, the World Bank, the European Bank for Reconstruction Development (EBRD), and the European Investment Bank (EIB). Thus, as can be noted, a large mix of operational strategies involving the Uzbek regime remains central, alongside the very specific strategy of targeting. These auxiliary aspects clearly form an essential part of the sanctions mix. However, in the official sanctions literature, these additional strategic dimensions are seldom considered.

Myanmar (Burma)

Myanmar has been in armed conflict since 1948. Various ethnic conflicts are still ongoing across the country. In May 1990, a free election was held in Myanmar, where the National League for Democracy (NLD) won 392 out of a total of 489 seats. However, the election outcome was not recognised by the sitting State Law and Order Restoration Council (SLORC) government, which refused to hand power over to the NLD. Being in power, the SLORC decided, as a substitute, to establish a new constitution through the process of a National Convention. This course, however, would never be realised. Instead, the issue became symbolically entwined with the political crisis, and the new constitution has not yet been implemented.[159] The political crisis has also escalated, with the government putting the NLD opposition leader, Aung San Suu Kyi, under house arrest for many years.[160]

Episodes Within this context, the EU decided in late October 1996 to impose a travel ban against the ruling SLORC elite (see Table 18 in Appendix 2).[161] In this first episode of holding specific targets accountable for their actions, no specific

158 European Commission, 'Joint Progress Report by the Council and the European Commission to the European Council on the Implementation of the EU Central Asia Strategy' (24 June 2008).

159 See Wallensteen et al. (2004).

160 Aung San Suu Kyi was imprisoned for the first time on 20 July 1989.

161 Common Position 1996/635/CFSP included a number of reasons for imposing targeted sanctions: 'The European Union is concerned at the absence of progress towards democratisation and at the continuing violation of human rights in Burma/Myanmar. It deplores, in particular, the practice of torture, summary and arbitrary executions, forced labour, abuse of women, political arrests, forced displacement of the population, and restrictions on the fundamental rights of freedom of speech, movement and assembly. It condemns the detentions in May and September 1996 of members and supporters of the National League for Democracy (NLD). It calls for the immediate and unconditional release of all detained political prisoners. The NLD and other legitimate political parties, including those from ethnic minorities, should be allowed to pursue freely their normal activities. It

list of names was issued. Instead, a more general provision for whom to target was included in the decision.[162]

On 15 November 1997, the EU renewed its sanctions position in order to reflect the fact that the SLORC had been dissolved and replaced by the State Peace and Development Council (SPDC).[163] In late April 2000, the EU agreed to strengthen the restrictive measures against the regime by imposing an assets freeze.[164] This marks the beginning of the name-specific sanctions lists. In September of the same year, Suu Kyi was again placed under house arrest after having been temporarily released. However, this arrangement was superseded by a deal brokered by the UN. Suu Kyi was released in early May 2002. With Suu Kyi having been free for less than a year, however, a crisis nearly occurred. Allegedly, the government sponsored an attack on an NLD rally. The subsequent NLD criticism of the government (both domestically and internationally) instigated the SPDC to return Suu Kyi to prison (30 May). Thus, in light of further deterioration on the ground, the EU increased pressure on the leadership. A cluster of episodes was triggered in 2003, marking the beginning of a policy that significantly increased the number of individuals being targeted, consequently in 2003, the UN Special Human Rights Rapporteur was expelled from Myanmar.[165] In March 2004, the UN Special Representative, Ismail Razali, resigned because he was denied entry into Myanmar. Ibrahim Gambari replaced Razali.

On 28 November 2005, Suu Kyi's house arrest was extended by an SPDC decision, and it was later prolonged again in 2006 and 2007. During these years, the EU's sanctions episodes bore more resemblance to annual extensions of sanctions than to a specific response to actions by specific members of the regime.

In October 2007, the UNSC issued a presidential statement deploring the use of violence by the government. This statement followed the government's clash with demonstrating Buddhist monks in September, where it was estimated that several hundred civilians had been killed. Following these clashes, the UN Special Envoy, Ibrahim Gambari, held direct talks with the Myanmar government. Later in the month, he travelled to the region to rally support for putting increasing pressure on the government.

The clash with demonstrators, as well as slow progress towards democratic reform, sparked renewed and expanded sanctions measures by the EU (as of 19 November 2007). Not only were more categories of individuals added to the target

---

calls on the SLORC to enter into meaningful dialogue with pro-democracy groups with a view to bringing about national reconciliation.'

162 Instead, the visa ban made a more general statement, providing for a ban on entry visas for senior members for the SLORC and their families, a ban on entry visas for senior members of the military and the security forces and their families, and the suspension of high-level bilateral governmental visits to Burma/Myanmar.

163 Council Decision 1998/107/CFSP.

164 Council Common Position 2000/346/CFSP.

165 Council Common Position 2003/297/CFSP.

list, but also several state companies and specific items and natural resources (such as jade, gold and timber). On 29 April 2008, the EU in its Council Conclusion expressed deep concern with regard to the political situation in the country, urging rapids steps towards a transition to a legitimate civilian government and national reconciliation. These measures are also noted in Episodes 23–7.

Auxiliary strategic tools Aside from an EU Special Representative for Myanmar (appointed in November 2007), the EU has had very little dialogue with the military regime since the imposition of targeted sanctions. Most of the dialogue is held via ASEM (Asia Europe Meetings), or through the EU and ASEAN (Association of Southeast Asian Nations). EU support is provided indirectly through the meetings of the International Labour Organisation (ILO) and the International Committee of the Red Cross (ICRC). Most of the EU's activities take place under the EC-Burma/Myanmar Strategy Paper for 2007–2013, which reviews and provides for the framework of the co-operation. The focus of the co-operation is based primarily on support for health, education and the economy following natural disasters. The role of targeted sanctions is mentioned in this strategy paper, but mostly with reference to the fact that they are put in place to target the regime, and not the population.[166] There is no bilaterally agreed co-operation programme with Myanmar, nor any direct involvement with nor financial support for the regime. Most support is granted via a number of NGO and UN projects. Moreover, EU companies are not allowed to make finances available to named state-owned enterprises. Judging from the character of the sanctions regime, it is difficult to foresee the EU being engaged with each listed person in order to modify their behaviour. This particularly holds true given the lack of personal identification regarding the individuals placed on the list.

Analysis and Conclusion

In his article 'On the Effects of International Economic Sanctions' (1967), Johan Galtung laid out the theoretical foundations for the impact of comprehensive sanctions. Galtung concluded that comprehensive economic sanctions, if not applied in a more refined way, could easily become a weak and vulnerable instrument. The main reason was that they did not make a distinction between the elite and the general citizenry of the target country. The approach, he suggested, could easily fail and have an opposite effect from what the sender had originally intended. Thus, unhappy about the possible negative consequences of comprehensive economic sanctions, Galtung rhetorically asked: 'What, then, can be done?'[167] One of the options that the international community could turn to would be to take actions

166 European Commission, *EC-Burma/Myanmar Regional Strategy Paper for Assistance to Central Asia for the Period 2007–2013.*

167 Galtung (1967): 414.

which would primarily be 'aimed at responsible individuals'.[168] Today, almost 40 years later, Galtung's vision in this regard seems more realistic than ever. As seen, the development of targeted sanctions, where individual decision-makers are held accountable, has been advanced by scholars, norm entrepreneurs and policy makers over the past 20 years. With the establishment of targeted sanctions, challenges to existing practice and theory on sanctions have been made, thus profoundly changing the general rules of the game. Today, however, one of the most fundamental challenges to targeted sanctions concerns effective implementation. The more refined the sanctions tool becomes, the more challenging it is for the sender to achieve impact, not least in terms of how sanctions fit and operate within a larger political strategy of coercion.

The overview of ongoing sanctions regimes in this chapter illustrates the plethora of coercive policies in operation. All of the above coincide with, accompany or embed targeted sanctions. While these larger background strategies are most likely to enable the performance of targeted sanctions, poor implementation or lack of co-ordination with this policy can also undermine its efficacy. Although much dependent on the larger strategic approach, targeted sanctions are in the end directly affected by the sender's effective implementation of this policy. Although much has been written about sanctions implementation problems, I will briefly bring up five aspects that can be observed from the overview in this chapter.[169]

First, the implementation, and consequently the impact of sanctions on individuals, are dependent on whether the government of the target country, as opposed to non-state actors, is being subjected to targeted sanctions. If the government and its members are themselves being subjected to sanctions, then the sending body needs the goodwill of the target's neighbouring states to enforce them. However, this is both costly as well as politically difficult. On the other hand, if targeted sanctions are imposed on a target that operates in a country without official support, the sender will have a much better capacity to enforce sanctions in co-operation with the host government. In fact, in terms of UN implementation, the impact of sanctions is dependent on member states having domestic sanctions legislation in place.[170]

Second, sanctions are likely to be more easily implemented the more economically and politically developed the host country is, as this makes it technically easier to monitor and interact with the target. Similarly, impact is dependent on the target's integration into the financial system, and its desire to travel legally on normal routes.

---

168 *Ibid.*: 415. Specifically, Galtung's third idea refers to global policing, in which an international police or some similar kind of force would arrest or topple leaders with failed policies (compare the activities of the ICC).

169 See the final report of the Stockholm Process on the Implementation of Targeted Sanctions, Wallensteen et al. (2003).

170 Chesterman and Pouligny (2003): 506.

Third, the proximity of sender and target is likely to have an impact on implementation. This seems particularly to be the case for the EU. In contrast to the UN, which has a global mandate, the greater the proximity between the sender country and the targeted entities, the more effective of the EU's targeted sanctions policy is likely to be. One explanation is that the closer the target is, the more vulnerable it is to the sender's monitoring and screening systems.

Fourth, in terms of differences in member state implementation, there is a clear difference between the EU and the UN. While the EU is mostly a 'club' of rich governments, the UN, although it has a global reach, is constituted of a large number of governments that lack resources for effective implementation. This suggests that EU governments have a sharp sanctions weapon, not only in terms of the refined capacities to ensure implementation and monitoring, but also because of the direct intimacy with member states' national interests. As seen above, the EU can also embed targeted sanctions in a number of other strategic policy tools, which it may operate simultaneously if it wishes. The obvious weakness in the EU's sanctions policy, however, is that it is limited to the territory of Europe. On the other hand, the UN is dependent on the political will of the UNSC and member states' interests, despite its advantage of having a global mandate.

Finally, it is worth noting that the UN and the EU differ significantly when it comes to sanctions implementation. Not only do their bureaucratic structures differ, but also their institutional practices as well as their cultures. Yet, interestingly, they are dependent on each other when it comes to the enforcement of sanctions. For instance, the EU implements UN sanctions automatically by adopting UNSC decisions. The EU's sanctions implementation (together with other non-European powers like the US) also gives much credibility to the UNSC. Yet despite the two-way dependency, there is, strangely enough, little active co-ordination on the ground between the EU and the UN in enforcing sanctions (for example, when it comes to monitoring travel ban and arms embargo evasion). One reason may be that that the EU, and more so the UN, lack sanctions co-ordination capacities within their various departments. Thus, little is to be expected in terms of co-ordination in the field.

With regard to listing and de-listing of natural entities, the number of individuals targeted with sanctions has continued to increase over the years following the introduction of new sanctions regimes. According to the analysis above, in mid-April 2009 there were a total of 1,186 individuals listed in all ongoing UN and EU sanctions regimes (based on the latest number of entities listed in each sanctions regime). This is a slight increase from the 950 targets listed in January 2008. Where the trend is going is still not clear, although signs suggest that fewer individuals are likely to be targeted in the years to come, given that the number of sanctions regimes is decreasing. The sum of targets presented in this chapter can also be compared to other estimates compiled in this context:

- Biersteker noted that in 2005 there were 929 individuals targeted by UN sanctions (of which 42 had been de-listed).[171] He further observed that there were 345 individuals listed on the UN Al-Qaeda Taliban terrorism list.
- In 2006, the Confederation of British Industries held that there were about 6,000 individuals listed for financial sanctions (including all US, EU and UN sanctions).[172]
- In 2006, the European Commission stated: 'To our knowledge, a calculation based on EU and United Nations lists suggests that the number of individuals amounts to something like 1,050, roughly, and the number of entities, groups or companies, to some 430.'[173]
- In 2006 HSBC Holdings Plc reported the following: 'There are approximately 6,000 individual and entity names specified by US, EU and UN sanctions. These consist of circa 470 names relating to Al-Qaeda and the Taliban; [and] circa 122 names, relating to suspected terrorist activity with the remaining names relating to individuals and bodies linked to [other] regimes or governments ....'[174]
- In 2005, a Swedish newspaper reported that the US government was keeping a sanctions list of individuals and companies numbering almost 80,000.[175]
- According to the US Department of Justice, as of April 2007 the US Terrorist Screening Database contained 700,000 records of more than 400,000 individuals who were 'known or appropriately suspected to be or have been engaged in conduct constituting, in preparation for, in aid of, or related to terrorism'.[176] This increases by about 20,000 records per month (that is, records, not newly added names). Estimates suggest that the records in early 2009 included 1 million entries.[177]

Despite these various estimates based on different definitions and focuses, it is safe to say that targeted individual sanctions cover a large number of individuals in a manner unprecedented in the history of EU and UN sanctions practice.

With regard to target engagement, as seen in the data presentation, both the UNSC and the EU have been actively engaged in putting pressure on specific individuals through various strategic frameworks. On the one hand, senders have sought to establish direct contact with specific entities when there is a clear reason for doing so. One typical case in this regard would be that of the ICTY sanctions

171 Biersteker (2008).
172 House of Lords (2007).
173 *Ibid.*, vol. 2: 91.
174 *Ibid.*: 147.
175 *Svenska Dagbladet*, 8 December 2005.
176 US Department of Justice (2007).
177 See American Civil Liberties Union Watch List Counter at <www.aclu.org> (accessed 11 February 2009).

regime, where the sender identified a set of actors which should be brought to trial. Typically, these individuals were easily identified and publicly well known. Moreover, targeted entities on their side were likely to have been well aware of the sanctions placed on them, not least through media attention.

Another example where the sender has shown an interest in interacting with targets is the Ivory Coast. Here as well, targets have been well known and have received public attention. In this regime, the UN has been actively involved in getting targets to sign and implement a peace agreement. Such contexts pave the way for direct sender–target contact. This is not to say that the sender necessarily wants to negotiate with the targets, or necessarily hold them accountable, but instead to keep them engaged in a dialogue. However, both the ICTY cases as well as the Ivory Coast case stand in sharp contrast to those regimes where targeted sanctions have been imposed on a group level.

The other extreme where the interaction between sender and target is almost absent are those situations where the sender has no immediate interest in interacting directly with the listed entities. In this case, the EU's targeted sanctions against the Myanmar elite serve as a typical example. The number of individuals targeted is very large (at least if compared to other sanctions regimes), while specific information about each targeted entity seems limited. At the same time, there are only a few dialogues taking place in which the sender can engage specific targets directly. Although the EU may encourage a dialogue, little interaction takes place with the entities on the sanctions list. There may be a variety of reasons for this. Governments of the sending bodies have no national interest in engaging the targets (the higher the national interest, the likelier it is for the sender to engage the target); governments of the sending body see a particular great power interest, and therefore do not want to intervene, or the sending body sees no need for a quick solution of the conflict as there are other more urgent conflicts that need to be resolved first.

Both extremes raise the question of impact. Are senders likely to experience more or less sanctions efficacy in those cases where targeted sanctions are imposed without there being any interaction with the targets? What determines in which cases individuals should be monitored and held accountable as opposed to others? Why, for example, did the former Serb leader Karadic receive more 'personal' attention, but not the listed general in Myanmar who is likely to have committed just as much human rights abuse?

Some insights into the impact of targeted sanctions can be noted. To begin with, the interviews presented in this chapter show that the imposed travel bans and assets freezes seem to have been evident in their daily lives.[178] This agrees with the findings of the Cosgrove study.[179]

---

178 This should be contrasted with the findings of the interview with the entity placed on EU's Transdniestria sanctions list who claimed that he was not aware about his inclusion.

179 Cosgrove (2005).

For instance, for some entities the travel bans and the targeted assets freezes seem to have affected targets in both their professional careers as well as their private lives. For instance, in terms of impact on the professional identity, one target reported that he was prevented from travelling, which was required in terms of being an elected official. Another effect of the imposition of targeted sanctions seems to be that a number of targets entered the Liberian Parliament, possibly in order to evade the impact of sanctions.

In terms of personal impact, most targets interviewed expressed the view that sanctions were both unjustified and unfair. There was often little understanding of why they had been put on the list. Most interviewees had their explanations, for example that it was simply for political reasons and because of their affiliation to other entities which posed more of a threat. Few recognised – or at least did not want to bring up – personal responsibilities (as seen in the case of the entity being placed on the Ivory Coast sanctions list). These perceptions were expected, however. Sanctions also seemed to have an impact on targets' relationships with friends and family, as the travel ban would sometimes prevent them meeting or sending money to one another. This must clearly be annoying.

None of the entities interviewed had been personally notified that they had been placed on the UN list. A number of entities had been notified that they were on the list via the media. In retrospect, one could ask whether personal notification would not make the target more aware of the sanctions, and thereby yield more pressure.

Moreover, as seen in the interviews, sender–target interactions were taking place: for instance, the chairperson of the Liberia Sanctions Committee had visited Monrovia to be informed about the effects of sanctions, and a number of entities had also been in contact with the UN Sanctions Committee to apply to be de-listed or to seek exemption from some of the sanctions measures. In the Ivory Coast, a number of informal contacts were made between UN officials and targets.

Lastly, in terms of the type of sanctions regimes that have been applied, the data above suggest that of the 18 ongoing cases examined above, 9 were aimed at non-state actors, while 7 were directed against government members (or persons closely linked to the government). In two cases, targeted sanctions were implemented on both sides of the conflict: both non-state and state actors. Obviously, this raises questions regarding the partiality and objectives of the sanctions. Should a collective security actor, such as the UNSC, side with one group and target the other, or stand impartial, targeting both sides? The result here suggests that siding with one party is a more common strategy. While sometimes the EU is a primary party to a conflict, it also ends up siding with a party in a conflict (becoming a secondary party). The role the sender takes obviously affects the kind of engagements it is prepared to be involved in, as well as its choice of actions. Usually the EU, in combination with UN actions, uses a policy mix that at the time most effectively contributes to solving the conflict at hand. Clearly, such actions are formulated because of the EU's short- and long-term interests. In terms of short-term actions, especially those aimed at conflict management and conflict resolution, the EU also provides support to mediation efforts, reconciliation talks and police missions. Often these go in tandem with UN actions. As illustrated, the goals here are primarily to enable conditions for changing behaviour and to achieve more reconciliatory attitudes from the parties to the dispute. In this realm, engaging actors forms a crucial goal, either through target support or by targeting spoilers. While the EU may pursue independent tracks, sanctions follow UN actions in tandem. The engagement by the EU is thus a blend of policies that seek either to support mediators and the priorities of the disputing actors, or through more punitive measures like 'drums beating in the background'.

Concerning long-term assistance, conflict resolution and putting pressure on parties, the EU operates through a number of policies, notably through country strategy papers, neighbourhood programmes, aid and humanitarian assistance, and so on. However, these tools function more like general forms of conditionality than targeting per se. In terms of applying targeted sanctions, the EU and the UN, as can be seen above, implemented *both* an assets freeze and a travel ban in 8 of the 18 sanctions regimes. When choosing between the two measures, senders prefer travel bans over targeted assets freezes (the latter being applied only in three of these cases). Interestingly, though, nowhere could it be established on what basis the sender determined the selection of one instrument over the other. Most probably, it is random.

In what contexts, then, are targeted sanctions applied?[180] A basic conflict classification suggests that actions taken by the sender to list entities usually either take place during an armed conflict or after a conflict has taken place. Based on the sanctions regimes examined here, the following categories can be noted:

- pre-conflict – Belarus, Iran and Uzbekistan;
- advanced crisis/early conflict – Zimbabwe;
- ongoing conflict – the DRC, the Ivory Coast, the Federal Republic of Yugoslavia (Serbia and Montenegro), Liberia, Myanmar and Sudan;
- post-conflict – Macedonia, Moldova, Serbia (the ICTY), Iraq, Liberia (both sanctions regimes) and Sierra Leone.

In almost all cases, there was an ongoing crisis or an armed conflict that triggered targeted sanctions. Another and perhaps different way of categorising these ongoing targeted sanctions regimes is by arranging them on the basis of conflict type, such as:

- democracy/human rights/governance – Belarus, Moldova, Uzbekistan and Zimbabwe;
- armed conflict – the Federal Republic of Yugoslavia, the DRC, the Ivory Coast and Liberia;

180 For an overview of contexts where the EU has implemented sanctions, see Kreutz (2005): 17–19. For an overview of where the EU has decided to suspend development co-operation as a form of sanctions, see Hazelzet (2005).

- peace negotiations – Macedonia;
- general negotiations/compliance/pressure – Iran, the ICTY, Iraq, Liberia and Sierra Leone.

In this context, it is also worth noting that the relatively large 'terrorism' category has not been accounted for.

A comparison here should be made with the data set presented by Charron (2009), in which she finds that of the 39 UN sanctions regimes existing in the period 1945–2007, 5 of them referred to inter-state conflicts, 19 to intra-state conflicts, 10 to rogue/pariah states and 5 to non-state/terrorism-related conflicts. With regard to strategic pressure, both the EU and the UN seem to complement each other. While the EU formally adopts UN sanctions, it also coerces targets with alternative tools, at least in cases where the EU and the UN are operating together.

The next chapter will discuss the role formal and informal decision-making structures play in shaping sanctions policies and their outcomes. The aim is to demonstrate how structural factors, as well as agents of the sanctions sending bodies, enable and constrain sanctions policies at the sender level, and what consequences this may have for the overall impact of sanctions.

Chapter 5
Decision-making, Perceptions and Complexity

Adopting and administrating a policy such as targeted sanctions is a complex institutional decision-making process that requires a large set of actors and institutional capacity. Not only is the strategy likely to be imposed in a highly politically sensitive context, but it also needs to be carried out with good timing and full legitimacy. In fact, at the outset of considering establishing a new sanction regime, the political and bureaucratic process involves not only deciding whether to adopt sanctions in the first place, but also taking the policy proposal through a number of intra-institutional environments. In general, such a process can be divided into three broad stages: (1) the design stage (based on the original policy initiated by senior politicians in which the main element of the sanctions regime is put in place); (2) establishing a political compromise (for example, negotiations in order to get the necessary number of member states on board with the policy), and (3) preparing the policy for management and implementation. As this chapter will argue, each of these stages involves a number of experts, bureaucrats, politicians and so on who are likely to shape the policy's effectiveness. It will analyse how formal and informal aspects of decision-making by sanctions senders contribute to shaping particular policy outcomes. While this complexity is not necessarily unique to the adoption and management of targeted sanctions, it is seldom scrutinised in detail nor accounted for in the sanctions assessment literature.

In contrast to conventional scholarly assessments of sanctions, where there is a tendency to compare the goals of a sanctions regime with the actual performance once the regime is terminated, the aim here is to examine how perceptions of the different decision-making processes and institutional units are likely to shape the policy process of targeting prior to the implementing stage. The argument advanced here is that even at this early stage, senders, through formal and informal rules, norms and institutional practice, shape sanctions at an early stage (this is examined further in Chapter 6 and 8).

Formal and Informal Decision-making Structures

In carrying out a targeted sanctions policy, there is a basic need for effective institutional co-ordination. While acknowledged in several policy studies, the complexity of sanctions co-ordination, as well as decision-making by senders, is seldom accounted for in sanctions assessment studies. During the Stockholm

Process on targeted UN sanctions, however, it was recognised that in order to make targeted sanctions effective, the policy had to be implemented through a chain of actions involving all levels of decision-making. As such, institutional bodies like the UN Security Council, its sanctions committees, the member states and their administrative agencies, international governmental organisations, the private sector, non-governmental organisations and so on needed to be co-ordinated more effectively.[1]

In the face of the various challenges at different stages of sanctions policy implementation, planning and management is considered a particularity important dimension in the process.[2] As was also pointed out by the Stockholm Process, decision-making needs to be pursued as logically and coherently as possible so that it can be translated into implementation.[3] In the case of the UN, this required the organisation to upgrade and rationalise its practices.[4] For example, it was noted that sanctions implementation did not have an institutional equivalent to the UN Department of Peacekeeping Operations (DPKO). Rather than being an effective process, it was pointed out, for instance, that a UN sanctions committee must act under numerous political, administrative and time constraints, which are sometimes exacerbated by poorly specified or incomplete UNSC mandates. Most often, the core tasks of sanctions monitoring – soliciting and receiving reports of sanctions measures undertaken by member states, and reviewing the work of the independent panels of experts – have taken priority over those of broader co-ordination and information dissemination.[5] This is clearly a problem. While improvements have been made, the UN still has far to go before it can ensure sanctions' effectiveness. Here is an excerpt from the sanctions manual illustrating this problem:[6]

> An integrated strategy requires more effective coordination both among the key sanctions bodies and between them and other relevant UN agencies and departments. Despite some notable exceptions … coordination among the Sanctions Committees remains sporadic. Coordination between Sanctions Committees, the Secretariat and other relevant UN agencies is likewise ad hoc. Among the Sanctions Committees and Expert Panels, this lack of systematic coordination can lead to unnecessary duplication of work, whereby Experts monitoring different sanctions regimes sometimes inadvertently pursue similar leads, make use of the same sources and make uncoordinated approaches to the same technical or regional organizations. While Sanctions Committees have undertaken periodic consultations with humanitarian agencies, the full potential

1 Wallensteen et al. (2003): iv.
2 *Ibid.*: vii.
3 *Ibid.*: 7.
4 *Ibid.*: 14.
5 *Ibid.*: 15.
6 *Ibid.*: 15–16.

> of other UN agencies and departments to assist in sanctions implementation and the implications of sanctions implementation for their own work has not been fully explored. Likewise sporadic are Sanctions Committee efforts to engage Member States, both directly, through briefings and consultations, and indirectly, through dissemination of information to the broader public and the mass media, in support of UN sanctions implementation.

As can be seen in this excerpt, effective sanctions require a great deal of intra-organisational co-ordination. What is left out, however, is that these institutional units, of which there are many, each have their own bureaucratic culture and procedures that do not always work in tandem. It is likely that differences in officials' understandings of what targeted sanctions entail also compounds these institutional challenges. As noted by Allison and Halperin when studying foreign policy actions, a government official is an individual in a unique position. His or her perceptions and preferences stem both from individual characteristics and from his institutional environment.[7] This needs to be considered when analysing the efficacy of a sender's policy. While the UN has sought to improve its institutional routines in this context, there are also additional challenges confronting the UN's sanctions capacity. For example, in a working group meeting held in March 2009, one of UN's member states' permanent officers observed that an 'astonishing lack of understanding' seemed to exist among member states regarding sanctions. Meanwhile, other participants at the meeting noted that the problems of co-ordination lay at different levels: at UN headquarters and in the field, among member states, within international agencies, among UN staff, and so on.[8] While it was also recognised that the UN Secretariat in recent years had taken steps to enhance co-ordination, there was a need for more focused and standardised procedures and greater institutional support mechanisms. For instance, participants mentioned the importance of greater co-operation among Secretariat departments on sanctions issues, and that co-ordination with international functional organisations needed to be expanded and standardised.[9] Obviously, these observations only highlight problems at the UN level, but there are similar problems at other levels of the sanctions implementation chain.

Similarly, the EU and its main institutions seems to be confronted with the same kinds of organisational challenges, as its sanctions framework features little or no co-ordination, assessment tools and follow-up capacities, and little shared understanding of what targeting entails among various branches of the EU Council, the Commission, Parliament, and so on.

Yet, having noted these challenges, there are still good reasons to support the claim that the policy of targeted sanctions nevertheless works, and that the

---

7 Allison and Halperin (1972): 48.

8 Statement made during the informal Working Meeting on United Nations Sanctions Coordination Mechanisms held in New York, 20 March 2009.

9 *Ibid.*

discrepancies between the various links in the sanctions policy chain are ultimately not that large. After all, targeted sanctions continue to be practised.

None the less, how can we prove that greater effectiveness through co-ordination and understanding will enable targeted sanctions senders to achieve greater impact? As seen in the policy debate, experts and practitioners acknowledge that: (1) there is an efficacy problem (as has been the case in the various international processes); (2) a lack of knowledge about how sanctions are meant to work means that practice is piecemeal (which empirical records suggest is true for both the EU and the UN); (3) established goals are not being, and cannot easily be, achieved (which is clearly demonstrated by the outcome of several sanctions regimes); (4) sanctions policies are mostly applied in a static way (which does not reflect the policy dynamic on the ground), and (5) there are increasing signs of side-effects, which suggests that the policy is not working as intended (as implied by the judicial listing/de-listing debate). All of this supports the argument that there is some degree of institutional awareness, and that steps are being taken to address these problems.

In this context, it is particularly useful to further distinguish two auxiliary categorisations that enable and constrain sanctions policies at the sender level: (1) formal, material factors, and (2) informal, intangible factors. The first category of formal factors implies that the policy is shaped by institutional resources and capacities, such as guideline documents, institutional budgets, competencies, staffing, arrangements for meetings, and decision-making structures. Factors like these set preconditions that determine how extensive a sanctions regime can be. Formal and material factors also influence the amount of resources at the disposal of senders to investigate sanctions evasion, and so on. Clearly, such boundaries effect the kind of impact that can be expected.[10]

On the other hand, the informal factors that shape the outcome include political will, norms, traditions, and the perceptions, preferences and biases of those units (and officials) engaged in targeting.[11] These aspects contribute to shaping the institutional culture of the sanctions regime that is being set up. For example, the UNITA targeted sanctions regime set up by the UN Security Council was greatly influenced by the work of Ambassador Fowler, who ensured that the targets were affected as much as possible by the sanctions imposed. In fact, this personal engagement was unprecedented in the history of targeted sanctions, and owes a great deal to Fowler's own conviction and perception of how sanctions should be designed. His activities influenced other team members' perceptions of how sanctions' impact could be interpreted within this informal framework.[12]

10 Academic work has been carried out on aspects of EU and UN formal decision-making. On the EU, see, for example, Hazelzet (2001) and Portela (2008), and on the UN, see Farrall (2007).

11 See Ameri (1996) and Galtung (1986).

12 See Möllander (2009).

However, the various bureaucratic units that deal administratively with sanctions policy further shape both formal and informal factors.[13] These administrative units are synonymous with the bureaucracies that adopt, enforce and manage sanctions on a daily basis, such as the UN Security Council, the UN Sanctions Committee, the UN Panel of Experts, the EU RELEX formation, the EU Council and its working groups (geographical and thematic), the EU Sanctions Policy Unit, banking groups (those implementing the financial sanctions), customs enforcement officials, immigration officials (those implementing travel bans) and any other private or public units engaged in the effort. In fact, one could argue that each of these units has its own very distinct understanding of what targeting means and how it should be enforced. Moreover, each unit is likely to shape the design of the overall sanctions. Often, the different bureaucratic and political units are likely to request the inclusion of particular aspects in the policy design which may contradict the perceptions and understandings of other units. For instance, the EU's Political Committee may want to see target compliance at any cost, while the Legal Department may require the inclusion of certain human rights clauses in the policy design. The Budget Department may also be concerned with keeping costs down by inserting financial ceilings and restricting budgets.

Moreover, each of these units through which the sanctions policy has to be processed is likely to shape the design of the policy according to its own specific needs, traditions (institutional cultures) and understandings of sanctions and their management. As a result of this process, the final policy may be very different from the originally formulation. However, the culture of each unit is not the only influential factor. If the analytical focus is shifted from the unit to individual desk officers (officials of the senders), their perceived understanding of targeted sanctions may also explain the formation and management of the sanctions policy.

As will be further demonstrated, each institutional unit, or each bureaucratic subject that makes up these institutional units, is likely to perceive itself as a policy performer, while thinking less of actual overall ownership of the policy (that it not to say that bureaucracies feel ownership of specific aspects of a more general policy). Most likely, a desk officer set to perform a particular policy task will seek to ensure that the policy is credible and achieve maximum impact, but ownership and responsibility for the entire rationale of the policy is likely to be perceived as lying somewhere else. One challenge to overcome, then, is how to reconcile the many different perceptions of the sanctions policies that are likely to exist in separate units throughout the sender's administration. These different understandings are likely to shape the policy of targeting in unpredictable ways, and the policy rationale is likely to be interpreted differently to what was perhaps originally intended by its initiators. The diversity of actors and special interests is therefore likely to have a significant effect upon the kind of policy that is ultimately pursued against the listed entities. In fact, one could make the case that disparities in sanctions policy are bound to arise given the plurality of perceptions held in

13 One could also conceptualise these as narratives, norms, cultures, and so on.

these various institutional units (or at least it will complicate the establishment, adoption, implementation and management of targeted sanctions). While bureaucratic processes like these are obviously likely to be complex, like any other policy process, this has not been investigated in the literature. This is surprising, since it does seem to have a profound effect upon sanctions outcomes.[14]

For this reason, Chapter 6 will examine the UN's formal and informal sanctions decision-making framework. While Chapter 8 will examine the EU's formal and informal sanctions decision-making framework. The aim is to demonstrate how such factors enable and constrain sanctions policies, and how they explain sanctions outcomes. Decision-making and the perception of the utility of targeted sanctions has so far been an under-studied area.

14 A RAND study notes: 'Every U.S. foreign policy agency has both a regional desk and a functional desk. The functional desk worries about such global matters as international security and becomes agitated about the slippery-slope consequences of allowing exceptions to international rules. The regional desk worries about relations with individual governments and rests about the consequences of allowing one issue to interfere with the resolution of other issues with that government. Almost every sanctions case brings to the fore this clash of objectives between functional and regional desks'; Speier et al. (2001): 4.

Chapter 6
UN Sanctions Decision-making

This chapter will examine the UN's sanctions management capacity. As explained in the previous chapter, any sanctions assessment method needs to take into account the institutional dynamic of the sanctions sending body in order to understand the policy's impact. To do so, we will first address the formal UN decision-making structure and how it shapes policy outcomes. Then we will examine the informal processes by which sanctions are shaped, by examining how UN desk officers themselves understand sanctions policies.

Formal Management

The UNSC has primary responsibility for ensuring that necessary action is taken to counter any threats to peace, breaches of the peace, or acts of aggression in the international system.[1] This means that in order to prevent an international crisis, the UNSC may impose sanctions under Chapter 7 (Article 41) of the UN Charter. Measures in this regard include the complete or partial interruption of economic relations and of rail, sea, air postal, telegraphic, radio and other means of communication, and the severance of diplomatic relations.[2] While historically sanctions have been conceived as an instrument *vis-à-vis* state actors, UN targeted sanctions have nowadays also become an accepted policy against individuals, groups, companies and specific commodities.[3]

Formally, UN targeted sanctions can be invoked in many different ways. Legally, however, the UNSC determines the existence of a threat to peace, a breach of the peace, or an act of aggression according to Article 39 of the UN Charter. Once the decision is made, it can invoke Article 41 for further legal justification.[4]

Commonly, the Secretary-General, or any of his designated subordinates, introduces a new item on the agenda of the UNSC. Frequently, the idea to use sanctions measures comes after informal negotiations over a draft UN resolution text brought to the UNSC either by the presidency or by any other UNSC member.

---

1 United Nations Charter, Chapter 7.

2 *Ibid.*

3 For an overview of these measures, see Doxey (1987): 10–12, Hufbauer and Oegg (2000) and Farrall (2007): 106–28.

4 *Ibid.*: 64–8.

In many cases, such drafts stem from a complex political and negotiation process involving the specific member state or states in the region of concern.[5]

From a formal and bureaucratic point of view, the UN sanctions committee operates the UN's sanctions programmes. It is now standard procedure to set up such a subsidiary committee for each sanctions regime. The composition of the sanctions committee mirrors that of the UNSC. Formally, the mandate of the committee is laid out in the founding UN Security Council Resolution setting up such a sanctions regime. The UNSCR also provides the committee with working guidelines. In this sense, all committees are unique. The committee is led by a chairperson and works behind closed doors, where decisions are made by consensus.[6] In those circumstances where committee members are in disagreement, the chairperson undertakes necessary consultations (sometimes reflected in committee reports that are issued now and then).

Decisive to the daily work of the committee is the Subsidiary Sanctions Branch at the UN Department of Political Affairs. The Sanctions Branch is important for several reasons. Being a form of 'service body', it supports the daily committee work on different tasks, for example by advising the sanctions committee chair and its members on practices and procedures; implementing committee decisions; managing and guiding expert groups mandated to monitor sanctions regimes; conducting sanctions-related analyses; screening reports coming in and out of the committee; disseminating information among committee members, as well as when needed through the wider UN system and to relevant field missions. Overall, the Sanctions Branch also provides the committee with a general institutional memory.

An important task for the Sanctions Branch is the administration of sanctions lists, especially regarding listing and de-listing matters (through the institutional structures set up to deal with procedural aspects relating to such issues).[7] While all sanctions committees are comprised of an equal number of states, formally the committees have enjoyed different degrees of activity and political support, which have affected sanctions implementation performance. For instance, UN Sanctions

---

5 As noted by Greenstock: 'On occasion this can happen in a formal meeting of the Council in the main chamber, but more frequently the first discussion of a new problem takes place in informal consultations in the side-room reserved for the Council. Here, the exchanges are restricted to Council members and relevant members of the Secretariat. The choice of topics is normally made in a common sense way and the discussion proceeds in an informed and sensible manner. It sometimes takes a day or two for all Council members to catch up with events and receive instructions from their Capitals .... The usefulness of informal consultations away from the public gaze is evident when sensitive information has to be included in briefing or when action to restrain a particular UN member states may be more effective without public fanfare'; Greenstock (2008): 252.

6 Farrall (2007): 156.

7 Procedures have been established in UNSCR 1730 (2006).

Committee 1267 (the al-Qaeda/Taliban sanctions programme) has received a lot of political attention.[8]

One of the core tasks of the committee is therefore to monitor compliance with targeted sanctions, whereas the UNSC assesses political developments within the framework of the objectives of the sanctions programmes.[9] To do so, the committee establishes monitoring teams and panels of experts.[10] Between 1995 and 2009 there were eight panels of experts associated with the sanctions committees.[11] Based on the provisions stipulated in the UN resolution, the UN Secretariat submits candidates for the approval of the committee, while the Secretary-General makes necessary appointments to these panels.[12]

Once in place, the panel of experts conducts investigations into all aspects of compliance and implementation (for example, by conducting interviews with key actors in the country of the target and in the region). The panel of experts then provides the committee with periodic reports. Over the years, these reports have become instrumental in documenting member state implementation of targeted sanctions.[13] Usually, these reports include elements of naming and shaming (for example, reporting on states, companies, organisations and individuals that do not ensure that sanctions are being enforced) of individual targets (such as evasions and circumvention). In pursuit of this, the UNSC can request impact reports on matters such as the economic, humanitarian or social impact of sanctions. In these cases, the UN Secretary-General would then make these assessments.[14] To date, such additional assessments have been few in number.

The committee is also responsible for identifying individuals and other entities it considers responsible for a crisis or conflict. Usually, names are provided by member states, but sometimes also upon the recommendations of the panel of experts or the UN special representative (if one exists). Names are placed on

---

8 Cortright et al. (2007).

9 In recent years, a number of studies and reports have looked at the institutional practices of some of these sanctions committees, especially the 1267 and 1373 Sanctions Committees. See, for instance, Angell (2004), Chesterman (2008), Flynn (2007), Foot (2007), Franck et al. (2007), Rosand (2004), Rosand et al. (2007), Lopez et al. (2006), Van Walsum (2004) and Ward (2005).

10 The first panel established was in conjunction with the arms embargo against Rwandan Hutu rebels; Cortright et al. (2008): 220.

11 Boucher and Holt (2009): 9.

12 For details of the UN panel of experts system, see *ibid.*, the Stimson Center report on UN panels of experts. This is the most comprehensive study on panels of experts to date.

13 Farrall (2007), appendix 3, collected all reports from sanctions-related expert and monitoring bodies to date.

14 At a seminar on the effectiveness of targeted sanctions, the former UN Secretary-General Kofi Annan said, 'Sanctions are not something that you can "fire and forget,"' thus indirectly calling for sanctions assessments; UN Press Release SG/SM/7360, 17 April 2000.

sanctions lists, which are then published on the committee website and distributed to all UN member states. The committee then subjects these lists to approval, a procedure that also applies when targets are being de-listed. The committee also grants targets and affected member states exemptions and waivers to ensure that practices and procedures are in line with UNSCR guidelines. Since its adoption, this process of listing has been controversial, especially regarding target accuracy, reliability and the human rights of the individual entities listed.[15]

Besides panels of experts, the committees is kept appraised of developments on the ground through UN missions. While the panels of experts do most of the work of providing the committee with information, direct contact and information collection on the ground can take place if the chair of the committee visits the country to obtain precise information from the field through access to the latest information from UN officers monitoring the local political dynamics. Sometimes members of the Sanctions Branch will also visit, together with the chair the UN missions in the target country, to discuss issues related to implementation. In practice, the committee chairs visit the target states to confer regarding difficulties related to implementation, while the UNSC sometimes undertakes missions to areas of conflict to discuss political issues more related to the various concerned parties.

However, the political aspects are usually of direct concern to the UNSC (it is occasionally also informally brought up to date on issues relevant to sanctions by other members of the Secretariat, such as the Department of Political Affairs, the Department of Peacekeeping Operations and the Office for the Co-ordination of Humanitarian Affairs). The head of the mission or the Special Representative of the Secretary-General (SRSG) reports to the committee when invited. Every now and then, the SRSG also investigates sanctions tactics on the ground officially, but this can also be carried out informally by interacting with listed targets, for instance by threatening more extensive listing or by offering de-listing if behaviour changes.[16] However, such a tactic is expected to conform with the Security Council Resolution.

There currently exist two factors in UN decision-making procedures which seem particularly important for sanctions impact. First, political will and institutional resources seem necessary to ensure the effective administration of sanctions-related practice. These aspects are likely to affect the work of the sanctions committee as well as the related branches dealing with sanctions matters. Nowadays it seems as if different committees have received different levels of institutional support as a result of varying political concerns among more influential member states. For example, institutional support (staffing, salaries, technical infrastructure, information, missions, and so on) has gone to those committees that are considered politically more important than others, as was the case with the Liberia Committee

15 Cortright et al. (2008): 223.

16 See interviews by the author with Ambassador Jan Eliasson (Eriksson, 2008) and Ambassador Pierre Schori (Eriksson, 2007a).

as opposed to the Sudan Committee (obviously, this is intimately bound up with interests of the five Permanent Members of the UNSC, P5). The Counterterrorism Committee (1373) and the committee dealing with al-Qaeda and the Taliban (1267) generally take political priority. Obviously, the political focus varies from time to time depending on the political interest of the P5 countries.

Moreover, particular skills and engagement by individuals in key positions in the sanctions administration, such as the chair of the sanctions committee, the head of the panel of experts team, officials of the Subsidiary Sanctions Branch, the SRSG, and the heads of monitoring groups, seem very important for sanctions implementation.[17] The reason is that they can take personal responsibility to initiate, plan and request, organise and assess the effectiveness of sanctions programmes.[18] Unless such actors have personal commitment, little sense of expediency, dynamics and ownership is likely to develop, which in the end has an overall impact on the credibility of the sanctions.[19] The perception of UN desk officers will be discussed in the next section.

Informal Management

Perceptions regarding UN targeted sanctions are likely to provide further insights into how the sanctions process shapes their impact. Individuals are responsible for actively practising and shaping the targeted sanctions policy, thereby determining how it is implemented its effectiveness. Each UN official has his or her own understanding, which feeds into a broader narrative of what targeted sanctions are meant to be like. In the end, knowledge of sanctions administration remains at the personal level.[20] It is therefore important to include such personal understanding in any sanctions assessment. Thus, one important issue that must be dealt with here is how relevant some UN officials working with sanctions perceive and understand this policy to be, and how their subjective views feed into the overall targeted sanctions policy. This chapter will report on a number interviews with UN desk officers.[21]

---

17 For example, in the UN sanctions discourse, several individuals have been seen as having made exemplary contributions in developing an efficient sanctions practice, such as Ambassador Fowler of Canada when he was chairman of the UNITA sanctions regime; see Möllander (2009).

18 To this one should add that professional capacity is essential. This has also been noted as a crucial point for sanctions implementation efficacy; Boucher and Holt (2009): 108.

19 For example, during the first eight years of the arms embargo on Sudan, the Sudan Sanctions Committee held only 15 formal meetings; Security Council (2008): 2.

20 Chesterman and Pouligny (2003): 514.

21 Those interviewed for this study represent only an illustrative sample among a broader number of officials and agencies working with targeted sanctions at the UN. In total, in-depth interviews were conducted with seven key officials. Interviewees were carefully

Policy Perceptions

The daily management and design of targeted sanctions – which is formally decided by the UNSC – goes hand in hand with the work of the subsidiary organs and the sanctions committees. Therefore, those engaged in this daily work play an important role in shaping the policy of targeted sanctions through their knowledge and commitments. Thus, one could anticipate that the way in which the policy is perceived may also contribute to the way it is implemented. What, then, did the interviewees refer to when asked to explain the policy of targeted sanctions?

During an interview session, a group of UN officials working on UN sanctions management, mentioned that while sanctions policy usually uses military vocabulary (for instance, words such as 'sharpness' and 'force'), the policy of targeting is perceived to be much more subtle than this. The position held by respondents was that targeting was perceived as contextually bound and had diverse meanings for different sanctions regimes. For example, the committees had dealt with diverse sets of target categories, some of which were seen as more difficult to handle than others. Some of the targets seemed extraordinarily committed to negative behaviour. Therefore, behavioural change was difficult to achieve. This was the case for those regimes or persons engaged in terrorism.

The interviews also brought to light recurring ideas regarding the strategic utility of the policy, describing it as an instrument used to avoid the cost of war. Sanctions were hence seen as an instrument that could also be used to 'mitigate the humanitarian impact'. For instance, this could be done by hitting the target where it hurt the most. However, the policy was not confined to specific kinds of explicit strategies per se. On the contrary, it was considered an effective tool on many other levels, as long as it was properly enforced. For instance, one respondent saw sanctions policy as a means to foster capacity-building in a more general sense, rather than as a strategic instrument by itself. In this sense, targeted sanctions could also be understood as a governance tool.

In addition, interviewees held that the implementation of targeted sanctions was not a problem-free process. Part of this had to do with the limitations of implementing current sanctions due to the lack of planning and engagement at the UN administrative level. This included a lack of political will, a lack of the expertise required to analyse sanctions implementation policies by the committees, and a disconnect between the recommendations of expert groups and committee follow-up. Another institutional shortcoming that was mentioned was the lack of institutional co-ordination among the committees (for example, regarding lessons

---

selected according to their degree of competence in political and institutional use of targeted sanctions. In addition, although not directly cited in this chapter, a number of UN officials working in specific contexts where sanctions have been applied were interviewed (such as UN sanctions committee chairs, heads of UN sanctions monitoring teams, UNSG special representatives and UN panel of experts members). All interviewees were guaranteed anonymity. A more detailed reference list can be located in earlier versions of this study.

learned) and between sanctions committees and country offices (although this interaction is on a more informal basis).

The Presence of a Sanctions Strategy

In several political settings where the UNSC is enforcing targeted sanctions, supplementary UN political measures are attached. Usually, some of these measures include peacekeeping missions, mediation efforts, and so on. One pertinent issue to address is whether these additional activities work as part of an intertwined strategic policy by the sender, or whether they work as stand-alone mechanisms. More specifically, do UN officials perceive sanctions as part of a larger political strategy when dealing with a particular crisis, or do they impose targeted sanctions separately?

Following a number of interviews, one respondent expressed the need to develop a broader approach to targeted sanctions. Another respondent said it was important to understand targeted sanctions as part of a larger toolbox: for example, as a complement to the Peace-Building Commission, as in the case of Liberia. Yet no answers were forthcoming as to how this could be done.

Regarding the importance of a larger strategy, one respondent also stated that targeted sanctions must be tailor-made in order for them to be context-sensitive. As explained, different conflict phases lead to different expectations, and one type of strategy will not work in every case. It was also too idealistic to think that everything could be accomplished through targeted sanctions, since the design of the sanctions was often adopted by a disunited UNSC. In a similar way, interviewees explained that it was important to abandon the belief that sanctions are the sole problem-solver: 'Sanctions, on their own, have little chance to be effective. It requires other tools as well, monitoring peacekeeping, carrot and sticks, and so on.'

Regarding possible ways to act more effectively, it was suggested that those UN bodies responsible for implementing sanctions should make more use of the information that had been collected over the years (for example, from different panels of experts). This had not yet been done.[22] The absence of lessons learned prevents future sanctions from being effective. In addition, there were also a number of institutional issues and practices that prevented the implementation of more effective sanctions regimes. For example, there was a lack of meetings between officials working with different sanctions committees (such as chairs), an unwarranted lack of transparency, over-sensitivity regarding the interests of members of the UNSC, as well as very little information-sharing. However, these factors were seen as part of a common culture. This lack of transparency has also been noted elsewhere.[23]

22 Actions are currently being taken at the UN to address this problem.

23 Farrall makes the following observation in his study of rule-of-law weaknesses regarding sanctions: 'Of the five principles of the rule of law analysed here, transparency is

Several respondents held a positive view regarding the need to analyse and use sanctions as part of a broader strategic framework. Respondents believed that using sanctions within the wider scope of political dynamics would lead to better results. While the UNSC imposes sanctions, the UN Secretariat helps implement them (which take place at different levels, including member state level). Although these two roles are separate but complementary, this does not prevent the Secretariat from designing a day-to-day 'tactic' under the specific UN Resolution framework. Yet, as noted, making targeted sanctions too much of a strategic instrument could risk pushing them out of the hands of the UN, and into the hands of particular member states at the UNSC.

Finally, comments were also made regarding the administrative performance of the UN, regarding the lack of information-sharing and political analysis. A better co-ordination capacity and information-sharing in order to develop a coherent sanctions policy with regard to implementation seemed preferred. Such improvement could also be used to better develop the strategic character of the sanctions policy.

Symbolic versus Direct Impact

The majority of the respondents understood that the policy of targeted sanctions must have both a symbolic and practical impact. Regarding the symbolic impact, some officials felt that a listed entity could experience a sense of being 'hunted', thereby feeling stigmatised. As explained, this could work by allowing the news media access to a specific UN sanctions list, thus increasing global attention and pressure upon the listed entity. It was perceived that this might also have a psychological effect on the target, as none of the listed individuals wanted to be targeted. Being listed can create an unpleasant sense of humiliation or a kind of 'pariah status'. Hence, listing functions well when it comes to 'naming and shaming' listed entities.

In addition to this symbolic perception, there was also the view that targeting could have a direct impact by restricting the target's room for manoeuvre. One official even suggested that this could be seen in the vocabulary used in Security Council Resolutions by the use of words like 'impede' and 'impel' in connection with targeting. For example, one respondent believed that certain commodity sanctions had directly contributed to mounting pressure against certain key parties, as it had moved them in a certain direction in the political reform process. In this context, it was believed that had the sanctions not been in place, the pressure would not have arisen.

One official explained that different restrictive measures could have different degrees of impact, and that it was the UNSC's role to ensure that these measures achieved their aim. It was also believed that the UN should seek to achieve as much impact as possible. However, this was not always easy to accomplish. According

---

arguably the one that is the least observed yet the easiest to remedy'; Farrall (2007): 230.

to one of the interviewees, not achieving the targeted impact represented a kind of failure for the UN, arguing that it was better to seek to have more of a direct impact than no impact at all. Having more of a direct impact would make the UN more credible in this respect.

While the impact of targeted sanctions is shaped by different factors at different levels among member states, much the impact of sanctions is still connected to political will and to administrative and institutional deficiencies. Not only is there a need for institutional support to develop credible sanctions, there is also a need for support from higher levels of the UN management. Senior management and those engaged in the decision-making and implementation processes need to be prepared to walk the extra mile.

One respondent suggested that sanctions had to be credible in order to achieve a direct and symbolic impact. If the threat of sanctions is used for too long without being implemented, the threat loses its credibility. Sanctions are also a policy to instigate 'movement' and to create an opportunity for things to happen. However, the opportunity for movement is time-bound, and the effectiveness of sanctions diminishes over time. Timing and credibility are therefore particularly important factors.

The Use of Assessment Tools

Part of administrating targeted sanctions involves ensuring that events on ground are responded to. One way of ensuring this is to have assessment capabilities available. If regular assessment is not pursued, there are good reasons to conclude that the symbolic application of sanctions plays a more important role than direct impact. Direct impact, in the sense of actually affecting targets (for example, by freezing targets' assets or preventing them from crossing boarders) requires a keen interest in sanctions efficacy. In general, the lack of assessments negatively affects the impact of both symbolic and direct sanctions.

Thus, the UN officials who were interviewed were asked whether they themselves engaged in evaluation and assessment of targeting. The responses signalled that the UN did not initiate such efforts. The onus fell mostly outside, on member states, and every now and then on academic institutions. However, as noted, there were mostly expert groups connected to the sanctions programmes that provided the committees and the Sanctions Branch with assessment reports on compliance and implementation. While the Sanctions Branch, for instance, did not invest as much time in assessing sanctions, it was noted that the UN Sanctions Branch was currently in the process of improving its capacity (for example, by establishing sanctions best practices, guidelines and procedures).

While it was argued that sanction assessments are important for any regime to be effective, there was little confirmation that serious reviews concerning the implementation and the results of sanctions were ever conducted. When asked whether there were assessment mechanisms in place, references were mostly made to panels of experts, UN special representatives, and so on.[24] It was also noted that sanctions assessment could become an obstacle for further UNSC involvement, since politically sensitive evidence in such assessment reports, such as failure to implement sanctions or adhere to legal principles, could restrain the committee members' future use of sanctions. While it was recognised that the committee did not conduct official assessments as it was not considered to be the role of the Secretariat (that is, it was not in their current mandate), there was also scepticism about the UN taking on such a task, as other actors were probably better equipped to do so.

In the end, some officials said that inaccuracies in the sanctions lists or the frequency of sanctions evasions (both aspects forming part of effective sanctions implementation), were not really a problem of the UN, but a problem for member state commitments. In fact, even deliberate imperfections could still affect sanctions implementation, as the nature of the list was to prevent other *potential* entities from challenging the UN. Respondents also believed that UN officials monitoring the implementation of sanctions lacked formal decision-making power. They had only advisory power, so it was usually up to UNSC members to keep sanctions up to date.

To conclude, it became clear that no formal assessments were conducted on a regular basis, either by the sanctions committees or by any other UN body. On the other hand, several interviewees believed that assessments were carried out indirectly by other actors, such as the panels of experts. Sometimes, references that were made to independent academic institutions outside the UN system suggest that they were engaged in such work. While several respondents believed that current forms of assessment were effective, a number of respondents also gave explicit examples of how they could be improved and that assessments should be seen as a shared responsibility by those who imposed them: the UNSC, the sanctions committee and the Secretariat. However, at least one respondent said that it was not only up to the UN to judge its own work, but that member states and independent institutions should also be involved.

One of the more imaginative comments in the interviews with regard to the use of an assessment was that the imperfections of the sanctions lists could in themselves actually function as a strategy (referring to a sanction list not being up-to-date). For instance, the Sierra Leone sanctions list, which was not updated for a number of years despite the fact that the conflict in that country had been resolved, was still in place. This was despite the fact that a number of those placed on the list had been killed or brought before the Special Court for Sierra Leone. The idea was that such a list would, by its mere presence, discourage actors from engaging in activities that could lead the UN to place them on the sanctions list.

24 However, it is worth noting here that these are assessments that are not built on a more scientific standard, nor encompassing other policies operating in conjunction with sanctions.

Another observation was that UN officials often have to be very sensitive to particular UN member states, so that decisions were not taken that would undermine their interests, which ultimately led influential powers to reduce their will to support and co-operate with those branches of the UN that were administrating sanctions on a day-to-day basis.

Targets and Behavioural Change

Few of the UN respondents believed that targeted sanctions had a direct and 'personal' effect on the behaviour of listed entities (as opposed to a symbolic impact or a group impact).[25] Still, there was a consensus that this could not be ruled out as a future strategy. One respondent even asserted that behavioural change takes place every now and then. However, it was unclear whether this person was referring to individuals or a group of targets.

Several respondents tried to explain that the possibility of a behavioural change not occurring had more to do with the limitations of implementation than anything else. Limited access to information about targets might be an example of this. Thus, the UN Secretariat did what it could with the information and instruments at its disposal. In many cases, the limitations on being effective were obvious. For example, respondents claimed that 'Though we impose a travel ban, a target can easily travel on false passports.' This, however, is closely linked to the political will of the states that implement sanctions.

Another reason that was put forward for the ineffectiveness of achieving behavioural change or directly constraining specific targets was simply that the targets themselves did not always know that they were designated as targets. Thus, if change is to take place, it is important that the targets know that they are on the sanctions lists.

Finally, an explanation was presented regarding the need to differentiate between the various sanctions measures. For example, it was held that an arms embargo is mostly used to change matters on the ground and limit and restrict a war, while targeted individual sanctions can help to draw specific individuals to the negotiating table. Thus, different measures are more or less likely to achieve behavioural change, as they operate differently and have different impacts. Such views should be contrasted with the common understanding that views targeted sanctions as a uniform policy instrument.

Comments during the interviews made little reference to the behavioural change of particular targets. However, few interviewees discarded the idea of using sanctions to change behaviour when asked to comment about this objective. Some respondents found it important to recognise that there is no general way to change the behaviour of a target, but that different sanctions measures (such as travel bans, assets freezes or commodity sanctions) address different aspects of the

25 Compare such a claim with the findings of Cosgrove (2005) and Wallensteen et al. (2006).

overall sanctions policy, and therefore different levels of impact must be expected, not only behavioural change.

Overview

The interviews showed that there existed different perceptions among the sanctions practitioners interviewed regarding the purpose and effectiveness of targeted sanctions. The diversity of comments discussed here should also be kept in mind, as there are potentially different understandings of sanctions among practitioners working at other levels of the sanctions implementation chain that are not analysed here (such as those working in other organisations outside the UN, those working in the banking industry, at customs checkpoints or at member state ministries). The nuances of sanctions are hence far more complex than has been displayed here.

Various comments could be considered subtle when it came to addressing the issues of what targeted sanctions can actually achieve. For some respondents, targeting was understood as a strategic policy to deal with a particular crisis, while for others, sanctions constituted something more than the restrictive measures, and were part of a broader strategy to deal with a particular crisis. Some respondents believed that targeted sanctions are very much dependent upon institutional capacities and effectiveness (that is, the administration of the policy).[26]

The interviews showed little evidence of the existence of a well-defined sanctions strategy, at least an explicit one that could be found in administrative environments such as the peacekeeping missions. Several respondents were open to such an approach. Some were also willing to analyse sanctions in a broader strategic sense. However, some observed that there were reasons to be cautious. First, connecting targeted UN sanctions to broader strategic tactics risked pushing sanctions out of the hands of those administrative units dealing with sanctions and into the hands of certain influential UN member states. Sanctions would then risk becoming an element of national policy rather than international policy. This suggests that targeting remains politically sensitive. Second, it seems as if there are currently too many institutional obstacles to such a strategic management of sanctions. For example, there are too many actors involved, too few mechanisms to share information, too little co-ordination, too much bureaucracy, too little sense of ownership, too little strategic thinking, too many quick and flexible response mechanisms to events on ground, and too much sensitivity towards more influential governments.

There were also repeated references to the threat of sanctions, suggesting that sanctions are mostly effective just before or immediately after they are imposed. The effects of targeted sanctions become more limited over time.

It also became clear that no formal assessments of sanctions have been carried out. Instead, this was reflected in other mechanisms operating in the sanctions

26 This has also been noted, although not fully explored, in an institutional analysis of the role of the UN Sanctions Branch; see Boucher and Holt (2009): 46–7.

programme (monitoring groups, panels, private academic and public evaluations, and so on).[27] Some respondents felt that more continuous and systematic assessments were needed to improve sanctions, but that formal and informal procedures did not permit this. At least one respondent believed that in-house assessments could be counter-productive, too subjective and too sensitive *vis-à-vis* more influential states. Critical in-house assessments could push sanctions practices into the hands of some UN member states, as governments may not be willing to support critical reports that are contrary to their interests.

Regarding the symbolic versus direct impact of targeted sanctions, the perception among the majority of UN practitioners was that the current policy fulfilled both roles. This seems to reflect a perception regarding both the rationale of targeted sanctions and actual practices. Nevertheless, there were different justifications for why it appeared one way or the other. Some believed that the conceptualisation of symbolic versus direct impact was not a focus for the practitioners (who concentrated instead on enforcing sanctions); others felt that the symbolic aspect had a sort of deliberate effect, while others pointed to institutional limitations.

Interestingly, this plurality of perceptions regarding symbolic and direct impact does not reflect an official policy per se, but is more of a perceived actuality. This obviously does not contradict the existence of a united official approach and policy from the UN, but reflects the fact that individual officials matter, and should not be mistreated or overlooked in sanctions assessment studies. The relevant issue, however, is whether these perceptions affect the daily management of sanctions. One answer was particularly interesting in this regard, suggesting that the type of effect that could potentially be inflicted upon the target was not something that was considered at the outset. On the contrary, when sanctions were adopted and implemented, the concern was to ensure that the policy was being implemented and would have some kind of impact. Hence, from this point of view, different measures must have different effects.

Based on the interviews, there was also an understanding that a symbolic impact was a result of ineffective policy management. Sometimes such troubles were caused by limited institutional capacities, co-ordination problems, lack of administration or personal commitments, and so on. Another explanation could simply be that the managers of sanctions did not share a common understanding of the potential of sanctions as an instrument, and they therefore acted differently. In the end, these are fairly subtle and fine-grained nuances when it comes to perception. Nevertheless, when taken together, they should not be underestimated, at least not from an academic point of view.

Finally, there was an understanding that the logic of targeting is very much related to timing, and to the credibility of the targeted sanctions threat. While most effective at the beginning, sanctions have less effect the longer a programme continues.

---

27 Several assessments to date have mostly covered comprehensive sanctions, or only been concerned with specific restrictive measures.

Conclusion

This chapter has offered illustrations of some complexities underlying the formation of targeted sanctions from an institutional perspective. Unlike sanctions assessment studies that take the decision-making process for granted – as a well-co-ordinated, rational and harmonised policy process – this chapter has examined how formal and informal decision-making procedures during the process of adopting, administrating and implementing targeted sanctions shape sanctions outcomes.

While the literature on targeted sanctions acknowledges the incompleteness of sanctions implementation, little effort has been made to try to review how this process actually looks when viewed in more detail. The findings here also need to be integrated into those analyses that want to achieve a better sense of sanctions' effectiveness and impact.

With regard to the formal decision-making system for UN targeted sanctions, these are still very much steered by the interests and political will of the members of the UNSC. What has been argued here, though, is that the impact of sanctions is also likely to be heavily dependent on formal institutional structures. Such formal structures include UN sanctions guidelines indicating best practices as well as general sanctions steering documents proscribing institutional procedures in administrating UN sanctions. Other formal procedures also include the influences of various sanctions management bodies, not least the work of UN sanctions committees. For example, over the last decade or so, UN sanctions committees have increasingly polished their procedures for administrating sanctions in order to respond effectively to events on the ground. Yet while there has been increasing awareness among the sanctions committees regarding the flexible use of targeted sanctions, there are still a number of institutional weaknesses that reduce the efficiency of the policy. For example, one aspect has to do with the political attention a sanctions committee receives. As noted, different sanctions committees have received different degrees of political attention (for example, an anti-terrorism committee may enjoy more support than a geographical sanctions regime); therefore, the support for targeted sanctions varies considerably across the sanctions regimes. Another example of how formal institutional structures shape outcomes lies in the role of administration by individuals in key positions of the sending body (for example, the sanctions committee chair, the panel of experts, members or special envoys). Unless these individuals act with commitment, the formal decision-making procedure risks losing swiftness, accuracy, ownership and accountability. Clearly, elements like these may reduce the efficacy of the sanctions programme as a whole.

As noted at the beginning of this chapter, the informal decision-making aspects are also important when trying to assess how targeted sanctions work. This has to do with the practitioner's attitude and perception of targeted sanctions and how these contribute to the formation and shape of the policy of targeting. While formal procedures have an impact upon outcome, institutional units as well as officials are likely to either hold views that conform to the officially expressed policy of targeted sanctions at the outset, or a more differentiated understanding. Views from desk officers are likely to be institutionalised, thereby creating different administrative cultures with their own distinct approaches to targeted sanctions. While the differences are not always very great, they do sometimes represent clear nuances which play a role in the overall operation of the sanctions policy. For instance, while some will take a legal approach, other units will take a more political approach to the targeted measures.

For a number of UN practitioners, targeted sanctions were perceived to be determined more by institutional practices than by anything else. For some, effectiveness and practice were very much dependent upon their senior officials' engagement. There was also an understanding that too much control or engagement by individual UN staff members could push the sanctions policy into the hands of more influential powers of the UN (for example, if member states consider that staff members are undermining their interests).

Moreover, given that many practitioners are involved in the entire chain of decision-making, these are also likely to establish separate bureaucratic cultures where the understanding of sanctions has particular connotations (for example, banking officials who have responsibility for implementing financial sanctions seldom get in touch with diplomats at the UN level who negotiate the sanctions text, and sanctions administrators at the UNSC level are never likely to interact with policy makers who operate sanctions on the ground). In sum, as a result of these many separate understandings, targeted sanctions may not in the end function as initially intended. This suggests that decision-making is as important a factor in the effectiveness of sanctions as the process of implementation itself.

While this chapter has focused upon the role of formal and informal UN sanctions decision-making by senders, the next will offer a more detailed analysis of what the policy dynamic looks like on the ground. This will be followed by an examination of the UN's former targeted sanctions regime adopted against UNITA.

Chapter 7
Episodes of UN Targeted Sanctions against UNITA

The crisis in Angola, which eventually led to an armed conflict between the government of Angola and UNITA (the National Union for the Total Independence of Angola; in Portuguese: União Nacional para a Independência Total de Angola), started at the time of independence from Portugal in 1975. According to the Uppsala Conflict Data Project, in comparison with other armed conflicts in the post-Second World War era, the conflict was one of the most intense in terms of number of battle-related deaths until its termination in 2002.[1] While scholarly attention on the dynamics of the civil war of Angola is well documented, less attention has been given to the role of UN targeted sanctions.[2] To fill this research gap, this chapter has two objectives. The first is to disaggregate the Angola sanctions regime into five distinct sanctions episodes based on the proposals suggested at the beginning of this book. A better understanding of the role, impact and effects of sanctions will be gained if we focus on those moments in time when targeting takes place, rather than on the entire sanctions regime era. The second is to present the findings of a number of interviews conducted with previously UN sanctions-listed UNITA members,[3] with the aim of analysing how targets perceived the sanctions.

The first section of this chapter sets out the background to the dynamics leading up to the introduction of targeted sanctions on UNITA. Thereafter follows a disaggregation of the Angolan sanctions regime into various episodes. These episodes represent the timing of the sender's decision to impose, renew and extend UN targeted sanctions lists. Each episode also covers the main political developments at the time of targeting. Next, we will turn to the role of targeted travel and financial sanctions, analysing the implementation aspects. To cover elements that fall outside the specific measures but which are likely to have a strong effect on political impact, we will also examine other strategic factors which

---

1 See Uppsala Conflict Database, <www.pcr.uu.se>, under 'Angola'.

2 Some research projects featuring the role of targeted sanctions in Angola can be found in Cortright and Lopez (2000, 2002a), Hodges (2001), and aspects of Malaquias (2007). Despite the limited focus on the role of targeted sanctions in Angola, the issue is well covered by a number of journalistic articles and policy reports produced by stakeholders to the conflict such as the UN. The reports produced by the UN Sanctions Committee on Angola and the panel of experts are particularly helpful in understanding the political events and the dynamics of targeting during the course of the sanctions process.

3 Targets were listed because they were considered as posing a threat to international peace and security.

influence the impact of targeted sanctions. This will include a classification and analysis of targets' reactions and behaviour based on these empirical findings.

Dealing with UNITA Non-violently

The point of departure for understanding UN targeted sanctions goes back to the years following the signing of the Bicesse Accord (Acordos de Paz) in 1991, as well as the 1994 Lusaka Protocol.[4] Both agreements provided the necessary ground for settling the Angola post-independence violence and offered a future based on stability. Regrettably, UNITA and the de facto Angola government never fully came to terms with these accords. Reconciliation efforts were slow and hampered by mistrustful acts contrary to the spirit of the agreements.

The international community considered acting within a culture of political distress and fatigue, especially concerning the inflexibility of UNITA in abiding by the stipulated principles of the peace agreement, with targeted sanctions as one alternative. For the UN and the Security Council, the targeted sanctions were originally considered 'a vehicle of peace to persuade the rebels to resume good faith participation in the process of national reconciliation'.[5] From the sender's (the UNSC's) point of view, the aim of the sanctions was not to 'punish' the UNITA leadership, but to promote a political settlement of the civil war.[6] The view of the UNSC on the role of targeted sanctions should therefore be regarded as part of a long-term project, in which the sanctions only played one part among a number of other strategies. More officially, the aim of the UN targeted sanctions was to have UNITA comply with the obligations it undertook when signing the Peace Accord, and to encourage the group to commit to a lasting peace.[7]

In this context, the UNSC was repeatedly informed by various member states that UNITA was actively working to promote its cause at all levels of international society, contrary to the spirit of achieving peace. What also became clear was that UNITA maintained pockets of guerrilla warfare inside Angola, supported by an international network of UNITA officials and representatives. Targeted sanctions became the main tool to dismantle such activities (see Table 7.1).[8]

4 S/2000/203, para. 2.

5 S/2001/966 (2001): 6.

6 S/2000/203.

7 Hartzell and Hoddie (2007): 110–25, recount the efforts made by the international community to have the parties settle the civil war in Angola.

8 It is clear that sanctions, both the 1993 (1994) embargo and the later 1997–98 targeted sanctions, were one-sided applications of measures on UNITA (siding with the government in Luanda).

Table 7.1 UNITA target categories

Episode no. Start date	1 29 October 1997	2 24 June 1998	3 18 April 2001	4 4 October 2001	5 6 April 2002
Military			n/a	54	n/a
Family			n/a	18	n/a
Students			n/a	4	n/a
Representatives			n/a	14	n/a
Secretary/ Political bureau			n/a	6	n/a
Other			n/a	61	n/a
Total	'All senior INITA officials and families'	'All senior INITA officials and families'	'De-lists 9, adds 3'	157	'De-lists 2'

Note: This table is based on all key UNSC resolutions and UN press releases, and a selection of other key documents related to the Angolan Sanctions Committee, which have been published (that is, official documents). I have not included decisions of UN Secretary-Generals' or the establishment and extensions of UN force deployment, or reports by UN envoys and so on which could work as intervening variables in sanctions impacts. Nor have I included all other measures that could impact the target, such as diamond bans, various types of preventive measures and the like. Note that press releases are important because these are the primary tool of information dissemination for the UN. These normally include updates and notifications on updates of listing procedures, people to be listed or de-listed, and so on. Documents were taken from the terminated Angolan Sanctions Committee homepage as of 1 October 2007. The start dates refer to dates of enforcement, or sometimes dates of publication.

Symptomatic of the UNSC's early efforts to adopt a strategy of targeted sanctions, with the implication that its implementation capacity was not yet fully developed, was that the actual targeting of individual members of UNITA did not become fully visible until 2001, when 157 individuals were placed on the list. While as early as 1997 the UNSC had adopted targeted sanctions against 'all senior UNITA officials and families', it took the UN Angola Sanctions Committee almost five years to adopt and publicly release a list of names of those who should be targeted. The delay in adopting the list was most likely perceived by UNITA as revealing that from an implementation point of view, the measure not very credible. After all, the UN was seen to be unable even to agree on which names should be included on the list.

If we look closer at the UNITA sanctions list, the single largest category of targets placed on it was military personal (54), followed by family members of UNITA targets (18), UNITA representatives (14), UNITA Party Secretaries (6),

UNITA students (4) and a large mix of unknown affiliations (61). There were 157 targets altogether.[9]

I will now examine each episode in detail, highlighting some of the key political developments during this period and indicating whether they led to progress or stalemate in achieving behavioural change.

Episode 1: October 1997

The UN Mechanism (an institutional body under the established Angola Sanctions Committee which collected information on the implementation of UNITA targeted sanctions) characterised the period between the second half of 1996 to May 1998 as a period of positive political development. The main development was the establishment of the Government of National Unity in April 1997. During this period, the UN Mechanism also stated that over the course of the conflict, it had become evident that Jonas Savimbi had abused the Lusaka Peace Process to undertake a 'major rearmament exercise for UNITA and that a significant number of UNITA combatants had kept in hiding in preparation for a major offensive'.[10]

The situation in Angola reached one of its lowest points during the conflict, prompting the UNSC to adopt UNSCR 1127 (28 August 1997), threatening UNITA with sanctions unless UN Secretary-General Kofi Annan could report by 30 September that it had complied completely with the 1994 Lusaka Protocol. The reaction from UNITA was not long in coming. On 1 and 5 September, UNITA promised to comply with the remaining conditions, while at the same time criticising the threat as a bad precedent'.[11] It is noteworthy, though, that as early as 1996, the UNSC had had threatened UNITA with stronger sanctions measures if it failed to comply with its demands. Given that subsequent threats were more or less a repetition of previous ones, UNITA learned that mere partial modification of behaviour, or public expression of compliance, would ease the UN's pressure, or at least postpone further sanctions measures (for instance, similar threats had been made in 1993–94). Hence, these threats of stronger sanctions delayed enforcement, giving UNITA a greater chance of evading or limiting the impact of these measures.[12] Unable to see a way through the impasse, and in the face of only limited compliance, the UNSC agreed to delay the implementation of UN targeted sanctions until 31 October 1997.[13] Yet on 30 October, targeted sanctions were imposed on UNITA because it had failed to fulfil its obligations under the Lusaka Protocol. In this first episode, no personal identifiers were released that could be applied to enforce sanctions in any credible way. The listing only referred to all

9 This categorisation is based on the UNSC 7162 press release (list of targets), 4 October 2001.

10 S/2000/1225, para. 8.

11 *Keesing's*, vol. 43, September 1997: 41,803.

12 See Cortright and Lopez (2000): 155.

13 S/RES/1130/1997.

senior UNITA officials and their families, and was in this sense highly symbolic. The response from UNITA officials was anger.[14]

For the rest of the year, fighting in Angola continued and intensified, while UNITA sent mixed signals to international mediators by ceding territory to the Movimento Popular de Libertação de Angola (MPLA) administration. The situation characterising the period at the imposition of targeted sanctions was one of great suspicions of UNITA's intentions.

In sum, much of the first episode seemed to have consisted of a cat-and-mouse game, where UNITA only tried to delay the UN's imposition of further measures. What was worse, however, was that the situation on the ground did not improve in any significant way despite the sanctions.

Episode 2: June 1998

Little progress with regard to the peace implementation took place during this period. Stumbling blocks included uncertainty about what political status the UNITA leader, Jonas Savimbi, would have in the future political life of Angola; how the handing over of territories by UNITA to the MPLA government would be worked through, and the demobilisation of UNITA soldiers (for instance, in June 1998 the MPLA government claimed that UNITA still controlled almost 30,000 armed men). Although UNITA was legalised as a political party on 11 March 1998 as a result of 'complete' demobilisation, the MPLA government concluded that the conflict was at its worst stage ever, with an intensification of fighting.[15] In late June, the UNSC decided to implement targeted financial sanctions on UNITA and its senior members.[16] As in the first episode, no explicit or detailed list was made available to the public, only the decision by the UN that all senior UNITA officials and their families were to be targeted.

On 26 June, a significant problem for the overall peace process erupted as the UN Special Representative, Alioune Blondin Beye, died in a plane crash. In light of this and other developments, the MPLA chairman of the Angolan National Assembly publicly declared that it had lost confidence in UNITA as a negotiating partner, suggesting that UNITA should be suspended from the National Assembly on grounds that UNITA had retained its army despite its agreement in the Lusaka Protocol to demobilise. This was, however, only one of several setbacks that

14 *Keesing's*, vol. 43, November 1997: 41,899.

15 *Keesing's*, vol. 44, November 1998: 42,321.

16 Moreover, on 12 June 1998 the UN, and later the EU (on 8 July), adopted targeted sanctions on diamonds. The fact that the EU adopted the diamond ban from UNITA-held areas was important because it also brought specific pressure to bear on the Belgian government of the time, one of the main traders of diamonds, to investigate and put an end to trade from UNITA-held territories.

UNITA would experience during the rest of the year.[17] On 15 September 1998, UNSCR 1195 (1998) also identified UNITA as the 'primary cause of the crisis in Angola'.[18] Perhaps even more problematic for UNITA's political efforts in the region was that the Southern African Development Community (SADC) in early October, sided openly with the MPLA government in Luanda, calling for a swift and concerted campaign to rid the region of UNITA fighters.[19] During the last months of 1998, fighting continued in several parts of Angola, prompting the UNSC to threaten UNITA on 12 January 1999 with further sanctions unless it returned to the negotiating table. The UN threat came in the context of two UN plane crashes in Angola (which led to a suspension of all UN flights over Angola and the withdrawal of peacekeeping troops from the war zones).

As major political events unfolded in these episodes, UN targeted sanctions continued to play a role, at least for the purposes of mobilising support against UNITA and encouraging UNITA to engage in talks. While targeted sanctions may have contributed to UNITA's decision to engage in dialogue with the MPLA, a host of other background factors need to be taken into account.

Episodes 3 and 4: April and October 2001[20]

On 17 January 1999, the UN Secretary-General deemed the situation in Angola to be on the verge of a catastrophic breakdown, blaming both UNITA and the sitting government for their failure to comply with previous agreements.[21] Operationally, UNITA was advancing in the field, and won a number of important and symbolic victories (for instance, by claiming to have shot down a government-owed plane in February 2001). Given this situation, on 26 January the MPLA government declared the November 1994 Lusaka Protocol dead.[22]

By April 2001, the UNSC reported that its overall assessment of targeted sanctions was that they continued to play an important part in resolving the Angolan

---

17 Meanwhile, various reports from the UN Angola Sanctions Committee continued to be presented, informing the international community about sanctions violations and further building up pressure on UNITA. For example, the Chairman of the Sanctions Committee, Ambassador Fowler, travelled extensively to the region to oversee sanctions implementation (travelling mostly to Africa and Europe). He later presented 19 points stressing the need for further measures to implement targeted sanctions; see S/1999/829.

18 Note that on 2 September 1998 UNITA split after Jorge Alicerces Valentim issued a communiqué in which he established an alternative UNITA Renewal Committee (later disbanded due to loss of support).

19 *Keesing's*, vol. 44, October 1998: 42,539.

20 Owing to limited information on the situation in Angola at this time, these two episodes have been merged.

21 *Keesing's*, vol. 45, January 1999: 42,711.

22 The MPLA government also said that it would only recognise the UNITA Renewal Committee, which at the time (12–14 January) held a congress in Luanda.

conflict, and that the policy should be maintained.[23] On 18 April, the Sanctions Committee decided to list nine individuals and de-list three.[24]

The month after the listing measures had taken place, fighting continued to increase. It took the UNSC until 4 October the same year to issue its first public detailed sanctions list. Little political progress took place during the remaining months of 1998. In fact, the war continued during most of 1999, and lasted until 22 February 2002. Finally, the sudden death of Jonas Savimbi (killed in battle), brought the civil war in Angola to an end.

These episodes suggest that targeted sanctions had a minor impact themselves in actually shaping battle outcomes. While travel bans and assets freezes, as well as the other sanctions measures imposed, certainly contributed to limiting UNITA's room for manoeuvre, the public blacklist per se did not solve the conflict, nor reduce its intensity. On the other hand, impossible to determine what the situation would have looked like if targeted sanctions had not been imposed.

Episode 5: April 2002

In the days following the death of Jonas Savimbi, the Angolan government ordered a halt to all offensives against UNITA in order to facilitate a dialogue with the established four-member management committee that would take over from Savimbi. The move came as the MPLA awaited reactions from the new leadership. This cease-fire came into effect on 13 March 2002. On 30 March, an official Memorandum of Understanding (MoU) was signed which ended the civil war. On 2 April, the government granted amnesty to all UNITA fighters. Four days later, the Angola Sanctions Committee issued a press release stating that two individuals had been de-listed. On 17 May 2002, through the adoption of UNSCR 1412 (2002), the UNSC decided to suspend the targeted sanctions imposed on UNITA members for 90 days in order to allow UNITA personnel to travel and reorganise with the goal of rapid reintegration into national life. Another 90-day suspension period was later approved on 15 August 2002 by UNSCR 1432 (2002), and the Angola cease-fire was concluded on 4 April 2002.[25]

Analysis

The episodes identified here suggest that there was no clear and direct correlation between the imposition of targeted sanctions and the political and military dynamic on ground. Nor was there a clear link between targeted sanctions and UNITA's

---

23 S/2001/363, 18 April 2001: 5. During this period, the UNSC also went public with the formal arrangements it had made with the services of Kroll Associates to further investigate UNITA's financial network.

24 No official list had been published until this point.

25 *Keesing's*, vol. 48, January 2002: 44,713.

reaction and willingness to engage in and commit to a sustainable Angolan peace. While targeting was sometimes followed by further commitments to peace by UNITA, it was mostly also met with continued or increased fighting. As a result, little can be said about the impact of targeted sanctions per se. On the other hand, it can by no means be concluded that sanctions did not help to improve the situation. One problem is that the various reactions by UNITA to the imposition of renewed targeted sanctions cannot safely be isolated from other strategic measures put in force by other actors such as the UN or independent states like the US, Russia, China and Cuba. UNITA's reactions were also likely to have been determined by a number of different UN policies, not just sanctions. Another problem is that some forms of impact, such as the psychological effects of being targeted, may not be clear in the short term, but only from a long-term perspective.

Although it is not the objective here to evaluate the sanctions, the episodes presented invite separate assessments for each of them, rather than assessing the entire regime as the scholarly literature to date has tended to do. Clearly, as demonstrated in this examination so far, each sanctions episode has its own specific dynamic process, involving a bargaining relationship between the sender and the target. In particular, one could note the following main events:

Episode 1 saw the establishment of the Government of National Unity; the continued rearmament of UNITA; the adoption of a UN resolution threatening UNITA with targeted sanctions; UNITA's promise to comply with these sanctions; the delay in implementation of targeted sanctions and increase in momentum between decision and implementation to evade them; the imposition of targeted sanctions and the unspecific nature of the list (no names included); the inclusion of UNITA family members; the continued military fighting; the role of international mediators, and the suffering of civilians.

Episode 2 featured slow progress in implementing the peace process; the slow handing over of territory to the central MPLA government; the slow demobilisation process of UNITA; the recognition of UNITA as a political party; the intensification of the armed conflict; the decision by the UN Security Council to impose targeted sanctions; the death of the UN special representative; the will of the MPLA to suspend UNITA from peace negotiations; the role of UNSCR 1195 (1998) and its attachment of guilt to UNITA for the ensuing crises; the siding of the SADC with the MPLA; the threat from the UNSC of further sanctions; the role of two plane crashes in Angola;, and the military's advances on the battlefield.

Episodes 3 and 4's main developments included the failure of the sender to keep the Lusaka Protocol alive; the active engagement of the Angola Sanctions Committee; the role of Ambassador Fowler; the positive endorsement of the targeted sanctions by the UN; the expansion of targeted sanctions to cover more individuals, and the death of the UNITA leader, Jonas Savimbi.

Episode 5 saw the termination of military engagements between the MPLA and UNITA; the establishment of the UNITA Management Committee; the signing of the MoU terminating the civil war in Angola; the continuation of the UN Angola Sanctions Committee despite the ending of the civil war; official support for the role of sanctions, and the ultimate UN suspension of targeted sanctions against UNITA.

The episodes above suggest that targeted sanctions were maintained despite the positive and negative developments that were taking place with regard to the resolution of the conflict. While the defined episodes above were negative, there were none the less plenty of opportunities for the sender to deploy positive sanctions as a reward for good behaviour. However, the episodes above suggest that the sender mainly assessed its own policy as not achieving much, given that it continuously decided to expand its policies and to punish UNITA. On the other hand, the sender did at times officially endorse the instrumentality of targeted sanctions.

Moreover, while the review above is concerned more specifically with the sender's more specific engagement with UNITA, one should not forget the fact that the UNSC was only one of many actors with strategic interests in the Angolan conflict. Not only were most other African governments concerned with, and one way or another active in, Angola, the major powers such as China, the US and Russia were actively pursing their individual interests. In addition to this, a number of private actors were also engaging with UNITA. All of these engagements are likely to have contributed the overall sanctions policy outcome.

Finally, it is worth noting here that the factors included in each episode are only a fraction of a host of other elements that contributed to the sanctions outcome. In any regard, each sanctions episode may be judged a success or a failure independent of the outcome of the sanctions regime as a whole.

The Impact of Targeted Individual Sanctions

This section will devote further attention to the impact targeted sanctions may have had on the listed entities. Judging from examples from several UN panel of expert reports documenting the implementation of targeted UN sanctions against UNITA, the process was weak at best.[26]

One explanation is simply that some poorer countries (such as Angola's neighbours) have difficulty enforcing sanctions because of their lack of governance capacities. Another reason is that it may be more difficult to enforce travel bans on particular targets engaged in civil war as the government is not likely to be in control of its country and the pressure on customs checkpoints is extreme. Angola also has a long and un-monitored border, so it is difficult to enforce implementation. Another explanation is that allies of UNITA often turned a blind in their dealings with UNITA. As noted in several UN reports, there were many instances of minimal efforts to fulfil the UNSCR stipulations. Various countries provided fake passports, pretended to expel targets or simply allowed UNITA members to continue with their political activities.

---

26 See Cortright and Lopez (2002a): 143.

Despite the evasion and circumvention of targeted sanctions, there was also another aspect suggesting that the UNITA leadership was more engaged by the UN because of sanctions, not least through its unprecedented investigation of sanctions evasion and campaigns of publicly naming and shaming governments that did not actively prevent UNITA's activities, but also because it had to respond politically to the sanctions policies.

The most important question remains, however, whether targeted individual sanctions had an effect in resolving the conflict. On the one hand, many of UNITA's activities continued as if no targeted sanctions had ever been implemented. Several UNITA members continued to be active around the world despite the sanctions regime. On the other hand, it is safe to say that the targeted sanctions contributed to undermining their activities as implementation was increasingly tightened. It is difficult to conclude how the personal impact on each listed target fed into the thinking of the UNITA leadership.

The Impact of the Travel Ban

On 28 August 1997, the UNSC introduced a travel ban. This prohibited entry into or transit through UN member state territories for all senior officials of UNITA and for adult members of their immediate families. UN member states were requested to suspend or cancel all travel documents, visas or residence permits issued to senior UNITA officials and family members, as well as ending contact with UNITA's leadership in occupied territories.[27]

As illustrated above, the need for the imposition of a travel ban had also become evident to the UNSC because of UNITA's ability to lobby openly for its cause to generate political, economic and moral support. Such lobbying also involved generating funding to buy weapons, which clearly did not comply with the spirit of seeking peace in Angola (besides the fact that it violated the arms embargo). A primary aim of the travel ban was this to put an end to UNITA's foreign representation. As noted in one of the UN's panel reports concerning the logic of sanctions, the UN:[28]

> developed a clear appreciation of the very close links between these vital aspects of UNITA's operation and the ability of UNITA personnel to travel and conduct UNITA business abroad. As an organisation UNITA conducts most of its business through direct personal contacts. This is in part a function of the clandestine activities in which UNITA is engaged ....

Stopping the activities of UNITA through the implementation of a travel ban thus became very important for the UN.

27 UNSCR 1127 (1997) and UNSCR 1173 (1998).

28 S/2000/203, para. 131.

Yet the record of implementation showed mixed results. There was ample evidence of circumvention and evasion, and implementation was rather weak, at least in the beginning. Targeted individuals were still able to travel between various countries without being stopped, and UNITA offices still operated abroad. In this sense, the targeted travel ban had no or little impact.

Over time, and mainly as a result of the various official UN reports on UNITA's sanctions-busting activities, it became increasingly difficult for host governments to continue allow UNITA operations on their soil. Several governments were repeatedly mentioned in the reports of the UN Mechanism and the Panel of Experts, naming and shaming them for not properly enforcing Security Council Resolutions.

Another explanation for the uncertain efficacy of the travel ban was administrative problems in implementing it. These ranged from lack of information about listed actors to problems in disseminating the lists to all UN member states and subsequent implementing bodies.

With regard to information about listed actors, the travel ban list was very poor in terms of lacking technical indicators such as names and passport numbers to make implementation effective in various screening systems (passport controls, financial transaction systems, and so on). In fact, most of the sanctions lists issued did not even contain the names of those meant to be targeted. Moreover, there were difficulties with the actual dissemination of the list. For instance, the UN Mechanism stated as late as October 2000 that of those countries it had been visiting in Africa, the list had only been distributed to Botswana, Namibia and South Africa.[29] Related to this was the problem of implementation. According to the UN Mechanism, even if a country did not have access to the sanctions list, this did not prevent their putting in place appropriate mechanisms aimed at controlling the movement of persons included on them (measures which the UN Mechanism found were lacking). But even if the list was in place, there were always many opportunities for those placed on the list to evade the sanctions. For example, there were no problems travelling to South Africa given the many airfields throughout the country. Consequently, UNITA officials did not have to proceed through required immigration channels, as smaller airfields did not have customs procedures. Instead, they could fly into a country illegally and simply go about their business.[30]

Besides the aim of preventing targets from travelling, there was also the aim of closing down UNITA's foreign representation. As noted above, during the course of the civil war, UNITA had several foreign representations despite their being prohibited. The most important UNITA representations were found in Lisbon, London, Paris, Rome, Bonn, Antwerp, New York and Washington, DC. In Africa, UNITA had important representative presences in capitals such as Lomé, Kinshasa (prior to the overthrow of President Mobutu Sese Seko), Abidjan and Ouagadougou.

---

29 S/2000/1026, 2000: 8.

30 S/2000/203, paras 130–38.

In principle, there were two types of UNITA representatives: ones that operated with the *acceptance* of the host government, and ones that usually operated with the *knowledge* of the host government, although not necessarily with its blessing.[31] The former included at times the representatives in Lomé, Abidjan, Kinshasa and Ouagadougou. Several countries were also providing senior UNITA officials with passports and facilitated their travel (sometimes with false names, sometimes under diplomatic protection).[32] For instance, in October 2001 it was reported that Ouagadougou was still used as a base for senior UNITA officials. Although several other countries of the UN had prohibited UNITA's official representatives and closed down several of its offices, the problem of evasion soon became clear to the UN Angola Sanctions Committee. Several UNITA representative bodies had transformed themselves into other kinds of NGOs, avoiding the label of UNITA in order to avoid being closed down.[33] The evasion was often difficult for host governments to counter because some UNITA individuals carried the host country's own citizenship and therefore, for constitutional reasons, could not be evicted.[34] This kind of problem was also noted by the UN Mechanism in its December 2000 report: 'The use of NGOs as front organisations is one important and efficient way of circumventing the sanctions, not least in view of the fact that freedom of association often is constitutionally guaranteed.'[35] The UN Mechanism was also able to demonstrate how UNITA still was able to operate in a number of countries despite the UN travel ban imposed four years earlier.

Besides various UN Resolutions, which in themselves became strong tools for mobilising public opinion against UNITA, the Angola Sanctions Committee built considerable pressure on UNITA through reports from panels of experts and the UN Mechanism which brought UNITA's activities out in the open. As expected, the effort to collect and present accurate information on UNITA's activities was confronted with numerous challenges. Not only were several UN member states unwilling to provide the UN with information, it did not fundamentally change its policy towards UNITA despite calls from the UNSC. For example, despite several sanctions evasion activities in Africa in clear violation of adopted resolutions, the UN Mechanism reported in December 2000, almost half a year after its earlier

31 S/2000/203, para. 132.

32 For example, the panel of experts noted in one of its reports that Savimbi's children in Lomé were under the direct protection of the president and his presidential guard, and when they wanted to travel, they were required to inform the head of the force in advance; S/2000/203, paras 130–37.

33 S/2000/1026, 2000: 9.

34 Cortright and Lopez (2000): 160.

35 Examples of some of these UNITA transformations into other organisations were: Commissao de Justica, Paz e Reconciliacao em Angola (CJPR) and the Center for Political and Economic Studies for Development in Angola, both clearly UNITA representatives; S/2000/1225, para. 75. Note also that similar transformations are currently occurring for terror-listed organisations, for example the Partiya Karkerên Kurdistan (PKK) changing its name to Kongra-Gel.

report, that: 'No information has reached the Mechanism indicating that any major changes in UNITA structures in Africa have taken place,'[36] and that despite previously disclosed findings, UNITA continues to operate through several front organisations in countries like Belgium, Portugal, Italy and Ireland. Furthermore, the UN Mechanism reported as late as April 2001 that it had 'not been informed about any action taken or efforts made to close the front organisations'.[37] In fact, it was noted by the UN Mechanism that UNITA's political campaign had intensified between May and October 2001.[38]

From the findings above, a set of typical evasion categories can be noted. The first type of evasion consisted of simple breaches of the ban by individual members of UNITA. As the examples show, several targets moved between different countries, with or without proper passports. The second type of evasion concerned the number of examples of UNITA representative bodies abroad (which, in a sense, were forbidden by the UNSCR). These UNITA operations were often conducted with the consent of the host government. A third type of evasion was the operation of front organisations actively campaigning for UNITA's cause. The final category comprised UNITA targets and allies that operated outside Angola in order to shore up support for the movement or to ensure that UNITA could operate smoothly (for example, by connecting sellers and buyers of UNITA diamonds or arranging covert travel for UNITA members).

The Impact of Targeted Assets Freeze Measures

On 12 June 1998, the UNSC imposed targeted financial sanctions on leading members of UNITA and their families. This action required UN member states to freeze all funds and financial resources of UNITA.[39] The move also reflected dissatisfaction with UNITA's unwillingness to comply with the Lusaka Protocol AND confirmed the UN's siding with and support for the MPLA government in Luanda.[40]

On the eve of the financial sanctions, the UN panel of experts found that Jonas Savimbi had ordered that UNITA's funds be withdrawn from banks and other

36 S/2001/363, 18 April 2001: 12.

37 *Ibid.*: 14.

38 S/2001/966, 2001: 12.

39 UNSCR 1173 (1998) stated: 'Decides that all States, except Angola, in which there are funds and financial resources, including any funds derived or generated from property of UNITA as an organisation or of senior officials of UNITA or adult members of their immediate families designated pursuant to paragraph 11 of resolution 1127 (1997), shall require all persons and entities within their own territories holding such funds and financial resources to freeze them and ensure that they are not made available directly or indirectly to or for the benefit of UNITA as an organisation or of senior officials of UNITA or adult members of their immediate families ...'.

40 Cortright and Lopez (2002a): 63.

financial institutions.[41] It was later discovered that as a result of targeted sanctions, UNITA had increasingly come to rely on trade in rough diamonds as part of its payment methods, and that some sums of money had been deposited with a handful of friends, supporters and key UNITA representatives abroad. Although it was also discovered that UNITA avoided using normal banking channels in order to minimise its economic exposure, the UN panel of experts none the less found that UNITA, and especially its senior officials, every now and then operated through bank accounts and credit card services. However, these were mainly used to complete and facilitate transactions such as monthly payments (for purchase of satellite communications equipment, and so on).[42]

In October 2001, it was reported that investigations made by the UN Mechanism had identified assets held in the names of UNITA officials in six countries: the Ivory Coast, Ireland, Italy, Portugal, Switzerland and the US. These assets were in the form of bank deposits, real estate properties and business entities.[43] In addition, it was established that offshore financial centres continued to play a major role as havens for UNITA funds and in facilitating financial transactions.[44]

Tracking UNITA assets was a cumbersome process for the UN's Angola Sanctions Committee. For instance, by December 2000 it was reported that 'Inquiries by Member States into UNITA assets had been severely hampered by the lack of available, validated information about UNITA's assets and membership.'[45] It was also reported that even where freezing of accounts had occurred, these had not contained substantial sums of money.[46] Another factor that made investigations difficult was that UNITA had separated its commercial and financial networks from its political activities.[47]

The role and impact of targeted financial sanctions cannot be properly understood without acknowledging the fact that trade in valuable minerals probably mattered more than simply using the financial system to sustain the economic activities of UNITA and its leaders. While the main purpose of the assets freeze was to prevent transactions between various aspects of UNITA's activities (for example, between its administrative headquarters and its foreign representatives), targeting UNITA's alluvial diamond trade became increasingly important for the UNSC's sanctions strategy.

---

41 S/2000/203, paras 120–21.
42 *Ibid.*, para. 118.
43 S/2001/966, 2001: 45.
44 Ibid.
45 S/2000/1225, para. 216.
46 *Ibid.*
47 *Ibid.*, para. 217.

The Role of Diamonds

Over the past two decades or so, the UN has devoted increasing attention to highlighting the role the trade in rough diamonds has played in funding civil wars.[48] In the case of UNITA, diamonds played a key role in sustaining its military operations. Angola has one of the largest diamond deposits in Africa. Although it owned assets and property, UNITA increasingly relied on the trade in diamonds throughout the war.[49] Diamonds were easy to trade and easy to hide. False certifications of origin were circulating and were easy to obtain. Diamonds from UNITA-held areas were easily smuggled to neighbouring countries, as well being sold from Luanda.[50] These actions did not have to be declared in the financial systems. As found by this research and elsewhere, the UN had many difficulties in tracing UNITA's financial activities, largely due to smuggling. Although it was able to block pockets of assets, the information discovered did not at all represent the full extent of the wealth of UNITA (whose illicit diamond trade had generated millions of US dollars over the years).[51] The fact that the diamonds were vital to UNITA is also reflected in the policy of the US during the peace negotiations. Part of this policy was to encourage a 'peace for diamonds' strategy. This was based on a similar calculation to that of the MPLA government – that UNITA was not likely to ever give up its diamonds, and that the only way to have it sign a comprehensive peace deal would thus be to grant it access to diamond mining fields.[52] Another relevant factor was that various tribes and ethnic groups had their own claims to the diamond-producing areas. These groups also had some loyalty to the fighting groups, in return for being granted access to a number of mines.[53]

The role of diamonds in financing UNITA was also mentioned in various UN reports. For instance, the UN panel of experts concluded that: 'The easy marketability of UNITA's diamonds also makes the hoarding of cash unnecessary for UNITA. There is also ample evidence regarding Mr. Jonas Savimbi's clear reluctance to deposit UNITA funds in banks, following the imposition of international financial

48 See Campbell (2002). For a good illustration of the role of conflict diamonds in the civil wars in West Africa, see Farah (2008).

49 It was also found that a significant amount of money was made by UNITA in the form of landing fees charged for aircrafts bringing in commercial products to UNITA-held territories. In 1997 and 1998, the panel of experts estimated that about US$5 million per month was made in such 'taxes'; S/2000/203, para. 117. Independent diamond diggers operating under UNITA-held areas also collected taxes. Moreover, money was collected by selling licenses to various diamond trading actors; Hodges (2001): 152.

50 *Ibid.*: 153.

51 Also worth mentioning is that during this period (by the end of 1999), UNITA lost its principal airport at Andulo in the Central Highlands. This loss led to further complications in importing arms and smuggling diamonds out of the country (the latter having an impact on the financial aspects of its activities).

52 Hodges (2001): 161–2.

53 *Ibid.*: 147.

sanctions against UNITA in 1998.'[54] After intensive investigation, the UN panel of experts concluded that diamonds were in fact the main source of income for UNITA, and that its assets were mostly kept in the form of rough diamonds. Diamonds were exchanged for cash and used to buy arms.[55]

The extent of UNITA's diamond trade is difficult to estimate. However, some researchers have argued that in 1999 alone, diamonds worth US$600 million were produced in Angola, and that an estimated 150,000 informal mine operators (*garimpeiros*) were active in UNITA-held areas.[56] This mining clearly gave UNITA financial strength. Other estimates suggest that between 1992 and 1998, UNITA's revenues amounted to US$3.7 billion, while the diamond industry claimed that US$2 billion was obtained by UNITA.[57] The real figure is still not known. Thus, undermining UNITA's diamond trade became even more crucial than simply investigating the conventional routes to trace the flow of money. This also explains why the panel of experts invested so much energy in tracking UNITA's activities in this sector. Meticulously investigated reports were published by the committee, detailing the trade in rough diamonds from Angola to diamond markets all over the world. Such reporting was clearly intended to counter and ultimately stop the continued smuggling of diamonds. As a result, diamonds were smuggled through many African countries such as Burkina Faso, Namibia, South Africa and Rwanda, and to several European countries, in particular Belgium and the UK (the panel of experts reports provide detailed accounts of these activities, as well as information concerning the lax controls on these activities by the governments concerned). What is particularly interesting is that the panel of experts identified how diamonds were used to buy friends and supporters. For example, the panel found 'first hand testimony from more than one source that large quantities of diamonds and cash were given by Savimbi to the former President of Zaire, Mobutu Sese Seko, in exchange for favours to UNITA, and also as a means of strengthening their existing "friendship"'.[58] Another illustrative example is the following:[59]

---

54 S/2000/203, para. 105.

55 For example, it was reported that 'In a typical arms transaction, UNITA prepares parcels of diamonds (allegedly valued between USD 4 million and USD 5 million each), and diamond experts provided by the arms broker and by UNITA agree on the value of each parcel based on the number and the quality of the stones presented. UNITA specifically seeks out arms dealers willing to accept diamonds as payment. In a typical non-arms related deal where cash is needed to purchase commodities, support operations, or assist family members, for example, the diamonds are usually carried to safe destinations outside Angola, and a meeting is arranged with interested buyers. The diamonds are then exchanged for cash'; S/2000/203, para. 81.

56 Malaquias (2007): 122. For a more personal and local account of the culture of the diamond trade in Angola, see Pearce (2005): 152–65.

57 Figure taken from Hodges (2001): 153.

58 S/2000/203, para. 100.

59 *Ibid.*, para. 102.

> UNITA's former representative in Togo described how on Savimbi's instruction he gave President Eyadema of Togo a 'passport sized' packet of diamonds when Eyadema agreed to allow Savimbi's children to come to Togo and be educated there. General Jacinto Bandau testified to having personally handed over packets of diamonds to Eyadema during private meetings between Savimbi and Eyadema.

A similar close friendship was identified between UNITA and the President of Burkina Faso. Examples like these illustrate the problems of enforcing targeted sanctions. These reports also highlighted a variety of sanctions evasion activities, for example by including names of individuals, companies and governments involved in selling and buying UNITA diamonds. These reports formed part of a strategy of naming and shaming both UNITA members and the governments that supported their activities.[60]

Importantly, though, judging from a number of UN reports, UNITA's reliance on cash and property diminished over time. Most of UNITA's financial activities were aimed at sustaining foreign representation, although some deposits of money were entrusted to various governments in case of emergency. As we have seen, the financial activity of UNITA was geared to buying friends and allies, and promoting its cause. Moreover, money was used to buy equipment for the military. No evidence exists that money was taken for UNITA members' personal gain.

In conclusion, it is safe to say that financial sanctions did have an impact on UNITA. For instance, in its analysis, the UN Mechanism concluded in October 2001 that since the implementation of sanctions, UNITA had experienced a decrease in liquidity. The financial sanctions could hence very well have led to a change in behaviour in both UNITA's general activities and in the case of some individual members. However, the impact may rather have been a behavioural change on the *strategic level* – in the sense of evasion or finding new ways to finance its activities, simply to survive. Less of an impact can be demonstrated in terms of a behavioural change in favour of compliance with the sender's goals. Yet the financial sanctions placed enormous pressure on UNITA and its activities, both domestically and abroad. Many of its activities in this area were made public by being placed on the table at the UNSC. In this way, the entire sanctions regime was characterised by innovative steps by the Angola Sanctions Committee and its active chair, along with willingness by the UN to develop new investigatory techniques to pinpoint target evasion.[61]

---

60 It was implicitly expected that the name-and-shame approach would have an impact. Note the following statement by the Mechanism: 'as a result of publicity and the "name and shame" campaign, we expect UNITA to seek new and unexpected friends and to explore more subtle and refined ways of evading the sanctions'; S/2000/1225, para. 20.

61 For example, the contracting of an independent investigation firm such as Kroll Associates, a US-based private financial investigation bureau contracted by the UNSC to

Other Factors that Had an Effect on the Impact of Sanctions

While it is in the nature of sanctions assessment to evaluate the role and the contribution of targeted sanctions in solving conflicts and disputes, there are a number of other factors that need to be included in the analysis when determining the overall impact of sanctions, and this is also the case with the UNITA sanction.

First, one important factor that was likely to shape the mindset of the UNITA leadership at the time of sanctions was the general situation of world affairs. Unlike current sanctions regimes, UNITA was a movement shaped by the logic of the Cold War. Although targeted sanctions were initially adopted in 1997, UNITA as a movement had been established almost 30 years earlier.[62] Founded as a guerrilla organisation (after training in various part of the world), its style and activities were very much steered by this guerrilla mentality and the role it could play in midst of the rivalry between the Soviet Union and the US. Beyond being just a guerrilla movement, UNITA was also a black nationalist movement, in the sense that it was fighting for the cause of black Angolans, and not primarily for a fixed revolutionary ideology. Hence, while ideologically restrained, UNITA did not follow a strict traditional political cause – capitalist or Marxist – but rather a cause that primarily put the interests of Africans first. Hence, the understanding of UNITA by the West and the more influential countries at the UNSC may have been somewhat complicated. UNITA's foundations as a non-state revolutionary black nationalist actor guided much of its thinking and actions. Thus, when trying to understand the political behaviour of UNITA *vis-à-vis* the UN, this history of UNITA's development needs to be borne in mind.

Second, UNITA entered into several different alliances during the Cold War, finding temporary allies offering shelter and protection. Angola was both geo-strategically and economically interesting for the major parties in the Cold War, thus attracting a lot of outside interest.[63] The experiences of being in the heart of the more heated conflicts in the Cold War also gave UNITA a strong will and capability to deal with various actors. In this context, it is worth noting the strong bond that existed between Angola and the US. American involvement in Angola on the side of UNITA prior to the sanctions was early on based on the Reagan Doctrine to counter anti-communist influence. This US support had an immediate effect on the civil war in Angola and the behaviour of UNITA.[64] American involvement had begun as early as the period of de-colonisation, but increased dramatically

---

scrutinise and report on UNITA's financial network, was a typical 'innovative' measure (alongside the Mechanism) which increased the pressure on UNITA.

62 For a very insightful account of UNITA's early establishment and search for legitimising and foreign support (especially from the Nordic countries), see Sellström (1999), vols 1 and 2.

63 Malaquias (2007): 72.

64 *Ibid.*: 42, 80–85; Crocker (1992).

as the US administration under Reagan adopted a pro-insurgency stance.[65] Over the years, UNITA had been a loyal partner in the struggle against the MPLA, and according to Schraeder, the US's support to UNITA amounted to US$60 million by the end of the 1980s.[66] However, this came to a halt in the early 1990s. Clearly, this had tremendous effect on UNITA. Instead of maintaining a close ally in the UNSC, UNITA was left with an influential country working against its interests. This needs to be kept in mind when assessing the efficacy of targeted sanctions.

Third, in order to understand the individual targeted sanctions, one also needs to keep in mind the wider political game. As it was imperative for the UN and some of its member states to have UNITA at the negotiating table, targeted sanctions became just one aspect of putting pressure on UNITA. For example, one interesting way of maintaining the pressure was the presence of the UN Angola Verification Mission (UNAVEM). UNAVEM had first been established in 1988, but was transformed into UNAVEM II to supervise elections. UNAVEM's presence in Angola was important for both the MPLA government and UNITA. For instance, not only could the government through UNAVEM verify that UNITA was being properly demobilised and disarmed, but also that it had properly handed over territories to government administration. For UNITA, UNAVEM certified that it was taking progressive steps, and prevented it being unjustly accused of failing to fulfil its part of the protocols. The UN did, however, on several occasions threaten not to deploy or not to prolong the UNAVEM missions. Clearly, this would have meant a return to full-scale war for both UNITA and the government. Not only did the opinion and decisions by the UNSC function as a tool to heighten the pressure, but also as an indicator of the political situation. If talks were successful and progress were made, UNAVEM's mission would have been prolonged. Similarly, if parties were uninterested in negotiations, threat was that the mission would cease.

Fourth, there was the important role played by the panel of experts and the UN Mechanism. After much unease in the UN about the impunity of UNITA in carrying out its activities, creative ideas were badly needed. Following Ambassador Fowler's fact-finding missions in early 1999, the UNSC decided in May that year (through UNSCR 1237), under the guidance of the Swedish Ambassador Anders Möllander, to establish a panel of experts to conduct investigations into violations of targeted sanctions in the areas of the arms trade, oil supplies, the diamond trade and the movement of UNITA funds. At the time, however, the cultural climate in the UN held that the work of the panel of experts was not expected to yield any results, so it faced some institutional challenges.[67]

The panel of experts met for the first time in New York in August 1999. Its role would be decisive, as it helped foster a debate in the UNSC on the role of targeted sanctions, sparking immediate implementation of some of the panel's

65 The US government's involvement was much influenced by the thinking of Henry Kissinger. For more on this, see Hanhimäki (2004): 403–26.

66 Schraeder (1992): 144.

67 Möllander (2001): 7.

recommendations to strengthening sanctions implementation.[68] During its investigation, the panel visited nearly 30 countries (meeting government officials, diplomats, NGOs, police and intelligence officials, journalists and industrial leaders).[69] Part of the investigation also included a number of interviews with UNITA defectors (which were taped at the UN Mission in Angola's headquarters, Villa Espa). The panel reports placed a lot of emphasis on the role of Jonas Savimbi in developments in Angola. In fact, his name is mentioned almost a hundred times in the 50-page report presented in 2000.

Understanding the evasion tactics is impossible without considering Savimbi's role. He was, after all, the leading intellectual figure in the movement. His views regarding political and financial operations (directly influencing the financial activities of UNITA and its members) were often obeyed in detail. Much of the work of the panel of experts had been prepared by the extensive reviews carried out by Ambassador Fowler, Chairman of the Angola Sanctions Committee. Ambassador Fowler worked hard to increase international awareness of the sanctions regime by engaging governments, regional organisations, international organisations and the private sector.[70] His work was considered groundbreaking for UN's efforts in strengthening the effectiveness of sanctions.

In retrospect, it has been concluded that the work of the panel of experts helped significantly to raise awareness of the situation and the sanctions.[71] The panel was also said to have had an impact on UNITA's capacity to pursue its war.[72]

Not to be underestimated for the sanctions outcome was the establishment of the UN Monitoring Mechanism by UNSCR 1295 (2000) of 18 April 2000. The purpose of this Mechanism was to collect additional information and investigate relevant leads related to any allegations of violations of measures contained in UNSCR 864 (1993), UNSCR 1127 (1997) and UNSCR 1173 (1998) on sanctions against UNITA. The establishment of the Mechanism followed the recognition that the imposition of sanctions alone, without the capacity to identify violators and monitor compliance, would be insufficient.[73] The UN Mechanism departed from the information which the panel of experts had collected. However, at the end of its work, one of the conclusions of the final reports of the UN Mechanism

68 Cortright and Lopez (2002a): 66–7.

69 S/2000/203, paras 7 and 8.

70 See, for instance, the work of Fowler in the Chairman's Report of the Angola Sanctions Committee: S/1999/829 and S/1999/64. The role of the Swedish Ambassador, Anders Möllander, should also be recognised here.

71 The importance of the UNITA Panel of Experts is also recognised in Boucher and Holt (2009): 10–11.

72 Möllander (2001): 8.

73 S/2001/966, 2001: 6. Further, the Mechanism not only reported sanctions-busting from its own investigations, but also co-operated with the Strategic and Operational Unit of the General Secretariat of INTERPOL, SADAC, the Wassenaar Arrangement, the World Customs Organisation, the UNDP, the UNHCR and the UN Office in Angola, and a private firm (Kroll Associates) to track UNITA's financial activities.

was that: 'the structures, objectives and strategy of the external representations remain to a large extent the same as those described in the report of the Panel of Experts'.[74]

These and the other factors considered above are merely the most basic and obvious ones that need to be included in any analysis seeking to determine the impact of targeted sanctions on the UNITA leadership. In order to further complement the analysis, we will now consider some insights from the perceptions of some former listed UNITA entities and their views on UN sanctions.

Interviewing Former Entities on the UNITA Sanctions List

During the Summer of 2007, a number of interviews were conducted with members of UNITA who had formerly been placed on the UNSC sanctions list.[75] The interviewees belonged to the inner elite of UNITA. Questions were open-ended in character, and were geared to deriving a better understanding of how sanctions were perceived and what kinds of impact they had.

Targets' Perceptions of UN Sanctions Policy

One important aspect of an effective sanctions regime is that targets must know that they are being watched by the UN. A relevant question in this context is to get a better sense of whether listed entities at the time of sanctions had actually been aware of their inclusion on the UN sanctions lists.

The responses revealed a varied set of experiences. For instance, one interviewee said that he never had access to the UN list. When he was shown the list during the interview, he said it was the first time he had ever seen it. This answer seems quite reasonable given that he had spent most of the time fighting in the Angolan countryside, and therefore would not necessarily have known about the list, let alone been in a position to react to it: 'I was a military commander throughout the war and was at the war front all time. I left for the bush in 1974 and stayed there until 2002.' The way he came to know about the UN sanctions was over the radio. In another interview, another former target was equally under-informed about the sanctions lists, stating that he had only limited information about the personal conditions set out the list, stating, inter alia, that he 'never knew that his name was on the list'. Further, he alleged: 'No one told me that my name was on the list. It is true that I on several occasions heard that sanctions had been put on UNITA and that there was a list of names, but I never saw it ....' What is clear here is that ensuring notification had not yet been an established practice in the UN's sanctions strategy.

74 S/2000/1225, para. 73.

75 All references to my interviewees have been kept anonymous. A more detailed reference list can be located in earlier versions of this study.

A rather sharp contrast regarding awareness of the sanctions policy became clear in another respondent's answer. On the specific question of how he was informed about the sanctions, he stated that he held an important position as a representative in Washington.[76] This gave him a close view of the US government's standpoint on the sanctions:

> In 1993, I was in good contact with the US State Department and especially with Mr. [X]. He informed me that I should be aware that a sanctions list was being created. He also wanted my passport in order to take a copy of it. The purpose was to provide the information to the UN Sanctions Committee. So I knew even from the beginning that I was being placed on the sanctions list. The process of establishing the detailed list started as far back as in 1997 .... We also had the [UN] list in its different stages ... we were very aware of the list. Perhaps the UN made sure that we knew of its formation as to involve us in a guessing game, a subtle threat if you want.

This comment suggests that the position of the target in the organisation could have a great bearing on his or her awareness about the targeted sanctions. Another respondent also revealed a similar level of awareness of the sanctions. He recalled being informed about them by UNITA's outside representatives, in particular at the UN, who followed daily events, but also via international broadcasts:

> The world is complicated, especially in the field of international politics. We all had our friends and enemies. We got the sanctions list very early on from the UN. One of the persons providing the information was our representative .... He used to get all information from the UN. In this way we knew all the steps of the sanctions policy, for instance which member state in the UN Security Council that supported us, even behind closed doors.

In view of this reply, it seems important that the sender consider the function as well as location of each target in a movement when seeking to achieve political impact, as such factors have a great influence on the actual impact of sanctions. For instance, if one is placed on a list while conducting military warfare on the ground, awareness of being included on a list does not seem very likely, thus impeding sanctions' impact.

The role and function of a target is also likely to affect the perception of the sanctions. For example, if the target is a military commander, it is not impossible that targeted sanctions will be considered just another means of warfare against the movement or the organisation. On the other hand, if the person listed is a diplomat, the sanctions could be understood as part of regular international affairs. However, random targeting may not prove to be the best option, as some persons may not be

76 On being asked who he thought had compiled the list, he replied that it was the Angolan government, which had later passed it on to the UN Sanctions Committee.

aware of their inclusion on the sanctions lists. This may reduce the impact of travel bans or assets freezes, and in the long run the prospects for behavioural change.

When asked about their general viewpoint on targeted sanctions and why these had been imposed, various perceptions were displayed. In particular, the interviewees brought up aspects such as their view of sanctions as more oriented towards UNITA as a group, rather than them personally, that sanctions had been unjustly imposed, that sanctions also led to a number of unintended consequences, and that the UNSC wanted to put pressure on the movement through the use of sanctions.

All of the interviewees perceived the UN's targeted sanctions to be directed against UNITA, and not against themselves as individuals.[77] For instance, one former entity formulated it in the following way:

> These sanctions were never personal, it was only collective sanctions. That was the case. Individual? No, not at all! I think that individual sanctions can only be applied if you are a government member. Only then can you be put on the list, that is, if you for example rob from the people, like in the case of Robert Mugabe of Zimbabwe.

The view that sanctions were not personally oriented was a recurring theme throughout the interviews. Another viewpoint of this kind was the following:

> The idea was to intimidate the individuals of UNITA into an agreement, but again these were not personal sanctions. It was a list to tell the UNITA that unless you negotiate the international community will ban you. These sanctions also became a tool for the government, a tool of their war against us. It was called targeted sanctions, but they were blunt sanctions. All the sanctions were placed on UNITA. It was not against me, but against the office.

Another former entity held that he was included on the list simply because he was a UNITA representative. The strategy was, from his point of view, based on the sender's desire to marginalise the movement.

As has been noted elsewhere, the shift from comprehensive to targeted sanctions came about because of the unintended consequences of broader sanctions. Despite such ethical aims, some respondents suggested that the measures directed at UNITA had broader consequences. For example, one

---

77 For example, one target said: 'I was really astonished by this. I did not know that people knew of me. We always believed ourselves to be so discrete, but suddenly your name gets mentioned on a list like this, that is public to the entire world. I was really surprised by this. I know now that some people in the UNITA had defected to the MPLA at the time, and that they helped the other side to localise us. The MPLA also made use of their embassies abroad to monitor our activities, that's why it became obvious that they knew about me.'

interviewee said that during the civil war, when UNITA held certain parts of Angola under its control, it was solely responsible for obtaining food, clothes, and war, school and hospital supplies for the population under its auspices. In fact, the population was dependent on UNITA. Another collateral consequence was that sanctions forced several Angolan students studying in different parts of Africa to end or interrupt their studies, partly because of the fact that UNITA – which was their main sponsor – could not support them under the sanctions ban. A third type of negative consequence was that UNITA's ability to pursue effective negotiation was impeded. One example of this is the following: 'Our diplomats could not move. For example, leaders of UNITA were prior to the sanctions working at the Vatican in Rome in order to find solutions to the war. But this work became much more complicated as a result of the sanctions.' One former target was convinced that the sanctions imposed had in fact contributed to prolonging the war, arguing that if sanctions had not been applied, a much earlier settlement could have been possible without the cost of so many lives.

In sum, then, contrary to the conventional wisdom in the scholarly literature on sanctions that suggests that *targeted* sanctions have a limited impact, it is apparent that the strategy had broader implications in practice.[78] Targeting the leadership of the organisation – by limiting the ability of UNITA representatives to acquire arms, food, petroleum, medicines, money, and so on – had an impact on UNITA's functions as a social movement providing services to the population under its control. On the other hand, this needs to be contrasted with the fact that the sitting government in Luanda could have provided for these needs had it not been under attack by UNITA. Another consequence, at least in the opinion of one interviewee, was that the targeted sanctions prolonged the conflict longer than necessary. Not only could sanctions motivate listed entities to take an even more stubborn attitude, they could also undermine effective negotiations by preventing targets from travelling to meetings that would seek further negotiations seeking a solution to the conflict. Although the responses do not represent all members of the movement, they do make the current understanding of targeted sanctions more complex.

Regarding the unfairness of the sanctions, one former listed entity compared the measures against UNITA to a boxing match, but one where the 'judge has tied the hands of one boxer so that the opponent could hit him as much as he wanted'. Another aspect relating to unfairness pin-pointed by the target was that although there was an arms embargo (on both sides), 'how come then that the MPLA could continue to import arms? The international community looked the other way.' A number of targets held the view that the UNSC sided with one party over the other.

---

78 Cortright and Lopez suggest that the humanitarian misery in Angola resulted primarily from war, not from sanctions: 'The sanctions were neither sufficiently broad nor comprehensive to cause serious humanitarian hardships'; Cortright and Lopez (2000): 158.

Moreover, there was also the view that sanctions came about in an untimely manner. One former target put it like this:

> I never understood why the United Nations put us under sanctions. We were in the midst of war with the MPLA. At the time when there was an election, the UN thought it would be very important to hold talks with the government. However, we were in a very difficult position because after the first round of the election we in UNITA were not satisfied. We wanted to speak with the government in order to discuss and set the conditions for peace in our country. However, the MPLA did not like this. In 1992, several members, especially the high-ranking members of UNITA were killed here in Luanda. While we had hoped that we after the election could find common ground with the MPLA in order to get peace, no such success took place ....

This statement indicates that talking and establishing mutual trust to settle differences is cumbersome and requires time. These efforts were undermined by the sanctions of 1993. This is in sharp contrast to the viewpoint held by the UNSC that UNITA did not want to engage in serious dialogue (because there was fatigue over UNITA's slow process in committing to peace).[79] Another former target felt that sanctions were put in place because it was considered by the UN that UNITA did not generally honour its agreements:

> [In 1996] ... I met with the UN Secretary-General. He complained to Dr. Savimbi that many of the issues which had been discussed and agreed upon [during the peace negotiations] were not respected, something that made the international community very upset. In my view however, it was the MPLA that forced the UN to expand the sanctions to cover also the UNITA representations abroad. But [the pressure] ... started very early. Even when I was in Bonn, the German government tried to expel me. [In this case,] it was the MPLA that pushed the German government to do so. They also actively lobbied the UN. Also, [a particular member] of the UK foreign office worked hard to make sanctions effective.

In their understanding of why sanctions were put in place, there was a clear viewpoint that the motivation had been to cut UNITA off from its political and economic activities. A typical remark was: 'It was a strategic move by the Angolan government to put us all on the list ... they wanted to cut off our activities.' A similar account was given by another former entity, suggesting that because of his extensive activities, which also included much travelling, he had to be targeted:

> I travelled a lot, I was travelling all over. This may be one reason, but everything was complex. States and organisations with great interest wanted to cut us off

79 UNSCR 864 (1993), 15 September 1993.

> from travelling. They did not want us to meet with influential people. During the introduction of the 1993 sanctions, I was in Angola, but I was travelling to various African countries. For instance, I went to Zambia on several occasions. The purpose was to get the negotiations to resume so that the conflict could be solved. Other similar journeys occurred between 1995 and 1999. Most of the time, however, I was in the bush together with Dr Savimbi.

Another comment pointed in the same direction: 'They put us on list because they wanted to cut our legs. They did not want us to give interviews abroad. You see, our colleagues abroad were so active.' The descriptions here suggest that the former UNITA targets were well aware that their political activity abroad was not contributing to the benefit of the UN, which sided with the MPLA in Luanda.

There were also some statements that suggested other reasons for the targeted sanctions. One respondent said that the Portuguese government had been particularly energetic in pushing for the sanctions, observing that the Portuguese ambassador to the UN was 'very emotional regarding the sanctions' and that 'It was almost personal for him.' He also said that the Portuguese policy smacked of racism: 'I also believe that the Portuguese view on this included a part of racism: "Let's punish the blacks since they are not listening to us."' A third view held that UNITA was targeted as a result of the policies of the two Cold War superpowers, which in their turn had been lobbied by groups with economic interests in the conflict, such as the oil industry.

In sum, the logic behind the UNSC's imposition of sanctions, at least in the view of some former listed entities, was to stop the activities of UNITA. They perceived sanctions as untimely, unfair and illegitimate. Now, in considering whether sanctions had an impact, one could argue that they sometimes did, albeit not precisely in the ways the international community intended.

Threat of Sanctions

One frequent argument in the sanctions literature is that the efficacy of sanctions is highly dependent on the existance of a prior threat.[80] If the sender threatens the target with sanctions, there is an opportunity for the target to reconsider its policies and adjust to the sender's demands to avoid their imposition. The opposite strategy to prior threat by the sender is to slap the target with a surprise (for example, to prevent the target from being able to move money around within the system or to deny a target passage through a customs airport). With such a policy, the target does not have the opportunity to comply. For both of these approaches to work effectively, though, they should preferably be applied on an individual basis.

In the case of UNITA, it seems that targeted sanctions were perceived more as targeted on the movement rather than against individuals. In fact, no interviewee

80 See the Threat and Imposition of Sanctions (TIES) dataset: <www.unc.edu/~bapat/TIES.htm>.

indicated that a personal threats had been made. With regard to prior threats, as one target described it:

> the international community thought in some sense that they could interact with the leadership [by publishing a sanctions list]. Anyway, we just saw it as the way the Security Council usually acted. From my point of view, sanctions were never made in the explicit form of a sanctions threat. On the other hand there was a kind of pressure on us to have us worry and thereby also to conform.

This comment suggests that sanctions were perceived as a more general form of pressure, and not a kind of bargaining strategy for each listed entity.

Reactions to Targeted Sanctions

One way of observing the impact of sanctions is to try to assess how individuals reacted to the realisation that they had been targeted. The interviews conducted on this aspect gave rise to quite disparate replies. For example, one target observed:

> Sanctions did not come as a surprise. We knew all along. In fact we got reinforced by the sanctions .... We were given a special status in international law. On the other hand, that sanctions were imposed was a normal evolution of politics that had only culminated with sanctions. The question for us, though, was how we should continue our work under them. Especially problematic was it that we could not travel easily.

Another former listed entity held that the sanctions did not really demand a response as they were seen more as a technical measures than anything else:

> It was a way to distribute our names to computer check-points all over the world. It was a way of saying that we were sanctioned. But the UN did not have any leverage on us. It was merely a political tool. How could they put pressure on us by including men that were out in the bush? These persons never travelled. They had no money in foreign accounts.

While these two comments do not necessarily capture the experience of all former targets, they still add to the general view that few persons included on the list were likely to make any particularly quick responses. Instead, sanctions were perceived as part of a general strategic calculation, and as a measure that was not likely to cause much pressure – or at least not too much. For instance, one strategy, which two of the targets referred to, was to convince the international community that sanctions were simply a bad policy adopted by the UN.[81] The

81 Interview conducted on 9 September 2007.

argument quite often relied on to promote this view was the suggestion that sanctions undermined dialogue:

> With sanctions you cut all lines of communications. Sanctions thus only meant more obstacles ... if the strategy of the UN on one side was a diplomatic move to put pressure on us, the consequences were more far-reaching as it also was perceived by the MPLA as a carte blanche for their activities in Angola. Having UN on their side, they could do whatever they wanted. Indirectly, the UN was responsible for killing many Angolans.

The question of whether they had a personal strategy to counter the sanctions gave rise to several comments. Most suggested that such responses never arose on a personal basis, but from the group as a whole. Moreover, reactions were seldom directed against specific measures imposed by the sender, but more as general policies to convince governments around the world to lift the sanctions. One former target suggested that the primary strategy was to contact various governments:

> Yes we had a strategy ... this consisted in contacting various European governments, Portugal, Russia, the US and others to clear our situation and to stop the sanctions. We also turned to African countries and friends to have them help us in lifting the sanctions. We talked to Mandela's South Africa, Togo, Ivory Coast, Burkina Faso, etc., in order to stop the sanctions.

Another strategy which was advanced was to try to sideline the impact of the sanctions through active evasion. This consisted of trying to circumvent the oil embargo in order to sustain UNITA's military capabilities:

> To survive, yes. We had a plan. We planned for them politically, diplomatically and economically. We had to. Internally, in Angola, this meant that we had to continue to do business in order to attain war material. For example, we had to get fuel for the war machinery. This was complicated with the sanctions. However, we had good experiences from the war with the Portuguese, experiences that we also used in the civil war. To get fuel we knew that business could continue with the MPLA generals. Also we would buy fuel from some wood cutters that worked in the countryside. With them we could do trade for petrol, etc.

Other details on this were also given:

> But you should also know that there were many affairs made between the generals of MPLA and UNITA. During the war, generals of the MPLA used to leave Luanda for example with fuel. In these cases, they said that they would dispatch these to their military bands. However, they took them to us in exchange for food and other things that they needed.

In examining these answers, two particular observations could be made. First of all, the interviewee was a field commander. His view of sanctions is likely to be seen through the lens of warfare – that is, sanctions are a military strategy by the opponent (the sender) aimed at undermining the capability of UNITA. Thus, it is quite rational, at least for a military commander, to try to get a hold of fuel to continue the war. Second, the interviewee never talked about personal strategies, but only tactics of the movement. This suggests that the separation between 'myself' (the target) and 'us' (the group or movement) is subtle.

When asked whether targeted sanctions had any kind of psychological impacts, either on those listed or the movement as a whole, a variety of answers were given. One interviewee said that the sanctions on UNITA forced him to lie low – that is, not to travel as he would otherwise have done – observing that, 'During these years, my prison was the whole of America.' Another former target said that the sanctions on him and his family made life as a foreign UNITA representative much more difficult:

> Personally, I had to leave my nice house in central Abidjan and find a smaller house for me and my family in the surroundings of Abidjan. This came as a result that we could not afford to pay the rent. Indeed I suffered because I noticed how sad my wife and children were. While initially the Ivorian President Houphouët-Boigny helped us with money, since he was generally favourable and supportive of UNITA, his follower, Henri Konan Bedie was not so helpful ....

Moreover, the former listed entity held that:

> Me and my family never saw the sanctions taking a human side ... moreover, I was not alone with my wife and my children in Abidjan, I also had under me the responsibility of several UNITA students studying there. I took care of them by providing them with scholarships as well as taking care of people which needed health care, especially at the time when we had problem of obtaining food and medicines. Many times I asked myself why the UN had taken such hard and inhumane decision, as many people were dependent on us and consequently suffering when we could not perform our role. I and my people suffered from the interest of foreign powers. The foreign powers were much more concerned with economic interests rather than the human beings that were affected by the sanctions ... the victims.

Other respondents suggested that the sanctions made them feel 'pushed up against the wall' and gave them the will to fight back harder, or that they boosted their morale, as was noted by one target:

> For me personally? No! I knew that this was part of our struggle. I could never let myself become frustrated. If you become frustrated, then you cannot take a step forward. I took the sanctions as part of an everyday struggle. I had to

> be prepared psychologically and physically for the struggle. Some members of UNITA got frustrated. Some died frustrated. I never become frustrated. We had reached the top of the mountain and we fell from it. This was very frustrating for some.

One of the interviewees also felt stressed by the fact that the UN embargo made it difficult for UNITA to acquire medicines, as he said he suffered from diabetes:

> I have diabetes and need insulin every day. But when under sanctions, it was not possible to attain these kinds of medicines. You know, [Mr. X on the sanctions list] died in the bush as he also suffered from diabetes.

When asked about the possible psychological impact of the UN's targeted sanctions, he replied:

> Yes they had. You know in order to function properly in world affairs, it is very important that you can travel. We had several UNITA students around the world, both in Europe and in Africa. Moreover, some people worked to get medicines for our country, but as they could not travel, these activities got disturbed and made the situation very difficult for us.

As noted in the literature overview, an important aspect of the current debate on sanctions is how targeted entities get listed and de-listed. This debate touches upon the procedures for removing a target from the sanctions list, in terms of the mechanisms and the target's rights. However, at the time of the Angolan sanctions regime, de-listing had not yet become a significant factor in the debate in the UN. With the opportunity to interview UNITA members, it was interesting to explore whether the former targets ever considered engaging the senders on this matter. The responses, however, pointed in the same direction as many others in this case study, namely that the perception of the targets was that sanctions were more directed towards the movement than them personally. Perhaps symptomatic of this is the answer given by one target on this matter, where he only referred to UNITA, and not to a personal effort to free himself from the measures:

> Frankly speaking, there was no space for this. We tried to denounce the sanctions on several occasions. For instance, we tried to explain to many foreign governments that imposing sanctions was a bad policy option. In a way sanctions brought out the worst out of UNITA I would say. It created among us a certain sense that the international community was against us, which also brought out the worst of us. For instance it made us not want to negotiate, and in this sense it destroyed chances to create solutions for negotiations. Playing the sanctions game was really bad for all sides I believe ....

If there ever was a strategy per se, this seems mostly to have consisted of trying to have UNITA as a whole removed from the list. As mentioned by several targets, the main tactic was writing letters to various government administrations (and not for personal reasons).

Part of the sanctions strategy towards UNITA was to put pressure not only on UNITA members, but also on their families. An analysis of the various responses during the interviews suggests that family impact did occur (though it is difficult to distinguish between direct impact and indirect, more abstract forms of impact). How this was manifested in events was very subjective and context-specific. For instance, one respondent said he had two sons in the Ivory Coast during 1997, but because of the sanctions they had to interrupt their studies. In most responses, though, there were signs of strong indignation when being asked about family impact. Comments in this respect included:

> I did not want my kids to be punished. I think sanctions like these mean that the international communities deprive people of their human rights. My kids were Americans, except my first daughter who was born in London .... In a way, sanctions penalized the kids through association.

and

> I don't understand how a child can be placed on a sanctions list just because of the activities of his father. In my view a child should not pay the price of what the father has done. Regarding my own activities, I was never really in contact with my family until the end of the war, when they came to Luanda. My family stayed in Brussels – my son was born there – but I could not come and visit them. It was terrible, especially for the kids. They wondered why they were put under sanctions. Perhaps one day we should raise this question again. It affected them psychologically.

Further, he also held that the family sanctions had been put in place because the supporters of the sanctions wanted those on the list to be flown back to Luanda. In his view, this would have led to a propaganda victory for the MPLA government (as had been the case, for instance, when Jonas Savimbi's son was forced back to Angola from Togo).

Targets' Perception of the Travel Ban

In several UN reports, it was claimed that some UNITA members were able to travel to various capitals around the world without major problems despite being targeted by the travel ban. However, one interviewee gave an example of an incident where one listed UNITA member had experienced problems when he could not leave Paris for London, where his family was living – something that he in retrospect found stupid. In a proportion of cases, the travel ban manages to prevent targets from travelling due to the chances of their being stopped at customs checkpoints, causing embarrassment and not least a general sense of insecurity. In addition, one interviewee said that he had tried to remain in his country of residence (outside Angola) in order to avoid the risk of being stopped and confronted at the border. In another case, the target had decided not to travel at all as a result of the travel ban (on the other hand, the target was already outside Angola, working as a representative for UNITA).[82] The decision not to travel, it seems, came as a result of being told not to do so by UNITA's leadership:

> For instance during my time in Abidjan, I was always able to travel to Togo. But as the sanctions came, the UNITA leadership told me to stay put. They did not want us to embarrass the authorities of the countries were we were staying. Personally, I did not dare to travel under different passports or different names ....

Clearly, the travel ban did matter, although its effects on targets varied. Given that the travel ban and the other measures of the sanctions had been put in place against UNITA, what was the concrete impact? One example of direct impact was given in the following account.

> Since sanctions were applied we could not travel and thus not be engaged in activities abroad. For instance, the government of Ivory Coast asked us in 1999 to close our bureau. You see, we never operated very visible, I mean, we did not have a sign stating that this was UNITA's bureau. We worked at the plateau of Abidjan. Our office was located next-door to the local Ivory Coast administration. Anyway, they told us kindly to close it down. Their argument was that 'the UN did not agree with you, and since we are members of the UN, we cannot allow you to work officially. If you want to stay then please provide us with your passports'. The government was very smart, I think, because they had our passports by telling us that they wanted to renew them, due to expiration. They said we could come back and pick them up in a few days. When leaving the office, we understood that we would never get them back.

Although some targets decided to lie low, others decided to continue with their activities as much as possible. For example, one respondent said that he was more or less a frequent flyer, and that the various UNITA representatives around the world would help him to travel (often with the consent of the local administration):

> I had several passports ... from Morocco, Ivory Coast and Senegal – you see we had a lot of friends in the world. In order to understand this, one has to analyse

82 Although it cannot be clearly determined whether he ever travelled at all, if he did not, then this could be construed as a change of target behaviour (although not on the level of change in the sense of compliance).

> things from a Cold War context. Everything worked during the Cold War. We had a lot of friends. The principle was simple. The allies' allies are my friends. We used to co-operate closely with many different security services .... If we wanted passports, then we just asked for [them]. I remember one time when I was travelling from Lisbon to Madrid on a passport that was Moroccan. I had an Arabic name in that passport. As I was waiting to go to the gate, I did not realise that the airport was calling out my passport name for the boarding procedure. I missed the plane ....

When asked whether it was a risky business for governments to receive targeted persons, the same respondent answered: 'Well, leaders in the region at this time were willing to help provide a solution to the conflict. Therefore they also helped to provide space for us.' When asked whether these friendly governments took immense risks receiving him, he answered:

> It is right that friendly governments took a risk in receiving us, but they also had an interest in helping us. By receiving us, they got informed about what was going on. Receiving us meant that they were given a platform. We were never able to travel to European countries though.

Another former target gave a similar account:

> Some of us travelled with passports from Zaire. We also had passport from Ivory Coast. Sometimes we even travelled with service passports [the second in rank from diplomatic passports]. Personally, I never travelled with different names ... other UNITA members did .... I always used my name. OK, the French mixed [up] my last and first name every now and then .... I personally never had problem to travel. For instance, I went to France, Germany, and Portugal on different occasion. The French government always knew, French President Mitterrand always knew .... We were vocal and we were all well known. We co-operated with many secret services. When we travelled we always saw them, but they pretended they never saw us.

It was even held that sometimes the targets' hosts benefited from having them around. One target also admitted to having ignored the travel ban:

> For instance, I was under sanctions ... but I did not leave Germany until 1999. I was not living as a hidden person. On the contrary, I was very vocal. The government tried to put pressure on me but not too seriously. They needed us. For example, the German government was given much information [from us] about what was going on in Angola. They knew that our information was more credible than the information provided by the Angolan embassy. The German government could easily confirm what we were saying. This is true. Kohl knew this also.

Hence, it seems that the imposition of targeted sanctions did not push him out of this role; rather, the contrary. The fact that UNITA had representation in Germany was obviously a breach of the UNSCR, but it also highlighted the type of information reciprocity that existed between UNITA and the host government. This perception certainly informs our general understanding of targeted sanctions.

To conclude, the travel ban seems to have made a difference in at least two aspects. On the one hand, travelling per se was not likely to be seen as a serious problem. Not only was this reflected in the interviews, but also reported by findings of the UN monitoring teams. In fact, some answers above disclose that there were often mutual relationships between targets and their host governments (such as on information exchange and/or strategic co-operation). On the other hand, while several targets were able to travel on fake passports (and seemingly were caught on occasions), some targets decided to keep a low profile because of the ban (for instance, in order not to upset allies). Judging from the interviews, it also seems obvious that the host government's attitude towards the target is vital when considering the role of target impact. As noted above, some interviewees maintained that they felt political pressure following international calls on UN member states to expel UNITA members, but several targets felt comfortable because of their host government's often relaxed attitude towards them. Yet other targets perceived an almost aggressive attitude from certain governments. In all, then, the host government's attitude towards the movement mattered a great deal, as it determined the success or failure of its enforcement activities.[83]

Targets' Perception of the Assets Freeze

During the course of the UNITA sanctions regime, the UN Monitoring Mechanism devoted a lot of resources to investigating UNITA's financial network. Despite such efforts, only small amounts of money were frozen. An obvious reason for this was that UNITA depended on informal economic processes. Rather than using the formal economic system, they often relied on cash or minerals . One respondent gave a few examples of how such a system worked:

> For the bureau in Abidjan, we used to get money directly through an aerial bridge. It was a plane that periodically took many people in and out of Angola carrying everything from journalists to students to politicians [suggesting that money was brought along during these trips]. As an outside representation, we had our budget. Every bureau had a budget. However, the money transferred stopped in 1998 as the aerial bridge stopped. On the eve of the sanctions, the

83 Note, though, that if a state is allowing targets to operate, the state is likely to be evading sanctions itself (as is forbidden by UNSCR). However, it should also be noted that aiding targets, for instance by giving them entrance into the country or lodging and harbouring them, may not only result from pure self-interest, but from a belief or perception of facilitating peace.

> UNITA gave us a higher amount of money than usual. The leadership told us to be careful with it. It was an amount that gave us a chance to survive one or two years ....

It was also argued that things would run more smoothly prior to the imposition of targeted sanctions, implying that the pressure resulting from this policy increased over time. This was particularly the case at the beginning of the sanctions regime, as UNITA was still sending money to its foreign representatives through transaction routes that had to be changed because of the measures.

Despite being asked about how the financial management was pursued, none of the interviewees members could provide information about the specific amounts of assets that had been frozen as a result of the sanctions. Although aware that the UN sanctions Committee and member states of the UN had searched for UNITA money all over the world, one respondent said that the international community never found anything except some money belonging to 'some kids in London and Lisbon'. He also felt that there was a relatively relaxed implementation of sanctions, saying: 'The US never went to implement personal sanctions. On the contrary they just wanted a general implementation.'[84] However, the interviewee did establish that specific targets had their private money caught up in the system:

> Personally, I had an account in Bonn at some stage ... about US$3,000–4,000. This money was never blocked or confiscated. Once, I experienced a problem when I was transferring money from Lisbon. This was in 2001. They blocked it and I lost the money. But it was just a small sum.

Despite being troubling for the target, these examples do not lend themselves to any observations on how it effected their political behaviour.

The absence of considerable economic damage to UNITA is further explained by the fact that UNITA did not hold much money in either banks or real estate:

> UNITA had no money and no buildings. So in this sense the sanctions did not affect us at all. It was Dr Savimbi's belief that we should not have money abroad. Only a little money was transferred and kept abroad, mainly to sustain our foreign representation. I think as little as US$2,000 was frozen.

Another reply also alluded to this:

> Well, during the sanctions period 1993–2002, the UNITA had no real money in the banks. There was only little money placed in banks during this time. Prior to the sanctions though, UNITA mainly had its money put into British banks. Our cashier, i.e. our secretary for financial matters, was himself based in London.

---

84 Interview conducted on 31 August 2007.

> From here, he could send money to various parts of the world. The money hence was mostly received by friendly nations as UNITA 'knocked doors'.

One of the main conclusions of the UN reports is that UNITA mostly used diamonds when paying for its activities:[85]

> It is true though that we received a lot of money from the diamonds. There were a lot of blood diamond and bloody oil around. If you are familiar with the French Falcone case, this illustrates much how it worked here. It illustrates the complexities of the Angolan conflicts. For example, if we needed arms, the sellers just came to us. In Andulo [Angola] we built a very nice airport. It was properly made. It was illuminated and 3,000 metres long. Even large Boeing airplanes could land there. So they just came there, landed, took money and we got the equipment that we needed. We kept a good registration of everyone coming and going.

Interestingly, diamonds were not only used to buy new arms, but also for other purposes:

> Well, even if we managed to get US$50 billion [from the diamonds] this would not cover the expenses to support a big part of the country. We had to administrate ourselves, schools, hospitals, armaments, medicines, communication equipment, administration, etc. This was indeed a demanding apparatus.

In conclusion, as reflected in these interviews, most targets maintained that little money was moved around in the established economic system. This suggests that a general assets freeze as a UN strategy may not be the best option, or at least should not be the only option, in cases where the sender wants to undermine individuals and groups constituting a real threat to international peace and security. Yet, as was noted above – and this probably had to do with the fact that the UN also tracked UNITA's dealings in the diamond trade – UNITA did suffer from sanctions. Not only are there indications that UNITA suffered on the group level, but also that it felt pressured on the personal level. The interviews also confirm both direct and symbolic impacts.

A Final Observation

Sanctions on UNITA seem to have had both a direct and an indirect impact. One example of direct impact is the fact that some targets refrained from travelling because of an unwillingness to embarrass allies' host governments through their presence. This obviously weakened, or at least undermined, UNITA's visibility, as

85 The role of diamonds in civil war is a well-covered topic; see, for instance, Billon (2005), Campbell (2002), and Cilliers and Dietrich (2000).

well as its capacity to campaign actively for its political cause. Another example is that various friends and allies seem to have refrained from contacting individual UNITA members, thus reducing personal contacts, and thereby limiting its various public support campaigns. Indirectly, or at a psychological level, sanctions seems to have caused annoyance, which means as impact was felt, but this did not necessarily contribute to a behavioural change or undermine UNITA's political activities. For example, the imposition of a travel ban caused some grievances among the targets and their families (for example, some children of listed entities had to abandon their university education). Situation like this, as well as other similar ones, may certainly have contributed to the target's experience of annoyance. Yet it is difficult to conclude that they changed their political behaviour because of the targeted sanctions. In fact, there are indications that some targets never understood the reasons for or the conditions of the sanctions.

Regarding target behaviour, two categories of reaction are particularly distinguishable: non-deliberate and deliberate. The non-deliberate behavioural strategies are actions that are not a deliberate response to the sender's measures, but are simply behaviour that seeks to find alternative avenues in order to ease their impact. Such moves could not be judged as a clear sign of defiance, but more as reasonable and realistic acts to circumvent impact. For instance, seeking citizenship in the country of residence at the time of targeting (as was done by one target) or lobbying for the de-listing by writing to various governments which may have leverage on the sanctions process (as had sometimes been done, although for the entire movement rather than on a personal level) are examples of reasonable behaviours rather than pure target defiance.

The more elaborate and calculated behaviours, on the other hand, were deliberate counter-sanctions strategic behaviours which involved, for example, travelling on different passports or under different names, placing money in safe havens, trading in rough diamonds to escape possible financial investigation and a targeted assets freeze, and using makeshift airports to transport money and people. These intentional moves, although defiant in nature, are not necessarily malevolent and defiant in themselves, but can be seen as rational and logical acts to enable activities to continue, despite the fact that others may not see it that way.[86]

Conclusion

Given the empirical aspects brought up in this chapter, answering the question of whether sanctions can be described as a success or failure in the UNITA targeted

86 Aside from these two active' behavioural strategies (intended or unintended), there is also the possibility of non-active target behaviour. This situation is likely to be observed when the target is not actually experiencing a direct impact, as would be the case, for instance, with a target that is out in the bush (not travelling or not involved in the modern financial system).

sanctions regime undeniably poses a difficult challenge. The reason is that there are so many inter-related variables that affect such a judgement. Not only are there an immense number of background variables affecting the political outcome, but there are also a number of variables that are determined by the sender and target independently of each other (those that are pre-determined by the sender's management of sanctions management and by the target's perceptions and decision to respond to the sanctions in a variety of ways). The complexity of all these inter-related factors simply does not allow for an either/or judgment. Yet where one is able to assign success or failure, the verdict would most likely point to a very weak decision, and one that is vulnerable to much criticism. Cortright and Lopez (2000) demonstrate an example of this difficulty, where they on one hand conclude that the UNITA regime was a failure,[87] yet two years later, after re-examining the case, they change their minds, concluding that the sanctions had begun as half-hearted measures, but they had become increasingly effective over time.[88] The judgement of a case as either a success or failure clearly presents a methodological problem. Most likely, such verdicts are highly subjective. The problem with assessing the impact of sanctions and understanding behavioural change is that it requires the exclusion of a number of variables in order to make the analysis manageable. By doing so, however, one also risks excluding a number of important explanatory factors.

Determining success or failure is also difficult as a measurement approach. The reason is that there are often many different types of factors that could be evaluated in a sanctions regime: the performance and decision-making of the sender, the ability of the sender to achieve its goals, the ability to cause target impact, the larger strategic paradigm operating in the background (the UNSC during different periods using directly or indirectly strategic measures such as containment, deterrence or coercion to put pressure on UNITA), and so on.

In the end, the overall goal is often forgotten: namely, that despite sanctions, civilians continue to be killed because of a war. This fact also raises the question that other indicators such as the number of refugees, food shortages, level of violence, number of displaced persons need to be considered in any serious sanctions assessment.[89] For instance, while the UNITA sanctions regime was highly successful in terms of detecting and reporting failures of implementation, this does not escape the fact that for instance in 1999, an estimated 200 people were killed every day because of the war. Such indicators suggest that the sanctions policy did not have the effect it should have done.[90]

Moreover, as was shown by looking into the various episodes, we cannot conclude that the personal sanctions (or indeed the UNITA sanctions) had

87 Cortright and Lopez (2000): 162.

88 Cortright and Lopez (2002a): 71.

89 Cortright and Lopez (2000) allude to some of these aspects; see, for example, ibid.: 157.

90 Prendergast (2000).

any particular effect on the dynamics of the armed conflict. This is at least the case if we see the goal of targeted sanctions as leading to behavioural changes that would lead to the resolution of armed conflict. Such an observation also relates to a wider methodological question of how one considers causality when determining the effectiveness of sanctions. On the other hand, it cannot be ruled out that the travel ban or the targeted financial sanctions did have implicit effects, as they were felt and continuously referred to by the targets. After all, we will never know how the war in Angola would have developed without the UN's adoption of targeted sanctions.

With regard to the travel ban's impact, targets could travel between different countries, with or without passports, or operate through various UNITA representatives, or behind the disguise of front organisations. Targets were also identified and pressured on the basis of their support functions for UNITA. With regard to financial sanctions, UNITA's access to money did begin to dry up over time because of the pressure exerted by the UNSC. There are several indications, both in the literature as well as the interviews, that money and property were frozen in practice. This was a strategic achievement for the sender. On the other hand, it is difficult to conclude that the targeting per se changed the behaviour of individual members of UNITA, or UNITA's official policy. The stigma of being included on a public name-and-shame list should not be underestimated. During the interviews, the psychological impact could be observed and seemed to matter a great deal, both on a personal level and on a movement-wide one.

The importance of other prevailing factors cannot be over-emphasised when seeking to better understand targets' reactions and behaviour, and how these are complementary to the effects of targeted sanctions. For example, one factor that could easily be overlooked is the nature of UNITA as a movement. Its identity as a black nationalist top-led insurgency group could partially explain the impact of sanctions. Operating during the Cold War, and as a product of it, UNITA's attitude towards international actors and the UNSC may well explain its political behaviour. UNITA was a skilful player, which over the years learned to deal with regional and international superpowers with great sophistication. Circumventing sanctions or finding temporary allies to help deal with increasing pressure were routes quickly adopted and used in various policy strategies. The influence of sanctions also needs to be assessed on the basis of the repeated threats made against UNITA. In particular, the deployment, or threat of deployment, of UNAVEM's forces seems to have had an impact on UNITA's political and strategic behaviour. Equally important was the role of the UN Mechanism and the panel of experts, which built international awareness and pressure on UNITA throughout the sanctions regime.

Finally, while the findings here (although not representing the views of the entire movement) suggest that targeted sanctions were imposed to put pressure on the movement rather than on the listed individuals, there are reasons to believe that personal impact also mattered a great deal. For example, the role of UNITA and its attitude towards the international or the regional community cannot be understood unless targeted sanctions against an individual such as Jonas Savimbi are taken into account. Although it operated as a group, UNITA needs to be understood through the behaviour and influence of separate individuals such as Savimbi.[91] To some extent, it could be argued that the leadership of UNITA, especially at the very top, de-individualised other members in the movement.[92] A number of activities and policies of UNITA must therefore be understood from the point of view of certain key actors.

Lastly, while measures were imposed to target the movement as a whole, there were also signs that the UN to a certain extent had individuals in mind when pursuing sanctions. In fact, the shift from publishing a general note stating that all senior UNITA members and their families should be targeted to a more specific list with names of individual targets suggests that the UNSC was, after all, interested in affecting specific individuals rather than the entire cadre. This is further strengthened by the fact that the UN Mechanism, the body that monitored and evaluated the implementation of the targeted sanctions, on a number of occasions publicly stated that the quality of the name list was a problem.

91 The argument for paying attention to individual leaders is contested. While it has been claimed here that sanctions' impact is shaped by target decision-makers, scholars such as Greenhill and Major (2007) suggest that it may be the circumstances that shape these entities role in the conflict (and not vice versa).

92 Malaquias even speaks of a 'personal cult'; Malaquias (2007): 97. Hodges also notes that Jonas Savimbi held absolute power in the movement, in the manner of a cult leader, and that his pre-eminent role also explains much of the dynamics of the conflict and the attitude UNITA held towards members of the UN: 'Besides the rivalry over access to resources and the general problem of mutual lack of confidence, a key factor has been the psychological make-up of Jonas Savimbi. His role in the Angolan conflict confirms the importance of the individual in history'; Hodges (2001): 19.

Chapter 8
EU Sanctions Decision-making

In recent years, an increasing number of academic studies have been devoted to EU restrictive measures (hereafter referred to as 'EU targeted sanctions').[1] Yet none of these has explained in detail how institutional design and practice in itself has shaped policy outcomes.[2]

Formal Management

The principles underlying the use of EU targeted sanctions are laid out in the *Basic Principles on the Use of Restrictive Measures (Sanctions)*,[3] where targeted sanctions are recognised as an important instrument for maintaining and restoring international peace and security in accordance with the UN Charter and the Common Foreign and Security Policy (CFSP). The use of targeted sanctions is specified to tackle issues like terrorism, the proliferation of weapons of mass destruction, and to uphold respect for human rights, democracy and the rule of law (that is, good governance). As stated above, targeted sanctions should be deployed in a flexible manner and on a case-by-case basis, and should be subject to regular review to achieve maximum impact.

Another document is the *Guidelines on Implementation and Evaluation of Restrictive Measures*.[4] Not only does this key framework lay out the strategic principles behind the use of EU targeted sanctions, but it also indicates how and when sanctions should be considered. Further to this, the EU Council has also distributed a best practice document, the *EU Best Practices for the Effective Implementation of Restrictive Measures*.[5] The recommendations it contains provide EU member states with a checklist of best practices, including suggestions on how to improve the process of designation and the identification of targeted entities (for example, the listing and de-listing of targeted entities).

---

1 See Anthony (2002), Hazelzet (2001), Portela (2008) and Giumelli (2009).

2 The Treaty of Lisbon, or the Reform Treaty, was signed by the EU member states on 13 December 2007 and entered into force on 1 December 2009. Some of the goals as well as working methods of in EU in the context of EU sanctions are currently being subjected to change.

3 Council of the European Union (June 2007).

4 Council of the European Union, (December 2005).

5 Council of the European Union (November 2005), since updated on several occasions.

These documents formulate the basis for the daily design of EU sanctions policies as well as contributing to synchronising the language for the establishment of various sanctions regimes (for example, by recommending standard wording in the official texts). In this sense, institutional features such as these documents and agreed-upon definitions play quite a substantial role in the design of the EU's sanctions programmes. One could even argue that they to some extent also determine the impact of sanctions, as guideline documents define the contours of the policy at an early stage. For instance, the inclusion of standard wording renders the sanctions policy static as opposed to flexible. This, for instance, makes it very difficult for the EU to be flexible in responding to continuously changing political dynamics on the ground. Clearly, this shapes the 'identity' of a sanctions regime.

The EU's Implementation of UN Sanctions Regimes

The Foreign Relations Counsellors Working Group (FRCWG) of the European Council carries out most of the daily work on sanctions in the EU (as well as the sanctions team at the Commission's Directorate-General for External Relations, DG RELEX). These national representatives negotiate the text of sanctions on the basis of instructions they receive from member states. In the FRCWG, representatives from the Commission and the Council are present. Depending on which aspects of the sanctions text are being negotiated, different representatives of DG RELEX take part. In addition to other CFSP-related issues on their agenda, the FRCWG is involved in all legal matters involving sanctions. The counsellors meet to draft policies and negotiate the texts of the positions outlining the sanctions regimes, almost on a daily basis.

To support the work of the Council, a Sanctions Formation has been established. This is constituted of the same members as the FRCWG, but usually seconded by national experts from relevant ministries of EU member states. The mandate to set up this formation was given by the Permanent Representatives Committee (COREPER) in early 2004. The task of the formation is further to monitor and evaluate the EU's restrictive measures.[6] This involves, for example, exchanging information and experiences concerning the implementation of specific restrictive measures regimes imposed by the EU. Since the establishment of this formation, a number of best practices has been developed, as noted above, to provide further guidelines on how to deal with different aspects of targeting (such as procedures on judicial freezing, identification of designated persons, claims concerning mistaken identity, and individual notification).[7] Yet work of the formation is based on a meeting format that rarely allows for any deeper reflective analysis, given the temporary arrangements (so far, it has only met about six times per year). For instance, there are no signs that the EU has developed any serious mechanism to evaluate and/or monitor targeted sanctions. Hence, many important sanctions

6 Council of the European Union (January 2004).

7 Council of the European Union (December 2004).

issues that require more substantive discussions by the FRCWG do not make it to the daily agenda of the formation because of a lack of time. Thus, several issues that really need attention tend to be overlooked. In all, the limited number of meetings is likely to undermine the effective management of sanctions, since the formation does not allow for the discussions needed to share and deal with the problems involved.

Besides having too narrow a mandate and limited time, there is also the problem – or perhaps the consequence thereof – that foreign relations counsellors have developed their own specific understanding of what a targeted sanctions policy should consist of. There is clearly a particular culture of norms and expectations of what language and actions a sanctions policy should contain. The special interests of each unit in combination with the culture of each member state (not least RELEX itself) shape the policy of targeting in a particular way that may differ from that envisioned by the other actors concerned. The problem is that the transition and end product from these negotiations may be quite distinct from the EU Council's ideas or understanding at the initial phase when it decided to impose sanctions. To give an example, in 2005 the EU imposed targeted sanctions on members of the Uzbek government. The aim was to force targeted entities to co-operate in investigations of events that led to the Andijan massacre of May 2005. While the Council had originally expressed fierce criticism of the Uzbek government for its 'excessive, disproportionate and indiscriminate use of force', such criticism was later diluted in order to secure a member state's national interest in the region (Germany had to preserve its military base in the country in order for the allies to pursue their war in Afghanistan more effectively). Thus, sanctions were dramatically relaxed, although not removed completely. Therefore, the general framework and resources to assess whether travel bans or assets freezes were attaining their goals (that is, the effects on the listed Uzbek regime members) were neither put in place nor ensured. As a result, the measures that were ultimately carried out differed from the original goal of acting decisively against Uzbek human rights abuses. Not only did member states disagree about the political role targeted sanctions should play, once they were imposed, they were relaxed and not implemented as an effective strategy. While it could be argued that the relaxation of the policy was in line with established Council decisions, one could also make the argument that the original intent did not correspond to actual practice. While national preferences played a crucial part, the differing perceptions and lack of enforcement capacities did not lead to meaningful pressure.

Returning to institutional structure and its impact on sanctions, how does the EU formally impose targeted sanctions? In principle, there are two different ways an EU sanctions regime can be put in place: they can either be based on a UN resolution (UN Chapter 7 sanctions provide for legally binding obligations under Community Law) or they can be based on autonomous EU procedures.[8]

8 For the legal framework, see Portela (2008): 60–63.

Given a UN Chapter 7 resolution establishing a new sanctions regime, the Council Secretariat asks DG RELEX at the EU Commission and its sanctions team at the Crisis Management and Conflict Prevention Unit (the sanctions team) to comment, usually on an informal basis, on how to word a first draft Common Position (in addition, the same unit consults appropriate units in other directorate-generals on the matter). In general, the regional council working group for the country concerned has an introductory role to play here, trying to find political agreement about the grounds for implementing sanctions. The working group also chooses which criteria to apply in targeting individuals, groups and entities. Thus, each institutional division shapes the policy according to its understanding.

The inclusion of the DG RELEX sanctions team at this stage is carried out informally in order to develop the appropriate language for the sanctions text. One reason is that the sanctions team at the EU Commission tends to carry a lot of institutional memory and expertise. In addition, it must bring forward a proposal to implement the Community aspects of the Common Position.[9]

As soon as the first draft of a Common Position text is established, generally on the basis of a presidential text (presented by the EU chair of the Council Secretariat), the sanctions draft is sent out to member states for their preparation and input prior to the first FRCWG meeting. After the initial meeting, in which all member states present their positions, a version of the text is negotiated until final agreement is achieved.

Later, when the major directions in the Common Position appear to have been agreed, the EU Commission will prepare a proposal for a regulation to implement Community aspects. The sanctions team prepares a draft, which is circulated among its various directorate-generals for comments before being adopted by the College of Commissioners and transmitted to the Council. The proposal is then defended within the Council against all the member states' proposals, where a number of different interests with regard to how the policy is to be applied come into play.

The next step is for the presidency to negotiate what are usually a number of diverse proposals from the member states, as well as seeking compromise on the viewpoints held by the Council and the Commission. This again is carried out with input from the Commission's sanctions team on the draft text.[10] The involvement of the Commission's desk officers also suggests the tacit influence they have in shaping the draft text.[11] For instance, if an officer has a technical and legal preference for targeted sanctions, the text being drafted will take on such a flavour, whereas if the officer perceives sanctions as a foreign policy tool, the text

9 In addition, the Commission's Legal Service Directorate-General, with its competence and understanding of sanctions, is involved at this early stage.

10 In this informal practice, the Commission is normally invited to a pre-meeting with the presidency before the member states meet in the Council plenary.

11 If the Commission agrees changes, then only a qualified majority vote is needed, while if the Commission objects, then the EU member states must be unanimous.

will reflect actions and mechanism that are more concerned with achieving target impact. In drafting the legal texts, the wording used should generally conform with what has been agreed in the basic guidelines (although member states can dissent). While a number of meetings may take place before a final text is arrived at, the EU presidency often closes the text at working level through a silent procedure.

Once member states have reached a Common Position, the text then goes to the Political and Security Committee (PSC) for scrutiny, and then to COREPER (the member states' ambassadors to the EU) for final approval. The final step is formal adoption by the Council (the ministers), and subsequent publication in the *Official Journal*. Legally speaking, a Common Position needs to be in place prior to (or simultaneously with) a regulation. Thus, once a Common Position is in place, a renewed drafting process to establish a regulation is initiated (this process corresponds to the drafting of a Common Position, and mostly coincides with it in terms of time). If the Council so decides, the Commission may be tasked with updating the regulation on its own.

While they share many similarities with the standard procedures for incorporating UN sanctions, the procedures for autonomous EU sanctions differ somewhat, particularly during the initial phase.[12] One of the EU member states usually brings up autonomous measures. Typically, one or several EU member states in this procedure suggest the policy of targeted sanctions at a Council meeting. Thereafter, the EU member state ambassadors in the country or region, if instructed by their capitals, initiate a meeting to establish a first set of recommendations of entities to be targeted with sanctions. The relevant forum under the Council, usually a regional working group, meets to discuss the criteria for the sanctions. After being deliberated upon, the issue is then transferred to the FRCWG, where a final document is worked out with the participation of the Commission. Once a negotiated text has been drafted, it continues to the PSC and COREPER, were the final version is completed. The text is then adopted by a Council meeting, and subsequently published in the *Official Journal*. Normally, country-specific sanctions are discussed in specific reviews, usually after a period of six months (for example, terrorism lists).

However, the complex formal and informal decision-making procedures can lead to numerous problems for the sanctions rationale. In fact, the many institutional steps from adoption to implementation and management are likely to

12 The EU also has its own autonomous restrictive measures in place in the field of terrorism. This is provided for in Common Position 2001/931/CFSP. In principle, a competent authority, most notably the judicial government body of a member state, can propose to the Council to designate or include an entity on the EU terrorist list. The recommendation to list or de-list certain targeted entities is made in the Clearing House formation at the EU Council. The Clearing House then makes recommendations to COREPER and the Council for designation of targeted entities. The decision to target an entity or a group must be taken unanimously. For a detailed analysis of listing and de-listing practices by the EU, see Eriksson (2009).

dilute the original intent and goal of the targeted sanctions and render the policy less powerful. In other words, the bureaucratic chain from adoption to implementation, adding here the lack of ownership and lack of feedback, make the discrepancies between the original intent of the sanctions policy (to achieve a behavioural change and to constrain targets) to its actual implementation very wide. In fact, the policy document may end up being so technical or vague, after rounds of negotiations, adjustments and bureaucratic interventions taking into account all the sub-units' interests and preferences, that there is little likelihood that the policy will be able to deal with the problems and dynamics on the ground. To give an example, the EU autonomous sanctions regime imposed on the Myanmar elite is never likely to succeed in achieving democratisation and putting an end to violations of human rights because the administrative process will simply not allow for it (despite the fact that the ambition is there and follows a particular logic). Needless to say, however, there are likely to be situations where policies are adopted which will never be realised. Besides the administrative differences and the processing of the sanctions policy (which can take several months and therefore not follow swiftly any events on the ground), major discrepancies can arise when an individual country desk officer has to implement the strategy in practice. We will return to this issue later.

In conclusion, then, over the last ten years, the formal and informal rule-based decision-making process of the EU has developed considerably. While we have highlighted only the most basic EU institutional practices when it comes to decision-making, the enforcement of sanctions requires even more actors (such as the banking industries, aviation authorities and customs inspectors).

As this review illustrates, the sanctions policy has to run through a number of bureaucratic units and institutional departments, such as national capitals, the EU Council, the Commission and its directorate-generals, regional committees, the legal service and COREPER before it can be adopted and properly managed. Although I have laid particular emphasis on the role of the foreign relations counsellors in this examination, the impact of many other administrative units, both within and outside the EU, will also shape the policy of targeting in their own particular ways. My argument here is that these enablers and constrainers do not necessarily strive in the same direction. What is particularly problematic in this regard, and what may explain the differences in how the various policy management units shape the policy, is that the long and complex chain does not seem to provide enough policy ownership. It is likely to be the case that several units operate independently without fully understanding how they relate to each other in the long and complex chain that shapes the overall sanctions policy.

While the EC/EU treaties provide for the overall framework, the Council and the Commission have more precisely been able to work out guideline documents on how to design and implement sanctions programmes. While these have led to a more uniform sanctions approach among the institutions as well as EU member states, by providing definitions, standards, models, procedures and best practices, this formalisation has come about at the expense of allowing the policies to become inflexible and static, and therefore not apt to address daily challenges which the targets are likely to pose. Sanctions model texts are more general than precise. In other words, while standard wordings and procedures are good in themselves, they come at the expense of failing to reflect the real political situation on the ground, as they do not allow daily interaction with local political events. An alternative would have been to set clearer criteria for what listed entities are expected to do in order to have sanctions lifted. In addition, there should be clear goals and criteria for how to use sanctions and where to allocate ownership of sanctions management. Above all, there need to be criteria that allow for more flexibility.

Best practices and sanctions guidelines also engender several other types of problems. For instance, while a number of documents have referred to the assessment, monitoring and so on of sanctions programmes (meaning that member states have informally agreed on the goals), these stipulations are not actively fulfilled. One reason for this is that the guidelines do not offer mechanisms to meet such demands, either by providing time or institutional resources.

Moreover, although EU counsellors are doing important work, such as drafting Common Positions and spending a great deal of time in designing sanctions policies, the formal and static approach many times leads to imprecise policies in relation to events on ground. There are several factors causing this, such as the formal decision-making system (diplomatic negotiations and institutional procedures), time constraints, understaffing and a lack of interaction with heads of mission on ground. A comparison can be made with the sanctions administrating unit of the US government, the Office of Foreign Assets Control (OFAC). OFAC has a very large department in comparison to the EU, working to ensure sanctions implementation on an entirely different level.

Finally, the language and phrasing of the Common Positions are often much influenced by the EU Commission. This is partly because the EU Council does not have as strong an institutional memory of past sanctions programmes as the EU Commission. This can be explained by staff rotation as well as the limits of having short-term presidencies (prior to the Lisbon Treaty entering into force, they changed every six months). Another explanation could be that the Council has transferred this task to the Commission (having previously taken responsibility for maintaining a public sanctions archive). Given that the number of EU Commission staff working on targeted sanctions is currently very limited, the personnel working with sanctions have a strong impact in shaping the policy of targeting. This, in the end, makes the entire EU sanctions process quite vulnerable. For instance, should something sudden happen, such as a reorganisation of the unit or the loss of personnel, this will have a major effect on the overall EU sanctions policy. One way to strengthen this particular frail link is to develop a unit that is much more resourceful and self-sustaining. Another would be to establish more ownership throughout the decision-making process to make the system more robust.

Informal Management

In addition to the formal aspects of EU sanctions decision-making processes (for example, negotiations, member state interests, resources and time restraints), there are also informal elements that are likely to shape sanctions policy. Here we will focus on the human factor and the impact individual EU officials have in shaping the outcome of sanctions through their perceptions of how to implement them by illustrating how different officials who work at desk officer level perceive sanctions, and how this perception is likely to feed into and shape the daily management of a sanctions regime. The following is a discussion, analysis and interpretation of some of the answers that were provided during a set of interviews with desk officers who manage sanctions on a daily basis.[13]

Policy Perceptions

An important aspect of understanding targeted sanctions is to examine how those people involved in targeting sanctions perceive the policy. For example, one would expect that the ways in which desk officers understand the policy would affect its implementation. If decision-makers do not understand or believe in the policy, the policy's impact is unlikely to be significant.

The interviews clearly demonstrated that officials perceived targeted sanctions as a way to coerce a set of identified entities, groups or governments by using a number of policy instruments. Several officials used words such as 'pressure', 'influence', 'punishment' and 'stigmatisation' when describing these tools. Answers like these reflect the perception that targeting often achieves what the sender wants it to achieve. Interestingly, some of the answers also seemed to imply that targeting could have negative consequences for the sender, causing a reverse effect, and generating support and sympathy for targeted leaders.

While targeting was considered by one desk officer as a way to apply pressure to targets (and commodities), it was also perceived to have clear limitations in terms of impact, including the fact that sanctions were sometimes unsuccessful. There could be several reasons for this: sanctions may not have been enforced

---

13 The interviews conducted here obviously do not serve as a complete inventory of the EU's institutional sanctions competence. Rather, the focus was on conducting a number of in-depth interviews with carefully selected experts. More specifically, interviewees were selected according to their degree of competence in the political and institutional use of targeted sanctions. The questions allowed for more profound explanations of different aspects of sanctions management. At the EU level, 17 officials were interviewed. In addition, although not cited directly in this chapter, a number of more informal interviews and discussions were conducted with EU officials (for example, heads of EU delegations and EU ambassadors, in contexts where sanctions had been applied). All interviews were conducted on an anonymous basis. A more detailed reference list can be located in earlier versions of this study.

properly, they may be easy to circumvent, or they may not have been discussed or evaluated.

In addition, some desk officers who were interviewed believed that targeting had more to do with sending signals or conveying messages than actually achieving a direct impact. In this regard, sanctions could be seen as a political signal to show disapproval or to pressurise leaders to take part in negotiations, to demonstrate a single-minded policy on the part of the EU, or to signal discontent. Specifically, as one interviewee maintained, a measure like this could inform a listed individual that he or she was personally responsible for his or her actions: 'It is not, and this is very important, a general signal of discontent, but a personal signal of disapproval of their responsibility.' This suggests that the immediate effect is of secondary importance to that of communicating the sender's political position. One respondent also suggested that the policy was intended to signal that the international community was 'watching' and that there would be no impunity for bad behaviour. This also suggests that targeting can be understood as a way to demonstrate and make visible a proactive stance towards a particular policy problem.

It was also argued by some respondents that targeted sanctions were only symbolic in nature. However, answers like these appear to contradict the basic guidelines that, as noted above, outline the EU's work regarding targeted sanctions (and perhaps answers like these may even suggest that the desk officers were not even aware of the existence of the basic guidelines). While these viewpoints may not be at odds with one another, the differing views say something about the credibility of the policy, given that not all officials understood how to use targeted sanctions.

A number of interviewee responses implied that the policy by itself signalled how serious the EU was in its views *vis-à-vis* the target and the target's behaviour. For example, one respondent explained that the imposition of sanctions signalled that something had to be done beyond traditional diplomacy in order to put pressure on the government to save the country. This suggests that the perception of sanctions reflected a desperate sense of helplessness. For example, there was a perception that targeting was the last resort given the fact that no other policies had worked. Similarly, targeting was understood as an instrument to be used when all other options were exhausted. Moreover, one respondent held that sanctions in themselves also signalled policy unity among the EU member states.

Another theme that emerged suggested that targeted sanctions might not work, but that the adoption and imposition of targeted sanctions might still prevent other actors from having relationships with the targeted country. As stated by one of the respondents: 'Another effect is that the market has experienced self-censorship. Several commercial operators are scared to invest or engage in commercial operations with the country of concern.' A more downbeat comment suggested that targeting had little direct or indirect impact because targeted actors could easily evade the sanctions. For instance, one official said that although he did not know how the targets perceived the sanctions, it was believed that 'travel sanctions do not really stop them', and that 'the assets freeze has not worked'. This view has also been noted in the recent sanctions literature.

An interesting point of view regarding the role of targeted sanction was that the policy was applied because there were few alternatives. Even if the policy did not achieve much, as one respondent claimed, it would be useless to remove it because domestic and international audiences could easily interpret such a measure as a concession.

There were also some reservations about the policy's usefulness in the first place. One of the respondents made such a comment regarding both sanctions strategy and implementation. It is difficult to know, however, whether this represented a general disbelief in sanctions, or merely scepticism regarding this country's specific sanctions programme. In contrast, there was also a clear belief among some of the interviewed desk officers that sanctions could have positive effects by pressuring those in decision-making roles while sparing the broader population from the negative effects of sanctions. For example, sanctions could encourage and facilitate further dialogue if the sender was open about the their objectives, giving targets an opportunity to respond.

To sum up, there were many different perceptions of targeted sanctions. While some officials projected a positive view of the potential of targeted sanctions, others were more sceptical, pointing to contradictions in the effects of targeting.

The themes can be classified into different categories of perceptions: sanctions having limited impact, sanctions conveying a message, sanctions as a symbolic measure, and sanctions as an expression of discontent. A number of themes also indicated that policy makers were fully aware of the limitations of targeting. However, the stated perceptions of targeted sanctions indicate that there were many diverse subjective views of the policy. Each official is likely to use sanctions strategically to suit his or her own political ends, without the leadership and guidance of an overall co-ordinator. Even these differences are not exaggerated; the mere fact that different perceptions exist may impair the management as well as the impact of sanctions.

A possible consequence is that targeting could be implemented differently against different countries, despite having the same initial goals and measures at the outset. For instance, if the European Council intended to respond to a particular situation with the aim of having a direct impact, it is not certain that this impact could be achieved simply because actors and policy makers have different opinions about what such a policy should accomplish.

A comparison could be made regarding how one thinks about the use of military force. It would be quite ridiculous to expect officers engaged in daily military warfare to have different perceptions of what warfare was actually meant to achieve. For example, it would be catastrophic for some officers to pursue symbolic warfare (unless this was their specific mandate) while other officers were engaged in operations in which adversaries were being killed.

The Presence of a Sanctions Strategy

The aim of any targeted sanctions policy is to design it in such a way that it achieves its goals. To do this, a clear and well thought out strategy is necessary. Such as strategy should be well planned and include elements of pre-assessments, evaluation capacities, and an implementation and co-ordination structure in order to affect targets.[14] However, when asked whether the respondents understood targeted sanctions as representing a strategic tool, a number of different responses were given.

To begin with, none of the interviewees had seen or created a strategy paper on how to examine and use targeted sanctions when faced with a crisis. The absence of such a strategy, as explained by one respondent, was not necessarily a key concern for the EU Commission. On the contrary, it was believed that the policy should probably be seen as something more ad hoc. Only one respondent clearly confirmed that there was a sanctions strategy in place for the specific regime in which he was involved. While several respondents had not explicitly worked on or seen any an outline of a sanctions strategy, their thoughts suggested that that the policy of targeted sanctions should be read as part of a more general strategy, for instance as a continuation of an earlier political step.

In response to a question on sanctions as a strategic tool, some desk officers tried to explain how they understood sanctions. Some of the remarks suggested that the policy should be interpreted as a reflection of EU member states' national interests rather than a common European interest. For instance, some respondents commented: 'Sanctions are partly the expression of satisfying home constituencies in Europe.'

Another view of sanctions as a strategy that stood out from the responses was that the current use of targeted sanctions reflected different visions of how to apply them. For instance, one official held that for some EU member states sanctions are about symbolism, whereas for others they are only about punishment. Similarly, one official portrayed the policy as a kind of stairway, while providing thoughts on how to proceed with targeted sanctions if the political situation deteriorated.

In conclusion, while several respondents did consider targeted sanctions as a strategy to be used in a rational and well thought out approach for a particular crisis (for example, that sanctions could be strengthened if needed, or applied as one out of many strategies), there was also a perception that targeted sanctions could be part of a policy that would continuously develop during the course of a crisis. This suggests that officials are likely to be working without a clear policy roadmap on how to use the instrument under a more general policy. This is likely to reduce the impact of sanctions. In the end, one could make the claim that while different understandings do not necessarily lead to a target impact, they could at least be improved through co-ordination and strategic streamlining.

---

14 An example here is the Treasury Department and OFAC. OFAC has a very active system to counter the efforts of targets seeking to evade financial sanctions.

Symbolic versus Direct Impact

One of the more central issues in the contemporary literature about sanctions is whether targeting should be understood in a symbolic sense, or whether the intention is to create a direct and concrete impact, or both. The difference between a symbolic impact and a direct impact is that the former entails causing an impact in psychological terms, which is not a controlled impact, while the latter means that the sender seeks to constrain or to achieve behavioural change by, for example, freezing assets or preventing travel.

There are a number of indicators that support the assertion that the purpose of the EU's targeted sanctions, at least formally, is about achieving a direct impact. First, the language and aims set out in the framework documents (basic principles and best practices) indicate that the intention of the EU's sanctions policy is to cause a direct impact. Second, the gravity of the situations that sanctions must address also implies that the EU seriously seeks to change behaviour, and not rely on potential symbolic effects (after all, sanctions are imposed in emergencies such as human rights abuses, the killing of innocents, torture, arbitrary arrests, and so on). Third, the fact that much time is invested in negotiating and drafting the policy also suggests that a direct impact is expected (otherwise, the policy process could be drastically reduced). Only a few respondents perceived targeting as an instrument that could have a direct impact, the majority suggesting that the instrument had more of a symbolic nature.

There were also some practical examples in support of some respondents' perception of targeted sanctions as a symbolic policy tool. For instance, one respondent said that he knew that some of the listed targeted rulers had been arrested or had already died. This implied that the targeting had to be more symbolic than anything else. In addition, two other comments claimed that: 'The assets freeze is symbolic, and they have no direct impact. Something like 500 euros has been frozen so far, and even if sanctions had 100 per cent success, we are still only talking about a limited number of people.' In one explanation, the respondent sought to explain the type of effects that targeting usually had:

> We started off our approach by only considering pure symbolic impact, and it has been quite successful in that sense. It has had a deterrent effect. This obviously was very good. We also found that it had a very strong psychological effect on the population because people thereby understood that EU was on their side.

The same respondent later stated:

> We implemented the first round of sanctions after a particular political event had taken place, then we came back to include even more persons, this had a strong psychological effect. These leaders are scared of the sanctions. They cannot travel nor do business as usual.

This line of reasoning was also described by another interviewee, who said that sanctions probably did have a tangible effect on targets.

While several officials were well aware of the limitations of the targeted sanctions policy, there were also suggestions that targeting sometimes had a greater impact if complemented by other strategies. The effectiveness of sanctions was also linked to political will and support. For instance, it was held that that the strategy depended upon the unity of EU member states. If member states held different views about sanctions, different effects of those sanctions would emerge.

For some respondents, targeted sanctions also represented a warning to those not included on the lists of what could happen if they did not change their behaviour. In this sense, targeted sanctions in effect set a type of threshold or benchmark for entities not included on the lists, rather than having an actual impact. Crossing this threshold would automatically lead to policy reactions. As one interviewee described it: 'In fact what is counting is not who is on the list, but perhaps those that are *not* on the list. Perhaps the list is there to persuade those outside the list not to cross the red line.' In this sense, targeting was mostly applied as a communicative tool.

Finally, comments were also made regarding the symbolic effects as being positive from the sender's perspective. One of the respondents put it in these terms: 'There is a cost to breaking the law. We are talking about symbolism, but this is good symbolism. It is not bad to talk about symbolic sanctions.'

In sum, there was a wide range of understandings of the role of sanctions because of differences in perception. This supports the notion that there are not one, but several different views of the purpose of targeting. Some argued that targeting was all about achieving direct impact, while others argued that it was all about symbolic actions. Notably, it seems far more accepted than expected that the policy can or should have a symbolic impact (such as a psychological one). The different perceptions also suggest that targeting is not as straightforward a process or instrument as one might believe. Officials seemed to lack a common understanding of what the actual policy of targeting means (especially if contrasted with the guideline documents discussed in the previous section). Whether or not this is the result of leadership shortcomings, institutional defects or simply different contexts and personal biases, the different types of answers suggest that current sanctions policies operate based on different understandings and expectations in the context of different countries.

Embedding Targeted Sanctions in a Larger Strategy

The question of what other strategic instruments need to be borne in mind when analysing the role of targeted sanctions generated a broad range of responses. Some frameworks typically referred to were: stabilisation and association processes (agreements, assistance and future EU member status), police missions, accession strategy, conditionality policies, suspension of assistance, restriction of ministerial contacts, the Cotonou Agreement (especially Articles 8, 9 and 96), development co-operation instruments and humanitarian assistance programmes. Hence, respondents perceived targeting as playing an important role in the overall sanctions strategy. As one respondent described it: 'The impact of sanctions is very limited. Perhaps one could see it in this way: travel bans play a 5 per cent role, the stabilisation and association agreements 20 per cent, the assets freeze 5 per cent, and so on.'

Besides an overall strategy embedding sanctions, some respondents explained that targeting was a problematic strategy in itself. For instance, one respondent stated that targeting is a bad choice: 'I don't think sanctions are a good tool to promote policies .... They are pointless.' In his opinion, targeting did not promote either dialogue or interaction with the targeted regime.

While the idea that targeted sanctions should form part of a larger political strategy is not necessarily new, it was, however, interesting to note how prominent many other strategies were in the minds of those working with sanctions regimes. This suggests that when assessing sanctions, these overall policies cannot be discarded.

Sender–target Interaction

An important aspect of targeted sanctions policy is to keep in close contact with events on the ground in order to achieve a targeted impact, in which context the role of sender–target interaction is important. Does such interaction exist, and to what degree? A number of themes emerged from the interviews.

First, the majority of the EU officials said that there was little or no interaction with entities placed on the EU's sanctions lists.[15] Likewise, there was little specific knowledge about each entity (this varied between some of the regimes, however). One official said that it was not up to the institutions to keep track of these, but rather it was the task of the EU delegations. There was no reporting requirement. A similar view also claimed that the heads of missions in the country of the listed targets were usually well aware of the listing.

Second, a number of respondents recognised that more target interaction was needed in order to influence the behaviour of targets, but that such this was currently lacking. While little interaction seems to take place with the targets, at least one respondent expressed a belief that targeting could lead to individual behavioural change and have a constraining effect: 'Sanctions could be used as a reward system. If you behave well, you could be taken off the list.' Another respondent implied that although there was not much interaction, there were, from time to time, personal notifications regarding why a particular regime or person had been targeted, in accordance with human rights standards. In this regard, it was

---

15 One could perhaps argue that it is not in their 'job description' to do so. Yet one might expect that awareness would exist under normal circumstances, especially given the weight restriction measures in the Common Foreign and Security Policy.

also held by one interviewee that the basis for listing a person or entity should be well founded and well argued. The same respondent also maintained that contact had been made with some listed members: 'People have contacted me because they could not transfer money because their names were on the lists.'

The majority of the respondents also implied that they did not assess the behaviour of each listed target. One reason for this, according to one official, was the belief that other actors were monitoring their behaviour: 'We rely on that they are being monitored by the forces on the ground (such as police and military forces, and so on).' Another explanation was that an individual assessment could be problematic: 'If we are opening a debate [by interacting with specific individuals on the list], we risk losing it [public legitimacy]. Instead, we want to remain open to a general dialogue. The stick approach has given nothing so far.' Claims like these support the notion that while targeted sanctions often seem to be *individually* oriented, there is often a de facto perception of a target *group*.

In sum, once targeted sanctions have been imposed, little political attention seems to be paid to the reactions and behaviours of the listed entities. Despite legal efforts, such as designing sanctions lists to ensure their accuracy, continuous assessment and monitoring of target behaviour does not take place. In fact, these interviews suggest that there are few assessments in general, which again suggests that some officials perceived targeting as a measure that affected groups more than specific individuals.

Targets and Behavioural Change

A common assumption held in the literature on targeted sanctions is that the more effective the policy of targeting, the more likelihood there is that it will result in behavioural change.[16] While in this respect behavioural change is a typical reference point, it is seldom demonstrated in practice. An important empirical exercise, then, is to see whether those engaged in sanctions programmes think in these terms in the first place, and if so, whether they actually believe in the idea of achieving change.

Most respondents said it was difficult to assess whether targeted sanctions had a direct impact on behaviour since they were not usually in contact with the targets. At least one official claimed that sanctions led to positive behavioural change (although it was unclear how this conclusion was reached). Some respondents also said that listing might cause other positive effects for the sender while not causing specific behavioural changes per se. Such additional effects could include annoyance, deterrence, change in public discourse, and anxiety. In contrast, there were also comments suggesting that targeting led to more negative behaviour, such as self-chosen isolation.

During the interviews, it was also suggested that behavioural change was likely to be conditional upon the effectiveness of targeting. For example, change

16 Cortright et al. (1998).

might be more likely to occur if the objectives were clearer and used as part of the strategy for specific purposes. In one particular case, the respondent meant that behavioural change was conditional upon the implementation of additional restrictive measures: 'Behavioural change will occur if a financial sanction is put in place. Financial transactions, blocking and freezing seems to have the potential to inflict damage on the regime. However, to have these effective, regional co-ordination is needed.'

Two interviewees thought that behavioural change, as a goal in itself, was problematic in the first place. First, if such change were to occur, it would not really make a difference, since individual behavioural change was marginal to the overall defiance of a regime. Second, the policy of targeting was more likely to shape behaviour than cause it. In fact, rather than changing it for the better, the experience usually made the target's behaviour more negative.

The general impression from these replies was that the aim of achieving change was not a policy that the EU seemed to practise day-to-day in managing targeted sanctions. On the contrary, different perceptions existed regarding what kinds of effect this policy should have. Even though some officials might have perceived and reasoned about behavioural change on the targeted entity's terms, there was not much evidence that such an approach was put into practice.

Conclusion

Based on the interviewees' responses, a number of preliminary observations can be made. In general, most comments about the role of EU policy were based on an attitude of 'them and us'. While this is a reasonable perception that can be expected, it also echoes an antagonistic view of the targets, as opposed to a more co-operative attitude and more constructive interaction with the targets. A position like this probably needs to be understood in the wider context of the role of targeted sanctions. If one accepts that targeted sanctions are primarily about changing behaviour, then taking an 'us versus them' approach may antagonise the target more than necessary. Thus, instead of thinking of targeted sanctions as a tool for punishment, sanctions could be adopted to keep entities engaged, something which could lead to positive or negative outcomes.

The answers also revealed that policy makers were somewhat aware of the complex inter-relationship between the limitations and potential of sanction policies. This supports the idea that there are a number of different institutional understandings (such as the institutional culture and the existing narratives) of what targeting is all about. These perceptions also seem to constitute elements of a grand narrative about the practice of sanctions as they affect the EU's Common Foreign and Security Policy.

There were nuances in decision-makers understanding of the purpose of targeting. As illustrated, the respondents saw many goals of sanctions, such as creating a tangible impact, conveying a message, creating a symbolic impact, and demonstrating or expressing discontent. While such nuances may seem innocent in themselves, these shifting perceptions do not necessarily conform to expectations of what sanctions are meant to achieve at a higher political level (for example, the intentions of the European Council). In other words, the way in which targeting currently works should be contrasted with how effective a more co-ordinated strategy could be.

From all this, one could also conclude that understandings and perceptions of sanctions are multifaceted and subjective. These differences in perception might also exist within each particular institutional unit or group, and they may operate at different levels of the policy chain, creating a plurality of understandings.

Several respondents thought of targeted sanctions as a strategic staircase, where the policy was implemented in a systematic approach, with pressure mounting on the target over time. Such a strategic notion also implies that targeted sanctions form part of other coercion measures.

Regarding the important issue of symbolic versus direct (concrete) impact, there was a wide range of comments. Some respondents perceived sanctions as having a direct impact, in contrast to the view that they were mostly symbolic. This supports the hypothesis that current sanctions policies do not work in a harmonised manner. This must be taken seriously in any assessment that seeks to understand targeted sanctions. Such a discrepancy could have certain consequences for individual cases, sanctions programmes, and more importantly, for the credibility of the EU's sanctions system.

One can also observe from the replies that only modest attention was paid to the reactions and behaviours of the listed entities. This contradicts much of the bureaucratic efforts devoted to ensuring that sanctions lists are accurate. Thus, conscious and systematic monitoring of target behaviour has not been undertaken (especially not on a person-to-person basis). This disregard for listed individuals was also demonstrated by many comments that suggested that most targeting was seen as being directed towards a group.

Another theme that emerged was that the policy of achieving behavioural change and directly constraining targets was not current practice as much as one might think. On the contrary, while some EU officials may certainly reason in such terms, there was little to suggest that such an approach was actually practised.

From the interviews conducted, one could detect that a majority of the respondents held a rather critical attitude towards the current practice of sanctions. While some EU officials believed that measures could be taken to strengthen a sanctions regime, other respondents believed that such improvements were limited by other conditions, such as institutional and procedural adjustments, or an explicit disbelief that situations could actually improve. However, this suggests a lack of sanctions ownership. To understand the nuances and varying concepts of sanctions reviewed and analysed here, one must contrast them with the various types of EU policies. As noted previously, it is worth examining military operations and how military force is managed.

Finally, the findings suggest that any serious attempt to assess the impact of sanctions cannot overlook the importance of personal perceptions and practices of officials in the sending body. Given these findings, further analysis is required in order to investigate how the sending actor's perceptions correspond with the target's perceptions and what such a dynamic means in terms of addressing the impact of sanctions.

Summary Conclusion

During the last decade, both the EU Council and the EU Commission have been able to agree on a set of formal documents to guide the EU in its daily management of various sanctions programmes. While these may have led to more streamlining of complex sanctions decision-making processes, providing definitions, standards, models, procedures and best practices, this formalisation has also been at the expense of letting the policy become too static. Rather than, for instance, agreeing to take a flexible and more dynamic approach towards events on the ground, a more legal and technical approach has been adopted by senders. In a sense, one could argue that the legalisation and institutionalisation of targeted sanctions management has become more about securing the role of the EU in its practice of doing right rather than designing policies that seriously address situations on the ground. This could easily trigger a critique of the EU, suggesting that it is not likely to get its foreign policy act together.

Moreover, from a sanctions perspective, this static approach has also led to a predetermination of policy, so that an outsider may know more or less what to expect from the EU without having access to insider knowledge about what exactly is going on. Thus, targets will quickly learn that in many cases, being exposed to targeted sanctions by the EU does not mean much in terms of punishment, and that it is quite easy to proceed unhindered. Another problem is that this trend of formalising policy documents is also likely to spread to future sanctions practitioners. However, this could go against the spirit of the guideline documents of the Council and the Commission, which express the will to take targeting seriously. Yet EU sanctions guidelines are no panacea either, as they do not specifically allocate the resources needed for achieving direct target impact, do not dedicate any ownership of the tasks, and do not specify what consequences should follow if the responsible unit or group fails to deliver on its responsibilities. Another problem seems to be that senior management has not made available enough time, staff or training for practitioners (in terms of harmonisation regarding what targeting is all about).

In fact, for both the EU and the UN (as seen in Chapter 6), the practice and the specific culture of decision-making in each unit, group or formation contributes to shaping the policy of targeting, as well as the degree of target impact. This is partly because of the static way in which the policy is designed, the institutional practices of decision-making, and guideline documents, and so on. What is needed to enhance the capacity and overcome a too static approach is to make sure that overall co-ordination exists among the units dealing with targeted sanctions, so that each unit has a sense of ownership and a feeling of responsibility to ensure target accuracy and efficacy.

Besides the formal aspects of EU decision-making, there are also informal aspects of EU policy formation that contribute to shaping sanctions outcomes. For instance, during the interviews, comments by the EU officials conveyed that in many cases they seemed unaware of their personal capacity to shape targeting policy.[17] In most cases, targeting was considered a procedural issue in which a task had been given to them to carry out. For several officials, ownership seemed to be perceived as to lying elsewhere. This view can also explain, in part at least, why few initiatives have taken place within the EU Council and the EU Commission to improve weaknesses in policy. Practitioners expect the initiation of change to take place elsewhere or higher up the hierarchy. It was also noted that few efforts were made to share experiences and information across the different sanctions programmes.

Another example of how decision-makers could influence sanctions outcomes had to do with fact that several practitioners perceived targeted sanctions as an 'us versus them' policy. Clearly, such thinking leads to a design of a policy that relies on a particular logic with this in mind. As discussed above, however, targeted sanctions do not need to depart from such a perspective, given that the essence of sanctions is to achieve a behavioural change and to constrain targets. On the contrary, imposing pressure does not need to mean punishment alone, but rather co-operation. Taking an 'us versus them' approach, which does not recognise co-operation, can cause both distance (where the practice of targeting does not match the reality on ground) and distortion (where listed entities can become targets, not acting humans) that in both cases can easily lead to a misguided sanctions policy. Again, this does not have be the case, since targeted sanctions can also be of a co-operative, strategic nature, as in the case of positive sanctions. While historically sanctions have often been associated with punishment or isolation, the more recent use of sanctions also relies on positive engagement.[18]

Furthermore, several EU officials did not think of achieving behavioural change and constraining listed individuals themselves, but more the groups they belonged to. This attitude is contradictory to the actual policy trend in EU targeting (not least in the judicial sphere), which usually calls for individual responsibility. Thus, the perception, policy and formalities do not work in conjunction with each other.

Another observation is that some EU officials in a number of cases also perceived targeting as more to do with sending symbolic messages and signalling than with causing direct impact. Once again, a decision-maker is likely to shape the policy through the way he or she understands sanctions. For example, if he or

17 This impact arises because each desk officer is able to define issue areas, actively solve problems, identify solutions, engage in the overall political dynamic of target compliance, provide resources for further management and carrying out assessments and recommendations within specific sanctions regimes.

18 For further reading, see Haass and O'Sullivan (2000).

she understands sanctions as having a limited impact, then limited impact is likely to become the practice of the sender. Similarly, if the official responsible for a particular sanctions programme only understands sanctions as part of a broader policy, then the policy of targeting is likely to be treated in such a way. In the end, there are many different competing understandings.

The next chapter will offer an examination of how the sanctions dynamic played out when enforced against the leadership of Zimbabwe. An important aspect here is to determine the target's perception *vis-à-vis* the sender, and how political behaviour is shaped as a result. It will emphasise how the EU, as a sanctions sending actor, is likely to interact with a target through the lens of a number of policy episodes.

Chapter 9

Episodes of EU Targeted Sanctions against the Zimbabwe Leadership

In mid-February 2002, the European Union imposed targeted sanctions ('restrictive measures') on the Zimbabwean leadership for its failure to conduct free and fair elections. Since then, a number of renewed and extended sanctions measures against individual members of the elite have been imposed. These actions followed the sender's assessment of whether political progress had been made with regard to the political and economic situation on ground in Zimbabwe, and whether they contributed to changing the behaviour of the targets included on the sanctions list. Today, the Zimbabwean elite have experienced almost a decade of EU sanctions, so a pertinent question to ask is what impact and achievements these measures may have led to.[1] More precisely, this chapter seeks to examine the EU's sanctions on Zimbabwe by discussing how they have worked and how they were constituted. Another aim is to demonstrate the complexity of the sanctions policy process by recognising the numerous factors senders need to confront in order to pursue a legitimate sanctions policy. This analysis intends to explore the implicit beliefs underlying much of the sanctions debate today, which adopts far too simple an approach when seeking to determine the effectiveness of sanctions.

Rather than engaging in a sanctions assessment, we will conduct a more in-depth examination of the Zimbabwe sanctions regime by disaggregating it into a number of episodes. While these episodes could be useful for scoring or assessing the EU's sanctions against Zimbabwe, as previously outlined, the intention here is to reflect the distinct dynamics within each sanctions regime. The disaggregation of the regime into episodes will provide a more detailed and clearer sense, not only of how the sender perceived the utility of the sanctions policy during the course of the sanctions management, but also the kinds of political challenges it had to confront at different stages.

The structure of this chapter is as follows. First, it will examine key developments in Zimbabwe prior to and immediately after the introduction of targeted sanctions, as well as the developments in the period immediately following their imposition. Nine separate episodes are identified. Next, it will look at the role the travel ban and the targeted financial sanctions measures played in this regime. One feature of this will be an explanation of how these measures personally affected the listed

1 While most studies take a unitary approach to target behaviour, there are some studies that come closer to addressing group behaviours; see Allen (2008) and Kirschner (1997).

entities. The final section includes an analysis based on interviews conducted with some Zimbabwean individuals targeted with sanctions.

An Emerging Crisis

During the years that immediately followed the overthrow of the Ian Smith regime and the first free elections held in February 1980, in which Robert Mugabe was elected president, Zimbabwe underwent an uneasy political and economic development. Politically, it did not come to terms with the new post-independence constitution, while economically, Mugabe was not able to fulfil his vision of a redistribution of land between the ethnically 'black' and 'white' communities. Two of the main problems for this uncertain period had to do with the future of the constitution and the land resettlement programme.

To begin with, it was held among some sections of Zimbabwean society that the Lancaster House Agreement, which ended white minority rule in Zimbabwe in December 1979, was the country's first constitution. Other segments regarded it simply as a cease-fire at the time it was signed, embedding a commitment for future negotiations concerning the political settlement in Zimbabwe. The issue proved to be increasingly complicated following Mugabe's attempt to modify this constitution by adding power to the presidential office, thereby amending it to his advantage.

Second, early on in the liberation struggle, Mugabe's government had committed itself to giving land back to the black population under a national land resettlement programme. Based on an interview with a senior inner-circle Zimbabwe African National Union – Patriotic Front (ZANU-PF) official, we can offer a brief summary of what the land reform was all about:[2]

> It was thanks to the British Prime Minister Margaret Thatcher, through her help in establishing the Lancaster House meeting that the Rhodesian question could finally be solved after many years of civil war. In terms of politics, the conservative Tories were more the 'implementers' while Labour put 'flesh' on their policies. Labour built the welfare state, while the Tories put out a post-war vision for society. The Conservatives knew how to deal with colonialism, which the Labour party did not. The Lancaster House Agreement called upon all stakeholders, and it even made us, the guerrillas, to come to the negotiation table. Thatcher and Mugabe were very close. During the negotiations, the UK promised to give financial help to the Zimbabwe government so that land could be bought from the commercial farmers on a 'willing seller – willing buyer principle'. In 1981, a new land reform policy was enacted, which granted government power to expropriate certain sectors. Thatcher sent us money every month, while we surveyed the land and planned for which farms to buy. In fact, we even got more

2 See also Eriksson (2007b).

> money than we could handle. At the time, the UK even said we were too slow in our land redistribution programme. Hence, as part of an agreement, John Mayor – once in office – made sure to send us five land experts to help us speed up the process. In fact, in 1988 there was an international conference on land reform, which got the support from all around the world. Thus, the Lancaster House agreement was much an issue of land.[3] The question of redistribution of land has been part of the problem in Zimbabwe for many years, but had remained unsolved. Even during the struggle for liberation, and the years to come after the unjust land situation against the black majority was still an underlying cause of frustration. The constitution also introduces the clause that the colonial power should pay for the land reform.

According to the UK, however, an evaluation of the land resettlement program had been carried out in 1988 (after having spent nearly £47 million on land reform, £20 million on land resettlement, and £27 million in the form of budgetary support during 1980–88). This evaluation suggested that further steps to improve the UK-funded programme had to be taken before further financing could be allocated. As a result, proposals to adjust the land resettlement programme were sent to the government of Zimbabwe for further elaboration. However, according to the UK Overseas Development Administration (ODA), the British government never received a reply to these adjustment proposals.[4] Regrettably, the dialogue was interrupted by illicit farm occupations.[5] Another element that complicated the land redistribution programme was the decision of the UK Labour Prime Minister of the time, Tony Blair, to revise Britain's policy towards Zimbabwe. Behind this new position lay suspicion of the existing Tory policy on Zimbabwe, which had been in place since the Lancaster House Agreement. It was believed that much of the land compensation paid to 'wealthy landowners' in Zimbabwe had generally close connections to well-off interests in the UK, by tradition allies of the Conservatives. The definitive policy change towards Zimbabwe came with a letter written by Secretary of State for International Development Claire Short in November 1997, stating that the UK was no longer prepared to continue to subsidise the Zimbabwe government's land reform initiative.

Faced with several political obstacles, including complicated economic, administrative, legal and demographic challenges, the Zimbabwe government

---

3 The position of the UK government has been that there is no provision in the Lancaster House Agreement of 1979 that provides for a specific fund to support land reform.

4 In addition to the proposed changes to the programme, the UK continued to provide aid to the Zimbabwe government, for instance by supporting the 1998 land conference that agreed on principles such as transparency, respect for the rule of law, and poverty reduction.

5 See the official policy on Zimbabwe in Foreign and Commonwealth Office (FCO), National Archive, 5 February 2008.

increased its efforts to nationalise and redistribute farms in the 1990s. Mugabe's policies was met with resistance, both from the white community (and interest groups from abroad) and from war veterans. The war veterans also formed an important interest group for President Mugabe going back to the early liberation struggle. However, they had begun to voice their concerns about the lack of economic support and compensation.

Nearly 20 years later, after his election as president, Mugabe was still entangled in the complexity of land redistribution and the question of the future of the Zimbabwean Constitution.

To deal with the growing criticism – domestic as well as from abroad – Mugabe supported a referendum to be held in held in 2000. The aim was both to speed up the continued land redistribution programme, which was marked by corruption and inefficiency, by proposing compulsory acquisition of land – a fast-track programme – and to strengthen presidential power through constitutional amendments.[6] When the constitutional referendum was held on 14 February 2000, surprisingly for ZANU-PF, Mugabe and his government lost, with 55 per cent voting against the new proposals and 45 per cent in favour. The outcome of the referendum unexpectedly signalled much stronger opposition to the sitting government than had been anticipated. Staggered by the election outcome, but clear in his vision, Mugabe declared his intent to continue with his policy of land redistribution and increase presidential power despite the public will reflected in the referendum. Immediately, the first farm occupations began. Following hardening rhetoric by the government, landless people, ZANU-PF loyalists and war veterans began to occupy land owned by white commercial farmers. Rather than condemning such occupations and trying to settle the matter in a judicial way, the government called the invaders 'Hungry Peaceful Demonstrators', thereby attaching official legitimacy to their actions. The Zimbabwean Supreme Court, declaring the acquisition of land in this way legal, later upheld the official government position.[7] As Good notes:

> Starting just days after the referendum, compelling evidence existed of the state's direct involvement in the invasions; government vehicles being used to transport occupiers to the farms; the engagement of CIO, army, and ruling party officials in the campaign; and reports of daily stipends paid to the occupiers.[8]

This official engagement further distressed the white farmer community.

The political support Mugabe had given to the land occupiers raised concerns in several democratic countries, most notably in the UK. The concern was that

---

6 Good found that much of the redistributed land had gone to public servants and politicians rather than to landless people; Good (2002): 13.

7 The policy was upheld by a visiting team from the SADC; *Keesing's* (Zimbabwe), vol. 47, December 2001: 44,492.

8 Good (2002): 14.

Mugabe, instead of taking the opportunity of address the land question through reconciliation, had dealt with it in a fairly hostile and unconstructive way, pitting white communities against black. The political events which unfolded in Zimbabwe, involving human rights abuses including the looting of private properties, also provoked worldwide reactions, leading various governments and regional organisations to reconsider their relations with Zimbabwe. For instance, the Commonwealth Ministerial Action Group (CMAG) issued a warning to the Zimbabwe government, declaring that the actions were contrary to the sprit of the Commonwealth statutes.[9]

In 2000, amidst all this turmoil, a parliamentary election was held in which the Movement for Democratic Change (MDC) won 57 of the 120 contested seats.[10] The political strength of the MDC in this election came as a surprise to Mugabe. To secure power, Mugabe later announced that he would be the ZANU-PF contender in the forthcoming election, scheduled for 2002. In this context, it is worth noting that during the days following this announcement, on 14 and 16 December, the Zimbabwean police arrested the main opposition leader, Morgan Tsvangerai of the Movement for Democratic Change (MDC), for possession of 'unlicensed radio equipment'.[11] In the run-up to the presidential election in 2002, the MDC leader was brought to trial, following footage transmitted by Zimbabwe state television on 13 February 2002 which showed Tsvangerai allegedly participating in a coup plot.[12] All these events led the EU to prepare targeted sanctions against Mugabe's government.[13]

Putting Targets under Pressure

Restrictive measures were imposed on the government of Zimbabwe on 18 February 2002. They were enacted just before the presidential election held in the country on 9–11 March 2002 after intense efforts by the EU to promote a reconciliatory political atmosphere in the days leading up to election day.[14]

9 There were also other policies causing annoyance, for instance the Public Order and Security Bill, and the General Laws Amendment Bill Acts giving the government power in a number of fields such as the security sector as well as tools to prevent foreign and independent election monitoring. On 31 January, the House also passed the Access to Information Bill, which restricted the media.

10 For more on the specific election result, see Kamete (2002).

11 *Keesing's* (Zimbabwe), vol. 47, December 2001: 44,492.

12 *Africa Research Bulletin*, March 2002: 14,758.

13 Discussions to implement sanctions had begun already in January. Reports suggest that in mid-January, the EU and the US had already formally begun to identify assets of the regime; *Africa Research Bulletin*, February 2002: 14,719.

14 For example, the EU in this context called for increased respect of human rights, democratic principles and an independent legal system.

Table 9.1 Zimbabwe target categories

Episode no.	1	2	3	4	5	6	7	8	9
Start date	18 February 2002	22 July 2002	13 September 2002	19 February 2004	13 June 2005	29 July 2005	19 February 2007	25 June 2007	22 July 2008
Defence/ Military/Air	4	4	4	7	6	5	5	5	26[1]
Family	—	1	1	1	1	1	1	1[2]	2
Government[3]	12	37	48	53	77	77	77	82	84
Parliament[4]	1	1	1	1	1	1	1	1	1
Police	1	1	1	1	1	4	4	6	8[5]
Prison	1	1	1	1	1	1	1	1	1
Central bank associates									3
War veterans									2
Media									2
Secretary/ Political bureau	1	27	23	25	25	30	28	29	30
Other	—	—	—	6[6]	8[7]	6[8]	8[9]	6	9[10]
Total	20	72	79	95	120	125	125	131	168

Notes: This table is based on a review of all key EU Council Decisions (CFSP) following the first adoption of the Zimbabwe sanctions regime in 2002. [1] A number of targets were added in this category following their participation in election violence. [2] Patric Zhuwao could also be considered a family member, as he is a nephew of Mugabe. He is listed here as part of the government in his capacity as Deputy Minister for Science and Technology. [3] Sometimes a minister may be the same person as the ZANU-PF Secretary. This can alter the categories slightly. [4] The Speaker of Parliament. [5] Two entities were added to the list, one of whom was a 'close cousin' of President Mugabe (which also allowed him to be placed in the family category). [6] Includes the Chairman of the Electoral Supervisory Commission, Chair of the Media Information Commission, Registrar General, Chair of the National War Veterans Association, Health Advisor in the Office of the President and the Chairman of the Presidential Land Review Committee. [7] In this episode, the Supreme Court Judge, the Chairman of the Delimitation Committee and the Chief Elections Officer were listed. [8] Includes the Chairman of the Supreme Court Judges, the Chairman of the Electoral Supervisory Commission, the Former Chairman of the Electoral Supervisory Commission, the Chair of the Media Information Commission, the Registrar General, the Chief Election Officer and the Former Chair of the National War Veterans Association. [9] Includes the Chairman of the Supreme Court Judges Delimitation Committee, the Chairman of the Electoral Supervisory Commission, the Former Chairman of the Electoral Supervisory Commission and the Chair of the Media Information Commission. [10] Includes the President of the World Medical Association, Zimbabwe Branch, the head of the Zimbabwe Cricket Federation and a Detective Inspector allegedly involved in torture and detention of MDC activists.

As late as February 2001, President Mugabe's representatives came to Brussels under a consultation process framework to discuss the situation in Zimbabwe.[15] Based on Article 96 in the Cotonou Agreement, signed in June 2000, the EU had called for the Zimbabwean regime to adhere to a set of conditions in order for the EU to recognise the election.[16] Despite the dialogue framework, the political climate inside the country did not change. The reluctance of the Zimbabwean government to agree to these stipulations led the EU to set out a number of benchmark conditions which the government would have to meet if the election were to be considered reasonably free and fair.[17] Unless the conditions were met, targeted sanctions (restrictive measures) would be imposed.[18] Despite the threat of sanctions, no change in the political situation took place, so a travel ban and an assets freeze policy was imposed (see Table 9.1).[19]

The Common Policy adopted by the EU aimed, at least in theory, to have an economic impact on the listed individuals:

> Funds, financial assets or economic resources of the persons listed in the Annex [referring to a list of names], who are engaged in activities that seriously undermine democracy, respect for human rights and the rule of law in Zimbabwe, will be frozen.

The policy continues: 'no funds, financial assets or economic resources will be made available directly or indirectly to the persons referred to in paragraph 1'.[20]

In addition, the EU withdrew its financial state-to-state support. Instead of providing financial support to the Zimbabwean government, the EU redirected its

---

15 The Cotonou Agreement is a global agreement signed in Cotonou, Benin on 23 June 2000 defining how the EU and ACP should co-operate on political, development and trade issues.

16 The conditions were: ending the political violence (and the public tolerance of such violence); allowing the EU to be invited to monitor the election and be granted unlimited access; allowing for the protection of the media; making the legal system more independent, and ending the illegal occupation of land; EU Commission, 26 October 2001.

17 These conditions are found the EU Council Conclusions of 28 January 2002.

18 The EU said that sanctions would be imposed if the government of Zimbabwe prevented the deployment of an EU election observation mission starting on 3 February 2002; if it prevented the mission from operating effectively; if the government of Zimbabwe prevented the international media from having free access to cover the election; if there was a serious in the human rights situation on the ground or there were attacks on the opposition, or if the election was judged not to be free and fair.

19 The EU Council also adopted an arms embargo on all supplies or sales of arms and related material to Zimbabwe.

20 See Council Common Position of 18 February 2002 concerning restrictive measures on Zimbabwe. Note that the amount of time that elapsed between the first official indication that the EU would implement sanctions (28 January 2008) and the de facto implementation (18 February 2002) gave the listed entities sufficient time to rearrange their private assets.

support to non-state operators.[21] In retrospect, one could ask whether this policy contributed to the increase of the financial crisis that would later plague Zimbabwe (as the state was on its own unable to cover public expenses due to the lack of foreign money and insecurity about future financial stability).

Zimbabwe Sanctions Episodes

I will now analyse the sanctions episodes that featured in EU's Zimbabwe sanctions regime. These episodes are based on the EU's official assessment of the sanctions policy process and the dynamics on the ground up to mid-2009,[22] reflecting some of the key political developments that took place during or immediately following, them.

Episode 1, February 2002

The decision to impose targeted sanctions on the Zimbabwean elite came when, prior to the election, the chairman of the EU election observer team, Ambassador Pierre Schori, informed the EU Council ministers that the government of Zimbabwe had failed to allow him to carry out independent election monitoring, stating that the mission could not operate with 'respect and credibility' under the terms imposed by the government.[23] The election went ahead despite the EU's imposition of targeted sanctions. On 13 March 2002, President Mugabe was declared the winner of the election, having received 56 per cent of the votes, while his opponent, Morgan Tsvangerai, claimed 42 per cent. Consequently, Mugabe was sworn in as president on 17 March, which would grant him another six years in office. Because of the conduct of the election, the MDC filed a complaint to the Zimbabwean High Court in which it challenged the outcome.

The EU deplored the fact that the political response from a host of other actors in the region did not go as far as it had wished in terms of denouncing the election results. While several governments in Europe criticised the Zimbabwean elections as fraudulent, a number of African governments accepted the elections as free and fair (among them, South Africa).[24]

21 'Imposition of EU sanctions', *Keesing's* (Zimbabwe), no. 41, February 2002.

22 Since, at time of writing, this is an active and ongoing sanctions regime, further episodes have followed in the period after mid-2009.

23 According to the government in Harare, however, Mr Schori was biased in his work; *Africa Research Bulletin* 2002: 14,758. See also Eriksson (2005): 115–19, and *Keesing's* (Zimbabwe), vol. 48, February 2002: 44,600.

24 Divisions were also noticed within the Commonwealth. For instance, some of its member states called for a tougher position on Zimbabwe (for example, Australia and New Zealand), while there was also opposition to the renewal of sanctions (for instance, from Nigeria and South Africa). Both Nigeria and South Africa wanted to deal with Zimbabwe in a manner of constructive engagement. South Africa's early policy of 'quiet and neutral

In order to prevent further deterioration into political violence following the election, ZANU-PF and the MDC met in April 2002, after mediation efforts by Nigeria and South Africa. It is difficult to conclude whether targeted sanctions contributed to ZANU-PF's decision to meet with the MDC.

Examining the list of targets referred to in the Common Position as of the 18 February 2002, some preliminary observations can be made. First, a majority of the individuals on the targeted sanctions list were government ministers (13 out of 20). However, the list seemed mostly to be symbolic in nature. For example, no explicit grounds were included in the Council Position to explain why these particular entities had been chosen in the first place.[25] Several ministers who could have been targeted were not included on this first sanctions list. One reason might be that the EU expected that omitting some members of the Zimbabwean regime might lead to friction within the government.[26] A more realistic explanation, though, is that the EU simply lacked coherent information. Second, the initial list did not include a single woman. This is somewhat extraordinary given that several influential women held positions in the Zimbabwean regime. Third, the Common Position also included a number of exemptions under which targeted individuals could, for instance, be granted permission to travel.[27] While these exemptions were included to take account of exceptional circumstances, there were ample indications that these waivers were misused, and in effect, were counter-productive to the EU's sanctions policy.[28]

diplomacy' later shifted to being supportive of Zimbabwe. In mid-October 2002, Australia introduced targeted sanctions on 77 Zimbabwe officials and ZANU-PF members, while at the same time underlining that the value of introducing the sanctions was only symbolic. During the same month, New Zealand expanded its sanctions list to cover 142 people; Reuters, 13 October 2002, and BBC News, 30 October 2002.

25 The EU heads of mission in Harare established the list.

26 For example, the EU omitted to place the two vice-presidents, Simon Muzenda and Joseph Msika, on the sanctions list, as they were not regarded as a hostile to the opposition; *News 24,* February 2002.

27 For example, Police Commissioner Augustine Chihuri, despite being placed on the EU sanctions list, could travel to Lyon to participate in an executive conference of Interpol; *BBC News,* 18 May 2002.

28 For example, Mugabe attended the UN General Assembly's Special Session for Children Conference in New York on May 2002. This caused anger among the opposition; MDC Press, 9 May 2002. Zimbabwe's Foreign Affairs Minister, Stan Mudenge, said sanctions would not prevent Zimbabwe leaders from carrying out diplomatic functions. Mudenge pointed out that despite the EU's imposition of smart sanctions, the president and his advisors flew to New York via Paris: 'we used Paris, an EU country … and were not hindered to use their international transit facilities'; *Zimbabwe Independent*, 17 May 2002.

Episodes 2 and 3, July and September 2002

During the Summer of 2002, the EU issued new sanctions lists. Both episodes followed a period in Zimbabwe, which did not show any signs of a change or constraint in behaviour on the part of the regime or its individual members.

Prior to the beginning of the episode, as early as in May 2002, representatives of ZANU-PF and the MDC met for a second time under the facilitation of Nigeria and South Africa to discuss their political differences regarding the election. The aim was to seek a solution to the political deadlock. Although this was seen as a positive step, the talks came to an abrupt end when the MDC filed a petition in the High Court challenging the election process and its outcome.

Meanwhile, the political situation worsened. The government intensified the eviction of the white farmer community under the fast-track land reform programme. The economic distress of those effected increased, and by July an estimated 2,900 farmers had been forced to leave their land. To cover the increasing food shortages, the World Food Programme (WFP) began to assist the government by delivering food. However, the situation was exacerbated even further when Zimbabwe's Deputy Minister for Foreign Affairs allegedly threatened the opposition more explicitly, claiming that food aid would not be available.[29] There were also other signs of an increasingly aggressive government policy towards the opposition, for example through the Zimbabwe government's increasing interference in the free press, as well as unwarranted prosecutions, in particular two high-profile cases relating to members of the Zimbabwean Law Society. These developments led the US government to set up its own sanctions regime.

In June 2002, the International Monetary Fund (IMF) adopted a declaration of non-cooperation with Zimbabwe. This followed a suspension of technical assistance. Unlike targeted sanctions, which were aimed at particular members of the regime, the move would also have an impact on both state and society.

Moreover, during the episode, public uproar erupted in June 2002 when the EU granted permission for President Mugabe to attend a UN summit meeting arranged by the Food and Agriculture Organisation in Rome. This decision caused divisions among the EU's member states between those in favour and those against letting Mugabe travel to Europe. One factor which certainly fanned this heated debate was media attention. While EU member states were well informed about the exemptions under which allowed a target to travel, the international media portrayed the EU as being slack in its commitment to sanctions as well as its implementation of them.

On 22 July 2002, the EU introduced an updated sanctions list.[30] This included two new categories of targets. Besides members of the military, parliament, police, prison and state security, which formed the bulk of the first list, a category of leading ZANU-PF members was also included. In addition, one family member

29 *Keesing's* (Zimbabwe), vol. 48, July 2002: 44,885.

30 Council Common Position 2002/600/CFSP.

– Robert Mugabe's wife – was added. The list had increased to nearly 50 entities. There may have been other reasons for the issuing of a new sanctions list. The first might have been to further isolate the entities that made up the power base of the Mugabe regime. Second, the EU might already have had plans for the second list when designing the first. Third, the EU might have had a pre-planned strategy to adjust to changing political dynamics on the ground in Zimbabwe (for instance, when it became clear that Mugabe had reshuffled the government since the first round of sanctions). However, the existence of such a refined EU strategy cannot be verified. Finally, it might be that the EU was better prepared to deal with sanctions evasion this time, and was responding to sanctions evasion more rapidly. A subsequent Council Decision added seven names, while two were removed. This revision took place against the background of a government reshuffle in Zimbabwe on 26 August.[31]

Episode 4, February 2004

During this episode, the situation in Zimbabwe continued to deteriorate, both economically and politically.[32] In late 2003, President Thabo Mbeki of South Africa met with President Mugabe following Mugabe's decision to withdraw his country from the Commonwealth on 7 December 2003 after one of the Commonwealth sub-committees (led by Australia, Canada, India, Jamaica, Mozambique and South Africa) had recommended that its members continue the suspension of Zimbabwe.[33]

During the episode, political developments in the Zimbabwean government continued to send signals to the EU that the listed entities were not considering

31 Council Decision 2002/754/CFSP.

32 This episode had been preceded by a number of events during 2003 that had further contributed to the deterioration of the relationship between Zimbabwe and the EU (and other concerned powers). In November 2002, when the government of Zimbabwe decided to impose a travel ban on all UK officials as a response to the UK's imposition of a visa requirement for Zimbabwean nationals, a diplomatic row also broke out over the failure to agree on new targeted sanctions for the leaders of Zimbabwe. The controversy occurred in late January 2003 because of France's decision to invite President Mugabe to attend the forthcoming Franco-African Summit in Paris on 19–21 February 2003. The invitation (and later attendance) of Mugabe was extended despite the UK's firm opposition. France's invitation followed concern that other African presidents had threatened to boycott the meeting unless Mugabe was be allowed to attend the meeting. Moreover, on 7 March 2003 US President George W. Bush signed an executive order imposing targeted sanctions on 76 high-ranking Zimbabwe government officials. A week later, the Commonwealth decided to renew the suspension of Zimbabwe from its organisation for another nine months. Finally, it is worth noting that during June 2003, the IMF decided to suspend Zimbabwe's voting rights; *Keesing's* (Zimbabwe), vol. 49, December 2003: 45,730.

33 *Ibid.*: 45,765.

changing their political course. On 19 January, the MDC's Tsvangerai appeared in court for to answer charges of treason for allegedly plotting to kill Mugabe.[34]

A month later, on 19 February, the EU extended its targeted sanctions against the regime for another 12 months following its political assessment that no progress had been made which would lead the country back to order. With the issuing of the list, a number of new target categories were added (such as members of Zimbabwe's army). This measure came ten days after Mugabe had carried out a reshuffle of his cabinet.[35] It is not clear whether the EU had anticipated this reshuffle or was simply responding to it on a routine basis.

Episodes 5 and 6, June–July 2005

A number of political developments prior to the fifth and sixth episodes provided the EU with sufficient reason to push for additional entities to be included on the sanctions list: (1) the instigation of Operation Murambatsvina (with the slogan 'Drive out Rubbish', or as it was officially called, 'Operation Restore Order'), and (2) the holding of a fraudulent election.[36]

The government's instigation on 23 May 2005 of Operation Murambatsvina provided additional justification for the continuation of the sanctions regime. This policy, which sparked fierce domestic and international outcry, was meant to clamp down on informal market activities and general lawlessness in the suburbs of Harare that, according to the government, had caused social distress. The policy also aimed to evict illegal settlers and clamp down on illegally built homes. The operations lead to violent clashes in various townships, notably in Harare. Reports later claimed that as many as 200,000 people were made homeless, while 25,000 were arrested.[37] A UN investigation claimed that about 2.4 million had been affected, and that an estimated 700,000 lost their homes because of this operation. The evictions (without any alternative housing being provided), the arbitrary arrests and clashes led to the establishment of the Broad Alliance (a formation of opposition groups as well as actors in civil society) to call for a general strike on 9–10 June. Fearing additional clashes, the strike was later called off.

Despite the mostly negative developments during these episodes, there were also a number of positive signs. For example, the Zimbabwe government suggested that white farmers would be allowed to return to the farmlands under certain land leases. While the government had been provocatively calling on all white people to leave their farms, more reconciliatory gestures were being signalled at the time. However, such moves were mainly interpreted as a sign of desperation due to the lack of agricultural expertise that resulted from the evictions, as agricultural

34 *Ibid.*, vol. 50, January 2004: 45,773.

35 *Ibid.*

36 *Ibid.*, vol. 51, May 2005: 46,611.

37 *Ibid.*

output declined rapidly, with food shortages as a result. Another such positive development was the invitation of the WFP back into the country.[38]

Besides these dynamics in Zimbabwe, there were also particular features during this episode that focused further attention on the EU's sanctions policies. For example, one row arose from Mugabe's wish to travel to the funeral of Pope John Paul II in Rome on 8 April 2005. As in earlier episodes, the travel exemptions sparked an intense international debate regarding the legitimacy of the sanctions.

On 13 June 2005, the sanctions list was expanded to cover an additional 25 individuals.[39] This list mainly followed the parliamentary elections held in March 2005, when the ZANU-PF took 78 seats and the MDC won 41. During the elections, the government of Zimbabwe had limited the number of independent election monitors and forbidden observers from 'unfriendly nations'. Most of the names added to the new sanctions list came under the 'government' category, along with a few more in additional categories. It must be noted here that the EU's listing measures had become almost a routine practice. Little innovative thinking took place. As an alternative, more family members could have been listed, or businesspersons personally connected to the regime could have been added.[40] Later in the Summer, on 29 July 2005, the list was lengthened by another five names, mostly police officers, for their involvement in Operation Murambatsvina.[41]

Episode 7, February 2007

On 16 December 2006, the ruling ZANU-PF declared that it wanted to hold the scheduled 2008 presidential election at the same time as the legislative election to be held in 2010 instead (this would ultimately lead to a prolongation of Mugabe's period in executive office). The objective of securing Mugabe's power fuelled further international criticism. Meanwhile, however, a more positive development was that the government indicated a policy change with regard to the land reform programme, suggesting that white people who had lost their farms could get them back on 99-year leases.[42]

38 Meanwhile, Mugabe declared that the land reform policy would continue and would only be determined as completed when there was not a single white-owed farm left; see *ibid.*, vol. 53, January 2007: 47,677.

39 Council Decision 2005/444/CFSP.

40 The inclusion of business sector targets has also been called for by the International Crisis Group: 'Those who have moved their assets abroad should be targeted quickly, especially those that that have helped bankroll ZANU-PF. The individuals and directors of companies that are the chief supporters and beneficiaries of Zanu-PF rule should be the next targets. A number of companies established by ZANU-PF officials and their close associates during the last decade receive most of the government contracts, get favourable treatment for import-export arrangements …'; *International Crisis Group*, no. 41, 2002: 13.

41 Council Decision 2005/592/CFSP.

42 *Keesing's* (Zimbabwe), vol. 53, January 2007: 47,623.

Targeted sanctions on Zimbabwe were renewed on 19 February 2007.[43] While the domestic political situation in Zimbabwe remain the same – indeed, it had slightly worsened – the extension was not triggered by any particular event besides the fact that President Mugabe carried out a cabinet reshuffle on 7 February (again with the possible intention of evading targeted sanctions by including ministers in the government who were not on the EU's sanctions list). In total, 125 names were added. For the most part, the same categories of targets remained, although there was a slight increase in the number of ZANU-PF members targeted. Calls were are made by international campaign groups to have the Reserve Bank Governor, Gideon Gono, added to the list, alleging that he had contributed to the economic decline of the country. Yet his name was not included at this stage.[44]

Episode 8, June 2007

Events in June 2007 were greatly affected by two particular events that took place some months prior to the episode. On 11 March 2007, a coalition called the Save Zimbabwe Campaign held a large demonstration in Harare which was met with government force. Receiving much international media attention, it attracted protests from a number of governments around the world. The other event that affected developments was the additional summit held by the Southern African Development Community, where African representatives met to discuss the near economic collapse of Zimbabwe. Contrary to expectations, instead of blaming the government for its lack of political and economic control, the SADC issued a statement reaffirming its solidarity with the government and people of Zimbabwe and called on the UK to honour its commitment to fund land redistribution under the Lancaster House Agreement.[45] This statement caused irritation among Western countries, most notably the UK.

More proactively, however, the SADC launched a mediation attempt to increase political co-operation between ZANU-PF and the MDC. A meeting facilitated by South Africa was held in mid-May. Both parties decided to meet again in early June.[46] Despite these fruitful moves to bring ZANU-PF closer to the MDC, continued persecution of opposition supporters forced the EU to impose additional targets on the sanctions lists.[47] In its decision, the EU Council noted in particular the responsibility of the police for these events.[48] As a result, on 25 June 2007 the EU increased the scope of targeted sanctions list to include 131

43 Council Common Position 2007/120/CSFP.

44 *International Crisis Group*, no. 122, 5 March 2007. One reason why was not included is that some EU actors considered him a man that they could talk to, and that therefore he should not be on the list.

45 *Keesing's* (Zimbabwe), vol. 53, March 2007: 47,795.

46 *Ibid.*: 47,911.

47 Council Decision 2007/455/CFSP.

48 Commission Regulation 2007/777 (2 July 2007).

regime-supporting entities. This was an increase of six entities compared to the previous list, adding categories such as government members, ZANU-PF officials and members of Zimbabwe's police force. During the episode, there were once again calls for the inclusion of the Reserve Bank Governor, Gideon Gono, on the sanctions list.[49] Notably, for the first time the EU made explicit reference in its sanctions list to why a particular entity had been placed on it by inserting a statement of the reasons for inclusion next to each individual's name.[50]

Finally, it is worth noting that during this episode, the Zimbabwe government was likely to have been further pressured by official estimates by South Africa that nearly 100,000 Zimbabweans were passing into South Africa every month as a result of the crisis.[51]

Episode 9, July 2008

Events during this episode were dominated by the presidential election held on 29 March 2008.[52] According to the state-led Zimbabwe Electoral Commission (ZEC), Tsvangerai did not win by an absolute majority (50 per cent), so he would have to take part in a run-off contest against Mugabe on 27 June 2008.[53] According to these official election results, Tsvangerai had won 47.9 per cent of the vote, while Mugabe had 43.2 per cent. However, on 22 June Tsvangerai withdrew from the second round, asserting that he had in fact won the first one and claiming that violence did not permit a fair election since almost ninety MDC members had been killed during the elections and several hundred opposition members had been wounded. Consequently, President Mugabe was declared winner of the presidential elections. Following Tsvangerai's withdrawal, the UN Security Council adopted a Presidential Statement which condemned the actions of the Zimbabwe government for its violence against the opposition.[54] Later, on 11 July 2008, the UN Security Council voted to impose an arms embargo, travel ban and

49 Various members of the UK Parliament called for the government to include the governor on the list. See 'UK Parliament debate on Zimbabwe', 19 July 2007.

50 The inclusion followed legal developments in the EU regarding judicially tight listing procedures.

51 *Keesing's* (Zimbabwe), vol. 53, July 2007: 48,029.

52 Note also that a number of important events took place in between the episodes. In particular, the second summit between the African Union and the EU was held in December 2007. However, UK Prime Minister Gordon Brown stayed away from the summit to object to President Mugabe's presence. During the meeting, though, Chancellor Angela Merkel of Germany issued a strong denunciation of the situation in Zimbabwe, which was supported by the Netherlands, Denmark and Sweden. Mugabe responded to the statement the day after, referring to his critics as 'Gordon's gang of four'. Several African nations sided with Mugabe; *Keesing's* (Zimbabwe), vol. 53, December 2007: 48,292.

53 *Ibid.*, vol. 54, June 2008: 48,620.

54 *Ibid.*

financial sanctions on the Zimbabwe government. This resolution was blocked by Russia and China.

Meanwhile, on 1 July 2008 the heads of state of the African Union called for 'a government of national unity' in Zimbabwe.[55] This statement was not fully endorsed by all member countries (for example, South Africa took a conciliatory approach, whereas Botswana called for further isolation).

On 22 July 2008, the EU issued an extended sanctions list including 36 new individuals. In this move, the EU added new categories of regime supporters, notably official members of the Central Bank, members of the War Veterans Association, members of the state-run media and individuals engaged in election violence. Moreover, on 25 July the US president signed an executive order which expanded its targeted sanctions, leading to further isolation of members of the regime.

On 21 July, Mugabe and Tsvangerai came face to face for the first time in ten years when formal power-sharing talks between ZANU-PF and the MDC opened in Pretoria. The negotiations were fruitful, and subsequently paved the way for a power-sharing agreement signed on 15 September 2008.[56] Slow implementation now led South Africa to threaten Zimbabwe with the withdrawal of aid unless it worked effectively to implement the power-sharing agreement. On 11 February 2009, Tsvangerai took office as Zimbabwe's prime minister, while Mugabe remained president.

Analysis

This section will discuss some of the main observations arising from the EU's implementation of targeted sanctions on Zimbabwe. The aim is to illustrate the complex political dynamics that contributed to shaping the sanctions outcomes.

Despite the implementation of targeted sanctions, the democratic situation in Zimbabwe continued to deteriorate over time, and individual members of the elite did not change their behaviour in the way European powers wanted. On the contrary, the elite repeatedly stepped up its violent treatment of the opposition, while at the same time growing increasingly hostile to the EU.

Episode 1 was marked by the failure to convince the target state to hold free and fair elections; the failure of the EU's prior sanctions threats; the failure of the consultation process; the impact of allowing a personal friend of Mugabe to serve as head of the EU's election observer team; a number of African governments' positive acceptance and legitimisation of the Zimbabwean elections, in contrast to the position of the EU; mediation efforts by Nigeria and South Africa; the role of the first, fairly limited and symbolic, sanctions list, and the impact of Australia's and New Zealand's imposition of sanctions.

---

55 *Ibid.*: 48,678.

56 *Ibid.*: 48,760.

Episodes 2 and 3 featured the sender's negative assessment of the target behaviour and its decision to expand targeted sanctions; the continued mediation by Nigeria and South Africa; the role of ongoing MDC High Court cases; the worsening of the general political and economic situation; the increasing food shortages; increasing interference with the Zimbabwean press; the IMF's adoption of non-cooperation; the role of travel exemptions; the negative media attention with regard to those travel exemptions; the role of new categories of targets included on the sanctions list, and the impact of the government reshuffle.

Episode 4's main features were the continued economic and political situation; the personal involvement and mediation of President Mbeki of South Africa; the court case involving MDC leader Morgan Tsvangerai; the role of new target categories; the negative relationship between Zimbabwe and the UK, and the impact of US targeted sanctions on Zimbabwe.

In Episodes 5 and 6 we note the failure to convince the Zimbabwean elite to hold democratic elections; the role of Operation Murambatsvina; the failure to deploy independent election monitors on the ground; the role of violent clashes in various places in Zimbabwe; the negative attention arising from allowing President Mugabe to travel to Rome; the EU's difficulties in persuading the African Union and SADC to reject the Zimbabwean elections; the role of US condemnation of the fraudulent elections; the positive developments with regard to allowing white farmers to return to the farmlands and the acceptance of World Food Programme aid; the role of new target categories, and the impact of Mugabe's insistence on continuing with the land reform policy.

Episode 7 is notable for discussions concerning Mugabe's desire to prolong his period in power; the role of the EU's expanded sanctions list, and the positive development of an official policy allowing white farmers access to land.

Episode 8's main features are the large-scale anti-government demonstrations held across Zimbabwe; the increasing brutality of the government; the increasing international media attention; the anti-sanctions campaign in Zimbabwe's state-run newspapers; the solidarity between the SADC and the ruling Zimbabwean elite; the SADC's mediation efforts; the expansion of the sanctions list; the inclusion of personal references to listed entities' responsibilities and reasons for being listed; the increasing collapse of Zimbabwe's system of government; the impact of the crisis on South Africa, and the concerns of members of the UK.

Episode 9 is notable for the failure of the EU to ensure a democratic election in Zimbabwe; the withdrawal from the second round of the election by MDC leader Morgan Tsvangerai; the large number of opposition members who had allegedly been killed during the elections; the involvement of the UN Security Council and the blocking of a Zimbabwe resolution by Russia and China; the official position taken by the AU; the expansion of the sanctions list and the inclusion of new target categories; the increasing economic collapse and high inflation; the negotiations between ZANU-PF and the MDC; the personal meeting between President Mugabe and Tsvangerai, and the seating of Tsvangerai as Zimbabwe's Prime Minister.

As seen from the empirical record, the implementation of EU targeted sanctions was not entirely in political harmony with the policies of neighbouring states. While the EU pursued an isolationist policy, countries such as South Africa and Nigeria adopted a more reconciliatory attitude towards Zimbabwe. While the EU pointed towards bad governance and human rights abuses, several SADC countries increasingly came to accept and support the view held by President Mugabe: that sanctions were the source of the crisis. For example, in various statements by the SADC, it expressed solidarity with the land reform and implicitly argued that the best way forward for Zimbabwe would be for the to EU reconsider its sanctions.[57] Even as late as Spring 2009, the SADC leaders continued to claim that the problems in Zimbabwe were being exaggerated and that all forms of sanctions should be lifted.[58] This standpoint held by the SADC led to an uneasy relationship with the EU.[59]

Based on the dynamics highlighted in these episodes, it is difficult to determine in what ways targeted sanctions contributed to solving the crises in Zimbabwe. While the sender had initially anticipated behavioural change among listed members leading to improvements in the domestic political and economic situation, the crisis none the less deteriorated. Moreover, despite the targeted nature of EU and US sanctions, the branding of Zimbabwe as a state in crisis scared off investors, which in the end had an effect on the entire country.

In terms of achieving behavioural change or constraining listed entities, targeted sanctions may have dissuaded targets from pursuing a more hostile policy than would have been the case without them. For example, knowledge of inclusion on the travel ban list may have led those targeted not to travel to public events where they could promote the government's cause. Such decisions not to travel, however, are non-explicit acts. The same argument could be made regarding the financial sanctions. The annoyance of not being able to buy personally, for example, certain products from London because of the fear of having money frozen may not be visible in the target's behaviour in the enduring political crisis. Nevertheless, it may cause the target to experience annoyance to such a degree that he or she will begin to behave differently. This, of course, is not obvious in the episodes.

While the EU adopted some sanctions targeted at individuals, it seems that most of the measures were group-based. Although in 2007 the EU decided to include personal 'statements of reasons' for why a particular person was included on a sanctions list, there seems not to have been any systematic bargaining rationale. In other words, personal listing was never really fully exploited by the EU to pressurise targets to modify certain behaviours. For example, the heads of mission in Zimbabwe could have taken advantage of the power struggles inside the ZANU-PF which took place during 2004 and 2007. A 'push and pull' approach could also have been used more strategically to foster a culture of dialogue, for instance in

57 Angola Press Agency, 4 October 2002.

58 *Keesing's* (Zimbabwe), vol. 53, August 2007: 48,071.

59 Agencia de Informacao de Mocambique, 8 November 2002.

connection with the mediation efforts by Nigeria and South Africa. In addition, the EU could have established a 'spoiler list' identifying and targeting those who were not able or ready to support the mediation strategy, as well as a 'reward list' of those who were prepared to do so.

One apparent difficulty with EU targeting strategy is that it has not dealt well with how to deal with travel ban exemptions. During certain episodes, the credibility of the EU's sanctions policy was undermined when listed entities were allowed to travel to Europe. As we have seen, this often caused public rows among the sender's member states, as well as among the democratic opposition and NGOs within and outside Zimbabwe. It also caused a political split among the EU's own member states over when to grant exemptions along certain policy lines. For example, in 2007 the British Prime Minister boycotted the EU-Africa summit because, despite the ban, President Mugabe had been invited to attend. In the international media, exemptions from the travel ban have also generally caused sensations as well as a belief that sanctions are more symbolic in nature than of serious political use. The fact that targets were able to travel despite being placed on travel ban lists could easily be perceived by the public as evasion by targets, or sloppy implementation of the travel ban regimes.

The examination of the impact of EU sanctions also reveals a more general methodological challenge in terms of assessment. One problem has to do with data collection concerning the target's behaviour. It seems unfeasible to collect systematic data to demonstrate that a particular behaviour has changed as a direct result of a particular restrictive measure. It is similarly difficult to assign a particular type of behavioural impact to targeted sanctions, such as 'sobering', 'restraint', 'repentance', 'victimisation' or 'repellence'. In this context, it is worth noting that local media are often limited and restrictive, thus making information difficult to obtain unless there are personal connections among those affiliated to the senders and the targets. A tentative review of target behaviour in the case of Zimbabwe suggests that travel ban violations are reported more widely in the media than evasion of financial sanctions.

While the imposition of a travel ban and a targeted assets freeze are meant to cause a political behaviour, or at least to constrain a target, it is surprisingly difficult to assign 'compliance', 'evasion' or 'do nothing' as a behaviour resulting from sanctions. Whereas evasion is generally observable, complicit behaviour is more difficult to observe. The 'do nothing' option is likely to be the least systematically reported behaviour. One reading is that this behaviour is good, as it means that the listed targeted is not actively challenging the sender. Another reading could be that 'do nothing' is a bad behaviour, in the sense that the target adheres to its earlier policy while keeping a low profile to avoid upsetting the sender.

A different methodological problem is that behaviour is time-dependent: a target can change its behaviour over time. Sometimes a target can be identified as evading sanctions, and at a later stage he or she can also be considered in compliance. Moreover, a listed entity can respond to the sender's demands on some issues but not on others. This clearly needs to be taken into account when assessing sanctions.

Finally, it is worth noting that the goals of the sender and the conditions for being listed were often connected to more general issues, such as the inability of the authorities to hold free and fair parliamentary elections. However, it is very difficult to ask each of the listed targets to relate to such conditions. This raises questions about the sender's intentions in using sanctions in the first place.

The Impact of Travel Bans

Travel bans have been adopted to put pressure on individual members of the Zimbabwean elite. Empirical evidence suggests that this measure has achieved a target impact in a number of cases. No longer can regime members placed on the EU sanctions list conduct shopping trips to European capitals. However, given that targeted sanctions are not globally enforced, shopping in non-European capitals can easily continue. As one interviewee from Zimbabwean civil society noted: 'Preventing those on the list from travelling is not so efficient since there are multiple alternatives, for instance by shopping over the Internet (using a Visa card). It is also easy to shop under different names.' Another problem is that it is difficult to have official targets banned entirely from European states because of the many exemptions included in the Common Positions. One technique to evade travel bans and pursue private pleasure is to attend international meetings and conferences, then stay on for a while. One problem with granting a travel ban exemption is that the presence of a listed individual in the EU is likely to signal to the public sloppiness in enforcement, as well as inconsistency. At least, this is how events could be interpreted from an outside perspective (that is, for those not involved in the sanctions game).[60] For instance, when the United Nations Development Programme (UNDP) arranged a meeting in Brussels to which some Zimbabwean parliamentarians had been invited, this created a great deal of debate in both the European media and in political circles in the EU, as the media had discovered that one of those invited was included on the EU sanctions list. While it was later decided that the target would not be allowed to travel to the venue of the meeting, the invitation had already undermined the legitimacy of the sanctions policy. On the other hand, it also annoyed the target, as it was revealed that the listed person had wanted to attend the meeting so that she could privately meet her children living in Brussels.

What is interesting is that the impact of sanctions could have effects beyond the more direct and physical ones that could be expected from the policy (such as preventing a target from travelling). Even if the targets did not always feel the

60 Government officials were likely to be more willing to reveal how their leaders could move around freely in European capitals rather than noting the fact that they were not welcome in European capitals.

impact of a travel ban directly, inclusion on a sanctions list seems to have led to stigmatisation, and thereby a psychological impact.

Targeting also had the (possibly unintended) effect of causing a sense of 'group feeling' among the listed entities. For example, being subject to sanctions could be seen as equivalent to being branded as a regime loyalist. Being labelled with the same target 'brush' could even have led to an increase in unity.[61] The more the leadership is targeted, the more the individuals in it tend to unite and resist the senders of the sanctions.

On the whole, though, it is difficult to verify whether travel bans led to a particular impact, alone or in combination with other specific measures.

The Impact of Targeted Assets Freeze Measures

While it is easy to find examples of situations where targets have been affected by travel bans, it is more difficult to assess the impact of an assets freeze. Figures are meant to be reported by EU member states to the EU Commission, but are not made known to the wider public.[62] In principle, EU member states are reluctant to hand out these kinds of figures (one explanation may be that few assets have actually been frozen).[63] Due to the scarcity of evidence concerning those cases where targets have had their personal assets frozen, it is not easy to conclude whether or not financial sanctions had any impact at all.

One problem with the adoption of a targeted financial sanctions policy is that there are many implementation loopholes, not to mention that they are easy to circumvent. While travel bans can only be verified through embassies, passport controls and other similar checkpoints, the myriad ways of transferring money in the financial system make it more complex. To start with, targeted financial measures require that financial institutions have accurate information about the senders, such as precise names, account numbers, personal social security figures and ID numbers. Nevertheless, even with this information, assets freezes can be easily evaded, for example simply by asking friends and families to conduct the financial transactions. This undermines their effectiveness.

While it is commonly assumed in the literature that it is more difficult to achieve success with regional sanctions compared to global mandatory UN

61 Explaining this logic, one interviewee said that there was even a particular word for this type of group cohesion based on external pressure: the 'laager', as used in by the Afrikaners in South Africa during the colonial era. It meant the way white settlers organised their camps in a circle, like a fortress of horses, so that they could better resist attackers following them during their trips. The same laager mentality thus seemed to prevail among those targeted.

62 The EU Commission in Brussels is also reluctant to publish such figures.

63 For example, it was acknowledged in a UK parliamentary debate on Zimbabwe that the UK government was looking for assets; Meg Munn, Parliamentary Undersecretary of State at the Foreign and Commonwealth Office. See 'UK Parliamentary debate on Zimbabwe', 19 July 2007.

financial sanctions, what seems to be a particularly important factor in shaping sanctions outcomes is the historic relationships and degrees of dependence that exist between senders and listed entities. In case of Zimbabwe, a number of listed entities have historically had close ties to the UK.

Other Factors Affecting the Impact of Sanctions

There are numerous factors, not covered here, that have shaped the effectiveness of sanctions. In this section, we will discuss two that seem important: the role of propaganda and the role of proportionality.

In the case of Zimbabwe, there has been a heated debate over whether to call the measures introduced by the EU 'sanctions' or 'restrictive measures'. According to the EU, there are no sanctions in place. Instead, the EU refers to 'targeted restrictive measures'. Members of the ZANU-PF government, however, continuously refer to these measures as 'sanctions', and claim that these are comprehensive and are put into place to harm the nation of Zimbabwe.[64] On the other hand, some of the targeted individuals project a narrative which asserts that what are in place are merely comprehensive sanctions. It is often claimed that comprehensive sanctions have led to dreadful suffering for Zimbabwe's population. The vocabulary used often speaks of 'illegal sanctions', and this view is further linked to side-effects – for example, that the policy makes international investors ignore Zimbabwe, thus having a long-term effect on the population as a whole.[65] On this point, it has been argued that several multilateral institutions have been blocked from having anything to do with Zimbabwe, as both the US and the UK have decisive influence in these institutions. The fact that 'sanctions' is part of the vocabulary when describing the situation in Zimbabwe, for instance, by IMF or the World Bank, scares international investors away from committing themselves to Zimbabwe markets. This has obviously had an enormous impact on the political and budgetary situation in Harare. In the end, this also affects

64 *The Zimbabwe Independent* of 22–28 September 2006 ran a story entitled 'Mugabe Still Blames Sanctions'. This is just one of many articles signal the government's blaming of the current crisis in the country on sanctions. Another such article is *The Herald*'s 'Sanctions: Zim soldiers on', which reported that: 'As Zimbabwe continues to face severe economic problems after six years of Western sanctions, President Mugabe says his country will continue its thrust to defend itself, with its people working hard to turn around the economy and prove the critics wrong'; *The Herald*, 14 September 2006. While the Zimbabwean government constantly blames sanctions as the cause of the country's problems, one interviewee noted that the government never mentions sanctions as a cause of evil during their day-to-day meetings with their European counterparts.

65 Dzinotyiweyi has also supported this view: 'No investor is happy to invest in a country where there is talk of sanctions of whatever form. Likewise few tourists are attracted to visit such a country. Thus the targeted sanctions may have missed their intended target but instead help create a negative perception about the country now avoided as a destination by both investors and tourists; Dzinotyiweyi (2004).

the life of ordinary Zimbabweans, leading to poverty and continued economic decline. As one interviewee from the NGO community described it: 'Targeted sanctions are a total failure. They have caused hardship to ordinary people. The targeted individuals own land and have access to foreign currency, which the poorer Zimbabweans do not have.' Whereas targets blame the senders for having introduced comprehensive sanctions, which according to this view primarily affect the Zimbabwean population, the senders claim that the only measures in place in Zimbabwe are travel bans, assets freezes and arms embargoes on the leadership. At the same time, it is argued that a great deal of development money is still being allocated to Zimbabwe (although not directly to the government).[66] These two narratives highlight a discrepancy between the technical vocabulary and the general perception of the effect of a policy. What is remarkable is that targets are able to project this narrative in the media, where more or less every week the government can discredit the sender's policy. Hence, one could describe the current situation as a sanctions media war.

Another factor that may influence the understanding of targeted sanctions is the issue of proportionality. It has been argued by some listed actors that the comprehensive economic sanctions imposed on Zimbabwe were out of all proportion to what was actually happening in the country. Referring to political events in other African countries, entities asked whether they deserved to be treated as harshly as they were. For instance, one interviewee asked:[67] 'Why are sanctions imposed on Zimbabwe while not on other African countries which are involved in wars?' Another interviewee maintained: 'The current sanctions are likely to be a smokescreen by the West. Why, for instance, is the international community imposing such strong measures on Zimbabwe, and not in other countries where conditions are much worse?'

Both these comments point to the question of proportionality – the role of unequal treatment by the EU. One human rights officer in Harare asked: 'What criteria were really used to come up with the listing of targeted individuals? If

66 'Article 96 in the Contonue Agreement suspends the development fund with about 108 million Euros. But we still use the fund for humanitarian purposes. There is no direct budget support to the government. It is a re-structuring of how we spend our money. We continue to support the people of Zimbabwe. For instance, there are several technical cooperation programs. Hence, there are several national cooperation programs, not only NGO cooperations. This is to counter the argument that sanctions stopped the aid to Zimbabwe. The restrictive measures are not an argument for having budget support restrictions. For instance, if the IMF had reservations on the conduct of economic policies, they would not – in any way – have been giving budget support. Thus, the money being spent here is just money being re-structured in terms of redistribution'; COM (2001), 623 final (26 October 2001).

67 An example of this is Namibia, which has also initiated a land redistribution policy. As noted by one interviewee: 'If other countries could be granted support in resettlement programs, why cannot the Zimbabwean government is allowed to the same without being punished?'

the listing was made as a consequence of abuses, then what are the criteria for inclusion?' In an informal interview conducted with an NGO representative working on women's legal rights in Zimbabwe, the interviewee said:

> Sanctions indeed have a taste of racism. Why, for instance, when the government already in 1998 chased away several black land owners, did the EU not impose sanctions, while only later, when the government took over several white-owned farms, did the international community care?[68]

Judging by the ongoing battle between sanctions narratives, it is quite clear that the parties are miscommunicating. While EU does not seem to have a platform to disseminate its sanctions policy, the government of Zimbabwe, on the other hand, does have such means. Moreover, while the EU is engaged in trying to explain the rationale for the restrictive measures – the failure of democratic governance, and human rights problems – the government of Zimbabwe can portray the comprehensive sanctions as yet another 'Rhodesia' (referring to the comprehensive sanctions imposed on Ian Smith) by connecting the policy to the question of land rights and sovereignty.

The fact that the EU is having a hard time conveying its version of the narrative is also reflected in comments made by two representatives of the human rights community, which would normally be supportive of the idea of having targeted sanctions. As noted by an officer of one of Zimbabwe's largest human rights NGOs:

> Sanctions may be targeted by nature, but do they really target the individuals placed on the list, or do they have unintended impact on ordinary civilians? It is likely that sanctions may indeed affect those that are not on the list.[69]

Another interviewee representing Zimbabwe's NGOs noted:

> Smart sanctions have worsened the livelihood of ordinary people. If you stigmatise the father you are also likely to stigmatise the son and the daughter. This is also what has happened with Zimbabweans. Furthermore, we do not believe that the targeted sanctions target those that should be targeted.[70]

The issues brought up so far have dealt with perceptions, legitimacy and proportionality. These factors indeed have an influence on the dynamics of sanctions in Zimbabwe. As noted, their common denominator seems to be the role of the media. One reason is that the media can help to explain the objectives of sanctions measures to the wider population. Implementing targeted sanctions in a

---

68 Interview conducted on 12 September 2006.
69 Interview conducted on 11 September 2006.
70 Interview conducted on 12 September 2006.

country like Zimbabwe, where the government is in control of most of the larger media channels, makes it difficult to promote EU-friendly narratives, while EU-hostile ones are more easy to propagate. Targeted sanctions can hence become a war over public opinion. As one senior ZANU-PF official observed:

> The issue of sanctions is really a matter of the media. Media is there to win the hearts and the minds of the people. This goes both for the sanctions imposer and for the targeted. As long as the sanctions imposers are unable to convince their own national citizens, or the citizens of the target country, sanctions are likely to fail.

In view of such a statement, one can conclude that access to the media is crucial. However, in Zimbabwe the sender lacks this access, as the media landscape is highly restrictive.[71] Since the EU does not have access to the Zimbabwean public in the same way as a government-influenced newspaper, the reaching out to the ordinary people is difficult. However, as indicated by a person working for the EU delegation in Harare, there are several alternative strategies for doing so: 'For instance, the EU holds many seminars in the country. During these seminars representatives try to inform the public of our views and our strategies.' There are also a variety of support programmes in the country. These are used as vehicles for promoting dialogue and informing people about aims of the sanctions. In addition to the local information, the head of delegations sometimes also makes statements. As noted by an official of the EU:[72]

> During our information dissemination we like to emphasise that we do not have trade sanctions. We try to counter some of the arguments of the government. We also try to publish some news articles every now and then, although this is very difficult. We also have workshops to convey our message. We are now becoming a bit more active than before. We are trying to make this [the restrictive measures] a bit more known.

The overall impression seems to indicate that the EU's efforts to counter anti-targeted sanctions propaganda need to be improved and be more vibrant to prevail in the asymmetric information battle.

Finally, in terms of being able to put pressure on the Zimbabwean elite, the EU has access to a number of different means. Not only can it use its influence in international bodies like the UNSC, the IMF and the World Bank (either officially or indirectly through its member states), but it can also rely on its influence to

71 For example, Raftopoulos has found that during the 2002 presidential election campaign, the Zimbabwean Broadcasting Authority (ZBC) devoted 94 per cent of its attention to the ZANU-PF candidates, but only 4 per cent to the MDC; Raftopoulos (2002): 48.

72 Interview conducted on 22 September 2006.

encourage African governments to support its policies towards the Zimbabwe elite. Such actions can be taken through a mix of classical forms of coercive diplomacy as well as positive sanctions and support. The EU can also use its influence to put indirect pressure on regional organisations that are important for the government of Zimbabwe (in terms of giving the elite legitimacy), such as the Commonwealth and the SADC, to go along with its policy. Another aspect relating to the larger strategic logic embedding targeted sanctions is the role of other international actors supporting the EU's policies. As we have seen, there are a number of international actors, such as the US, Australia and New Zealand, which enforce targeted sanctions. The dynamic in which these are engaged also needs to be brought into the analysis if one wants to achieve greater understanding of target behaviour.

Conclusion

The EU's current targeted sanctions policy against Zimbabwe seems to lack proper implementation, monitoring and analysis. Few systematic assessments are carried out to respond strategically to listed individuals' behaviour.

As we have seen, members of the Zimbabwean elite have been able to propagate its view of the EU's sanctions policy relatively unhindered, convincing the Zimbabwean people that the EU's sanctions are comprehensive and punitive in nature. In fact, the Zimbabwean government during this period has seemed very sanctions-aware and actively engaged in countering EU sanctions. Given its control of the media, it also has an 'interpretation advantage' with regard to the effects sanctions have had on the population. This poses a fundamental challenge to the EU. Unless the EU can convince the people of Zimbabwe that its restrictive measures are meant to put pressure on individual members of the regime, and not to coerce the wider population, then the sanctions strategy will simply become an empty shell.

Perceptions of Targeted Individuals

To develop a better understanding of the role of sanctions targeting individuals and to relate this aspect to the overall EU policy towards Zimbabwe, I will turn our attention to listed entities' own perceptions of senders' sanctions policies. Therefore, the analysis below aims to link micro-political dynamics with micro-political events.

The starting point for examining listed targets' perception of sanctions is that the general literature on sanctions often overlooks the role listed entities themselves play in shaping the efficacy of sanctions. None of the core readings in the area, such as *Economic Sanctions Reconsidered* (Hufbauer et al., 1985) or *The Sanctions Decade* (Cortright and Lopez, 2000), gives a systematic account of listed targets' perception of sanctions and their impact. This suggests a profound limitation in our current understanding of sanctions. However, tackling the question of the impact of targeted personal sanctions from the receiver's point of view is methodologically difficult, as the data collected by interviewing such actors is difficult to validate. Yet, while bearing this in mind, it is still important to at least let targets themselves have a chance to explain their point of view.[73] To make the analysis more accessible for the reader, I have divided my findings into two categories: (1) targets' more general understanding of EU targeted sanctions, and (2) targets' private accounts of their experiences regarding the impact of these sanctions.

Targets' Understanding of EU Sanctions Policy

Asked about their general perception of targeted sanctions, a number of common features emerged. These will be summarised here as the target's perception of comprehensive sanctions, the legitimacy of sanctions, and the root causes of the conflict.

Concerning the role of comprehensive sanctions, it was repeatedly held by most interviewees that the policy imposed had comprehensive rather than selective in character. That is to say, several targets, contrary to the actual goal of the sender, considering the sender's sanctions as detrimental to the Zimbabwean society at large, rather than being affected personally. One interviewee said:[74]

> I don't know where to start. It is important to understand the background. In my view there are sanctions. The problem with these is that they should be targeted, which they are not. Instead, there are targeted sanctions on the entire country. It targets vulnerable people. They are targeting those that have nothing. As such, I don't think that there are any targeted sanctions. It targets the ruling party and the population in general ....

73 Interviews with members of the Zimbabwean elite were carried out during the Summer of 2006 and included various levels, such as a senior ZANU-PF secretary; a senior government minister; a deputy minister; a deputy ZANU-PF secretary; a senior member of the judiciary; a ZANU-PF senator in parliament, and a senior Politburo Committee member. Interviews were also conducted with various sections of civil society; see Eriksson (2007b). Questions were open-ended in character and contextualised to the crisis in Zimbabwe at the time of the interview. It should be noted that the interviews only represent sample views, and should not be further generalised. Answers were clustered around the questions posed: general perception of sanctions and why they came about; the political context at the time of targeting, personal knowledge of being listed; specific personal experiences of being targeted; experiences of sanctions' impact on the target's family, the possible experiences of the threat of sanctions, possible attempts by the target to de-list him or herself; possible experiences with regard to assets freeze measures or travel bans and other general impacts.

74 Interview conducted on 21 September 2006.

This view was anticipated, in the sense that listed persons are likely to have a high degree of aversion towards the EU sanctions list. From this point of view, discrediting the policy thus makes sense. Beyond rhetoric, however, the responses do broaden and challenge the theory of targeting and its 'smartness' because targets are still able to turn the policy around against the sender. This becomes even clearer in the following answer from one of the targets:[75]

> We have now noticed a pattern. Besides the EU and UK's bilateral isolation, there is also an isolation of Zimbabwe in other contexts, for instance in forums such as IMF [International Monetary Fund], the ADB [African Development Bank] and so on, in order to oppose our agenda. For example, the EU and the West are issuing travel warnings; and the media is portraying us as a dangerous country. All these actions to isolate us hinder us from receiving tourists and investments. Hence, we are likely to suffer from a shortage of foreign currency.

As was alluded to in the answer above, the policy of targeting was perceived as tagged on to a broader sanctions strategy, in this case to isolate Zimbabwe completely. The typical reference to comprehensive sanctions represents a fundamentally different understanding of sanctions than what the sender intended. While targeting, at least in the 'smart' sense, is construed as a measure directed at a specific individual, the broader policy of isolation, which often results from targeted sanctions, affects other persons than those listed.[76] For example, while restrictive measures against individuals are in place, de facto exclusion from some regional and multilateral organisations will also have an impact on the general population. This could easily be exploited by listed entities. Moreover, even if there is no explicit strategy of isolation, the very act of imposing sanctions is likely to scare off foreign economic investors, with implications for the people of Zimbabwe. For example, having targeted sanctions in place in the Zimbabwe sanctions bill implemented by the US government prohibits American companies from trading with Zimbabwe. Although the aim is to target certain economic interests, this will in the end lead to an overall loss of investment in Zimbabwe and to a reduced inflow of foreign currency. This is likely to have a broader negative effect on Zimbabwe's population. However, lack of data makes it difficult to draw significant correlations between the implementation of sanctions and the increasing crisis in Zimbabwe.

Another aspect brought up by an interviewee which also referred to comprehensive sanctions related to the policy of preventing members of the elite from representing the people of Zimbabwe in international organisations. For instance, one target explained:[77]

75 Interview conducted on 19 September 2006.

76 This finding is further strengthened by studies of EU's Burma/Myanmar sanctions, where some side-effects of targeting were also noted; see Wallensteen et al. (2004).

77 Interview conducted on 19 September 2006.

> Although I am apparently on a list ..., there is no such thing as targeted sanctions. Let me give you an example: An ACP-EU meeting was supposed to be held in 2003. I was recommended to attend this meeting. The EU, however, did not allow me to participate. Because of this, the ACP launched a protest. They argued that unless Zimbabwe was allowed to participate, there would be no meeting. This standpoint affected the entire shape of the meeting .... My point is that if one is excluded for a personal sanction, then as a consequence, the entire population is excluded, and as such the entire country.

The view held here hints at another problem with targeted sanctions. Whereas the EU in its Commons Positions and Council Regulations clearly stipulates the exemptions that allow listed individuals to attend meetings which are for the benefit of the Zimbabwean people, such decisions can also be made arbitrarily. Sometimes this could be a problem for Zimbabwean society, for example when it do not have official representation at certain venues. At other times, it can be problematic for the EU. For instance, the decision to allow President Mugabe to attend the EU-Africa summit in Lisbon in 2007 was subject to prior debate that caused internal divisions. It was felt by some EU members, such as the UK, that granting Mugabe access to the meeting could easily be interpreted as a sign of a softer policy towards the Zimbabwean regime.

Some interviewees also maintained that although sanctions may be targeted on them in a personal capacity, their inclusion on a sanctions list could also indirectly have negative side-effects on immediate family, friends and colleagues. For example, one interviewee said that several of his employees were affected, as his own company suffered from some aspects of the US assets freeze:[78]

> Not only am I affected by it [the assets freeze], but also all those citizens and economic operators that fall under the provisions of this sanctions bill. For example, I am a shareholder in a mining company. We export, among other things, chrome. During a certain period, we cooperated with a Swiss company and had entered a business contract. One day, however, the chairperson of the Swiss side called me and said we had to cancel the contract. The reason was that they could not cooperate with us, arguing that we on our side fell under the American Zimbabwe sanctions bill. Hence, what I had to do was to call off about 500 workers. Thus, not only was I affected, but also several hundred families. This is unfair.

Because of income dependency, employees could be affected if a target is affected.[79] The example given here could certainly be the case in many other situations as

78 *Ibid.*

79 What is also interesting here is that targets were not only exposed to EU sanctions, but also to sanctions imposed by the US.

well. A related question, then, is whether this type of side affect is worthy the policy (the alternative being smarter sanctions or comprehensive sanctions).

In examining the role of listed individuals' perception and understanding of targeted sanctions, one recurring theme was the legitimacy of the sender's sanctions policy. In fact, the question of legitimacy underpinned several responses from targets when asked what sanctions 'were all about'. In particular, two aspects were mentioned: lack of legitimacy of the EU's sanctions policy among ordinary Zimbabweans, and lack of legitimacy within the sender constituencies (the EU's own member states).

The strategy of targeted individual sanctions is intended to address issues such as legitimacy. When the comprehensive sanctions against Iraq were criticised for not being legitimate, members of the international community decided to bring in targeted sanctions to better achieve behavioural change among those in power. However, in the case of Zimbabwe, as argued by some interviewees, sanctions were likely to fail because they did not convince the wider population. One quote is typical in this regard:

> If sanctions are to be successful, the population needs to be convinced that they are right. Convincing the population needs to be done domestically in Zimbabwe as well as internally in the EU. If sanctions are not successfully understood or reliable, then they will not be effective either.[80]

Hence, it is argued that as long as the population does not accept the EU's sanctions policy against Zimbabwe, the policy will never work. The EU's bargaining leverage would certainly be more effective if the level of support were be higher. What was not brought up by the targets, though, was the role of propaganda inside Zimbabwe. While it may be the case that the EU's policy would be more effective if it enjoyed further societal support (on the basis of legitimacy), the current lack of such support does not stem from a lack of legitimacy, as claimed. Rather, it looks like the impact of targeted sanctions, at least as portrayed in the government-controlled media, brought about negative effects on the people of Zimbabwe.

With regard to the EU's sanctions towards Zimbabwe, it was also felt that the policy suffered from a lack of legitimacy because, in their view, it was driven by the UK, and not necessarily by other EU member states:

> The [Zimbabwe] sanctions do not fit here. The population is not convinced by the underlying arguments of them. You see, this is a fight with the UK and it is about land reform issues. However, we got support internationally about the land issue. You see, the white population took the best land. They occupied the land.[81]

80 Interview conducted on 13 September 2006.

81 *Ibid.*

Another similar statement was made:

> What we do not understand is why EU does not force the UK, which we have the bilateral dispute with, to deal with us directly. What we constantly articulate is that we don't have a direct dispute with the EU.[82]

Therefore, targets saw the sanctions as somewhat hypocritical, in the sense that UK and its policy towards Zimbabwe was likely to obliterate the EU's policy. In this sense, targets found the sender to be lacking in credibility. While the literature on sanctions is often concerned with the importance of having legitimacy on the ground in the target state as well as in the wider region, less consideration is given to the importance the sender being united in its viewpoint while imposing sanctions.

In the interviewees' accounts, the notion of root causes was also brought up in their perception of why the EU's sanctions policy had come about. Since sanctions had been applied because of the government of Zimbabwe's failure to conduct free and fair elections, one could have expected the targets to concentrate on criticising this particular aspect of the policy. However, as was implied by several targets, the perception was that the EU's sanctions were part of a deeper policy of injustice. Rather than only arguing about personal injustice as a result of being included on the EU's sanctions list, several interviewees directed attention to a deeper historical injustice, going back to colonialism. In particular, several interviews made special reference to the UK. As one target claimed:[83]

> The EU sanctions do not have the support of the UN. In fact, a majority of the EU countries know that this is a UK fight, but because they are part of the European Union, they have to show solidarity. Here in Zimbabwe there is no support of the sanctions. The farmers are upset because of the land issue. However, the UK makes a large mistake here. Instead of dealing with us on the land issue, they imposed sanctions.

The same interviewee linked the implementation of targeted sanctions to a historical isolationist policy towards Zimbabwe, also linking the issue to racial aspects:[84]

> Cecil Rhodes is the root cause of this situation. He told some of his men, while discovering Zimbabwe that they could go two hours with horse in one direction, and then turn and go two hours at the other direction, and take the land therein .... But the colonisers did not only take land, they also took our cattle. My father had some cattle. It was our family's life insurance. We were six persons in the

82 Interview conducted on 19 September 2006.
83 Interview conducted on 13 September 2006.
84 *Ibid.*

> family. In order for us to attend school, my father butchered one animal every year, and with this money, he paid our school fees. Life was pretty simple and comfortable at that time. Then came the 'white' people. Today it is completely different. School fees are high and there are generally high costs to live. In fact the white people have created much problem for indigenous people.

Another interviewee alleged that sanctions were only connected to the land issue:

> It was the British that chased away our ancestors. Those who not fled had to work on the white man's farm, and they were not even paid for this work. We would like to have our land back. I am not happy with the sanctions.[85]

As can be seen from these answers, some targets perceived sanctions as just one additional injustice from the West (arguing, among other things, that there had been many broken promises on the part of the West, and the UK in particular). Rather than addressing specifically the failure to conduct free and democratic elections, the perception of sanctions was that they had more to do with a failure among the senders to recognise their need to shoulder their own historical responsibility, especially with regard to the land programmes.

In several replies, the historical ties between sender and target seemed to matter a great deal. Hence, a lesson to be learnt from these views is that when designing targeted sanctions against a certain elite, historical connections and previous policies need to be considered. In the case of the EU's sanctions against the Zimbabwean elite, experiences of the long involvement of the British, the connection to colonialism, previous political and financial support, the memory of previous sanctions (those sanctions put in place towards Ian Smith) and other related factors need to be included in a more refined sanctions analysis.

Personal Impact

Besides general understanding of sanctions, and why these were put in place, there were also a number of accounts of how the EU's targeted sanctions policy had affected the interviewees personally.[86] Here, answers were clustered along targets' perception of personal impact, perception of the nature of that impact, and how targets were notified that they were on the list.

In order to have a proper strategic effect – that is, for the sender to achieve behavioural change – the sender needs the target to understand the rationale for its policy. In particular, the policy and its communication need to be clear. Unless this is ensured, the policy of the sender is likely to fail even at the outset of its implementation. Hence, perception is crucial. What, then, was the perception of

85 Interview conducted on 22 September 2006.

86 It is possible to draw a distinction between the public and the private with regard to target impact.

the targets when it came to the selective and target-oriented nature of the EU's sanctions policy, and how did the interviewees regard its personal impact?

To begin with, one of the most interesting aspects of some members of the elite's accounts had to do with the impact of symbolic versus concrete sanctions. Three quotes are significant here:

1. 'I don't think that the targeted or the personal sanctions lead to a behavioural change. It mostly has symbolic effect. On the contrary, it will probably harden them, and increase the resolve of the persons ....';[87]
2. 'The sanctions are a challenge to me, but I will manage. I really don't feel affected by them';[88]
3. 'Sanctions do not take much of my attention. My friends are encouraging me. For me these measures only have a symbolic effect.'[89]

These quotes summarise some important aspects which the sanctions literature has yet to deal with. While much of the literature on targeted sanctions has addressed implementation aspects, less is known about the role of the symbolic use of targeted sanctions. It is interesting to note that some of the persons included on the sanctions list recognised the symbolic impact of sanctions. Still, we know less about the extent to which symbolic targeting matters, as well as how it affects the target from a psychological point of view. One aspect in the first quote indicates that listing individuals actually strengthens the targets' resolve. This is certainly an unwanted consequence from the sender's point of view.

Besides the targets' perception of the role that selective sanctions play, how did those on the Zimbabwean sanctions list get to know about their inclusion? This issue is increasingly being addressed in the legal debate on sanctions. First, all interviewees knew that they were included on the EU's sanctions list. While some had been informed by friends or had read about it in a newspaper, others had received a personal letter from the US Embassy.

For example, one interviewee said: 'I learnt about the black-list from the press. I learnt that I've become a black sheep. We have not reattributed on this. We are too big for that kind of behaviour. They will be embarrassed by the sanctions themselves.'[90] Another interviewee reported that: 'I found out that I was on the list in December .... I was notified that I was on EU's list by a friend.'[91] And a third answer referred specifically to the US sanctions: '[I was] notified of the American sanctions list by a letter from the American Embassy here in Harare. The letter also stated that my children were targeted. Regarding the EU sanctions, I was informed

87 Interview conducted on 22 September 2006.
88 Interview conducted on 19 September 2006.
89 *Ibid.*
90 Interview conducted on 13 September 2006.
91 Interview conducted on 19 September 2006.

by reading the news.'[92] What is interesting here is that the EU and the US adopted different approaches to informing the targets that they were subject to travel bans and assets freeze measures. Finally, another interviewee said the Internet had played an indirect role. In recent literature on sanctions, the issue of notification has been one of the more important legal aspects under discussion regarding the implementation of sanctions.[93] The reason for the interest in this aspect is that notification is part of the listed individual's rights. Everyone subjected to sanctions has a right to be informed about the specific measures that have been put in place towards him or her, and for what reasons. The issue of notification has also, particularly in the legal context, been intimately connected to the reasons why a person has been listed. Not only should the target be informed of listing, but also about the accusations (the motivation) that prompted it.[94] Closely related to the question of listing is the issue of de-listing – the procedure by which the sender removes a person from the sanctions list. Until the early 1990s, the procedure for adding a person to a list or removing them from it had been made ad hoc and without proper procedures. Since early 2000, however, the topic has gained increasing importance because it involves the legal protection a target enjoys. The topic grew particularly important as it was much debated in the sensitive area of counter-terrorism listing efforts. Hence, as part of the interviews, the question was also posed how common it was among the targets to request de-listing. As expected, few targets had tried to do so:[95]

> We have asked our friends [the EU] to remove the sanctions. However, the response is always that if we want to be removed from the list, we need to 'take away this bill and withdraw that bill', and so on. But you see, we need to have certain security laws in our country to have security. The British government said that they want regime change. Are we just to sit down and say 'Yes, master'?

It was quite common for targets included on the Zimbabwean sanctions list to speak in favour of a general policy of having the EU reconsider its targeted sanctions, rather than being individually taken off the list. Thus, it is possible to draw the

92 Interview conducted on 21 September 2006.

93 Moreover, the issue of notification has been discussed in various legal contexts, as well as in relation to sanctions cases brought before the European Court of First Instance. One explanation is that since 11 September 2001, when the UN Security Council adopted personal sanctions towards a number of potential terrorists and terrorist organisations, the legal basis for issuing the list was unclear. Listed entities had no legal recourse to turn to in order to make complaints about inclusion. Only now are the legal procedures at the UN as well as the EU level becoming clearer. Clarifications on listing and de-listing procedures have been made through various national and regional court decisions, hence the legal interest.

94 This is also why the EU Zimbabwe sanctions list in Episode 8 for the first time set out the reasons why each of the targets had been included on the sanctions list.

95 Interview conducted on 19 September 2006.

conclusion that targets were still unaware that they could take legal action against the sender. Finally, the language of the targets also revealed that targets considered sanctions as an 'us and them' instead of a 'me and them' dichotomy.

Targets' Perception of the Travel Ban Policys

According to Conroy (1999), travel sanctions should have two main operational effects. The first is to create a symbolic sense of isolation and send signals of disapproval. Isolating the target from international processes can de-legitimise the target's behaviour and/or claims to authority. The second is to make the target's policy of non-compliance more costly and difficult to sustain.[96] Based on the interviews with targeted entities in Zimbabwe, this impact was achieved, at least in some cases. Here is one example:[97]

> I am the minister of [X], and I get many invitations to travel abroad. However, when I now get these invitations [unclear whether he was referring to EU, US or Commonwealth invitations], I just put them aside and don't think about it. We now have the 'Look East' policy. I can go to Japan, China, Russia etc., although I cannot go to Australia – which is unholy. I don't have to go to a country where I am not wanted. You don't go to a home where you are not welcome. Sanctions were so abrupt, we were not prepared. The credit line from the financial institutions where swiftly caught off. We cannot by chemicals, medicine, hospital equipment, and so on. We have an open door policy on Europe. But we now turn to our friends that helped us during the war, China. They also help us now. Europe can come on board whenever. I'd love to go to London, I love their people. But the government is unjust. Italy and France we are already dealing with, on a bilateral level. I also meet with the EC on informal occasions, such as over some lunches.

Another example is the following: 'My best friend is in Canada. I am afraid to travel there, I don't know if I am allowed.'[98]

This case suggests that even if targets themselves are not physically prevented from travelling, the mere fact that they could be apprehended may prevent them from doing to. In some of the accounts given by the targets, they did travel despite the chance of being apprehended, but experienced humiliation and annoyance, as they were not allowed into the destination country. These cases seemed to strengthen their political resolve against the sender. One way to evade the desired outcome of the travel ban was to send a representative instead:

96 Conroy (1999): 1.

97 Interview conducted on 21 September 2006.

98 Interview conducted on 22 September 2006.

> I would not be prevented to attend international conferences like the ACP or the UN, and so on. In those cases were I would be prevented [due to a ban], I would simply send someone to represent me. We generally work in a team.[99]

On the basis of the interviews, one could also observe that the travel ban measure seem to have caused uncertainty, economic costs, indignation and annoyance. For instance, a degree of annoyance can be noted in this quote:[100]

> I cannot travel to Europe, but would this be a big deal for me? – I won't travel there anyway! They [member countries of the EU] target the entire population. However, tarnishing Zimbabwe will have implications for tourism, foreign investment and so on, which will affect ... Zimbabwe [as a whole]. In theory, they are targeted, but not when it comes down to real matters. [For me personally] it is really not a big deal. I don't sleep worse just because I am on a sanctions list.

There were also several other examples of the travel ban being effective. One interviewee gave the following illustrative description (though with regard to US targeted sanctions): [101]

> My wife wanted to attend my daughter's student graduation in the US, and for this she got a visa. But when my wife came to the airport in Los Angeles, she was told that she was not allowed access to the country and that she had to return back. Can you imagine this! Why did they not tell her here in the first place, why wait for her to fly all the way over there? It was also expensive. At the airport she complained saying that 'I am an adult and you cannot treat me this way.' She protested also by saying 'Treat us as individuals, as God does.' The intention [of the sanctions] is surely to split families, but that failed for us. We are a strong family. Yeah, she got true a bitter experience. But she came back strengthened and more experienced. To hell with America. They talk about justice, 'But I see no justice in this,' she told them. Is this really justice?

Besides targeting individual entities, the travel ban also had a broader impact on the government's ability to participate in international conferences:[102]

> I want to go to London and Europe, but I am not allowed. But it doesn't harm me. I simply avoid going there. I just heard that the we [the government] had some troubles going to the Non-Alliance Movement meeting in Havana, Cuba [in 2006], and then to the General Assembly meetings in New York. We sent an advance team – two persons – before our president. It was difficult. They told

99 Interview conducted on 25 September 2006.

100 *Ibid.*

101 Interview conducted on 21 September 2006.

102 Interview conducted on 13 September 2006.

> me to arrange for a direct connection to Havana. However, the only possible way with established air companies was to go via Madrid. That is the best way. However, this could not work. Therefore, instead we had to arrange for a direct flight to Havana with Air Zimbabwe. It made a short stop in West Africa. The costs were high and caused a lot of irritation. We do not blame President Mugabe for this, we blame the British. It is not fair to impose sanctions just because of animosity of a leader. President Mugabe and PM Blair share much animosity.

It is possible to assume that several targets had had many different experiences of sanctions. In the end, though, it is difficult to tell what is likely to be achieved with regard to changing political behaviour – that is, whether this is what the sender wants to accomplish (in the case of Zimbabwe, signalling may be a goal).

Targets' Perceptions of the Assets Freeze Policy

According to the Interlaken Process, a targeted assets freeze is defined as being targeted in the sense that it applies only to a subset of the population, financial in the sense that it involves the freezing or blocking of funds and other financial resources, and a sanction in that it is a coercive measure applied to bring about change. Overall, there were several different types of target perceptions and forms of impact. Most of them suggested that the EU's targeted financial sanctions were counter-productive or less efficient than could have been anticipated (on the other hand, these cases are not representative of all cases).

First, financial sanctions work best by surprise. This suggests that targets should not be notified in advance of these measures, because they are, they will transfer money or assets to safe locations. In the case of Zimbabwe, though, the EU made several threats of targeted sanctions ahead of the elections. This pre-signalling of sanctions certainly limited their impact. This aspect, however, highlights a paradox. On the one hand, targeted sanctions could be used as a bargaining tool, as was done in Zimbabwe. In fact, as often argued, sanctions work best by threat. On the other hand, sanctions have to work through surprise, otherwise they lose their efficacy. If targets are aware of financial sanctions because of a prior threat, then it is not likely that targets will keep their assets exposed in vulnerable environments where they run the risk of having them frozen. This also limits their impact. Moreover, in the Zimbabwean case, there seems to have been only a general threat of targeted sanctions (as discussed previously), and no personal sets of sanctions. For instance, one listed entity gave the following account when asked about a prior personal threat of sanctions:

> I was never personally threatened with sanctions. These sanctions are a blessing from God. It taught us to survive. It is a blessing in disguise. We used to get everything, and we got used to it; education, health and infrastructure. God

> blesses people in different ways. God also misinformed Tony Blair. Just for the purpose of strengthening us.[103]

Second, several targets were likely to have less wealth inside the EU than in Zimbabwe, which suggests that targets could be financially unaffected by EU sanctions. One target gave the following example:

> I came to the government from the private sector. I worked for the World Bank. I have travelled all over the world. I set up a bank company, but now I have sold my shareholdings. My wife she runs a few shops. Our family also has some farms. I work mainly with import. I have not been punished by sanctions.

Without stating whether he had assets in EU member states, the quote above suggests that even if that was the case, the wealth and business inside Zimbabwe would go unharmed, so the target would not be seriously affected.

Third, as part of the smart sanctions rationale, the listing of family members could be effective. This is particularly true when it comes to financial sanctions. Not only is the rationale to effect the elite (those directly responsible, but also their immediate dependants), but also to make sure that a target subject to financial sanctions does not sign over his or her wealth to another family member. However, little evidence or information was found to clarify this.

Fourth, another aspect of targets' perception of financial sanctions was, as one interviewee put it, that they were imposed on the wider population of Zimbabwe. In common with the previous examples, financial sanctions were seen by various targets as part of a broader campaign against Zimbabwe:[104]

> I participated in the struggle. During this war I lived in a concentration camp. Ian Smith committed a number of atrocities. Many of my country fellowmen were killed and butchered. Ian Smith used chemical weapons against innocent people. However, this is part of the capitalist structure. North sees this as an economic struggle, and creates darkness so that money dries out for us the people in the south.

This perception of the target is obviously far away from the idea of targeted personal sanctions. In fact, the EU's sometimes unarticulated sanctions policy undermined the efficiency of the policy. It was also evident from the interviews that US financial sanctions at times mattered more than the EU's. This is not surprising, however, since the international economic system is dominated by US trade. In this context, one interviewee gave the following example:[105]

---

103 Interview conducted on 21 September 2006.

104 *Ibid.*

105 Interview conducted on 19 September 2006.

> Another case is the one that happened quite recently: I bought a tractor from a farming company. The tractor was about to be imported from the US. The price of the tractor was 36,000 USD. The company asked me to deposit the money into an account of theirs. Soon after this was done however, it was discovered that the money was frozen [unclear if he actually got the tractor of not/and unclear if the deposit had actually reached the company's account. Hence they lost their money. They wanted their money back, but I said I was not responsible for this and that they should have had an assurance of this. Now, what needs to be remembered here is that although I was indirectly affected by the missed opportunity, also several families that would have benefited from the use of the tractor were also affected.

Whether or not the sender considers this side-effect is unclear. On one hand, it causes annoyance, which is a sender strategy; on the other hand, it hinders government officials in carrying out policies of representation. This is also likely to have an impact on the people of Zimbabwe as a whole.

Conclusion

With regard to the political developments that took place in Zimbabwe during each of the sanctions episodes, a striking pattern of deterioration could be observed. However, the examination suggests no correlation between the actual implementation of targeted sanctions and the resolution of the crisis. Despite this, one cannot conclude that targeted personal sanctions did not have any effects. As we have seen, targeting could play out in many unforeseen ways. For instance, personal sanctions may have prevented entities from travelling or led to their taking decisions that they would otherwise not have made (for instance, to maintain their power base). Personal listing measures could, for example, have assisted in undermining targets' room for manoeuvre, which in the end could be of benefit to the sender. This counterfactual possibility is not easy to prove.

Moreover, what was noted was that the sender did not explicitly engage individual targets in bargaining situations during the course of the episodes. Yet there were a number of indirect sender–target interactions going on. For instance, some targets travelled to Europe under particular exemptions. Thus, while individual considerations of specific persons on the list were made, they had little value in assessing the overall policy of the sender to constrain, isolate and achieve a behavioural change in government policy. As was further noted, some of these exemptions were very problematic, as these decisions could easily have a tendency to divide the sender states. Instead of using the exemptions to bargain with the separate targets, the issue of temporary suspensions of the travel ban for a particular individual became a burden by provoking controversy about the legitimacy of the sender's policy. This legitimacy aspect often received widespread media attention, as well as causing diplomatic rifts. The provisions for temporary suspensions also had the effect that over the course of time, the view seems to have developed that individual sanctions were mostly of a symbolic nature.

Regarding the travel ban and the financial sanctions, it was also found that listing measures could create group cohesion among the targets. Being targeted meant that individuals were, or became, core regime loyalists. Specific examples of situations were found where targets experienced an impact in the form of annoyances. Yet, again, it is difficult to claim that this impact changed the behaviour of the targets.

Concerning other prevailing factors, the examination pointed to the importance of the perception of sanctions. This became most clear with regard to targeted actors' view that comprehensive sanctions were in force, while the sender claimed to have imposed targeted restrictive measures. Through the eyes of some of the listed entities, sanctions were thus seen as a kind of punishment of the people of Zimbabwe, while the sender felt that restrictive measures referred to a selective number of policy measures against specific individuals in the government. This obviously displayed a very different viewpoint regarding the source of the crisis in conflict. The importance of perception was specially noted in the Zimbabwean media. It is clear that the media played an important vehicle for targets' perceptions, advancing a sanctions narrative. The fact that the elite could advance its own perception of sanctions undermined the sanctions policy of the EU. The Zimbabwean population became convinced that the crisis was due to the EU's sanctions.

Besides the question of direct and indirect consequences of sanctions, the examination also reveals that the targets in some cases often did not see the EU's sanctions as proportional. While the sender had issued a list of official decision-makers because of their involvement in bad governance, the targets (and to some extent civil society) claimed that the sanctions were disproportionate, as they were often connected to other broader policy measures with wider negative impacts on the Zimbabwean people.

Interviews with targets revealed that there seemed to be a strong awareness of sanctions. Either consciously or unconsciously, sanctions did seem to figure in the life of targets. While sometimes they had a direct impact, they also at times had a clear psychological impact, for instance by causing frustration and uncertainty, as well as indignation.

Finally, it could be observed that the main benefit of using targeted sanctions on Zimbabwe was that it opened up the possibility of a dialogue with the target regime and listed individuals. While some measures did not cause a direct impact, or even symbolic one, they did allow the EU to engage the elite. However, it is difficult to say whether this prolonged or delayed the crisis that sanctions were actually meant to resolve. Such an observation also confirms the conclusions found in studies such as those by Cortright and Lopez that suggest that the type of impact (positive or punitive) on the targets is not as relevant as the value of actually creating a bargaining environment.[106]

---

106 See Cortright (2001): 118.

Chapter 10
Rethinking Targeted Sanctions

While diplomacy prior to the 1990s was constrained by rules and norms arising from the Cold War, the security landscape that has evolved since has made it possible for practitioners involved in political and economic statecraft to come up with new tools to address human rights abuses and challenges to peace and security. One such invention, which has now become an essential element in international relations, has been the design of targeted sanctions. Compared to the historic use of comprehensive sanctions, which were mostly state-oriented and undifferentiating in terms of coercing the ruling elite and the society of a country, targeted sanctions have deliberately been developed to be more 'ethical' and 'smart'. Actors such as the UN Security Council and the EU continue to invest confidence in the utility of this policy, convinced that its successful application can address a wide range of politically complicated issues in different geographical contexts. To date, the number of UN and EU sanctions regimes established has increased every year.

In recent years, though, the confidence vested in this policy has been somewhat eroded, especially following the many negative side-effects of the so-called war on terror that in many ways came to be associated with targeted sanctions. For instance, in a recent assessment of unilateral targeted sanctions, it was concluded that:[1]

> The impact of economic sanctions makes it clear that previous attempts … to apply economic sanctions against other countries have backfired … that sanctions used in isolation from other forms of diplomatic pressure are unlikely to force major policy change and may even be counterproductive.

Such conclusions obviously hint at mistrust of the sanctions tool. There are also signs of criticisms among scholars and practitioners with regard to the inability of targeted sanctions to be sufficiently focused, so that instead of achieving their goals, they in fact accentuate problems through unintended consequences. Such side-effects have also been noted in several court cases where listed entities have brought their placement on sanctions lists to appeal because of violations of their human rights. In many of these court cases, former targets have won their appeal, forcing governments to change their listing procedures. In all, this has also led sanctions scholars to suggest that targeted sanctions may be slowly beginning to enter a legitimacy crisis. While scholars sometimes maintain that targeted sanctions

1 House of Lords Select Committee on Economic Affairs (2007).

are a policy maker's dream, there are signs suggesting quite the opposite.[2] From a scientific point of view, however, the question is how the policy has been assessed in the first place, in order to give rise to a positive or negative conclusion about its relevance.[3]

Moreover, the sanction field has in recent years has been marked by several policy innovations. For instance, much scholarly as well as policy attention has been given to technical policy development – that is, how collective security actors like the UN and the EU can improve their institutional procedures to make them more effective, especially in terms of implementation. Moreover, the focus of academic attention has also come in the form of assessment studies seeking to determine the efficacy of sanctions by looking at the outcomes of particular sanctions cases. Although organisational as well as implementation problems are acknowledged, diagnosed and even provided with policy proposal 'treatment', the efficacy of targeted sanctions is seldom studied in terms of the underlying and enabling rules and norms that shape the policy in the first place. More studies of this kind are needed in future.

This study, however, has examined some common assumptions in the sanctions literature on how best to assess the sanctions instrument. A starting point for reconsidering targeted sanctions is to define what the new policy is all about and what distinguishes this from other studies. Therefore, an alternative definition of targeted personal sanctions has been put forward, one that is more inclusive than more general definitions of sanctions:

> The implementation of targeted sanctions is a flexible and multivariate process embedded in a larger strategic context involving a sender and a target, where the decision-making, perception and interactions between these actors, during well-defined episodes in a sanctions regime, shape impact, leading to a new political outcome.

Targeted Sanctions as a Multifaceted Policy

One of the main arguments put forward in this study is that the introduction of targeted sanctions has paved the way for a new way of thought with regard to sanctions in general. Not only have new actors and issues entered the sanctions agenda, at least compared to comprehensive sanctions, but also new forms of relationships among these constitutive elements forming part of the targeted sanctions policy. It is fair to say that today, perhaps more than previously acknowledged, the imposition of targeted sanctions is a multifaceted and complex process. It is multifaceted in the sense that the nature of the policy attracts many different actors with a variety of

2 Craven (2002): 47.

3 At time of writing, an international consortium of sanctions scholars and policy makers around the world has begun joint efforts to assess UN targeted sanctions.

strategic interests, which are often linked. It is complex both because of the depth of the areas of application, as well as the institutional practices that are required to administrate this policy.[4] In addition, the fact that governments often tend to have high expectations of what the policy can achieve makes the policy management of targeted sanctions even more complex. All these aspects also structure the policy outcome in unforeseeable ways. None the less, while the sanctions literature recognises that sanctions are both multifaceted and complex, such intricacy is rarely the point of departure in studies seeking to determine their efficacy.

Having been in place for nearly two decades, a number of studies have broken new ground on the role and practice of targeted sanctions. Yet, despite the shift to targeted sanctions, which could have invited new thinking on how we treat and understand sanctions from an epistemic point of view, there are a number of profound problems with the ways we tend to look at the utility of this tool. In fact, it seems that the conventional way of addressing comprehensive sanctions continues in the same way when we seek to analyse the effectiveness of targeted sanctions. In view of the ontological shift that has taken place in the move from comprehensive to targeted sanctions, one would have assumed that policy makers and scholars of sanctions measures would have adapted to this. Yet this seems not to have occurred. On the contrary, conventional assessment approaches have until now continued in the same tradition.

As a result, this study has sought to question the conventional way of assessing sanctions. This has been done by illustrating the multiplicity of processes and relationships between decision-making procedures and policy consistency, by bringing forward relevant factors such as: the various goals and phases which sanctions regimes usually go through; how broader strategic paradigms tend to embed and shape targeted sanctions, and how targets themselves perceive sanctions and what role this may have. These factors, and others, will affect the sanctions outcome, and therefore need to be accounted for independently and in combination in any serious sanctions assessment. In this context, it is worth repeating that this study has deliberately chosen not to assess any single UN or EU targeted sanctions regime. Doing so would significantly change the scope and focus of the study, and engaging in sanctions assessment here is likely to be of little value to policy makers, given that their agenda may include a wider variety of considerations than such an assessment would ever be able to cover. None the less, to counter often misguided sanctions assessment approaches, the objective here has been to demonstrate, by disentangling various segments of the sanctions policy process, the kind of political complexity that occurs when applying sanctions, and how this shapes a particular

4 In addition to this, there are a number of enduring problems that targeted sanctions are unable to solve, for example: the fact that sanctions are always confronted with a large-scale collective action problem when implemented on the ground; the problems of dealing with the target's learning capacity and adjustments to the pressure of the sender, and the scientific problem of demonstrating causality between the application of sanctions and the political outcome. To this can be added a host of other issues not covered in this study.

sanctions outcome. For this reason, close attention has been paid to linking together conflict-level, institutional-level and sender/target-level factors of sanctions practice. Not only does such an approach offer an alternative conceptualisation of targeted sanctions, but also an alternative and refined methodological approach to how to go about understanding sanctions' effectiveness.

Refining Sanctions Assessment Approaches

Following the literature review on the shifting practice of targeted sanctions, a number of problems relating to sanctions assessment methodology and sanctions conceptualisation were identified. These related to (1) the sanctions literature's conventional reliance upon the 'case' as a unit of analysis; (2) the conventional methods used to assess sanctions regimes; (3) a reliance upon the unitary state-based approach, and (4) the problem of using scoring methods. As an alternative to such cruder methods, I offer a more refined approach, placing further emphasis upon the process within a case, by thinking more about the separate episodes it contains; the role of the strategic paradigms that enable sanctions practice, by looking at enabling strategic frameworks, and finally, the role of the sender's decision-making processes as 'shapers' of sanctions utility, by looking at both formal and informal sender practices.

Rethinking the case Following some limitations of current sanctions assessment approaches, this study has suggested the need to reconsider the conventional notion of a sanctions case and its constitutive elements. Given the new reality-based dynamics that targeted sanctions bring into sanctions analysis, the cruder and conventional state-based approach needs to be reconsidered as in its current form, it is much to imprecise, at least if one looks at what it claims to explain. To do so, one needs to begin by rethinking the level of analysis. Instead of focusing only on official state or group behaviour, one needs to focus more closely on the persons who are being targeted. Devoting greater attention to individual decision-makers also provides for a new way of thinking strategically about the logic of a sanctions strategy. In contrast to official state-responses, listed actors can 'think', 'act' and 'feel'.

Second, once the level of analysis has been shifted, there are also good reasons to rethink the unit of analysis. Rather than thinking of a conventional sanctions case, and mistakenly assessing the utility of sanctions by evaluating the sender's stated goals against a regime outcome, one needs to think of sanctions' impact in terms of the ongoing process within such a case. In order to do so in a systematic way, we have proposed a disaggregation of cases into a number of more refined and tighter time episodes. In this way, new trends and patterns of targeting as well as impact can be determined. Each episode hence covers the main political developments during the targeted sanctions regime. Moreover, as opposed to conventional large-*n* studies or particular case studies based on static sanctions approaches, each episode reflects the sender's viewpoint on the efficacy of sanctions. The more refined these episodes are, the better they account for dynamics on the ground.

As has been discussed, a sanctions regime comprises a collection of sender 'judgements'. Each episode reflects the specific political goals that were initiated in the period before the adjustment of the sanctions list (the listing or de-listing of entities). Overall, the disaggregation of the regime into episodes provides for a more detailed and clearer sense of the contextual difficulties experienced while the sanctions played out. In addition to thinking of the sender's assessment of target behaviour, one can also evaluate the sender's perception of how well it considered its commodity-based sanctions. After all, the overall value of assigning particular cases and episodes to crises and conflicts is to make them easier to assess and compare. However, the definition of a case (and its episodes) is purely a construct, and does not necessarily reflect developments on the ground.

Enabling strategic frameworks This study has also proposed thinking about sanctions as part of a broader strategic framework. The aim was to get a better sense of what factors shape and enable sanctions' impact. Rather than thinking of targeted sanctions as a stand-alone measure, it seems more accurate to acknowledge and take into account the larger strategic framework that enables targeted sanctions to function in a particular way. Although targeted sanctions may direct certain attention and pressure on particular actors, it is the combination with other strategic measures – that is, the overall strategic framework – that is likely to determine the outcome of both sanctions and the conflict. The need to look at targeted sanctions in a broader strategic framework follows from the observation that the policy has different degrees of impact in different contexts, despite the fact that the same restrictive measures are applied. This suggests that targeted sanctions cannot be understood in isolation from a broader strategic framework, but need to include the constant interplay between the sanctions instruments.

As noted, each sanctions regime has its own strategic and political dynamics. This makes it difficult to compare different sanctions cases simply because the rules and constraints enabling targeted sanctions rest upon different grounds. This is seldom acknowledged in comparative assessment studies. Another observation is that it is difficult to confirm that the sender, when setting up a sanctions regime, has done so with a broader strategic framework in mind. While there are on the one hand clear empirical records that show that targeted sanctions are connected to a number of other coercive policies to put pressure on a target and the target country, it is on the other hand impossible to find operative and well-articulated (official) *strategic* principles regarding how the overall approach was meant to work.

Moreover, when keeping in mind the larger strategic framework embedding sanctions, the rationale of the strategy can also be better understood, and consequently better administrated. For instance, similar to the way the policy of deterrence can deter a state from engaging in a particular actions, senders can also actively pursue deterrence with regard to each listed individual. However, such a strategic approach requires much political sophistication.

In the end, the question of whether targeted sanctions are meant to work as a stand-alone measure or as part of a wider strategic approach follows a common point of debate in the sanctions literature. In this context, it is worth recalling debate regarding what results sanctions have on their own and/or in connection with other instruments, as pursued by Pape and Elliott.[5] None the less, the policy implication for targeted sanctions is that there is a continued clear need to take a more holistic approach to examining the role of sanctions, especially when assessing sanctions regimes. Such calls are also being echoed at the UN, where officials working with targeted sanctions find the debate to be too narrow in terms of the role of targeted sanctions, and that it fails to take into account other policy measures the sender attaches to the sanctions instrument.

To sum up, whereas targeted sanctions has long been seen as an instrument to achieve political change and resolve a number of complex emergencies, targeted sanctions cannot be seen as a stand-alone measure, nor assessed in isolation.

'Black Box' Processes

One important but often under-studied area of targeted sanctions is the role of the sender's 'black box' and the effect it has on sanctions implementation. This study has made a case for the need to take institutional decision-making seriously, as the processes here are very likely to influence outcome in ways that are less widely acknowledged in the sanctions assessment literature. More precisely, it has argued that there are formal and informal rules and norms that shape sanctions policy at a very early stage, and which will predetermine the degree of sanctions impact that is to be expected when they are implemented. This argument should be contrasted with the approach that seeks to determine the efficacy of sanctions only by comparing the officially stated goals of the sender and the outcome of the sanctions regime.

An in-depth examination of the sanctions decision-making of the UN and the EU was conducted by looking at the use of travel ban and assets freeze measures applied to specific individuals. Differentiation was made between the formal and material boundaries shaping sanctions outcomes, and the informal and more subjective management of sanctions by individual officials. It was found that both formal and informal decision-making procedures seem to complement and exhaust each other during the policy process of adopting, enforcing and implementing targeted sanctions. In terms of the formal rules shaping the outcome, it was found that practitioners in the sender body often have problems ensuring that the pressure of sanctions is maintained and that measures are adapted to developments in the political situation on the ground. While targeted sanctions policies may be effective (partly following the relevance of the use of a prior threat), they have a tendency to become misplaced and less precise over time. This raises the question of the sender's flexibility. As found in this study, one explanation for this problem is that the formal rules shaping sanctions policies are often too static, and cannot

5 Pape (1998) and Elliott (1998).

be continuously adjusted to suit events on ground. For instance, while the EU in recent years has been adopting policy guidelines (for example, to establish standard language and best practices) for the design and practice of targeted sanctions, such bureaucratic moves to ensure decision-making harmony among member state governments have come at the expense of sanctions policies not always reflecting the real problems on the ground. While a static process for designing sanctions regimes increases the degree of unity among EU member states and may lead to faster decision-making procedures, it comes at the expense of more precise and timely sanctions that truly deal with the challenges the sender and its allies encounter on the ground.[6]

For UN sanctions impact, the formal decision-making system is still very much steered by the interests of the members of the Security Council. Over the last decade or so, UN sanctions committees have increasingly polished their procedures in order to be able to respond to events on the ground. Part of this has to do with the institutional support provided by administrative units such as the subsidiary sanctions branch and the creativity of the permanent staff in co-operation with associated experts in the academic field.

Yet, while there has been an increasing awareness among the sanctions committees, especially with regard to the flexible use of targeted sanctions, there are still institutional weaknesses that seem to predetermine sanctions outcomes. As argued in this study, however, to overcome the specific problem of having a sanctions policy approach that is too static, senders should enhance its institutional capacity and invest more attention to open-ended sanctions mandates that will allow for more flexible response procedures. This includes senders ensuring that there is overall co-ordination and streamlining of the policy. As demonstrated here, desk officers working with sanctions on a daily basis usually have a great deal of leverage with regard to shaping the impact of sanctions. For example one factor that seems to explain these differences in sanctions management practices is the lack of policy ownership among those actors operating at different stages of the policy management process. This leads to different expectations for policy implementation, as well as different consequences. In fact, the question of ownership seems to be a particularly important factor in achieving target impact. In terms of the informal rules enabling sanctions, the examination suggested the need to look at the 'culture of understanding' that exists among officials of the sending body regarding targeted sanctions, and how this will shape target impact. Thus, with regard to the sender's ongoing informal rules and processes, findings suggested a need to pay further attention to the practitioner's outlook and perception of targeted sanctions. While, for instance, at the UN the formal

6 It is interesting in this context that aspects of the formal sanctions procedures are being copied by other regional organisations. In 2010, the African Union was in the process of institutionalising a sanctions mechanism under its Peace and Security Council. In this regard, the AU is looking closely at both EU and UN sanctions management; see Eriksson (2010).

decision-making system is largely steered by the interests of the members of the Security Council, it is informally shaped by individual administrative officials. It was found that the role and creativity of individual UN officials working on sanctions have independent leverage in shaping sanctions impact. It is therefore possible to conclude that part of the explanation for sanctions efficacy involves looking at official desk officers and their management of the sanctions file. In fact, one can even argue that sanctions will not be more effective or create more impact than the sanctions file of the sending body allows. This also supports the findings of previous studies.

Furthermore, it was established in this study that officials working with the policy of targeted sanctions often demonstrate nuanced views regarding how they perceive this tool. Thus, perceptions of sanctions policy among officials contribute to the overall effect of sanctions. While these differences may not be enormous, they do have consequences for the policy outcome. Given that such nuances matter in the overall management of sanctions policy, they cannot be ignored in any serious sanctions assessment study. Considering that targeted sanctions rarely function as initially envisaged with regard to long-term crisis management or conflict resolution, one explanation may therefore be that practitioners' perceptions and management of sanctions, especially when put together, shape the policy in unexpected ways. In this regard, decision-makers play an equally important role in sanctions implementation as the many other dynamics involved in sanctions management. All this suggests that rules and norms on the sender side contribute to shaping sanctions policies, and thus particular sanctions outcomes. In particular, it seems that sanctions efficacy, or target impact, is very much dependent upon the role decision-makers are willing to play in ensuring sanctions are effective. A desk officer of the sending body can more or less make the policy either symbolic or direct in effect. While such explanations may have been pointed to elsewhere, they have never been demonstrated per se. The policy implications of this further suggest that those political leaders who seek to respond to a particular crisis therefore need to make sure that the officials engaged in adopting, implementing and administrating sanctions are well co-ordinated and streamlined, and have a flexible cognitive attitude when using targeted sanctions. In addition, the policies need to assign the necessary resources, political will, and above all, a sense of ownership of who does what. To increase sanctions effectiveness, ownership should be assigned to those units that are engaged in overseeing the sanctions process. Political leaders who wish to impose targeted sanctions need also to ensure that other actors, both public and private operators, are in full understanding of what is expected by the policy.

An interesting paradox with regard to both the formal and informal rules and norms shaping sanctions policies is that, while on the one hand the policy seems to suffer from cultural differences in personal and departmental understanding of sanctions, what they are and how they work, senders still manage to carry out their policy work relatively effectively – or at least so it seems. Why? As discussed earlier, this paradox can probably be best explained by the fact that there is seldom a well-established and objective evaluation mechanism in place that can account for all sequences along the policy chain, bearing all its actors, rules and procedures in mind. The playing out of sanctions is simply the result of a combination of rational, irrational and random procedures and practices. Since no scale or comparative measurement is applied, it simply looks as if the policy outcome is as expected. This should be contrasted with a policy that is carried out in a similar way to a military mission, where doctrines, strategic principles, operational guidelines, procedures, decision-making systems, co-ordination and segmental ownership are in place. It should be noted, however, that the role of decision-making procedures is not unique to the adoption, management and implementation of targeted sanctions. On the contrary, it is seems to be a common factor for most policy tools operating in a similar setting and for a similar purpose. Usually, policies are adopted with a functional ideal in mind, where the policy is expected to work in a particular way. Seldom are such policies likely to work as expected, though. Neighbouring academic fields (decision-making theory, organisational theory and policy evaluation theory) bear witness to this. The decision-making and implementation involved in targeted sanctions are no exception.

In all, then, a theory of sanctions needs to include the underlying reasons why the sender is acting, since they predetermine policy outcome. The observations made here are therefore relevant to the theory of sanctions, as they add additional dimensions to the ways in which we think about targeted sanctions. The theoretical implication of this is that further research into the 'black box' of the sender is necessary to establish a deeper understanding of the factors that constrain and enable sanctions outcome.

Trends in Targeting

This study examined new data on the number of targets listed under UN and EU sanctions regimes. There were two goals in doing this. The first was to see whether the listing of entities was becoming more or less common in practice, and the secondly was to see how personal sanctions fit the strategic rationale that embedded each of these current sanctions regimes.

This study found that 1,186 individuals were subject to targeted sanctions in mid-2009. While some sanctions regimes displayed very limited sender–target interaction (for example, Uzbekistan), others regimes featured many more actions, not least in terms of the number of entities placed on the list (for example , the ICTY). In terms of listing and de-listing, there were, as expected, clear signs that UN and EU sanctions usually start by listing a rather limited number of entities, this number normally increasing over time. This illustrates that sanctions commonly work in a gradual way. One explanation for this may be that the sender has a strategy prepared to include further targets unless the official policy of the government is changed. Another explanation may be that new actors enter the political game and need to be listed as they pose a threat to the sender and its interests.

Trends in targeting also gives further support to the notion that actors such as the UN and the EU are increasingly seeking to hold individual decision-makers accountable for their political deeds. This supports both the notion of a broader trend of humanisation in international law and politics, as well as an ongoing 'justice cascade'. Another observation is that in the majority of sanctions regimes, the sender prefers to implement both an assets freeze and a travel ban. When it chooses to impose only one of these measures, the UN seems to select travel bans rather than assets freezes.

Of the sanctions regimes currently being applied to natural entities, about half are aimed at non-state actors, while the others are directed against government members (or persons closely linked with the government). In two cases, targeted sanctions were implemented on both sides of the conflict (on both non-state and state actors). In terms of the target category that is applied when these sanctions lists are being established, there are no specific or objective criteria that run across the sanctions regimes. On the contrary, each sanctions regime is unique in this regard. Observation suggests that senders are prepared to apply a whole host of target categories if necessary. For instance, in the case of Zimbabwe, the EU has applied sanctions against target categories such as: the military, air force, targets' families, government, parliament, police, prison, election officials, central bank associates, war veterans, the media and political bureau members (ZANU-PF). New categories may be added in future episodes.

An intriguing question running throughout this study has been to what extent targeted personal sanctions actually had any impact upon those listed. Here, the argument is made that sanctions can achieve impact in two ways: direct and symbolic. One finding of this study is that some regimes randomly seem to operate symbolic sanctions, while other regimes seem more inclined to strive to achieve a more direct target impact. There are probably several explanations for this, such as lack of political will, lack of resources for implementation, or because of the sender's (and its many departments') diverging sets of administrative cultures for operating sanctions policies. However, a consequence of sometimes adopting a policy with more symbolic aims while at other times seeking to interact directly with the target is that the sending body risks undermining its legitimacy, as it may be perceived, both by insiders and outsiders, as incapable of achieving its aims. To solve this problem, senders need to develop a more refined strategy for communicating the rationale for engaging in one or the other strategy to international audiences.

In terms of using targeted sanctions as part of an operational strategic approach, there have been few signs of an explicitly stated doctrine to use targeted sanctions in interaction with other parallel and broader strategic frameworks. This is somewhat surprising. While it was clear that targeted sanctions were embedded in a number of accompanying strategies, such as neighbourhood programmes, co-operation agreements, assistance efforts, and so on (that is, sanctions were often mentioned or referred to in such documents), there were seldom documents describing how they would be strategically applied. This gives further support to the idea of targeted sanctions being embedded within a larger strategic logic, although seldom part of operating procedures. For example, while the UNSC has imposed arms embargoes in a number of contexts, it has not co-ordinated such measures with for example ongoing military operations on the ground. If a sender instead instructed its peacekeeping forces active in the field to, let's say, work to prevent arms embargo violations, then the overall goals of the sender would be easier to achieve.

In summary, a general policy implication is that there is a clear need to think of the role of sanctions as part of a holistic sanctions approach rather than a stand-alone policy. Whereas UN and EU targeted sanctions have long been seen as instruments to achieve political change and resolve a number of complex emergencies, targeted sanctions should not be assessed in isolation. Inclusion of broader strategy would therefore improve sanctions theory in general.

Recognising Targets

In this study, a number of interviews were also carried out with individuals on sanctions lists. The starting point was to bring to the forefront some of those individuals who collective security actors of the international community have branded as posing a threat to peace, security and human rights. It was hoped that bringing the perception and behaviour of targeted individuals into sanctions analysis would lead to a better understanding of how the sanctions policy tool might work.

A general finding was that the entities targeted by the EU and UN were quite 'anonymous', in the sense that little information existed about them in the international media (for example, little is known about the targeted entities in Myanmar).[7] One explanation for this may be that targets are only 'visible' in their own local environments, and not so much on the international scene. In fact, several sanctions lists examined included individuals who had been killed or imprisoned (for example, the UN's Sierra Leone sanctions list).

Moreover, it was found that the impact of targeted sanctions on specific individuals does seem to play an important role. There were many different examples of how both travel bans and assets freezes have been 'present' in the daily life of the entities. While the findings do not necessarily suggest that sanctions achieved a behavioural change in those interviewed (making them abide by the rules of the sender), they did prove to have achieved different kinds of impact. For some entities, the impact was related to their professional and official career (which sanctions often disturbed), while other entities felt the impact privately, in terms of the strain upon relationships with their friends and families (for example, travel

7 However, there are a number of high-profile cases where targets have been very vocal and visible (for example, Zimbabwe and Liberia).

bans sometimes prevented targets from meeting with them). Also interesting, and perhaps more important, is that targeted sanctions also seemed to function as an annoyance, creating insecurity, stigmatisation and frustration. There were many different accounts of this in the interviews.

The interviews also gave reasons to think further about the role of target behaviour and ways to categorise it: for example, 'sobering', 'restraint', 'repentance', 'victimisation' or 'repellence'.[8] Such a categorisation fits the kind of answers provided by the targets. Yet this does not mean that their actual behaviour always changed. On the contrary, sanctions could also make targets more obstructive *vis-à-vis* the sender. Such contrary notions add to the complexity of the argument. It is also possible to categorise the political behaviour of targets according to their reactions to the sender: 'comply', 'evade' or 'do nothing'. However, the lack of data and information does not allow any systematically based conclusions – more data are needed.

The interviews conducted here, as well as an analysis of reports looking at compliance and evasion elsewhere, suggest that in the cases of Zimbabwe, Angola, Liberia, the Ivory Coast, Moldova (Transdniestria) and Sierra Leone, most targets either tried to evade or do nothing, while there were only few signs of compliance. However, just because targets did not respond positively by changing their behaviour following targeted sanctions does not mean that the goals were not achieved. In fact 'doing nothing' could mean that the sender actually succeeded in constraining the target. An important aspect of targeting is that it does not always intend to achieve behavioural change, but sometimes also to constrain targets. Here it should be recognised that targeted sanctions play very different roles depending on the contexts they are intended to address. While the same types of restrictive measures may be put in place across different sanctions regimes, the outcomes vary considerably.

Finally, albeit not surprisingly, the interviews conducted revealed that targeted sanctions were seen as both 'unjust' and 'unfair'. There was often little understanding of why an individual had been put on the list. In some cases, the interviewees had their own specific explanations – such as for political reasons or because of their affiliation with other entities that might be of more threat to the sender and its interests – but entities rarely took personal responsibility for being listed. The sender was often blamed. In all, such comments reveal that sanctions were felt to be imposed on a personal basis. While senders can usually be sure that there is enough 'evidence' to impose sanctions on a target, there are also a number of entities that are innocent. Such errors contribute to making sanctions inefficient. All of this suggests a further need to look beyond the state and the group when analysing the impact of targeted sanctions.

8 Wallensteen et al. (2006).

Experiences from Zimbabwe and Angola

In order to give further empirical evidence for the need to rethink existing sanctions theory and assessment methodology, a closer empirical examination of the EU's targeted sanctions against the current Zimbabwean elite as well as the former UNITA leadership was made. Particular attention was paid to the kinds of episodes occurring within this case, the kinds of target categories that the sender placed on the sanctions list, the perception of targeted sanctions by the sender, the potential impact of a travel ban and financial sanctions on the targets, and the general impact sanctions had on the conflict.

In general, the examination found no correlation between the implementation of personal sanctions and the resolution of the overall crisis (conflict) which would have proven the efficacy of sanctions. On the contrary, following the introduction of targeted sanctions, economic and political deterioration continued over time in both cases. Establishing a correlation is impossible given the extreme number of direct and indirect factors that one would have to take into account. None the less, it was argued that it was not feasible to claim that targeted individual sanctions did not play any part at all. In contrast, it is possible to argue that personal listing measures limited listed entities' room for manoeuvre, and in that sense had a constant effect. One could argue that this could be beneficial in terms of conflict resolution. Concerning the perceptions of the targets, it was also observed that there was well-developed sanctions awareness among actors on the ground, both among listed entities and the larger population. Targeted sanctions seemed to have both a direct and indirect impact upon the targets interviewed.

In the case of Zimbabwe, some of the interviewees at times displayed frustration, and sometimes also indignation. If the Zimbabwean entities' behaviour was categorised according to 'comply', 'evade' or 'do nothing', most targets seemed to 'do nothing' *vis-à-vis* the EU in order to improve their situation. Another finding from the study of the Zimbabwean elite was that the policy enabled a dialogue with regime officials in a way that might otherwise not been possible. Although the sender publicly seemed to refrain from interacting directly with targeted actors, there were still several examples of indirect strategic engagement with members of the regime by listing and de-listing target categories and by making statements regarding the behaviour of listed entities.

Other such kinds of interactions included, for instance, keeping targets notified that they were on the list and what the main arguments were for their inclusion (by writing public letters to targets). While achieving a change in target behaviour is crucial from a sanctions assessment point of view, another decisive factor seemed to be the sender's ability to encourage targeted actors interested in pursuing dialogue or contact. This enabling effect of targeted sanctions has also been confirmed in studies undertaken by Cortright and Lopez, which suggest that the type of impact (positive or punitive) on the targets is not as relevant as the value of creating a bargaining environment.[9] This also suggests that future sanctions assessment studies should take into account how senders manage to utilise such an enabling momentum, instead of over-focusing on what outcomes sanctions have led to in comparison to the initial goals. Such a capacity could be a good criterion for success.

Other findings in the examination of the Zimbabwean case include that a travel ban and financial sanctions could augment group cohesion among the targets; that targets in a number of cases experienced impact in the form of annoyances, and that a strong anti-sanctions narrative had rooted itself among the elite on the ground, which undermined the EU's sanctions policy. Findings like these suggest the need for sanctions scholars to be more context-sensitive when seeking to determine sanctions impact. It follows that there are a number of 'local' rules, norms and processes that enable or constrain sanctions.

Similarly to the Zimbabwean case, the UNITA sanctions regime was also divided into a number of distinct sanctions episodes based on the sender's adjustment of the sanctions lists. The review of the UNITA sanctions suggests, not surprisingly, that targeted sanctions did not seem to contribute directly to conflict resolution. As we saw, the violent conflict continued for many years. Yet it would be wrong to conclude that targeted sanctions were a failure. On the contrary, there are good reasons to suggest that without targeted sanctions, the situation would have been much worse, as the pressure it mounted against UNITA's operations clearly undermined its ability to pursue 'business as usual'.

With regard to the personalisation of targeted sanctions, there were several indications that both the sender and a number of targets perceived sanctions as an instrument to be imposed upon the political movement as a whole, rather than upon specific individual entities. Yet, while there was a notion that it was the group that was under pressure and not specific individuals, this did not rule out that personal experience did matter in the UNITA sanctions regime. There were several statements from former listed entities implying that they felt personally affected, not least on the psychological level. While it did not change the behaviour of those listed, it did at least seem to constrain and annoy some of them. The importance of stigmatisation because of the sanctions should therefore not be underestimated. In fact, such psychological impact was evident, and seemed to matter a great deal. Moreover, the effects of stigmatisation could be noted both at the personal and the group level. Such an impact was also likely to change over the course of the sanctions regime. The findings therefore suggest that there should be greater focus upon the political behaviour of the targeted actors. In view of the findings of this case study, it is also important to pay further attention to other ongoing sender strategies which may be equally important as targeted sanctions in constraining and coercing targets. Far too often sanctions assessment looks only at sender-related aspects and at particular

9 Cortright (2001): 118. See also Cortright and Lopez (2000).

sanctions implementation difficulties. The perception of the targets is crucial to the effectiveness of a sanctions regime.

Finally, it is worth noting that the Angola sanctions regime further demonstrated that when conducting sanctions assessments, there is a need to pay attention to the continuous interaction that takes place between the sender and the target during the course of the conflict. In contrast to other sanctions regimes, the Angola sanctions committee, and in particular its chairman (Ambassador Fowler), was very active in holding press conferences, issuing reports, and so on. Not only did such actions signal to the international community that the UN was watching developments on ground closely, it also communicated resolve to the targeted actors. Thus, much of the success of a sanctions regime depends upon the sanctions sending body's active and clearly signalled commitment to making sanctions effective and peace possible.[10]

10 Möllander (2009).

Appendix 1
Operationalisation and Definition of Targeted Sanctions

Decision-making: The process by which a sender maintains a sanctions regime.

Implementation: The enforcement of a sanctions policy by a sanctions sending body.

Multivariate process: All the applicable variables that exist in a specific sanctions case, leading to a particular sanctions outcome. For example:

- *nature of the international system* – distinct periods containing a set of structural features in the international system that may have an impact upon a target's decision-making behaviour (for example, institutions, norms and values);
- *location of the targeted actor in the international system* – the geopolitical location of the targeted actor (the regional dimension); this can also encompass the 'mental' location of the target (for example, support from different political actors);
- *sender factors* – the number of actors in the international system imposing targeted sanctions, upon the immediate target (or his or her affiliates) at a given point in time.

Perception of sanctions: Both the sender and the target perceive sanctions subjectively. This perception shapes their understanding of sanctions, which also shapes the impact of sanctions:

- *sender's perception* – the sender is likely to shape the design of the sanctions policy following its understanding of how the policy is meant to work; such understanding affects daily sanctions impact;
- *target's perception* – the way the target frames the sender's political intentions and credibility.

Political behaviour/target reaction: The reaction the target displays when being targeted by sanctions. Three types of behaviour can be identified: 'compliance', 'evasion' or simply 'do nothing'. The behaviour follows sanctions measures (change of political behaviour can be identified by actions or the absence thereof, or verbal or written comments by the target).

Relationship between the target and sender: The general or specific relationship that exists between the target and the sender:

- *general relationship* – a historical relationship encompassing political, economic, social and cultural ties;
- *specific relationship* – the immediate conflict history that unfolded and led the sender to adopt and implement sanctions. The specific relationship is also linked to the sender's and the target's expected relationship in the future.

Sanctions episodes: The number of policy entry points by the sending body in a particular sanctions regime to adopt, adjust and replace sanctions measures *vis-à-vis* the target. Each episode displays a success or a failure.

Sanctions impact: Impact can be thought of in three ways:

1. target impact (for example, physical or psychological impact on an individual or group);
2. sender impact (for example, counter-productive or instrumental);
3. conflict/crisis impact (for example, achievement of goals or resolution of problems).

Sanctions regime: The duration of a sanctions policy. Each regime is divided into a number of sanctions episodes.

Sender: The implementing body:

- The sender is constituted of a number of sanctions-implementing bodies, as well as individual decision-makers (for example, ministers, administrative units, officials, sanctions experts, and so on).
- Decision-makers are those officials who deal with sanctions on a daily basis (for example, UN and EU officials). They also include other implementing actors such as customs officials and financial operators.

Sender–target interaction: The interaction that takes place between a sender and a target during a sanctions regime. This interaction can take different forms (for example, political, economic or military). The most notable forms are policy modifications, demands and interventions (for example, UN Security Council Resolutions or EU Common Positions or regulations). This interaction also defines the number of episodes within a sanctions regime.

Strategic context: The overall strategic logic that embeds targeted sanctions (for example, deterrence, compliance and containment).

Success and failure: The aggregated impacts and effects of each separate episode in a given sanctions regime.

Target: The receiving end of the restrictive measures; the entity being placed on the sanctions lists (for example, an individual entity, a group or a company).

- *targeted sanctions*: Restrictive measures imposed on an individual, a company or a commodity (for example, travel bans and assets freezes).

Appendix 2
Sanctions Regime Episodes

Table 1 Belarus

Episode no.	Decision	Total entities	Travel bans	Assets freezes
1	24 September 2004	4	4	
2	13 December 2004	6	6	
3	10 April 2006	37	37	
4	18 May 2006	37	37	36
5	18 May 2006	36		36
6	23 October 2006	35	35	
7	23 October 2006	40		40
8	19 April 2007			
9	7 April 2008			
10	10 November 2008			

Table 2 Former Yugoslav Republic of Macedonia

Episode no.	Decision	Total entities	Travel bans	Assets freezes
1	16 July 2001			
2	10 February 2004	12	12	
3	10 February 2005	19	19	
4	10 February 2005	21	21	
5	10 February 2006	19	19	
6	10 February 2007	16	16	
7	10 February 2008	17	17	

Table 3 Serbia and Montenegro

Episode no.	Decision	Total entities	Travel bans	Assets freezes
1	13 March 1996			
2	19 April 1998	10	10	
3	27 April 1998			
4	7 May 1998			
5	22 June 1998			
6	8 June 1998			
7	29 June 1998			
8	24 July 1998			
9	10 August 1998			
10	7 September 1998			
11	23 April 1999			
12	29 April 1999			
13	10 May 1999			
14	10 May 1999	279	279	
15	21 May 1999			
16	1 June 1999	287	287	
17	15 June 1999	290		290
18	19 July 1999			
19	28 June 1999	288	288	
20	3 September 1999			
21	13 September 1999	305	305	
22	15 September 1999			
23	4 October 1999			
24	11 October 1999			
25	22 October 1999			
26	15 November 1999			
27	6 December 1999	588	588	
28	22 December 1999	795	795	
29	24 January 2000			
30	1 February 2000			
31	28 February 2000			
32	28 February 2000	795	795	
33	20 March 2000			
34	6 April 2000			
35	24 April 2000	793		793
36	18 May 2000			
37	22 May 2000	793	793	
38	24 May 2000			
39	29 May 2000			
40	5 May 2000	754	754	

Table 3 (continued)

Episode no.	Decision	Total entities	Travel bans	Assets freezes
41	30 June 2000			
42	20 July 2000			
43	20 July 2000			
44	26 July 2000			
45	3 August 2000			
46	3 August 2000	811	811	
47	9 October 2000	626	626	
48	9 October 2000			
49	9 October 2000			
50	10 November 2000	626	626	
51	10 November 2000	626		626
52	20 November 2000			
53	26 February 2001	13	13	
54	19 June 2001	13		13

Table 4 EU measures in support of the mandate of the ICTY (against supporters of indicted entities)

Episode no.	Decision	Total entities	Travel bans	Assets freezes
1	16 April 2003	2	2	
2	27 June 2003	14	14	
3	30 March 2004	14	14	
4	28 June 2004	27	27	
5	31 January 2005	36	36	
6	16 March 2005			
7	10 March 2006			
8	5 March 2007	35	35	
9	23 July 2007	42	42	
10	13 April 2008			
11	15 September 2008	34	34	

Table 5 EU measures to bring indicted entities before the ICTY

Episode no.	Decision	Total entities	Travel bans	Assets freezes
1	16 March 2004			
2	11 October 2004	3		3
3	11 October 2004	3		3
4	15 November 2004			
5	15 November 2004	21		21
6	22 December 2004	19		19
7	22 December 2004	19		19
8	21 February 2005	17		17
9	22 February 2005	17		17
10	18 April 2005	13		13
11	18 April 2005	13		11
12	30 May 2005	10		10
13	6 June 2005	10		10
14	11 October 2005	9		9
11	9 October 2005	9		9
12	21 December 2005	8		8
13	9 January 2006	10		10
14	10 March 2006	7		7
15	10 March 2006	7		7
16	11 July 2006	6		6
17	4 July 2006	6		6
18	1 October 2007			
19	24 July 2008	3		3
20	28 July 2008	3		3
21	12 September 2008	2		2
22	15 September 2008	2		2
23	29 September 2008			

Table 6 Moldova (Transdniestria)

Episode no.	Decision	Total entities	Travel bans	Assets freezes
1	27 February 2003	17	17	
2	23 February 2004	17	17	
3	26 August 2004	27	27	
4	21 February 2005	27	27	
5	12 December 2005	29	29	
6	12 February 2006			
7	12 February 2006	29	29	
8	19 February 2007	29	29	
9	27 February 2008	29	29	

Table 7 Iraq

Episode no.	Decision	Total entities	Travel bans	Assets freezes
1	7 August 1990			
2	29 October 1990			
3	10 December 1996			
4	10 December 1996			
5	25 July 2002			
6	7 July 2003-07-07	55		55
7	22 May 2003			
8	29 April 2004	71		75
9	6 September 2004	77		77
10	28 June 2004			
11	8 July 2005	78		78
12	3 August 2005	84		84

Table 8 Iran

Episode no.	Decision	Total entities	Travel bans[1]	Assets freezes
1	27 February 2007	12	12	12
2	19 April 2007	12		12
3	20 April 2007	27		27
4	23 April 2007	42	42	42
5	23 April 2007	42		42
6	25 April 2007			
7	5 June 2007			
8	28 January 2008			
9	11 March 2008	55		55
10	23 June 2008	60	15	60
11	23 June 2008	60	60	60
12	24 June 2008			
13	7 August 2008	68	68	68

Note: [1] Entities subject to travel bans are the only ones listed, and remain the same throughout the regime – for this reason, they should not be added as a separate category to the total.

Table 9 Sierra Leone

Episode no.	Decision	Total entities	Travel bans
1	8 December 1997		
2	28 January 1998		
3	8 January 1998	57	57
4	5 June 1998		
5	18 February 2000		
6	1 February 2001	56	56
7	6 June 2003	48	48
8	25 February 2004	46	46
9	20 September 2004	30	30
10	28 January 2008		
11	9 June 2008	6	6

Table 10 Liberia 1 (prior to Charles Taylor)

Episode no.	Decision	Total entities	Travel bans
1	8 May 2001		
2	4 June 2001	136	136
3	26 December 2001	131	131
4	18 March 2002	129	129
5	7 May 2002		
6	10 July 2002	126	126
7	22 July 2002		
8	9 September 2002	122	122
9	5 November 2002	118	118
10	7 May 2003		
11	9 June 2003	116	116

Table 11 Liberia 2: Travel bans

Episode no.	Decision	Total entities	Travel bans
1	22 December 2003		
2	16 March 2004	47	47
3	16 April 2004	46	46
4	12 July 2004	49	49
5	26 August 2004	51	51
6	2 May 2005	57	57
7	30 November 2005	59	59
8	1 December 2005	59	59
9	15 December 2006	58	58
10	12 February 2007		
11	28 November 2007	57	57
12	12 February 2008		
13	31 March 2008	56	56
14	21 May 2008	55	55
15	13 June 2008	54	54
16	10 September 2008	53	53
17	10 November 2008	52	52
18	4 December 2008	51	51
19	15 December 2008	50	50

Table 12 Liberia 2: Assets freezes

Episode no.	Decision	Total entities	Assets freezes
1	12 March 2004		
2	10 February 2004		
3	10 February 2004		
4	29 April 2004		
5	29 April 2004	3	3
6	22 June 2004	23	23
7	18 August 2004		
8	8 September 2004	26	26
9	22 December 2004		
10	2 May 2005		
11	9 June 2005	26	26
12	30 November 2005	28	28
13	12 December 2005	28	28
14	23 December 2005		
15	23 January 2006		
16	24 July 2006		
17	24 July 2006		
18	11 December 2006		
19	12 February 2007		
20	11 June 2007		
21	23 July 2007		
22	11 December 2007	27	27
23	2 October 2008[1]	26	26
24	10 November 2008	25	25
25	4 December 2008	24	24
26	15 December 2008	23	23

Note: [1] A number of UN press releases concerning de-listing of assets freezes have not yet been reflected in EU regulations.

Table 13 Ivory Coast

Episode no.	Decision	Total entities	Travel bans	Assets freezes
1	13 December 2004			
2	31 January 2005			
3	12 April 2005			
4	12 April 2005			
5	13 February 2006	3	3	3
6	27 February 2006	3	3	3
7	14 February 2006	3	3	3
8	11 July 2006	3	3	3
9	16 December 2006			
10	22 November 2007			
11	18 November 2008			

Table 14 Democratic Republic of Congo

Episode no.	Decision	Total entities	Travel bans	Assets freezes
1	21 October 2002			
2	29 September 2003			
3	29 September 2003			
4	13 June 2005			
5	13 June 2005			
6	18 July 2005			
7	9 November 2005	15	15	15
8	18 January 2006			
9	13 June 2005			
10	15 September 2006			
11	23 February 2007			
12	12 April 2007	17	17	17
13	3 August 2007			
14	20 September 2007			
15	7 November 2007	19	19	19
16	28 April 2008	18	18	18
17	14 May 2008[1]	17	17	17
18	19 December 2008	16[2]	16	16

Notes: [1] The Common Position replaces the previous list, which was not in line with previous UN lists. [2] This figure is based on the consolidated lists kept by the UNSC Sanctions Committee on the DRC. The last list issued by the UN had 18 targets listed. The number is now 16, meaning that another two targets must have been de-listed without press releases confirming this. One problem is that press releases from the various sanctions committees do not always include references to the correct consolidated lists (sometimes referring to older lists), leading to difficulties in counting.

Table 15 Sudan

Episode no.	Decision	Total entities	Travel bans	Assets freezes
1	15 March 1994			
2	9 January 2004			
3	26 January 2004			
4	10 June 2004			
5	26 July 2004			
6	30 April 2005			
7	30 May 2005			
8	30 May 2005			
9	18 July 2005			
10	18 May 2006	4		4
11	1 June 2006	4	4	4
12	17 August 2007			

Table 16 Zimbabwe

Episode no.	Decision	Total entities	Travel bans	Assets freezes
1	18 February 2002	20	20	
2	18 February 2002	20		20
3	22 July 2002	72	72	
4	13 September 2002	79	79	
5	18 February 2003			
6	18 February 2003			
7	19 February 2004	95	95	
8	19 February 2004	95		95
9	13 June 2005	120	120	
10	15 June 2005	120		120
11	29 July 2005	126	126	
12	1 August 2005	126		126
13	30 January 2006			
14	19 February 2007	125	125	
11	25 June 2007	131	131	
12	2 July 2007	131		131
13	18 February 2008			
14	22 July 2008	168	168	168
15	23 July 2008	168		168
16	31 July 2008			

Table 17 Uzbekistan

Episode no.	Decision	Total entities	Travel bans	Assets freezes
1	14 November 2005	12	12	
2	14 November 2005			
3	13 November 2006			
4	14 May 2007	8	8	
5	13 November 2007	8	8	
6	10 November 2008	0	0	

Table 18 Burma/Myanmar

Episode no.	Decision	Total entities	Travel bans	Assets freezes
1	28 October 1996			
2	29 April 1997			
3	20 October 1997			
4	27 April 1998			
5	26 January 1998			
6	26 October 1998			
7	11 October 1999			
8	26 April 2000	140	140	140
9	22 May 2000	140	n/a	140
10	9 October 2000			
11	22 April 2002			
12	28 April 2003	115	115	115
13	20 June 2003	269	269	269
14	22 December 2003	178	178	178
11	26 April 2004	178	178	178
12	26 April 2004	179	n/a	179
13	25 October 2004			
14	25 October 2004			
15	21 February 2005			
16	22 February 2005			
17	25 April 2005	390	390	390
18	28 April 2005	390		390
19	27 April 2006	392	392	390
20	29 May 2006	392		392
21	23 April 2007	379	379	379
22	27 April 2007	386		386
23	19 November 2007	428	428	428
24	25 November 2008	432		432
25	11 March 2008			
26	29 April 2008	523	523	523
27	29 April 2008	513		513
28	30 April 2008			

Bibliography

Books and Articles

Abdelal, Rawi and Kirshner, Jonathan. 'Strategy, Economic Relations, and the Definition of National Interests', in Blanchard, Jean-Mark F., Mansfield, Edward. D. and Ripsman, Norrin. M (eds), *Power and the Purse: The Political Economy of National Security*, 119–56 (London: Frank Cass, 2000).

Abi-Saab, Georges. 'The Concept of Sanction in International Law', in Gowlland-Debbas, Vera (ed.), *United Nations Sanctions and International Law*. Graduate Institute of International Studies (The Hague: Kluwer Law International, 2001).

Ahtisaari, Martti. *Report to the Secretary-General on Humanitarian Needs in Kuwait and Iraq in the Immediate Post-crisis Environment by a Mission to the Area. Report led by Mr. Martti Ahtisaari, Under-Secretary-General for Administration and Management, March 1991* (New York: United Nations, 1991).

Albright, Madeleine K. 'Economic Sanctions and Public Health: A View from the Department of State', *Annals of Internal Medicine*, vol. 132, no. 218, 155–7 (2000).

Ali, Mohamed and Shah, Iqbal. 'Sanctions and Childhood Mortality in Iraq', *The Lancet*, vol. 355, no. 9218, 1851–7 (May 2000).

Allen, Susan Hannah. 'Political Institutions and Constrained Response to Economic Sanctions', *Foreign Policy Analysis*, vol. 4, 255–74 (2008).

Allison, Graham T. and Halperin, Morton. 'Bureaucratic Politics: A Paradigm and Some Policy Implications', *World Politics*, vol. 24, 40–79 (1972).

Almqvist, Jessica. 'Human Rights Critique of European Judicial Review: Counter-terrorism Sanctions', *International & Comparative Law Quarterly*, vol. 57, no. 2, 303–31 (2008).

Alsnasrawi, Abbas. 'Iraq: Economic Sanctions and Consequences, 1990–2000', *Third World Quarterly*, vol. 22, no. 2, 205–18 (2001).

Ameri, Houshang. *Politics of Staffing the United Nations Secretariat* (New York: Peter Lang, 1996).

Andersson, Torbjörn and Cameron, Ian. 'EU Blacklisting: The Renaissance of Imperial Power, but on a Global Scale', *European Business Law Review*, vol. 14, 111–41 (2003).

Andreas, Peter and Nadelmann, Ethan. *Policing the Globe: Criminalization and Crime Control in International Relations* (Oxford: Oxford University Press, 2006).

Angell, David J.R. 'The Angola Sanctions Committee', in Malone, David M. (ed.), *The UN Security Council from the Cold War to the 21st Century* (Boulder, CO: Lynne Rienner, 2004).
Annan, Kofi. *Annual Report on the Work of the Organization* (New York: United Nations, 1998), <www.un.org/Docs/SG/Report98>.
Annual Review of Global Peace Operations. Center on International Cooperation (London: Lynne Rienner, 2008).
Anthony, Ian. 'Sanctions Applied by the European Union and the United Nations', *SIPRI Yearbook 2002: Armaments, Disarmament and International Security*, Stockholms Internationella Fredsforskningsinstitut, Solna (Oxford: Oxford University Press, 2002).
Arnove, Anthony (ed.). *Iraq Under Siege: The Deadly Impact of Sanctions and War* (London: Pluto Press, 2003).
Askari, Hossein, Forrer, John, Teegen, Hildy and Yang, Jiawen. *Economic Sanctions: Examining their Philosophy and Efficacy* (Westport, CT: Praeger, 2003).
Bahgat, Gawdat. 'US-Iranian Relations: Sanctions and the Caspian Sea', *Security Dialogue*, vol. 32, no. 2, 231–43 (2001).
Baldwin, David A. 'The Power of Positive Sanctions', *World Politics*, vol. 24, no. 1, 19–38 (1971).
——. *Economic Statecraft* (Princeton, NJ: Princeton University Press, 1985).
——. 'Success and Failure in Foreign Policy', *Annual Review of Political Science*, no. 3, 167–82 (2000).
—— and Pape, Robert. 'Evaluating Economic Sanctions', *International Security*, vol. 23, no. 2, 189–95 (1998).
Baram, Amatzia. 'The Effect of Iraqi Sanctions: Statistical Pitfalls and Responsibility', *Middle East Journal*, vol. 54, no. 2, 191–223 (2000).
Barber, James. 'Economic Sanctions as a Policy Instrument', *International Affairs*, vol. 55, 367–84 (1979).
Beehner, Lionel. 'Council on Foreign Relations. Iran Undeterred by DPRK Sanctions', *Daily Analysis*, 24 October (2006).
Bianchi, Andrea. 'Assessing the Effectiveness of the UN Security Council's Anti-terrorism Measures: The Quest for Legitimacy and Cohesion', *European Journal of International Law*, vol. 17, no. 5, 881–919 (2007).
Biersteker, Thomas. *The Emergence, Evolution, Effects, and Challenges of Targeted Sanctions*, paper prepared for the conference 'Sanctions Economiques: Vers de Nouvelles Pratiques', Paris, 14 June 2004 (Providence, RI: Watson Institute for International Studies, Brown University, 2004).
——. 'Routes to Enhanced Respect: Reflections on Recent Experiences and Realistic Alternatives', unpublished presentation prepared for the Dag Hammarskjöld Symposium 'Respecting International Law and International Institutions', Uppsala, Sweden (June 2005).
——. 'Targeted Sanctions and Human Rights'. Paper prepared for presentation at the Annual Meeting of the International Studies Association (ISA), San Francisco, CA (March 2008).

—— and Eckert, Sue. *Strengthening Targeted Sanctions through Fair and Clear Procedures.* Report commissioned by the governments of Germany, Switzerland, and Sweden (Providence, RI: Watson Institute for International Studies, Brown University, 2006).

—— and Eckert, Sue (eds). *Countering the Financing of Terrorism* (New York: Routledge, 2008).

——, Eckert, Sue and Reid, Natalie. *Targeted Financial Sanctions: A Primer.* Background Paper for the Targeted Financial Sanctions Simulation Exercise at Naval War College, New Port, Rhode Island, 11–13 May 2000.

Billon, Philippe L. *Fuelling War: Natural Resources and Armed Conflicts* (London: Routledge, 2005).

Blake, Charles H. and Klemm, Noah. 'Reconsidering the Effectiveness of International Economic Sanctions: An Examination of Selection Bias', *International Politics*, vol. 43, 133–49 (2006).

Blanchard, Jean-Marc F. and Ripsman, Norrin M. 'Asking the Right Question: When do Economic Sanctions Work Best?', *Security Studies*, vol. 9, no. 1–2, 219–53 (1999).

Blanchard, Jean-Marc F., Mansfield, Edward D. and Ripsman, Norrin M. 'The Political Economy of National Security: Economic Statecraft, Interdependence, and International Conflict', in Blanchard, Jean-Marc F., Mansfield, Edward D. and Ripsman, Norrin M. (eds), *Power and the Purse: Economic Statecraft, Interdependence, and National Security.* Cass Series on Security Studies (London: Frank Cass, 2000).

Bonn-Berlin Process. *Design and Implementation of Arms Embargoes and Travel and Aviation Related Sanctions: Results of the 'Bonn-Berlin Process'.* Bonn International Center for Conversion, no. 6 (Baden-Baden: Nomos Verlagsgesellschaft, 2001).

Boucher, Alix J. and Holt, Victoria K. *Targeting Spoilers: The Role of United Nations Panels of Experts.* Report from the Project on Rule of Law in Post-conflict Settings. Future of Peace Operations Program, Stimson Center Report no. 64, rev. 1 (January 2009).

Brooks, Risa A. 'Sanctions and Regime Type: What Works, and When?', *Security Studies*, vol. 11, no. 4, 1–50 (2002).

——. 'Putting More Teeth in UN Arms Embargoes', in Cortright, David and Lopez, George A. (eds), *Smart Sanctions: Targeting Economic Statecraft* (Lanham, MA: Rowman and Littlefield, 2002).

——. 'From Dumb to Smart: Recent Reforms of UN Sanctions', *Global Governance*, vol. 9, 519–35 (2003).

——. 'Measuring the Effectiveness of Arms Embargoes', *Peace Economics, Peace Science and Public Policy*, vol. 14, no. 2 (2008).

Bures, Oldrich. 'EU Counterterrorism Policy: A Paper Tiger?', *Terrorism and Political Violence*, vol. 18, no. 1, 57–78 (2006).

Cameron, Iain. 'European Union Anti-terrorist Blacklisting', *Human Rights Law Review*, vol. 3, no. 2 (2003a).

——. 'Targeted Sanctions, Legal Safeguards and the ECHR', *Nordic Journal of International Law*, vol. 72, no. 2 (2003b).
——. *The European Convention on Human Rights, Due Process and United Nations Security Council Counter-terrorism Sanctions* (Council of Europe, 2006).
——. *Respecting Human Rights and Fundamental Freedoms and EU/UN Sanctions: State of Play*. Report commissioned by the European Parliament, Policy Department External Policies, Directorate-General for External Policies of the Union (October 2008).
Campbell, Greg. *Blood Diamonds: Tracing the Deadly Path of the World's Most Precious Stones* (Boulder, CO: Westview Press, 2002).
Center for Economic and Social Rights. *UNsanctioned Suffering: A Human Rights Assessment of United Nations Sanctions on Iraq* (New York: Center for Economic and Social Rights, 1996).
Chan, Steve and Drury, Cooper (eds). *Sanctions as Economic Statecraft: Theory and Practice* (New York: Palgrave, 2000).
Charron, Andrea. *UN Targeted Sanctions: Changing the Lens from Sanctions to the Crisis Context.* Paper presented to the International Studies Association conference (ISA), New York (2009).
——. *UN Sanctions and Conflict: Responding to Peace and Security Threats.* Routledge Studies in Security and Conflict Management (London: Routledge, 2010).
Checkel, Jeffrey T. 'Why Comply? Social Change and European Identity Change', *International Organization*, vol. 55, no. 3, 553–88 (2001).
Chesterman, Simon. *The UN Security Council and the Rule of Law: The Role of the Security Council in Strengthening a Rules-based International System*. Final Report and Recommendations from the Austrian Initiative, 2004–2008 (New York: Institute for International Law and Justice, New York University School of Law and Federal Ministry for European and International Affairs, 2008).
—— and Pouligny, Béatrice. 'Are Sanctions Meant to Work? The Politics of Creating and Implementing Sanctions through the United Nations', *Global Governance*, vol. 9, no. 4, 503–18 (2003).
Cilliers, Jakkie and Dietrich, Christian (eds), *Angola's War Economy* (Pretoria: Institute for Security Studies, 2000).
Conroy, Richard. 'Implementation Problems of Travel Bans: Practical and Legal Aspects', paper presented at the 'First Expert Seminar, on Smart Sanctions: The Next Step – the Debate on Arms Embargoes and Travel Sanctions within the "Bonn-Berlin Process"' (Bonn, 1999).
——. 'The UN Experience with Travel Sanctions: Selected Cases and Conclusions', in Cortright, David and Lopez, George A. (eds), *Smart Sanctions: Targeting Economic Statecraft*, 145–70 (Lanham, MD: Rowman and Littlefield, 2002).
Conte, Alex. *Handbook on Human Rights Compliance while Countering Terrorism* (Washington, DC: Center on Global Counterterrorism Cooperation, 2008).

Cortright, David. 'Powers of Persuasion: Sanctions and Incentives in the Shaping of International Society', *International Studies*, vol. 38, no. 2, 113–25 (2001).
—— and Lopez, George. *Economic Sanctions: Panacea or Peacebuilding in a Post-Cold War World?* (Boulder, CO: Westview Press, 1995).
—— and Lopez, George. 'Are sanctions Just? The problematic case of Iraq', *Journal of International Affairs*, vol. 52, no. 2 (1999).
—— and Lopez, George (with Wagler, Julia, Conroy, Richard W. and Dashti-Gibson, Jaleh). *The Sanctions Decade: Assessing UN Strategies in the 1990s* (Boulder, CO: Lynne Rienner, 2000).
—— and Lopez, George (with Gerber, Linda). *Sanctions and the Search for Security: Challenges to UN Action* (Boulder, CO: Lynne Rienner, 2002a).
—— and Lopez, George (eds). *Smart Sanctions: Toward Effective and Humane Sanctions Reform* (Lanham, MD: Rowman and Littlefield, 2002b).
—— and Lopez, George (eds), *Uniting against Terror: Cooperative Nonmilitary Responses to the Global Terrorist Threat*, 23–50 (Cambridge, MA: MIT Press, 2007).
——, Lopez, George A., Minear, Larry, Wagler, Julia and Weiss, Thomas G. *Toward More Humane and Effective Sanctions Management: Enhancing the Capacity of the United Nations System*. Occasional Paper no. 31 (Providence, RI: Thomas J. Watson Jr. Institute for International Studies, Brown University, 1998).
——, Lopez, George and Conroy, Richard. 'Are Travel Sanctions "Smart"? A Review of Theory and Practice', in *First Expert Seminar, 21–23 November 1999. Smart Sanctions: The Next Steps – the Debate on Arms Embargoes and Travel Sanctions within the 'Bonn-Berlin Process'* (Bonn: International Center for Conversion, 2000).
—— Lopez, George and Rogers, Elizabeth S. 'Targeted Financial Sanctions: Smart Sanctions that Do Work', in Cortright, David and Lopez, George A. (eds), *Smart Sanctions: Targeting Economic Statecraft*, 23–40 (Lanham, MD: Rowman and Littlefield, 2002a).
——, Millar, Alistair and Lopez, George A. 'Smart Sanctions in Iraq: Policy Options', in Cortright, David and Lopez, George A. (eds), *Smart Sanctions: Targeting Economic Statecraft*, 201–24 (New York: Rowman and Littlefield, 2002b).
——, Lopez, George, Millar, Alistair and Gerber-Stellingwerf, Linda. 'Global Cooperation against Terrorism: Evaluating the United Nations Counterterrorism Committee', in Cortright, David and Lopez, George (eds), *Uniting against Terror: Cooperative Non-military Response to the Global Terrorist Threat*, 23–50 (Cambridge, MA: MIT Press, 2007).
——, Lopez, George and Gerber-Stellingwerf, Linda. 'The Sanctions Era: Themes and Trends in UN Security Council Sanctions since 1990', in Lowe, Vaughan, Roberts, Adam, Welsh, Jennifer and Zaum, Dominik (eds), *The United Nations Security Council and War: The Evolution of Thought and Practice Since 1945* (Oxford: Oxford University Press, 2008).

Cosgrove, Erica. 'Examining Targeted Sanctions: Are Travel Bans Effective?', in Wallensteen, Peter and Staibano, Carina (eds), *International Sanctions: Between Words and Wars in the Global System* (New York: Frank Cass, 2005).

Craig, Gordon and George, Alexander. *Force and Statecraft: Diplomatic Problems of Our Time*, 2nd edn (New York: Oxford University Press, 1990).

Craven, Matthew. 'Humanitarianism and the Quest for Smarter Sanctions', *European Journal of International Law*, vol. 13, no. 1, 43–61 (2002).

Crawford, Neta C. and Klotz, Audie. 'How Sanctions Work: A Framework for Analysis', in Crawford, Neta C. and Klotz, Audie (eds), *How Sanctions Work: Lessons from South Africa*, 25–44 (New York: St. Martin's Press, 1999).

Crocker, Chester. *High Noon in Southern Africa: Making Peace in a Rough Neighbourhood* (New York: W.W. Norton, 1992).

Crumm, Eileen. 'The Value of Economic Incentives in International Politics', *Journal of Peace Research*, vol. 32, no. 3, 313–30 (1995).

Daoudi, M.S. and Danjani, M.S. *Economic Sanctions: Ideals and Experience* (London: Routledge & Kegan Paul, 1983).

Dashti-Gibson, Jaleh, Davis, Patricia and Radcliff, Benjamin. 'On the Determinants of the Success of Economic Sanctions: An Empirical Analysis', *American Journal of Political Science*, vol. 41, no. 2, 608–18 (1997).

de Chazournes, Laurence Boisson. 'Collective Security and the Economic Interventionism of the UN: The Need for a Coherent and Integrated Approach', *Journal of International Economic Law*, vol. 10, no. 1, 51–86 (2007).

De Vries, Anthonius. 'EU Sanctions against Yugoslavia, 1998–2000', in Cortright, David and Lopez, George A. (eds), *Smart Sanctions: Targeting Economic Statecraft*, 87–108 (New York: Rowman and Littlefield, 2002).

Department of Political Affairs (DPA), UN. 'The Experience of the United Nations in Administering Arms Embargoes and Travel Sanctions: An informal background paper prepared by the United Nations Sanctions secretariat, Department of Political Affairs January 2000', in *First Expert Seminar, 21–23 November 1999. Smart Sanctions: The Next Steps – the Debate on Arms Embargoes and Travel Sanctions within the 'Bonn-Berlin Process'* (Bonn: International Center for Conversion, 2000).

Dewulf, Steven and Pacuée, Didier. 'Protecting Human Rights in the War on Terror: Challenging the Sanctions Regime Originating from Resolution 1267 (1999)', *Netherlands Quarterly of Human Rights*, vol. 24, 607–40 (2006).

Doxey, Margaret P. *Economic Sanctions: Past Lessons and the Case of Rhodesia* (Toronto: Canadian Institute of International Affairs, 1968).

——. *Economic Sanctions and International Enforcement* (New York: Oxford University Press, 1971a).

——. 'The Rhodesian Sanctions Experiment', *Year Book of World Affairs*, vol. 25, 142–62 (1971b).

——. 'International Sanctions: A Framework for Analysis with Special Reference to the UN and Southern Africa', *International Organization*, vol. 26, no. 3, 527–50 (1972).

——. 'Sanctions Revisited', *International Journal*, vol. 13 (1976).
——. *International Sanctions in Contemporary Perspective* (London: Macmillan, 1987; New York: St. Martin's Press, 1996).
——. *United Nations Sanctions: Current Policy Issues* (Halifax, NS: Centre for Foreign Policy Studies, Dalhousie University, 1999).
——. 'Sanctions through the Looking Glass: The Spectrum of Goals and Achievements', *International Journal, Canadian Institute of International Affairs*, vol. 55, no. 2, 207–22 (2000).
——. *United Nations Sanctions: Trends and Problems* (Halifax, NS: Centre for Foreign Policy Studies, Dalhousie University, 2007).
Drezner, Daniel W. *The Sanctions Paradox: Economic Statecraft and International Relations* (Cambridge: Cambridge University Press, 1999).
——. 'The Hidden Hand of Economic Coercion', *International Organization*, vol. 57, no. 3, 643–59 (Summer 2003).
Drury, Cooper. 'Revisiting Economic Sanctions Reconsidered', *Journal of Peace Research*, vol. 35, no. 4 (1998).
Dzinotyiweyi, H.A.M. 'Targeted Sanctions: A Call for Enforcement or Removal', in *Crises Coalition, The Zimbabwean Crisis: 2005 Elections and the Role of the International Community* (Harare: National Think Tank, 18 March 2004).
Eaton, Jonathan and Engers, Maxim. 'Sanctions: Some Simple Analytics', *American Economic Review*, vol. 89, no. 2, 409–14 (1999).
Eeckhout, Piet. 'Community Terrorism Listings, Fundamental Rights, and UN Security Council Resolutions: In Search of the Right Fit', *European Constitutional Law Review*, no. 3, 183–206 (2007).
Elliott, Kimberly Ann. 'The Sanctions Glass – Half Full or Completely Empty?', *International Security*, vol. 23, no. 1, 50–65 (1998).
—— and Hufbauer, Gary. 'Same Song, Same Refrain? Economic Sanctions in the 1990's', *American Economic Review*, vol. 89, no. 2, 403–8 (1999).
Eriksson, Mikael. 'EU Sanctions: Three Cases of Targeted Sanctions', in Wallensteen, Peter and Staibano, Carina (eds), *International Sanctions: Between Words and Wars in the Global System* (London and New York: Frank Cass, 2005).
——. 'Interview with Pierre Schori, UN Special Representative to Côte D'Ivoire', *NEWS*, Website of the Nordic Africa Institute, <www.nai.uu.se> (Uppsala: Nordic Africa Institute, 2007a).
——. *Targeting the Leadership of Zimbabwe: A Path to Democracy and Normalization?* (Uppsala: Department of Peace and Conflict Research, Uppsala University, 2007b).
——. 'Sanctions and the political process for Darfur: An interview with Jan Eliasson', *Accord*, no. 19, *Incentives, Sanctions and Conditionality: An International Review of Peace Initiatives* (London: Conciliation Resources, 2008).
——. *In Search of a Due Process: Listing and Delisting Practices of the European Union* (Uppsala: Department of Peace and Conflict Research, Uppsala University, 2009).

——. *Supporting Democracy in Africa: African Union's Use of Targeted Sanctions to Deal with Unconstitutional Changes of Government*, FOI Report no. 3,000 (Stockholm: FOI, 2010).

Farah, Douglas. 'Al Qaeda and the Gemstone Trade', in Biersteker, Thomas and Eckert, Sue (eds), *Countering the Financing of Terrorism*, 193–206 (New York: Routledge, 2008).

Farrall, Jeremy Matam. *United Nations Sanctions and the Rule of Law*. Cambridge Studies in International and Comparative Law (Cambridge: Cambridge University Press, 2007).

Fassbender, Bardo. *Targeted Sanctions and Due Process The Responsibility of the UN Security Council to Ensure that Fair and Clear Procedures are Made Available to Individuals and Entities Targeted with Sanctions under Chapter VII of the UN Charter.* Study commissioned by the United Nations Office of Legal Affairs, Office of the Legal Counsel, March (New York: Office of the Legal Counsel, United Nations, 2006).

Finnemore, Martha and Sikkink, Kathryn. 'International Norms: Dynamic and Political Change', *International Organization*, vol. 52, no. 4, 887–917 (1998).

Fitzgerald, Peter L. 'Smarter "Smart" Sanctions', *Penn State International Law Review*, vol. 26, no. 1, 37–56 (2007).

Flynn, E.J. 'The Security Council's Counter-terrorism Committee and Human Rights', *Human Rights Law Review*, vol. 7, no. 2, 371–84 (2007).

Foot, Rosemary. 'The United Nations, Counter Terrorism, and Human Rights: Institutional Adaptation and Embedded Ideas', *Human Rights Quarterly*, vol. 29, 489–514 (2007).

Franck, Thomas, Chesterman, Simon and Malone, David. *Law and Practice of the United Nations: Documents and Commentary*, 1st edn (New York: Oxford University Press, 2007).

Freedman, Lawrence. *Strategic Coercion: Concepts and Cases* (Oxford: Oxford University Press, 1998).

Fruchart, Damien, Holtom, Paul, Wallensteen, Peter, Wezeman, Siemon and Strandow, Daniel. *United Nations Arms Embargoes: Their Impact on Arms Flows and Target Behaviour* (Stockholm International Peace Research Institute and the Department of Peace and Conflict Research, Uppsala University, 2007).

Galtung, Johan. 'On the Effects of International Economic Sanctions: With Examples from the Case of Rhodesia', *World Politics*, vol. 19, no. 3, 378–416 (1967).

——. 'On the Anthropology of the United Nations System', in Pitt, David and Weiss, Thomas G. (eds), *The Nature of United Nations Bureaucracies* (London: Croom Helm, 1986).

Garfield, Richard. *Morbidity and Mortality among Iraq Children from 1990 to 1998: Assessing the Impact of Economic Sanctions.* CASI Internet version, July 1999. Other print versions available (i.e. Occasional Paper Series, 16, no. 3. Paper Commissioned by the Joan B. Kroc Institute for International Peace Studies at the University of Notre Dame and the Fourth Freedom Forum (Notre

Dame, IN: University of Notre Dame, 1999), <www.casi.org.uk/info/garfield/dr-garfield.html>.

Geiss, R. 'Humanitarian Safeguards in Economic Sanctions Regimes: A Call for Automatic Suspension Clauses, Periodic Monitoring, and Follow-up Assessment of Long-term Effects', *Harvard Human Rights Journal*, vol. 18, 167–99 (2005).

George, Alexander L. *Forceful Persuasion: Coercive Diplomacy as an Alternative to War* (Washington, DC: United States Institute for Peace, 1991).

—— and Simons, William E., with contributions from Hall, David K. et al. *The Limits of Coercive Diplomacy*, 2nd edn (Boulder, CO: Westview Press, 1994).

Giumelli, Francesco. 'Coercing, Constraining and Signalling: Explaining UN and EU Sanctions after the Cold War', unpublished thesis (Florence: Institute of Humanistic Sciences, 2009).

Good, Kenneth. 'Dealing with Despotism: The People and the Presidents', in Melber, Henning (ed.), *Zimbabwe's Presidential Elections 2002: Evidence, Lessons and Implications*. Discussion Paper 14, 7–30 (Uppsala: Nordic Africa Institute, 2002).

Gottemoeller, Rose. 'The Evolution of Sanctions in Practice and Theory', *Survival*, vol. 49, no. 4, 99–110 (2008).

Gowlland-Debbas, Vera. *United Nations Sanctions and International Law* (The Hague: Kluwer Law International, 2001).

Greenhill, Kelly and Major, Solomon. 'The Perils of Profiling: Civil War Spoilers and the Collapse of Intrastate Peace Accords', *International Security*, vol. 31, no. 3, 7–40 (2007).

Greenstock, Jeremy. 'The Council in the Post-Cold War World', in Lowe, Vaughan, Roberts, Adam, Welsh, Jennifer and Zaum, Dominik (eds), *The United Nations Security Council and War: The Evolution of Thought and Practice Since 1945*, 248–64 (Oxford: Oxford University Press, 2008).

Gregory, Frank. 'The EU's Response to 9/11: A Case Study of Institutional Roles and Policy Processes with Special Reference to Issues of Accountability and Human Rights', *Terrorism and Political Violence*, vol. 17, 105–23 (2005).

Griffiths, Aaron and Barnes, Catherine (eds). 'Powers of Persuasion: Incentives, Sanctions and Conditionality in Peacemaking', *Accord*, no. 19 (London: Conciliation Resources, 2008).

Haass, Richard N. (ed.). 'Sanctioning Madness', *Foreign Affairs*, vol. 76, 74–84 (1997).

——. *Economic Sanctions and American Diplomacy* (New York: Council of Foreign Relations, 1998).

—— and O'Sullivan, Meghan L. (eds). *Honey and Vinegar: Incentives, Sanctions and Foreign Policy* (Washington, DC: Brookings Institution Press, 2000).

Halliday, Dennis J. 'The Impact of the UN Sanctions on the People of Iraq', *Journal of Palestine Studies*, vol. 28, no. 2, 29–37 (1999).

Hanhimäki, Jussi. *The Flawed Architect: Henry Kissinger and American Foreign Policy* (Oxford: Oxford University Press, 2004).

Harbom, Lotta and Peter Wallensteen. 'Armed Conflicts, 1946–2009', *Journal of Peace Research*, vol. 47, no. 4 (2010).

Hartzell, Caroline A. and Hoddie, Matthew. *Crafting Peace: Power-sharing Institutions and the Negotiated Settlement of Civil Wars* (Pittsburgh, PA: Pennsylvania State University Press, 2007).

Harvard Study Team. 'The Effect of the Gulf Crisis on the Children of Iraq', *New England Journal of Medicine*, vol. 325, no. 13, 977–80 (1991).

Hawkins, Darren and Lloyd, Joshua. 'Questioning Comprehensive Sanctions: The Birth of a Norm', *Journal of Human Rights*, vol. 2, no. 3, 441–54 (2003).

Hazelzet, Hadewych. 'Carrots or Sticks? EU and US Reactions to Human Rights Violations 1989–2000', unpublished dissertation (Florence: The European University Institute, 2001).

——. *Suspension of Development Cooperation: An Instrument to Promote Human Rights and Democracy?* European Centre for Development Policy Management Discussion Paper no. 64 (2005).

Hodges, Tony. *Angola from Afro-Stalinism to Petro-diamond Capitalism* (Oxford: James Currey, 2001).

Hoffman, Fredrik. 'The Function of Economic Sanctions: A Comparative Analysis', *Journal of Peace Research*, vol. 2, 140–59 (1967).

House of Lords Select Committee on Economic Affairs. 'Memorandum submitted by the European Commission to the House of Lords Economic Affairs Committee. Witness examination on the Impact of Economic Sanctions, of Mr Karel Kovanda and Albertus Straver, External Relations Directorate-General, European Commission', in *House of Lords Select Committee on Economic Affairs, 2nd Report of Session 'The Impact of Economic Sanctions', 2006–2007* (London: SO, May 2007).

Hovi, Jon, Huseby, Robert and Sprinz, Detlef F. 'When Do (Imposed) Economic Sanctions Work?', *World Politics*, vol. 57, 479–99 (2005).

Hufbauer, Gary C. and Oegg, Barbara. 'Targeted Sanctions: A Policy Alternative?', Peterson Institute Symposium on 'Sanctions Reform? Evaluating the Economic Weapon in Asia and the World' (Washington, DC: Peterson Institute for International Economics, 23 February 2000), <http://www.iie.com/publications/papers/paper.cfm?ResearchID=371>.

Hufbauer, Gary C., Schott, Jeffrey and Elliott, Kimberly. *Economic Sanctions Reconsidered: History and Current Policy*, 2nd edn (Washington, DC: Institute for International Economics; Cambridge, MA: MIT Press, 1990).

Hufbauer, Gary C. and Schott, Jeffrey, assisted by Elliott, Kimberly. *Economic Sanctions Reconsidered: History and Current Policy* (Washington, DC: Institute for International Economics; Cambridge, MA: MIT Press, 1985).

Hufbauer, Gary C., Schott, Jeffrey J., Elliott, Kimberly and Oegg, Barbara. *Economic Sanctions Reconsidered*, 3rd expanded edn (Washington, DC: Peterson Institute for International Economics, 2007).

Hurd, Ian. *After Anarchy: Legitimacy and Power in the United Nations Security Council* (Princeton, NJ: Princeton University Press, 2007).

Jakobsen, Peter Viggo. 'The Strategy of Coercive Diplomacy: Refining Existing Theory to Post-Cold War Realities', in Freedman, Lawrence (ed.), *Strategic Coercion: Concepts and Cases* (New York: Oxford University Press, 1998a).

——. *Western Use of Coercive Diplomacy after the Cold War: A Challenge for Theory and Practice* (Basingstoke: Palgrave Macmillan, 1998b).

Jentleson, Bruce W. 'Economic Sanctions and Post-Cold War Conflicts: Challenges for Theory and Policy', in Stern, Paul C. and Druckman, Daniel (eds), *International Conflict Resolution after the Cold War*, 123–77 (Washington, DC: National Academies Press, 2000).

—— and Whytock, Christopher. 'Who "Won" Libya: The Force-diplomacy Debate and Its Implications for Theory and Policy', *International Security*, vol. 30. no. 3, 47–86 (2006).

Jimeno-Bulnes, Mar. 'After September 11th: The Fight against Terrorism in National and European Law. Substantive and Procedural Reforms: Some Examples', *European Law Journal*, vol. 10, no. 2, 235–53 (2004).

Kaempfer, William and Lowenberg, Anton. 'The Theory of International Economic Sanctions: A Public Choice Approach', *American Economic Review*, vol. 78, no. 4, 1,304–6 (1988).

Kaempfer, William and Lowenberg, Anton. 'International Sanctions', *Journal of Economic Perspectives*, vol. 17, no. 4, 233–5 (2003).

Kamete, Amin. 'The Rebels Within: Urban Zimbabwe in the Post-election Period', in Melber, Henning (ed.), *Zimbabwe's Presidential Elections 2002: Evidence, Lessons and Implications.* Discussion Paper 14 (Uppsala: Nordic Africa Institute, 2002).

Kelley, Judith G. *Ethnic Politics in Europe: The Power of Norms and Incentives* (Princeton, NJ.: Princeton University Press, 2004).

Kirshner, Jonathan. 'The Micro Foundations of Economic Sanctions', *Security Studies*, vol. 6, no. 3, 32–64 (1997).

Knight, Andy. 'Improving the Effectiveness of UN Arms Embargoes', in Price, Richard M. and Zacher, Mark W. (eds), *The United Nations and Global Security* (London: Palgrave, 2004).

Knorr, Klaus. *The Power of Nations: The Political Economy of International Relations* (New York: Basic Books, 1975).

Kratochwil, Friedrich. 'Looking Back from Somewhere: Reflections on What Remains "Critical" in Critical Theory', *Review of International Studies*, vol. 33, 25–45 (2007).

Kretzmer, David. 'Targeted Killing of Suspected Terrorists: Extra-judicial Executions or Legitimate Means of Defense?', in *European Journal of International Law*, vol. 16, no. 2, 171–212 (2005).

Kreuger, Alan B. and Laitin, David. 'Misunderestimating Terrorism', *Foreign Affairs*, vol. 83, no. 5, 8–13 (2004).

Kreutz, Joakim. *Hard Hard Measures by a Soft Power? Sanctions Policy of the European Union.* Bonn International Paper 45 (Bonn: Bonn International Centre for Conversion, 2005).

Kulessa, Manfred. 'Potentials, Problems and Prospects of Various Types of Travel Sanctions', in *First Expert Seminar, 21–23 November 1999. Smart Sanctions: The Next Steps – the Debate on Arms Embargoes and Travel Sanctions within the 'Bonn-Berlin Process'* (Bonn: Bonn International Centre for Conversion, 2000).

Lavranos, Nikolaos. 'Judicial Review of UN Sanctions by the Court of First Instance', *European Foreign Affairs Review*, no. 11, 471–90 (2006).

——. 'UN Sanctions and Judicial Review', *Nordic Journal of International Law*, vol. 76, no. 1, 1–17 (2007).

Lektzian, David. *Making Sanctions Smarter: Are Humanitarian Costs an Essential Element in the Success of Sanctions?* (Oslo: Norwegian Red Cross and International Peace Research Institute, 2003).

Lindsay, James M. 'Trade Sanctions as Policy Instruments: A Re-examination', *International Studies Quarterly*, vol. 30, no. 2, 153–73 (1986).

London School of Hygiene and Tropical Medicine (1996), Letter to *The Lancet*, *The Lancet*, vol. 347, no. 8,995 (1996).

Lopez, George and Cortright, David. 'Containing Iraq: Sanctions Worked', *Foreign Affairs*, vol. 83, no. 4 (2004).

Lopez, George, Millar, Alistair, Ipe, Jason, Cortright, David, Marbarger, Anne and Lawall, Kathryn. *Standards and Best Practices for Improving States' Implementation of United Nations Counter-terrorism Mandates.* Report prepared for the Netherlands Ministry of Foreign Affairs (2006).

Lotrionte, Catherine. 'When to Target Leaders', *The Washington Quarterly*, vol. 26, no. 3, 73–86 (2003).

Luck, Edward C. *Choosing Words Carefully: Arms Embargoes and the UN Security Council.* Paper presented at the 'First Expert Seminar on Smart Sanctions: The Next Step – the Debate on Arms Embargoes and Travel Sanctions within the "Bonn-Berlin Process"' (Bonn, 1999).

Mack, Andrew (ed.). *The Human Security Report 2005* (Oxford: Oxford University Press, 2005).

—— and Khan, Assif. 'The Efficacy of UN Sanctions', *Security Dialogue*, vol. 31, no. 3, 279–92 (2000).

Malaquias, Assis. *Rebels and Robbers: Violence in Post-colonial Angola* (Nordiska Afrikainstitutet, Uppsala 2007).

Manners, Ian. 'Normative Power Europe: A Contradiction in Terms?', *Journal of Common Market Studies*, vol. 40, no. 2, 235–58 (2002).

Martin, Lisa. *Coercive Cooperation: Explaining Multilateral Economic Sanctions* (Princeton, NJ: Princeton University Press, 1992).

Marty, Dick. *United Nations Security Council and European Union Blacklists.* Report by the Council of Europe, Committee on Legal Affairs and Human Rights, Doc. 11,454 (2007).

Mastanduno, Michael. 'Economic Statecraft, Interdependence, and National Security: Agendas for Research', *Security Studies*, vol. 9, 288–316 (1999).

Meron, Theodor. *The Humanization of International Law* (Leiden: Martinus Nijhoff, 2006).

Millar, Alistair and Rosand, Eric. *Building Global Alliances in the Fight against Terrorism.* Report Commissioned by the Better World Campaign of the UN Foundation (Washington, DC: Center on Global Counterterrorism Cooperation, 2006).

Millar, Alistair et al. *Report on Standards and Best Practices for Improving States' Implementation of UN Security Council Counter-terrorism Mandates.* Report prepared for the Netherlands Ministry of Foreign Affairs (Washington, DC: Center on Global Counterterrorism Cooperation, 2006).

Mueller, John and Mueller, Karl. 'Sanctions of Mass Destruction', *Foreign Affairs*, vol. 78, no. 3, 43–53 (1999).

Möllander, Anders. 'Can sanctions work? The case of Angola', *News from the Nordic Africa Institute*, no. 3 (Uppsala: Nordic Africa Institute, 2001).

——. *UN Angola Sanctions: A Committee Success Revisited* (Uppsala: Department of Peace and Conflict Research, Uppsala University, 2009).

Newcomb, Richard. 'Targeted Financial Sanctions: The U.S. Model', in Cortright, David and Lopez, George A. (eds), *Smart Sanctions: Targeting Economic Statecraft* (Lanham, MD: Rowman and Littlefield, 2002).

Niblock, Tim. *'Pariah States' and Sanctions in the Middle East: Iraq, Libya, Sudan* (Boulder, CO: Lynne Rienner, 2001).

Nincic, Miroslav and Wallensteen, Peter. *Dilemmas of Economic Coercion: Sanctions in World Politics* (New York: Praeger, 1983).

Nossal, Kim Richard. 'International Sanctions as International Punishment', *International Organization*, vol. 43, no. 2, 301–22 (1989).

O'Sullivan, Meghan L. *Shrewd Sanctions: Statecraft and State Sponsors of Terrorism* (Washington, DC: Brookings Institution Press, 2003).

Pape, Robert, 'Why Economic Sanctions Do Not Work', *International Security*, vol. 22, no. 2, 90–136 (1997).

——. 'Why Economic Sanctions Still Do Not Work', *International Security*, vol. 23, no. 1, 66–77 (1998).

Pearce, Justin. *An Outbreak of Peace: Angola's Situation of Confusion* (Claremont, South Africa: David Philip, 2005).

Porretto, Gabriele. 'The European Union, Counter-terrorism Sanctions against Individuals and Human Rights', in Miriam and Mathew, Penelope (eds), *Protection: Fresh Perspectives on the 'War on Terror'*, 235–68 (Canberra: ANUE Press, 2008).

Portela, Clara. 'Where and Why Does the EU Impose Sanctions?', *Politique Européenne*, no. 17 (2006).

——. 'The Efficacy of Sanctions of the European Union: When and Why do they Work?' unpublished dissertation (Florence: The European University Institute, 2008).

Prendergast, John. *Angola's Deadly War: Dealing with Savimbi's Hell on Earth* (Washington, DC: United States Institute of Peace, October 2000).

Rackow, Peter and Stegmiller, Ignaz. 'EC Regulations: Targeted Sanctions', *Journal of Criminal Law*, vol. 71, no. 1, 25–8 (2007).

Raftopoulos, Brian. 'Climbing out from the Rubble', in Melber, Henning (ed.), *Zimbabwe's Presidential Elections 2002: Evidence, Lessons and Implications*, Discussion Paper no. 14 (Uppsala: Nordic Africa Institute, 2002).

Rodman, Kenneth A. *Sanctions Beyond Borders: Multinational Corporations and U.S. Economic Statecraft* (Lanham, MD: Rowman and Littlefield, 2001).

Rosand, Eric. 'The Security Council's Efforts to Monitor the Implementation of Al Qaeda/Taliban Sanctions', *American Journal of International Law*, vol. 98, no. 4, 745–63 (2004).

——, Millar, Alistair and Ipe, Jason. *The UN Security Council's Counterterrorism Program: What Lies Ahead?* (Washington, DC: Center on Global Counterterrorism Cooperation and International Peace Academy, 2007).

——, Millar, Alistair and Ipe, Jason. *Human Rights and the Implementation of the UN Global Counter-terrorism Strategy* (Washington, DC: Center on Global Counterterrorism Cooperation, 2008).

Rudolf, Peter. *Sanctions in International Relations: On the Current State of Research* (Berlin: Stiftung Wissenschaft und Politik, 2007).

Rydell, Randy. *Monitoring United Nations Arms Embargoes*. Paper presented at the 'First Expert Seminar on Smart Sanctions: The Next Step – the Debate on Arms Embargoes and Travel Sanctions within the "Bonn-Berlin Process"' (Bonn, 1999).

Schelling, Thomas C. *Arms and Influence*, 12th edn (New Haven, CT: Yale University Press, 1976).

Schimmelfennig, Frank and Sedelmeier, Ulrich (eds). *The Politics of European Union Enlargement: Theoretical Approaches* (London: Routledge, 2005).

Schimmelfennig, Frank, Engert, Stefan and Knobel, Heiko (eds). *International Socialization in Europe: European Organizations, Political Conditionality, and Democratic Change* (Basingstoke: Palgrave Macmillan, 2006).

Schraeder, Peter J. 'Paramilitary Intervention', in Schraeder, Peter J. (ed.), *Intervention into the 1990s: U.S. Foreign Policy in the Third World* (Boulder, CO: Lynne Rienner, 1992).

Sellström, Tor. *Sweden and National Liberation in Southern Africa, Volume 1: Formation of a Popular Opinion (1950–1970)*, and *Liberation in Southern Africa – Regional and Swedish Voices: Interviews from Angola, Mozambique, Namibia, South Africa, Zimbabwe, the Frontline and Sweden* (Uppsala: Nordic Africa Institute, 1999).

Shagabutdinova, Ella and Berejikian, Jeffrey. 'Deploying Sanctions while Protecting Human Rights: Are Humanitarian "Smart" Sanctions Effective?', *Journal of Human Rights*, vol. 6, no. 1, 59–74 (2007).

Sikkink, Kathryn. 'From State Responsibility to Individual Criminal Accountability: A New Regulatory Model for Core Human Rights Violations'. Paper presented at the Annual Meeting of the American Political Science Association, Boston, 28–31 August 2008.

Simons, Geoff. *Imposing Economic Sanctions: Legal Remedy or Genocidal Tool* (London: Pluto Press, 1999).
Speier, Richard H., Chow, Brian G. and Starr, Rae S. *Nonproliferation Sanctions*. National Defense Research Institute, Office of the Secretary of Defense (Arlington, VA: RAND, 2001).
Stedman, Stephen. 'Spoiler Problems in Peace Process', *International Security*, vol. 22, no. 2, 5–53 (1997).
——. 'The Former Yugoslavia', in Haass, Richard N. (ed.), *Economic Sanctions and American Diplomacy*, 177–96 (New York: Council of Foreign Relations, 1998).
Stenhammar, Fredrik. *Riktade FN Sanktioner och Rule of Law i Folkrätten*. Dissertation on targeted UN sanctions and the rule of law (Stockholm, June 2008).
Stiles, Kendall W. and Thayne, Adam. 'International Law on Terrorism at the United Nations', *Cooperation and Conflict*, vol. 41, no. 2, 153–76 (2006).
Strandow, Daniel. 2006. *Sanctions and Civil War: Targeted Measures for Conflict Resolution*. Uppsala: Uppsala University, Department of Peace and Conflict Research.
Sutterlin, James S. *The Untied Nations and the Maintenance of International Security*, 2nd edn (Westport, CT: Praeger, 2003).
Tierney, Dominic, 'Irrelevant or Malevolent? UN Arms Embargoes in Civil Wars', *Review of International Studies*, vol. 31, 645–64 (2005).
Tostensen, Arne and Bull, Beate. 'Are Smart Sanctions Feasible?', *World Politics*, vol. 54, 373–403 (2002).
Van Bergeijk, Peter. 'Economic Sanctions: Why Do they Succeed; Why Do they Fail?', in Van Genugten, Willem J.M. and De Groot, Gerhard A. (eds). *United Nations Sanctions: Effectiveness and Effects, Especially in the Field of Human Rights* (Antwerp: Intersentia Law Publishers, 1999).
Van Brabant, Koenraad (ed.). *Sanctions: The Current Debate. A Summary of Selected Readings*. Report of a Conference held in London, 16–17 December 1998 (London: Overseas Development Institute, 1999a).
——. 'Report from Working Group 1 Travel Sanctions', in *First Expert Seminar, 21–23 November 1999. Smart Sanctions: The Next Steps – the Debate on Arms Embargoes and Travel Sanctions within the 'Bonn-Berlin Process'* (Bonn: International Center for Conversion, 1999b).
Van Genugten, Willem J.M. and De Groot, Gerhard A. (eds), *United Nations Sanctions: Effectiveness and Effects, Especially in the Field of Human Rights* (Antwerp: Intersentia Law Publishers, 1999).
Van Walsum, Peter. 'The Iraq Sanctions Committee', in Malone, David M. (ed.), *The UN Security Council from the Cold War to the 21st* Century, 181–94 (Boulder, CO: Lynne Rienner, 2004).
Vaux, Tony, Bewa, Anaia and Sampson, Peter (2007). *Aid and Conflict in the Democratic Republic of Congo: Strategic Conflict Assessment* (London: Department for International Development, 2007).
Vines, Alex. 'Can UN Arms Embargoes in Africa Be Effective?', *International Affairs*, vol. 83, no. 6 (2007).

von Sponeck, Hans. 'Iraq: International Sanctions and What Next?', *Middle East Policy*, vol. 7, no. 4, 149–62 (2000).

——. *A Different Kind of War: The UN Sanctions Regime in Iraq* (New York: Berghahn, 2006).

Wallensteen, Peter. 'Characteristics of Economic Sanctions', *Journal of Peace Research*, vol. 5, no. 3, 248–67 (1968).

——. (ed.) *International Sanctions: Theory and Practice.* Proceedings of the Nordic Conference on Sanction Research, Sigtuna, Sweden, 27–28 April 1968, Report no. 1 (Uppsala: Department of Peace and Conflict Research, 1969).

——. *A Century of Economic Sanctions: A Field Revisited.* Uppsala Peace Research Papers no. 1 (Uppsala: Department of Peace and Conflict Research, Uppsala University, 2000).

——. 'Positive Sanctions: On the Potential of Rewards and Target Differentiation', in Wallensteen, Peter and Staibano, Carina (eds), *International Sanctions: Between Words and Wars in the Global System*, 229–41 (London: Frank Cass, 2005).

——. *Save the Arms Embargo.* Joan B. Kroc Institute Policy Brief no. 14 (January 2008).

—— and Staibano, Carina (eds). *International Sanctions: Between Words and Wars in the Global System* (London: Routledge and Frank Cass, 2005).

——, Eriksson, Mikael and Staibano, Carina (eds). *Making Targeted Sanctions Effective: Guidelines for the Implementation of UN Policy Options.* Report from the Stockholm Process (Uppsala: Uppsala University, 2003).

——, Eriksson, Mikael and Staibano, Carina. *Routes to Democracy in Burma/Myanmar: The Uppsala Pilot Study on Dialogue and International Strategies.* Report presented to the Swedish Foreign Ministry (Uppsala: Uppsala University, 2004).

——, Eriksson, Mikael and Staibano, Carina. *The 2004 Roundtable on UN Sanctions against Iraq: Lessons Learned* (Uppsala: Department of Peace and Conflict Research, Uppsala University, 2005).

——, Eriksson, Mikael and Strandow, Daniel. *Sanctions for Conflict Prevention and Peace Building: Lessons Learned from Côte d'Ivoire and Liberia.* Report presented to the Swedish Foreign Ministry (Uppsala: Department of Peace and Conflict Research, 2006).

Ward, Curtis. 'The Counter-Terrorism Committee: Its Relevance for Implementing Targeted Sanctions', in Wallensteen, Peter and Staibano, Carina (eds), *International Sanctions: Between Words and Wars in the Global System* (New York: Frank Cass, 2005).

Watson Institute. *Targeted Sanctions Bibliography.* Maintained by the Targeted Sanctions Project (Providence, RI: Watson Institute for International Studies, Brown University, 2007), <www.watsoninstitute.org/pub/Targeted_Sanctions_Bibliography.pdf>.

Weiss, Thomas G. 'Sanctions as a Foreign Policy Tool: Weighing Humanitarian Impulses', *Journal of Peace Research*, vol. 36, no. 5, 499–509 (1999).

——, Cortright, David, Lopez, George A. and Minear, Larry (eds). *Political Gain and Civilian Pain: Humanitarian Impacts of Economic Sanctions* (Lanham, MD: Rowman and Littlefield, 1997).

Wendt, Alexander E. 'The Agent-structure Problem in International Relations Theory', *International Organization*, vol. 41, no. 3, 335–70 (1987).

Woodward, Susan L. 'The Use of Sanctions in Former Yugoslavia: Misunderstanding Political Realities', in Cortright, David and Lopez, George (eds), *Economic Sanctions: Panacea or Peace building in a Post-Cold War World?* (Boulder, CO: Westview Press, 1995).

Zaidi, Sarah and Smith-Faz, Mary C. 'Health of Baghdad's Children', *The Lancet*, vol. 346, no. 8,988, 1,485 (1995).

Zucconi, Mario (ed.). *The Effects of Economic Sanctions: The Case of Serbia* (Milan: FrancoAngeli, 2001).

News Sources

Africa News Update. *Zimbabwe Elections Special* (14 March 2002), <www. afrika.no/links/>.

Agencia de Informacao de Mocambique (8 November 2002).

Angola Press Agency (4 October 2002).

BBC World News. 'Savimbi "died with gun in hand"' (25 February 2002).

BBC News. 'Zimbabwe leaders face financial probe' (23 January 2002).

——. 'Zimbabwe police chief flouts EU ban' (18 May 2002).

——. 'New Zealand extends Zimbabwe travel ban' (30 October 2002).

The Daily Telegraph. 'EU Talks Moved so Zimbabwe Can Attend' (24 October 2002).

The Financial Gazette. 'Martial Law Looms' (8 September 2001).

——. 'Zimbabwe: Government fights back on sanctions' (1 August 2002).

—— (1 September 2002).

——. 'Inflation to hit 4000%: IMF' (21–27 September 2006).

Financial Times. 'N Korea leader raises a glass to Gibraltar' (2 February 2007).

Global Policy. 'The Trafficker Viktor Bout Lands US Aid for Services Rendered in Iraq' (original source *Le Monde*, 18 May 2004), <www.globalpolicy.org/security/issues/iraq/contract/2004/0518bout.htm>.

The Herald. 'Anti-Zim Crusade: UK Prosecutes Businessman Over "Sanctions-Busting"' (11 November 2002).

——. 'Full List of Persons Placed Under Zim Sanctions' (9 November 2002).

——. 'Sanctions: Zim soldiers on' (14 September 2006).

—— (18 September 2006).

IRIN. 'Mugabe should let them take over, not these MDC puppets' (March 2007).

MDC Press. 'Threats on Passports is Futile Primitive Revenge' (1 August 2002).

News 24 (South Africa). 'Smart Sanctions Spare some Vets' (21 February 2002).

Reuters. 'Australia to impose sanctions on Zimbabwe' (13 October 2002).

——. 'Zimbabwe claims victory after EU talks boycotted' (26 November 2002).
Sunday Times. 'Probe into highlife of Mugabe's elite' (2 February 2002).
——. 'Smart sanctions will hurt but don't expect to recover riches' (2 February 2002).
The Standard. 'Mugabe's livestock relocated', 'Christian Alliance leads the Save Zimbabwe Campaign', and 'Namibia land Reforms: Following in Mugabe's heavy footsteps' (10–16 September 2006).
——. 'Mugabe still Blames Sanctions' (22–28 September 2006).
Svenska Dagbladet. 'Flera svenskar på terrorlistan' (8 December 2005).
Turkish Weekly. 'Uzbekistan: Oil and Human Rights on the Table' (9 April 2007).
University World News. 'Zimbabwe: Mugabe's daughter to stay at Hong Kong University' (8 February 2009).
Voice of America (online). 'On the Line: Iran Threatens Israel', News VOA.com (5 November 2005).
Washington Post. 'Administration seeks to block suit against Zimbabwe leader' (26 February 2001).
Zimbabwe Independent (17 May 2002).
——. 'EU Plans Direct Intervention in Zimbabwe' (15 November 2002).
—— (22–28 September 2006).
Zimbabwe Standard. 'US Freezes Mugabe and Cronies' Assets' (10 March 2002).

Other Media

Africa Research Bulletin. Political, Social and Cultural Series, vol. 39, no. 2 (1–28 February 2002).
——. vol. 39, no. 3 (1–31 March 2002).
Africa Confidential, vol. 43, no. 5 (8 March 2002).
Keesing's Record of World Events (formerly *Keesing's Contemporary Archives*). Internet edition, <www.keesings.com>, vol. 43 (September 1997).
——. vol. 43 (November 1997).
——. vol. 44 (October 1998).
——. vol. 44 (November 1998).
——. vol. 45 (January 1999).
——. vol. 47 (December 2001).
——. vol. 48 (January 2002).
——. vol. 48 (February 2002).
——. vol. 48 (July 2002).
——. vol. 49 (December 2003).
——. vol. 50 (January 2004).
——. vol. 51 (May 2005).
——. vol. 51 (June 2005).
——. vol. 53 (January 2007).
——. vol. 53 (February 2007).

——. vol. 53 (March 2007).
——. vol. 53 (May 2007).
——. vol. 53 (June 2007).
——. vol. 53 (July 2007).
——. vol. 53 (August 2007).
——. vol. 53 (November 2007).
——. vol. 53 (December 2007).
——. vol. 54 (January 2008).
——. vol. 54 (March 2008).
——. vol. 54 (April 2008).
——. vol. 54 (May 2008).
——. vol. 54 (June 2008).
——. vol. 54 (July 2008).
——. vol. 54 (September 2008).
——. vol. 54 (October 2008).

EU Council Common Positions

1996/635/CFSP.
1998/240/CFSP.
1999/318/CFSP.
1999/318/CFSP.
2000/346/CFSP.
2001/542/CFSP.
2001/931/CFSP.
2002/145/CFSP.
2002/600/CFSP.
2002/600/CFSP.
2003/139/CFSP.
2003/280/CFSP.
2003/297/CFSP.
2003/495/CFSP.
2004/133/CFSP.
2004/137/CFSP.
2004/622/CFSP.
2004/661/CFSP.
2004/661/CFSP.
2004/848/CFSP.
2004/848/CFSP.
2004/852/CFSP.
2005/411/CFSP.
2005/792/CFSP.
2006/276/CFSP.

2006/276/CFSP.
2006/362/CFSP.
2006/362/CFSP.
2006/787/CFSP.
2007/120/CFSP.
2007/173/CFSP.
2007/338/CFSP.
2009/788/CFSP.
Council Common Position on the Control of Arms Brokering and the List of Dual-use Items and Technology (see the last Council Regulation 2006/394 of 27 February 2006 amending the Community Regime for the Control of Exports of Dual-use Items and Technology, <http://ec.europa.eu/trade/issues/sectoral/industry/dualuse/index_en.htm>).

EU Council Regulations

2002/2368.
2005/1184.
2173/2005.
310/2002.

EU Council Decisions

1998/107/CFSP.
2002/145/CFSP.
2002/754/CFSP.
2005/444/CFSP.
2005/592/CFSP.
2006/56/ CFSP.
2006/718/CFSP.
2007/455/CFSP.

Other EU Council Documents

Basic Principles on the Use of Restrictive Measures (Sanctions) (Brussels, June 2007).
Common Military List of the European Union. Equipment Covered by the European Union Code of Conduct on Arms Exports, 2006/C 66/01 (Brussels, 17 March 2006).
'Council Conclusions on Uzbekistan'. 2,897th External Relations Council Meeting, Luxembourg, 13 October 2008 (Brussels, 2008).

'Council Conclusions on Zimbabwe'. 2,886th External Relations Council Meeting, Brussels, 22 July 2008 (Brussels, 2008).

'Council Conclusions on Zimbabwe'. 2,889th External Relations Council Meeting, Brussels, 15 and 16 September 2008 (Brussels, 2008).

Council Joint Action 2006/319/CFSP. 'On the European Union Military Operation in Support of the United Nations Organisation Mission in the Democratic Republic of the Congo (MONUC) during the Election Process' (27 April 2006).

EU Best Practices for the Effective Implementation of Restrictive Measures (Brussels, November 2005).

European Union Code of Conduct on Arms Exports, 8675/2/98 (Brussels, 5 June 1998).

Guidelines on Implementation and Evaluation of Restrictive Measures (Sanctions) in the Framework of the EU Common Foreign and Security Policy (Brussels, December 2005).

Presidency of the European Union. 'Declaration by the Presidency on behalf of the European Union on Zimbabwe', Brussels, 4 July 2008. ST 11447/08 (Presse 198). P 082/08 (2008).

Other EU Council General Secretariat Documents

European Union and Central Asia: Strategy for a New Partnership (Brussels, October 2007).

Spokesperson of the Secretary General. High Representative for CFSP. S202/06. *Elements of a Proposal to Iran as Approved on 1 June 2006 at the Meeting in Vienna of China, France, Germany, the Russian Federation, the United Kingdom, the Unites States of America and the European Union* (Brussels, 2006).

European Commission

Commission Regulation (EC), No. 702/2008 of 23 July 2008 Amending Council Regulation (EC) No. 314/2004 Concerning Certain Restrictive Measures in Respect of Zimbabwe (Brussels, 2008).

Commission Staff Working Document. *Serbia 2006 Progress Report*, COM (2006) 649 final, SEC (2006) 1389 (Brussels, 11 August 2006).

Commission Staff Working Document. *Serbia 2007 Progress Report Accompanying the Communication from the Commission to the European Parliament and the Council. Enlargement Strategy and Main Challenges 2007–2008*, SEC (2007) 1435 (Brussels, 6 November 2007).

Commission Staff Working Document. *Serbia 2008 Progress Report, Accompanying the communication from the Commission to the European*

Parliament and the Council: Enlargement Strategy and Main Challenges 2008–2009, COM/2008/674 (2008).

EC-Burma/Myanmar Regional Strategy Paper for Assistance to Central Asia for the Period 2007–2013.

Enlargement Strategy Paper: The EU's Enlargement Policy, COM (2005) 561 final (Brussels, 9 November 2005).

EU-Uzbekistan: The Partnership and Cooperation Agreement.

European Neighbourhood and Partnership Instrument. *Belarus Country Strategy Paper 2007–2013 and National Indicative Programme 2007–2010.*

European Neighbourhood and Partnership Instrument. *Republic of Moldova Country Strategy Paper 2007–2013* (Brussels, 2007).

Ferrero-Waldner, Benita. 'Statement of Commissioner for External Relations and European Neighbourhood Policy on latest developments in Belarus'. Speech. IP/06/321 (Brussels, 16 March 2006).

——. European Commissioner for External Relations and European Neighbourhood Policy, *What the European Union Could Bring to Belarus* (Brussels, 21 November 2006).

Joint Progress Report by the Council and the European Commission to the European Council on the implementation of the EU Central Asia Strategy (Brussels, 24 June 2008).

Message from the European Commission on Initiating Consultations with Zimbabwe According to Article 96 in the Cotonou Agreement, COM (2001), 623 final (Brussels, 26 October 2001).

Republic of Liberia-European Community: Country Strategy Paper and Indicative Programme for the Period 2008–2013.

The Eastern Partnership: An Ambitious New Chapter in the EU's Relations with its Eastern Neighbours, IP/08/1858 (Brussels, 3 December 2008).

What the European Union Could Bring to Belarus (26 November 2009), <http://ec.europa.eu/delegations/belarus/documents/eu_belarus/non_paper_1106.pdf>.

Other EU Documents

General Affairs and External Relations Council (GAERC). *Conclusions* (21–22 November 2004).

——. *Conclusions* (7 November 2005).

Judgment of the Court of First Instance in Case T-228/02 *Organisation des Modjahedines du Peuple d'Iran* v. *Council of the European Union* (12 December 2006).

Kadi Judgment on 3 September 2008. Judgment of the Court of Justice in Joined Cases C-402/05 P and C-415/05 P Regarding *Yassin Abdullah Kadi and Al Barakaat International Foundation* v. *Council and Commission* (2008).

UN Documents

UN Security Council Resolutions (UNSCR)

UNSCR 811 (1993).
UNSCR 827 (1993).
UNSCR 864 (1993).
UNSCR 841 (1993).
UNSCR 903 (1994).
UNSCR 914 (1994).
UNSCR 1045 (1996).
UNSCR 1127 (1997).
UNSCR 1130 (1997).
UNSCR 1132 (1997).
UNSCR 1173 (1998).
UNSCR 1195 (1998).
UNSCR 1237 (1999).
UNSCR 1267 (1999).
UNSCR 1291 (2000).
UNSCR 1295 (2000).
UNSCR 1343 (2001).
UNSCR 1373 (2001).
UNSCR 1412 (2002).
UNSCR 1432 (2002).
UNSCR 1483 (2003).
UNSCR 1484 (2003).
UNSCR 1493 (2003).
UNSCR 1521 (2003).
UNSCR 1521 (2003).
UNSCR 1552 (2004).
UNSCR 1564 (2004).
UNSCR 1572 (2004).
UNSCR 1591 (2005).
UNSCR 1593 (2005).
UNSCR 1596 (2005).
UNSCR 1671 (2006).
UNSCR 1672 (2006).
UNSCR 1718 (2006).
UNSCR 1730 (2006).
UNSCR 1737 (2006).
UNSCR 1769 (2007).
UNSCR 1829 (2008).
UNSCR 1836 (2008).
UNSCR 1853 (2008).

UNSCR 1862 (2009).
UNSCR 1865 (2009).
UNSCR 1907 (2009).

Other UN Reports

S/1995/300. *Letter Dated 13 April 1995 from the Permanent Representatives of China, France, the Russian Federation, the United Kingdom of Great Britain and Northern Ireland and the United States of America to the United Nations Addressed to the President of the Security Council* (13 April 1995).

S/1999/64. *Letter Dated 4 June 1999, from the Chairman of the Security Council Committee Established Pursuant to Resolution 864 (1993) Concerning the Situation in Angola Addressed to the President of the Security Council* (4 June 1999).

S/1999/516. *Letter Dated 6 May 1999 from the Permanent Representative of Germany to the United Nations Addressed to the President of the Security Council* (6 May 1999).

S/1999/829. *Letter Dated 28 July 1999, from the Chairman of the Security Council Committee Established Pursuant to Resolution 864 (1993) Concerning the Situation in Angola Addressed to the President of the Security Council* (28 July 1999).

S/2000/203. *Letter Dated 10 March 2000 from the Chairman of the Security Council Committee Established Pursuant to Resolution 864 (1993) Concerning the Situation in Angola Addressed to the President of the Security Council. Final Report of the Panel of Experts on Violation of Security Council Sanctions against UNITA, from 28 February 2000* (10 March 2000) (The Fowler Report 2000).

S/2000/1026. *Letter Dated 24 October 2000, from the Chairman of the Security Council Committee Established Pursuant to Resolution 864 (1993) Concerning the Situation in Angola Addressed to the President of the Security Council. Interim Report of the Monitoring Mechanism on Angola Sanctions* (24 October 2000).

S/2000/1225. *Letter Dated 21 December 2000 from the Chairman of the Security Council Committee Established Pursuant to Resolution 864 (1993) Concerning the Situation in Angola Addressed to the President of the Security Council. Final Report of the Monitoring Mechanism on Angola Sanctions* (21 December 2000).

S/2000/1225. *Note by the President of the Security Council* (23 February 2001).

S/2001/363. *Addendum to the Final Report of the Monitoring Mechanism on Sanctions against UNITA (Note by the President of the Security Council)* (18 April 2001).

S/2001/966. *Letter Dated 12 October 2001 from the Chairman of the Security Council Committee, Transmitting the Supplementary Report of the Monitoring Mechanism* (12 October 2001).

S/2006/65. *Final Report of the Panel of Experts: Report Submitted in Accordance with Resolution 1591 (2005)* (30 January 2006).

S/2006/250. *Final Report of the Panel of Experts* (19 April 2006).

SC/6472. 'Security Council Committee on Sierra Leone Releases List of Junta Members Affected by Sanctions' (28 January 1998).

SC/7162. UN Press Release SC/7162. 'Security Council Committee on sanctions against UNITA issues revised list of UNITA officials and adult members of their immediate families' (4 October 2001).

SC/8546. 'Security Council Committee issues list of individuals and entities subjected to measures imposed by Resolution 1596 (2005)' (1 November 2005).

UN Security Council, 1267 Sanctions Committee. *Individuals, Groups, Undertakings and Entities that have been Removed from the Consolidated List Pursuant to a Decision by the 1267 Committee*, <www.un.org>.

UN Press Release SG/SM/7360. 'Secretary-General reviews lessons learned during "sanctions decade" in remarks to international peace academy seminar' (17 April 2000).

Other UN Documents

Annan, Kofi. *Annual Report on the Work of the Organization* (New York: United Nations, 1998).

Food and Agricultural Organization of the United Nations. Evaluation of Food and Nutrition Situation in Iraq (Rome: UNFAO, 1995).

Ki-moon, Ban. 'Sanctions Work Best When there are Carrots and Not Just Sticks' (New York: UN News Center, 30 April 2007).

Oil-for-Food Programme. *Report on the Manipulation of the Oil-for-Food Programme. Issued by the Independent Inquiry Committee into the United Nations Oil-for-Food Programme (2004–2006)*, <www.iic-offp.org/documents.htm>.

The Children are Dying: The Impact of Sanctions on Iraq. Reports by UN Food and Agriculture Organization and world leaders, 1st edn (New York: World View Forum, 1996).

The Children are Dying: The Impact of Sanctions on Iraq. Reports by UN Food and Agriculture Organization, Ramsey Clark and world leaders, 2nd edn (New York: International Action Center, 1998).

Non-governmental Reports

Conciliation Resources. *Incentives, Sanctions and Conditionality: A Review of International Peace Initiatives*, *Accord*, no. 19 (London: Conciliation Resources, 2008).

Global Witness. *A Rough Trade: The Role of Companies and Governments in the Angolan Conflict* (London: Global Witness, 1998).

Security Council Special Research Report on UN Security Council. *Autonomy of a Sanctions Regime: A Case Study of Sixteen Years of Failed Efforts to Effectively Implement Sanctions in Somalia*, no. 4 (New York: United Nations, 2008).

International Crisis Group (ICG) Reports

Africa Report. *Zimbabwe: An End to the Stalemate*. No. 122 (5 March 2007).

Africa Report. *Zimbabwe at the Crossroads: Transition or Conflict*. No. 41 (2002).

Other Multilateral and Regional Organisations

International Atomic Energy Agency (IAEA). Board of Governors. *GOV/2009/8 Date: 19 February 2009, (GOV/2009/6) Implementation of the NPT Safeguards Agreement and relevant provisions of Security Council resolutions 1737 (2006), 1747 (2007), 1803 (2008) and 1835 (2008) in the Islamic Republic of Iran Report by the Director General 1* (2009).

UK

Foreign and Commonwealth Office. Official policy on Zimbabwe: 'Zimbabwe: UK Approach to Land Reform', UK National Archive, <www.fco.gov.uk> (5 February 2008).

UK Parliamentary Debate on Zimbabwe, 'Zimbabwe', *Hansard* (19 July 2007), <www.publications.parliament.uk/pa/cm200607/cmhansrd/cm070719/debtext/70719-0011.htm#07071991000003>.

USA

US Department of Justice. *Follow-up Audit of the Terrorist Screening Center*. US Department of Justice, Office of the Inspector General Audit Division Audit Report 07-41 (September 2007).

US Department of State. *Country Reports on Terrorism 2007* (April 2008), <www.state.gov/s/ct/rls/crt/2007/index.htm>.

US President. 'State of the Union Address'. The United States Capitol, Washington, DC (29 January 2002).

White House transcript. 'President Bush Announces Major Combat Operations in Iraq Have Ended: Remarks by the President from the USS Abraham Lincoln at Sea Off the Coast of San Diego, California' (1 May 2003), <http://georgewbush-whitehouse.archives.gov/news/releases/2003/05/20030501-15.html#>.

Sanctions Reports

Bonn-Berlin Process. *Design and Implementation of Arms Embargoes and Travel and Aviation Related Sanctions: Results of the 'Bonn-Berlin Process'*. Bonn International Center for Conversion, no. 6 (Baden-Baden: Nomos Verlagsgesellschaft, 2001).

Interlaken Process. *Expert Seminar on Targeting UN Financial Sanctions* (Interlaken, Switzerland: Swiss Federal Office for Foreign Economic Affairs, Department of Economy, 17–19 March 1998a).

Interlaken Process. *2nd Interlaken Seminar on Targeting United Nations Financial Sanctions* (Interlaken, Switzerland: Swiss Federal Office for Foreign Economic Affairs, Department of Economy, 29–31 March 1999b).

Wallensteen, Peter, Eriksson, Mikael and Staibano, Carina. *Making Targeted Sanctions Effective: Guidelines for the Implementation of UN Policy Options*. Report of the Stockholm Process, Swedish Ministry for Foreign Affairs (Uppsala: Uppsala Department of Peace and Conflict Studies, 2003), <www.smartsanctions.se> (accessed 15 June 2010).

Index

www.ingramcontent.com/pod-product-compliance
Ingram Content Group UK Ltd.
Pitfield, Milton Keynes, MK11 3LW, UK
UKHW020016200926
475702UK00014B/1921
* 9 7 8 1 1 3 8 2 7 3 7 8 8 *